PRINCE
Freya

1

CONTENTS

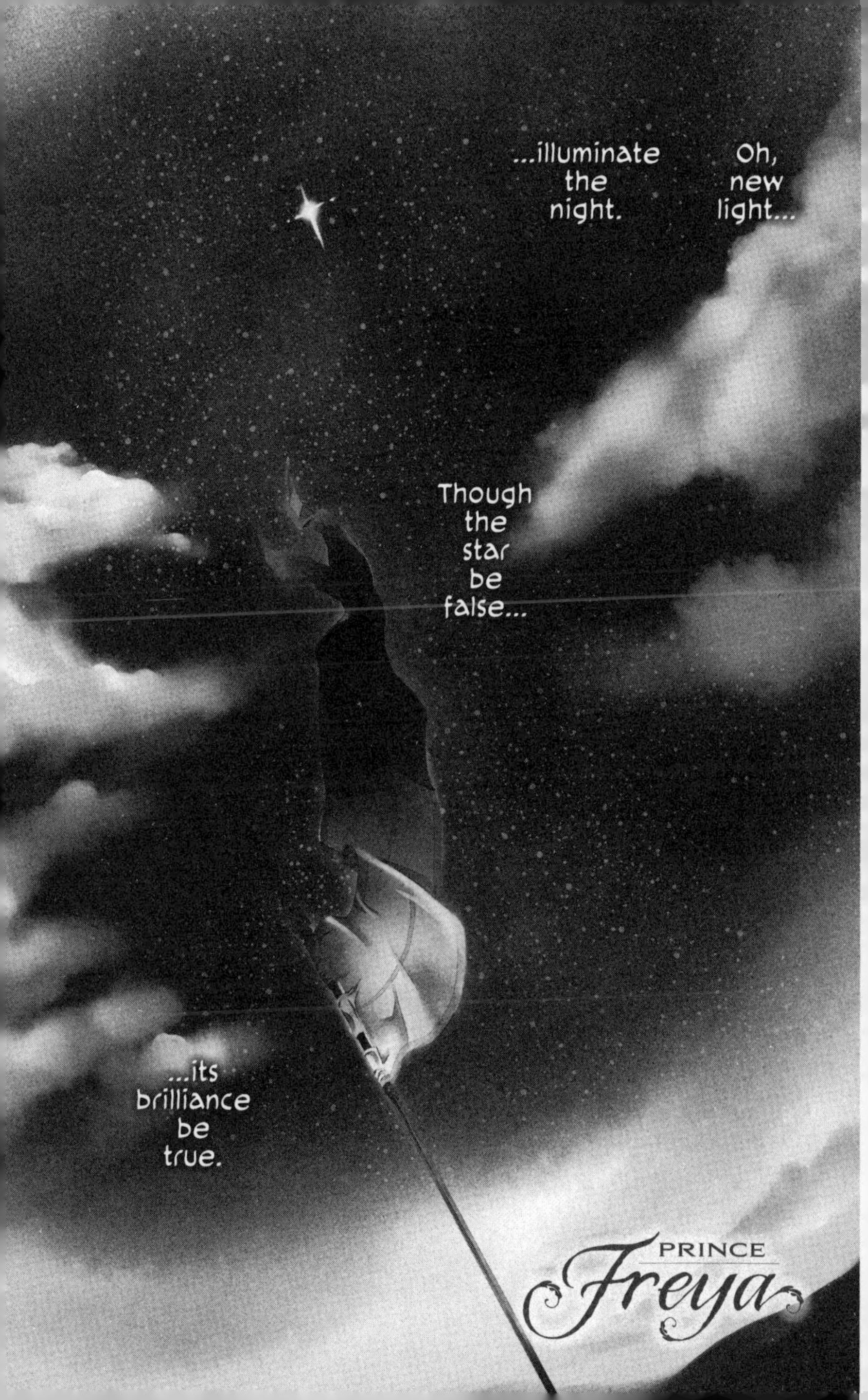
Oh, new light...
...illuminate the night.
Though the star be false...
...its brilliance be true.
PRINCE Freya

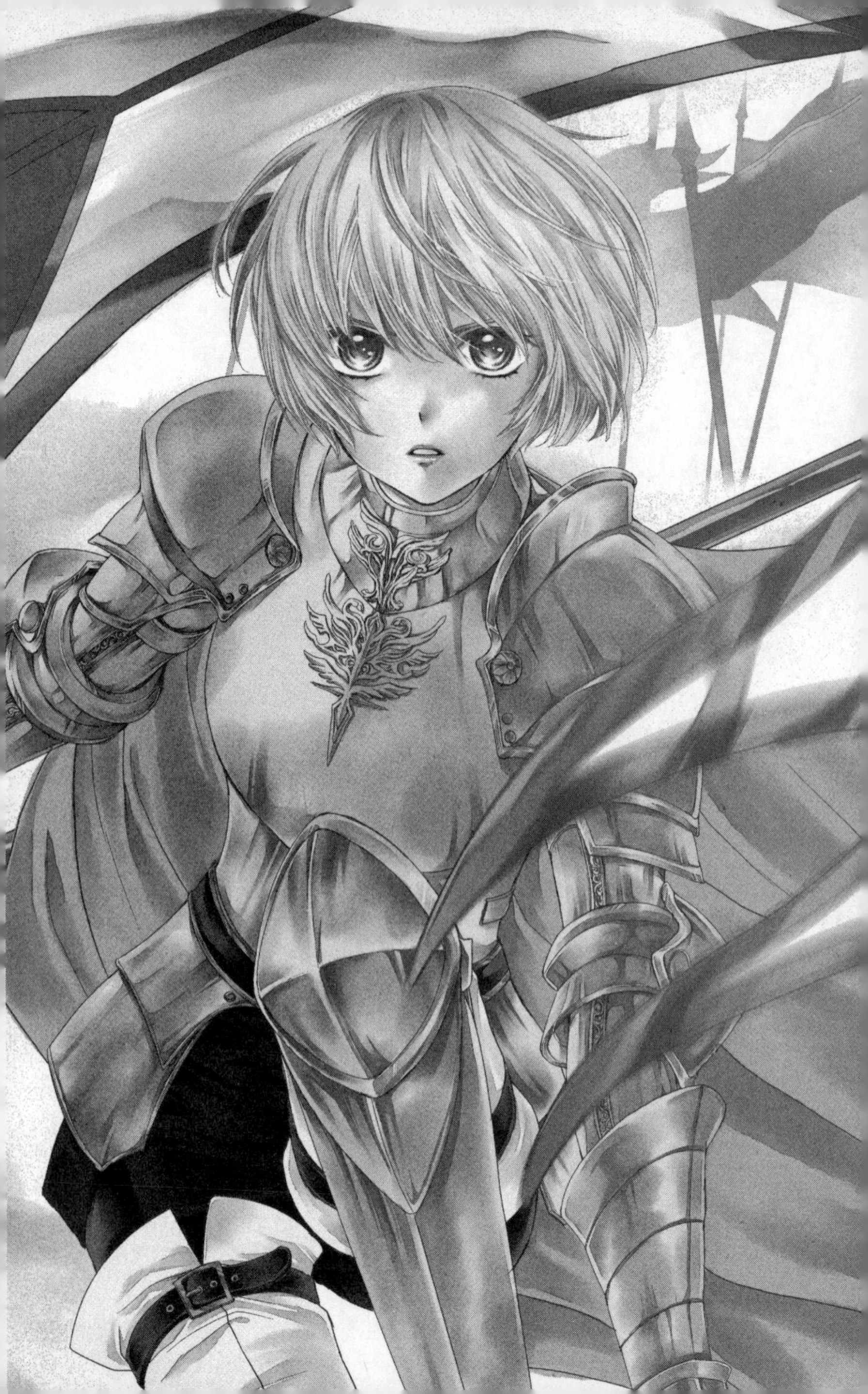

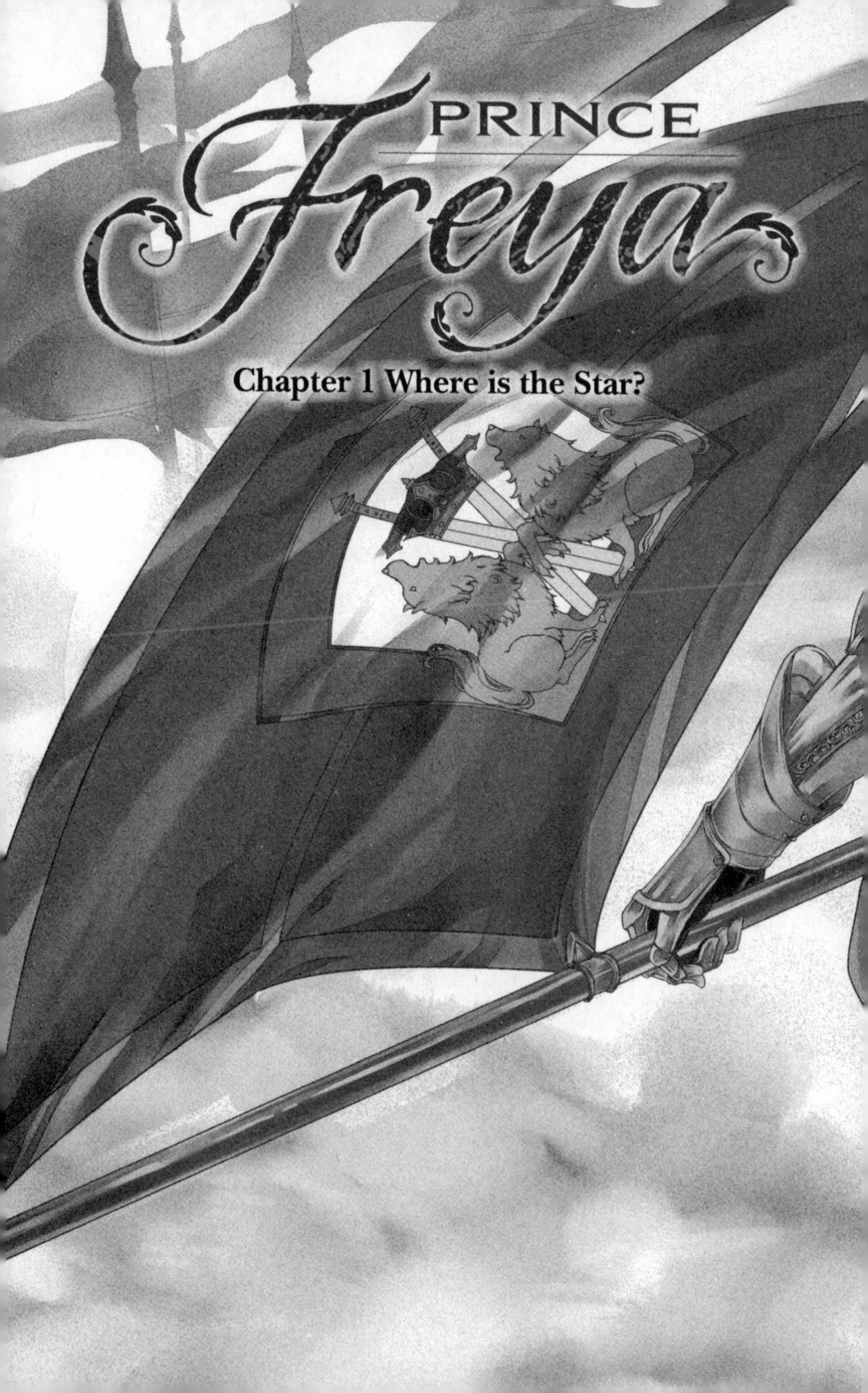
PRINCE
Freya
Chapter 1 Where is the Star?

PRINCE

Freya

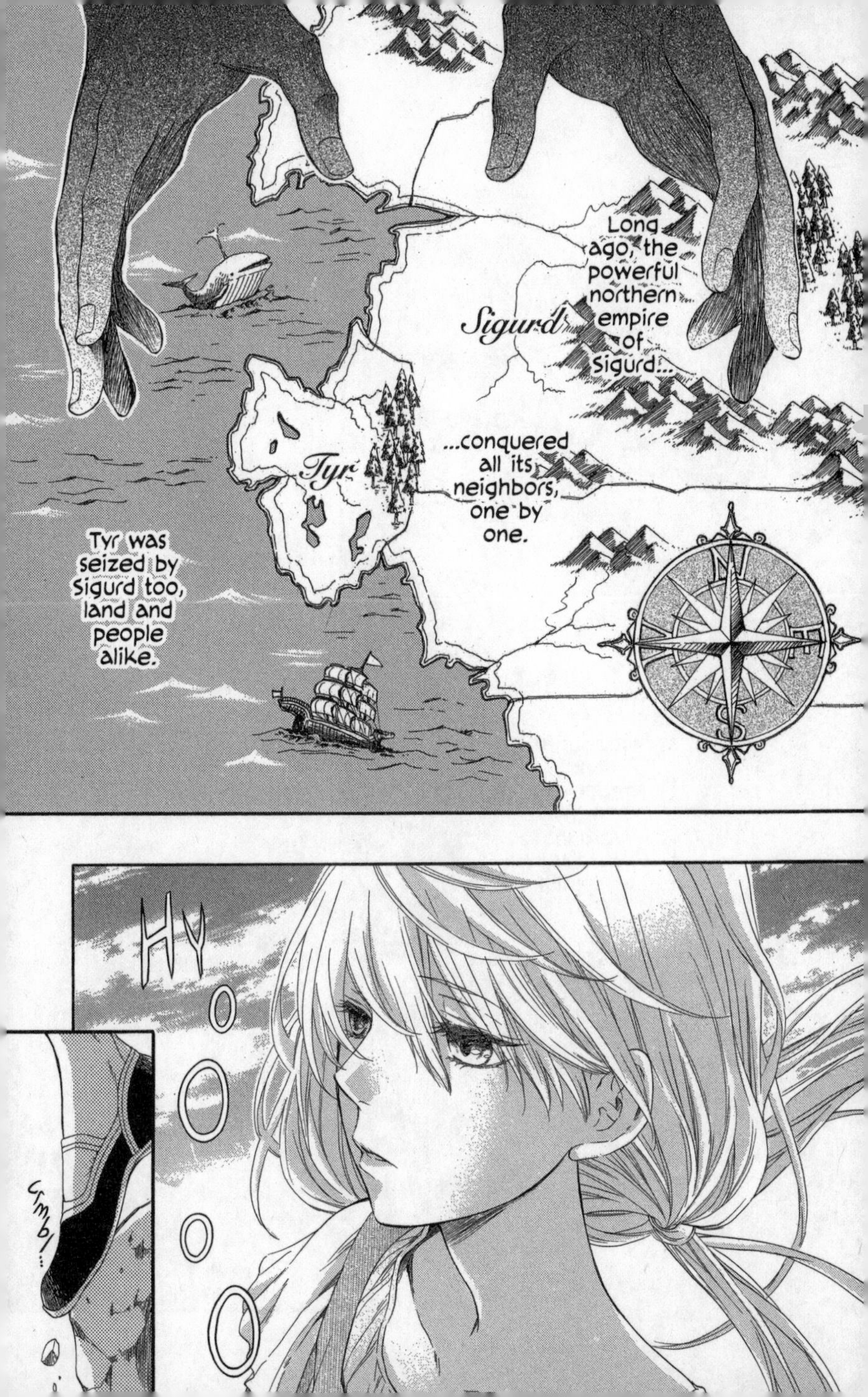
Long ago, the powerful northern empire of Sigurd...
Sigurd
...conquered all its neighbors, one by one.
Tyr
Tyr was seized by Sigurd too, land and people alike.
HYOOOO
crmbl...

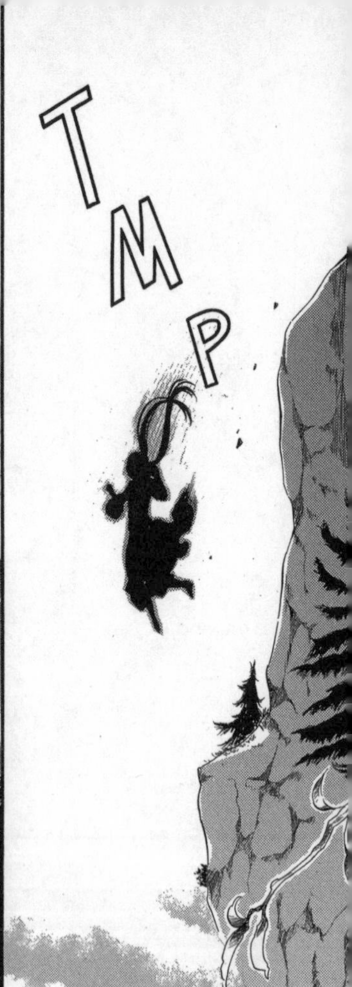
TMP

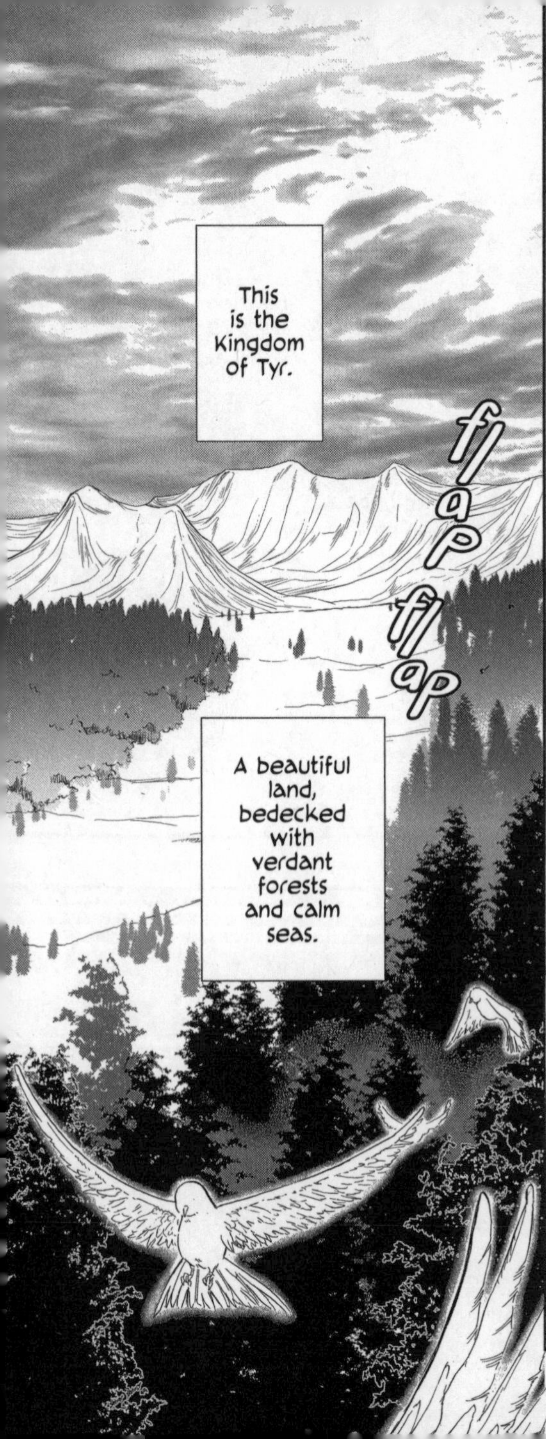
This is the Kingdom of Tyr.
flap flap
A beautiful land, bedecked with verdant forests and calm seas.

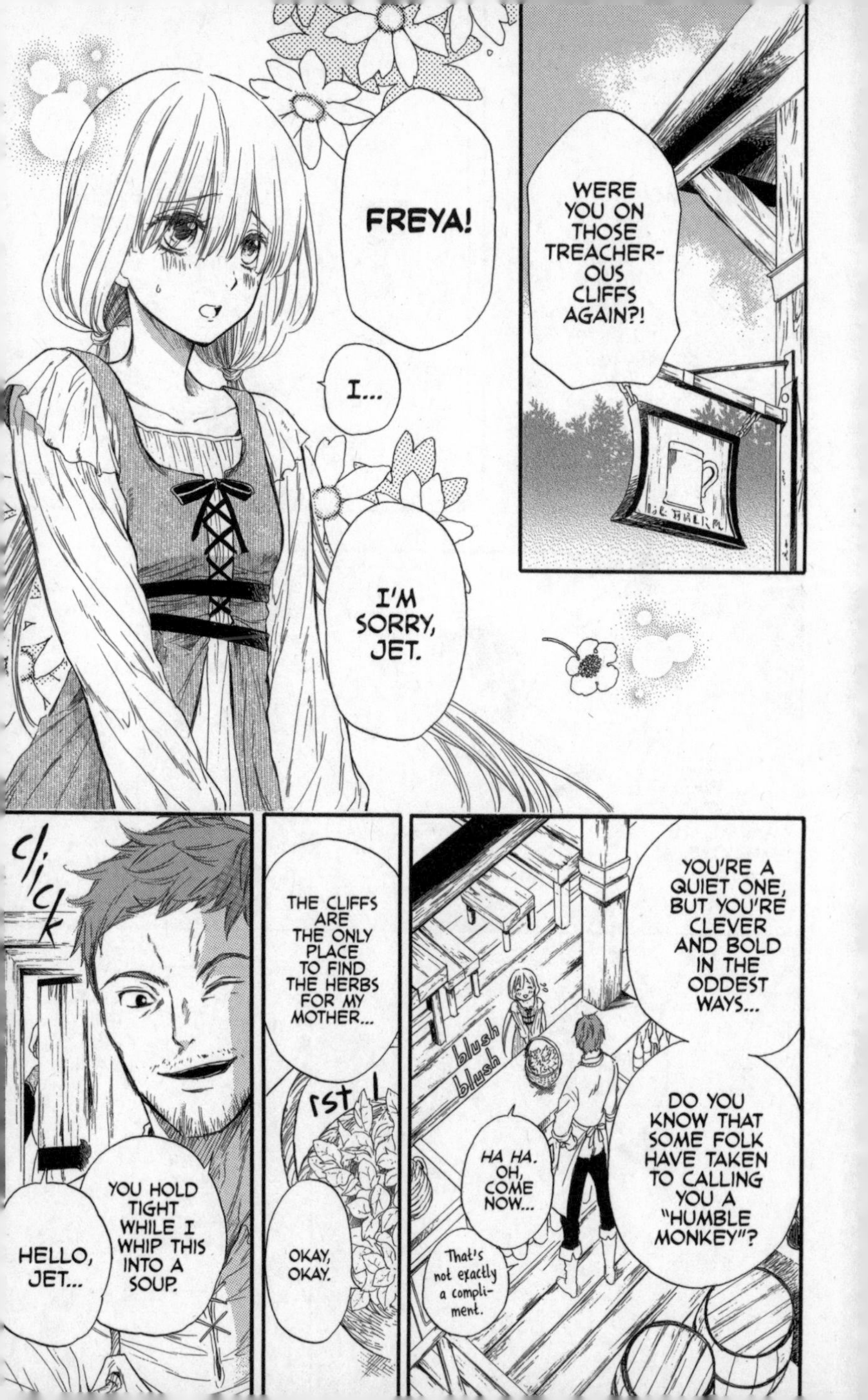
WERE YOU ON THOSE TREACHER-OUS CLIFFS AGAIN?!
FREYA!
I...
I'M SORRY, JET.
YOU'RE A QUIET ONE, BUT YOU'RE CLEVER AND BOLD IN THE ODDEST WAYS...
blush blush
DO YOU KNOW THAT SOME FOLK HAVE TAKEN TO CALLING YOU A "HUMBLE MONKEY"?
HA HA. OH, COME NOW...
That's not exactly a compli-ment.
THE CLIFFS ARE THE ONLY PLACE TO FIND THE HERBS FOR MY MOTHER...
rst
OKAY, OKAY.
click
YOU HOLD TIGHT WHILE I WHIP THIS INTO A SOUP.
HELLO, JET...

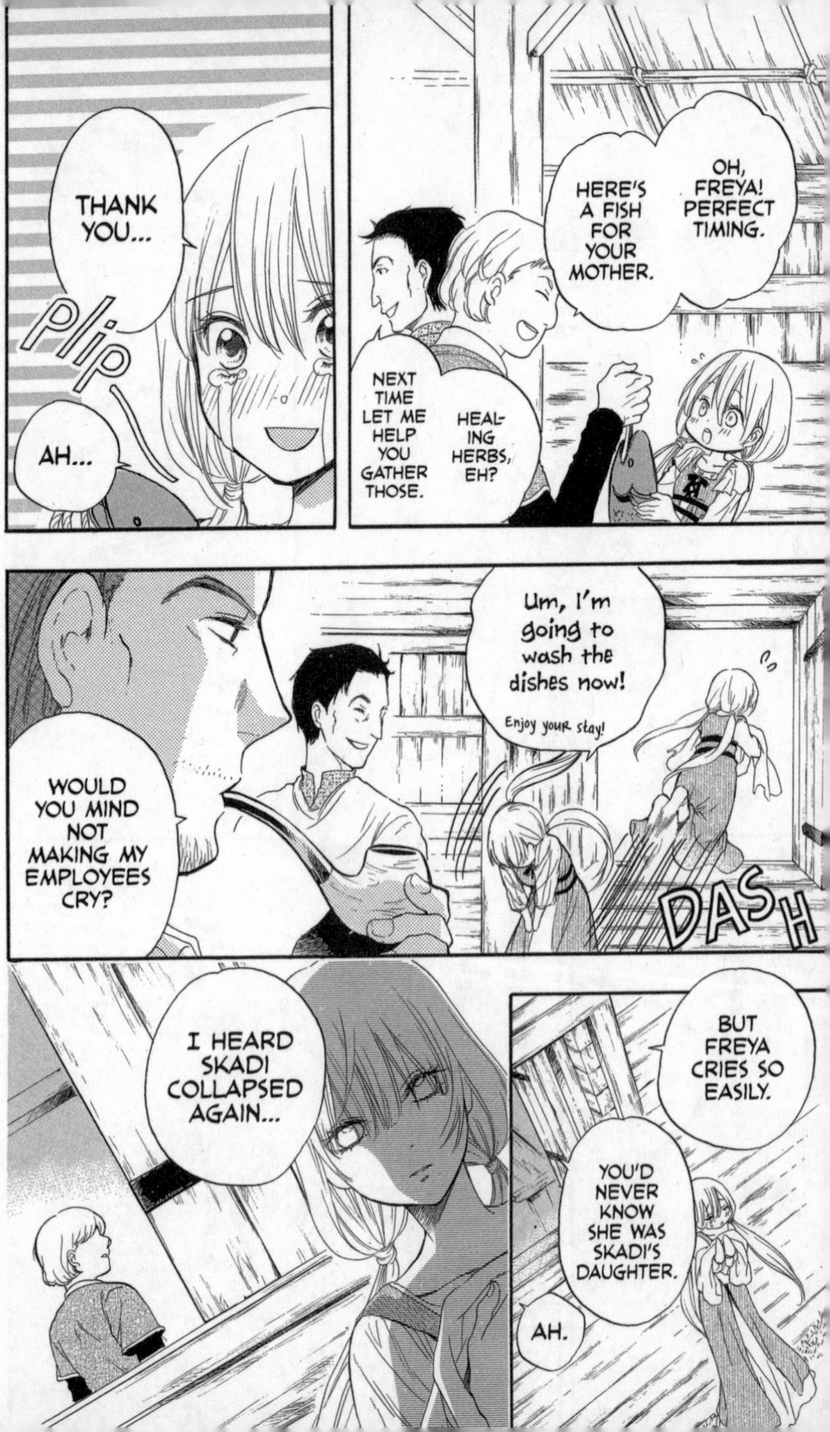
OH, FREYA! PERFECT TIMING.
HERE'S A FISH FOR YOUR MOTHER.
HEAL-ING HERBS, EH?
NEXT TIME LET ME HELP YOU GATHER THOSE.
THANK YOU...
Plip
AH...
Um, I'm going to wash the dishes now!
Enjoy your stay!
DASH
WOULD YOU MIND NOT MAKING MY EMPLOYEES CRY?
BUT FREYA CRIES SO EASILY.
YOU'D NEVER KNOW SHE WAS SKADI'S DAUGHTER.
AH.
I HEARD SKADI COLLAPSED AGAIN...

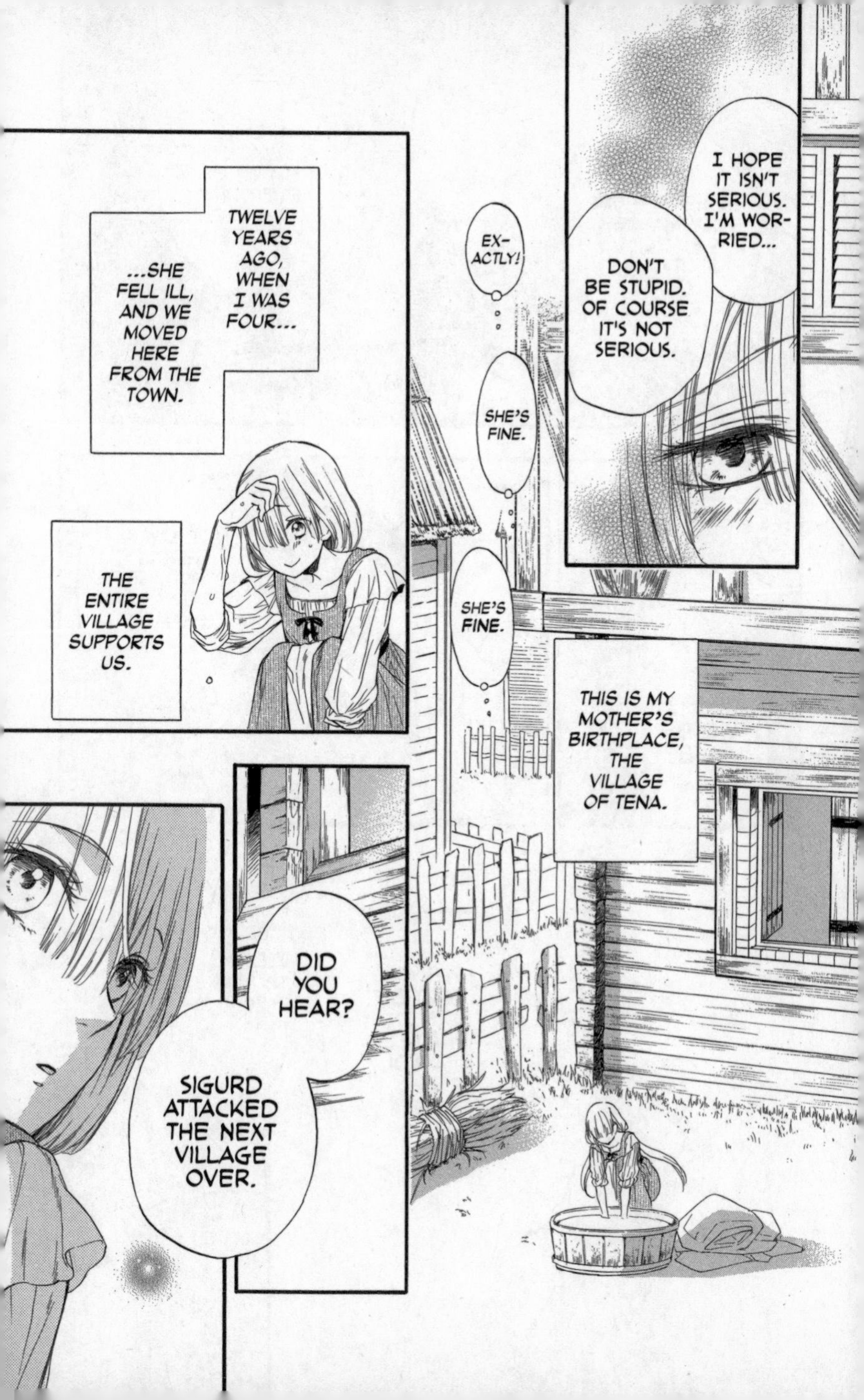
I HOPE IT ISN'T SERIOUS. I'M WORRIED...
DON'T BE STUPID. OF COURSE IT'S NOT SERIOUS.
EX-ACTLY!
SHE'S FINE.
SHE'S FINE.
THIS IS MY MOTHER'S BIRTHPLACE, THE VILLAGE OF TENA.
TWELVE YEARS AGO, WHEN I WAS FOUR...
...SHE FELL ILL, AND WE MOVED HERE FROM THE TOWN.
THE ENTIRE VILLAGE SUPPORTS US.
DID YOU HEAR?
SIGURD ATTACKED THE NEXT VILLAGE OVER.

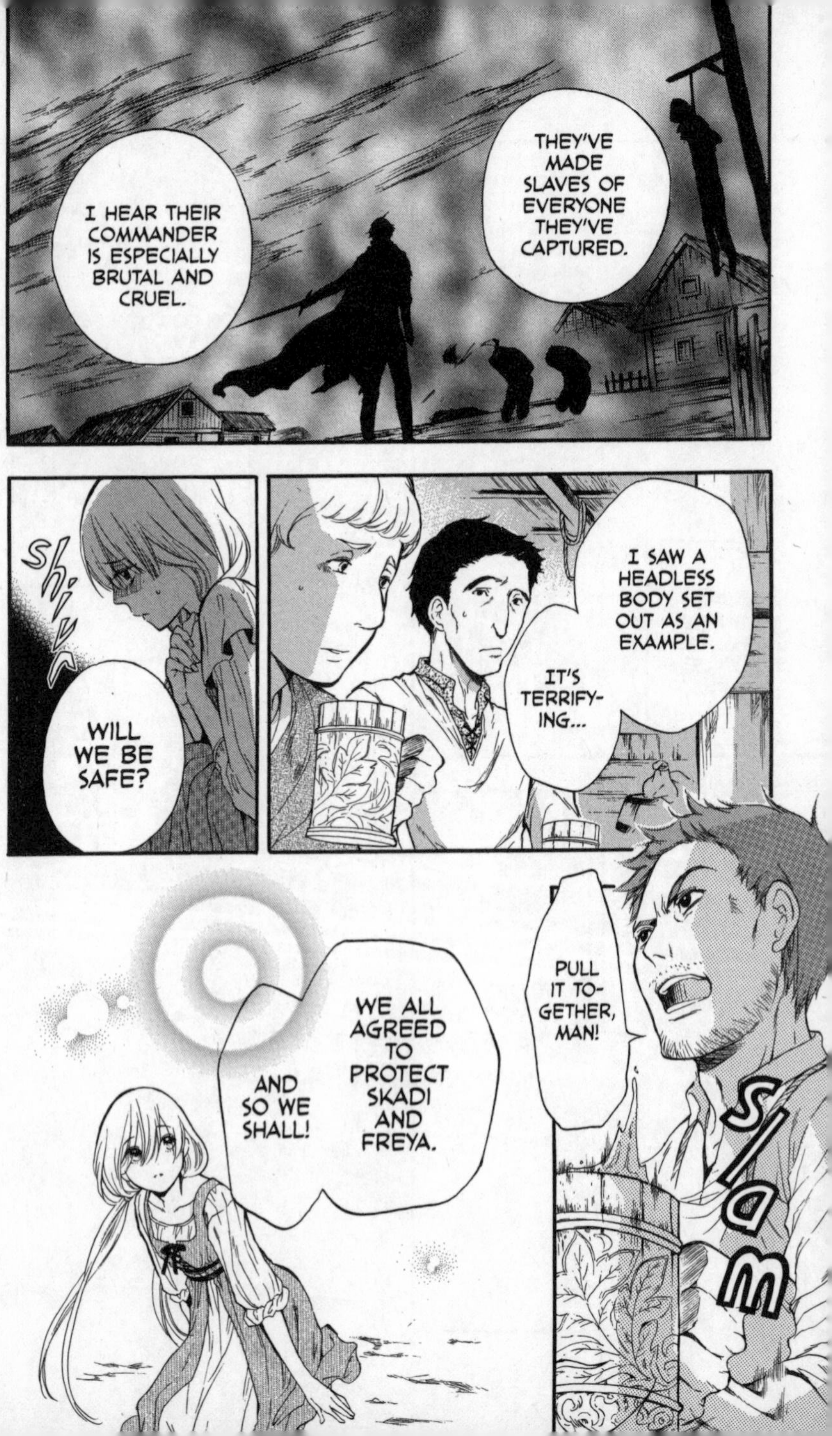

THEY'VE MADE SLAVES OF EVERYONE THEY'VE CAPTURED.
I HEAR THEIR COMMANDER IS ESPECIALLY BRUTAL AND CRUEL.
I SAW A HEADLESS BODY SET OUT AS AN EXAMPLE.
IT'S TERRIFYING...
shivvr
WILL WE BE SAFE?
PULL IT TOGETHER, MAN!
Slam
WE ALL AGREED TO PROTECT SKADI AND FREYA.
AND SO WE SHALL!

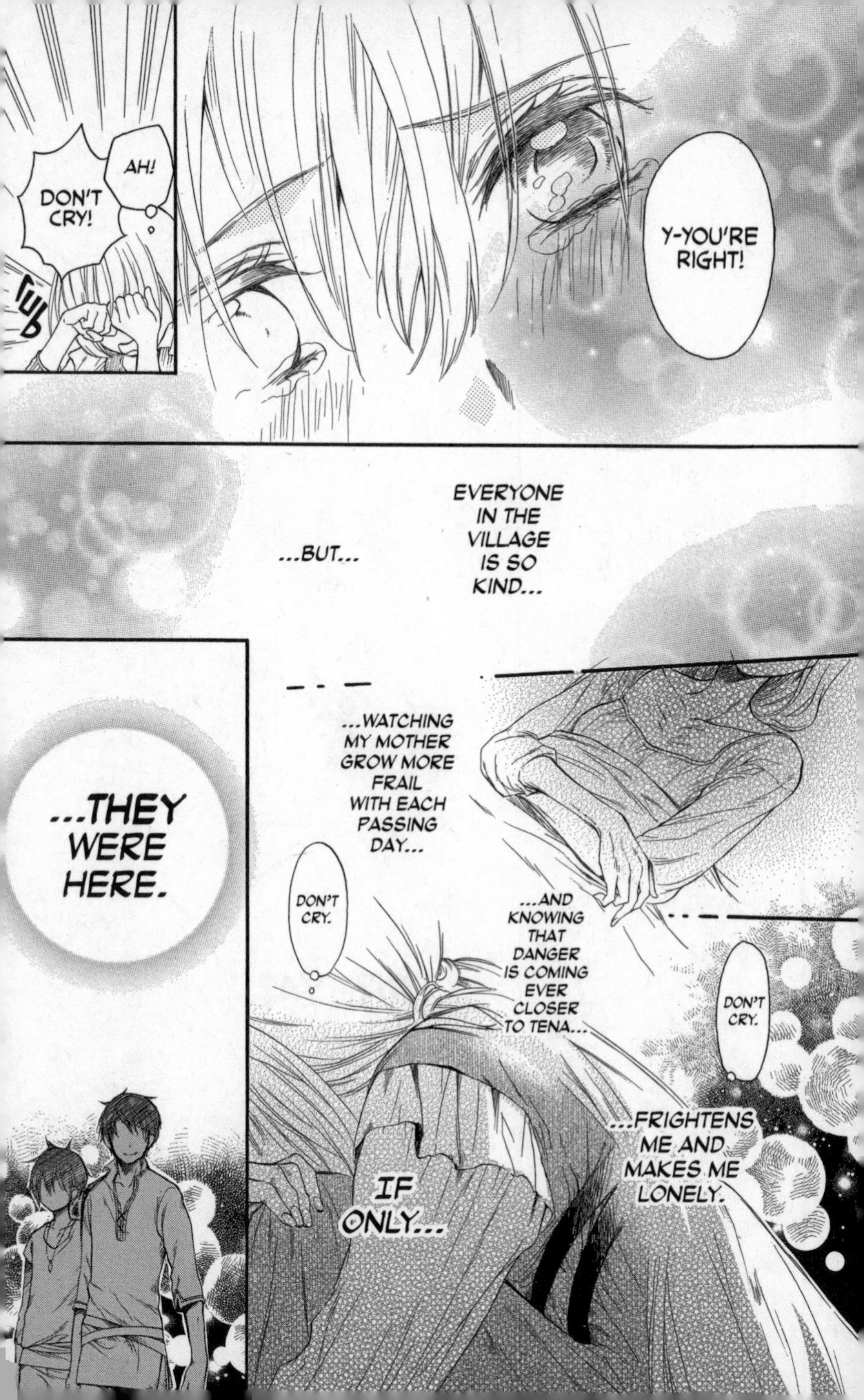
Y-YOU'RE RIGHT!
AH!
DON'T CRY!
rub
EVERYONE IN THE VILLAGE IS SO KIND...
...BUT...
...WATCHING MY MOTHER GROW MORE FRAIL WITH EACH PASSING DAY...
...AND KNOWING THAT DANGER IS COMING EVER CLOSER TO TENA...
DON'T CRY.
DON'T CRY.
...FRIGHTENS ME AND MAKES ME LONELY.
IF ONLY...
...THEY WERE HERE.

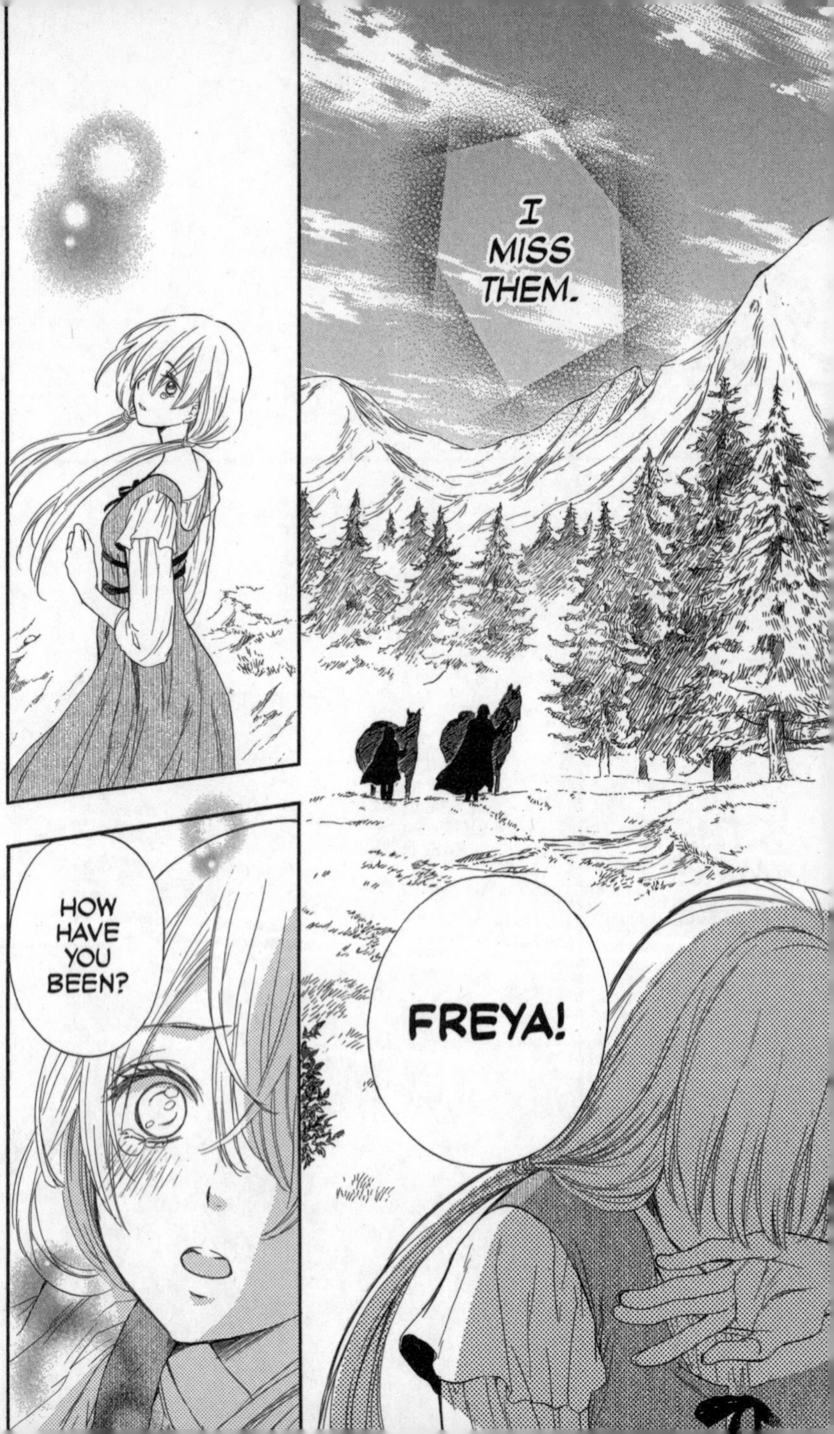
I MISS THEM.
FREYA!
HOW HAVE YOU BEEN?

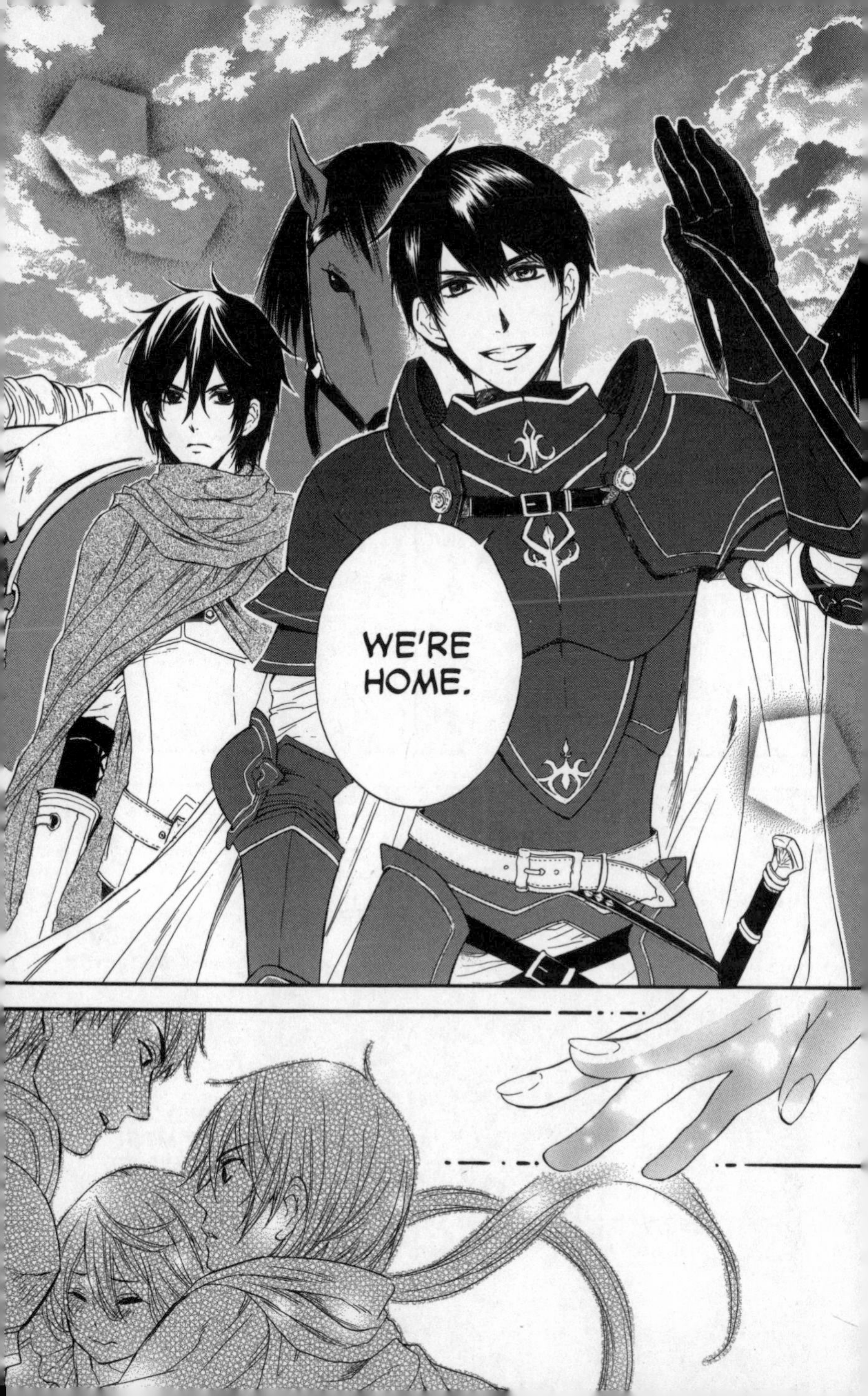
WE'RE
HOME.

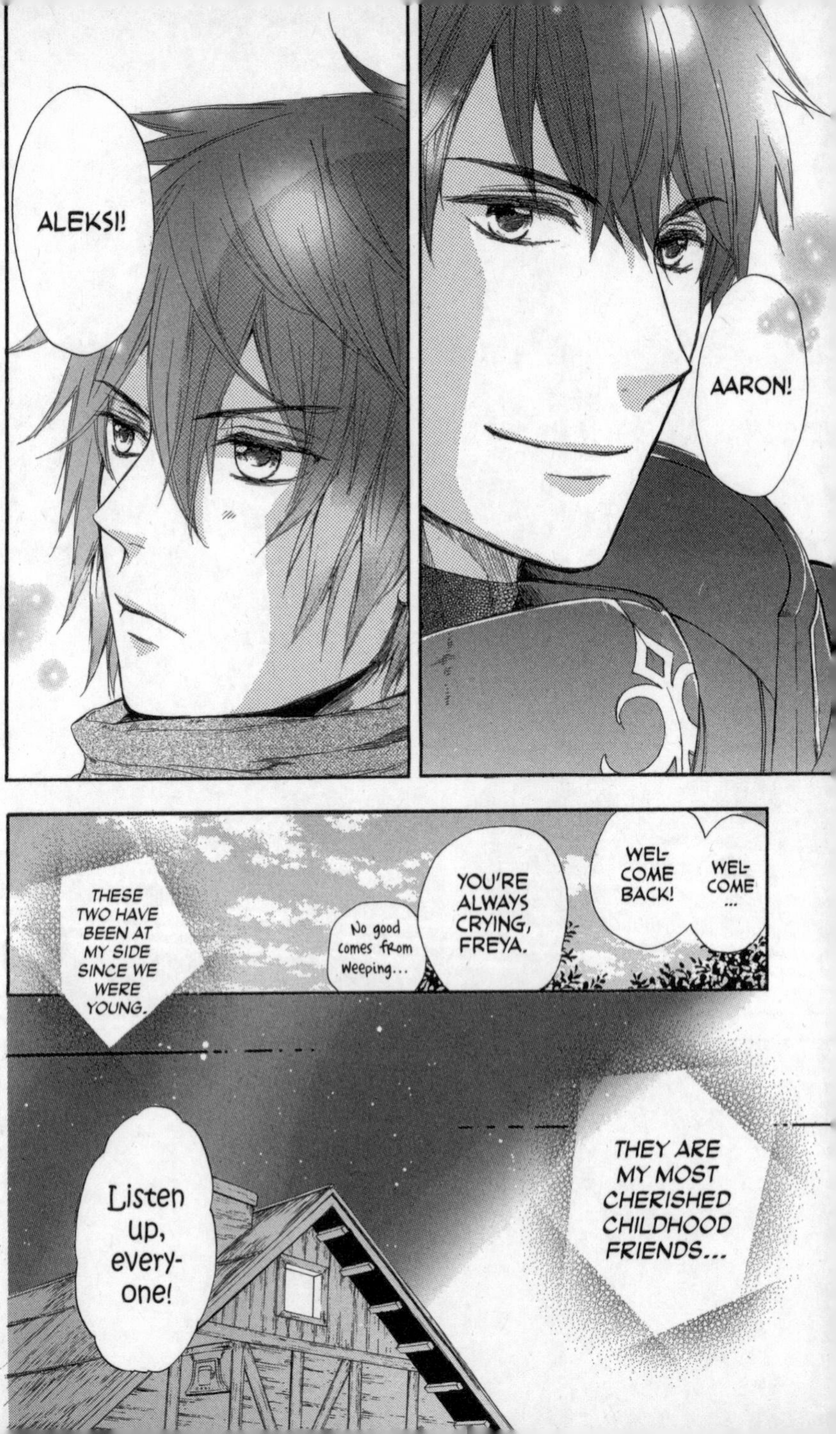
AARON!
ALEKSI!
WEL-COME...
WEL-COME BACK!
YOU'RE ALWAYS CRYING, FREYA.
No good comes from weeping...
THESE TWO HAVE BEEN AT MY SIDE SINCE WE WERE YOUNG.
THEY ARE MY MOST CHERISHED CHILDHOOD FRIENDS...
Listen up, every-one!

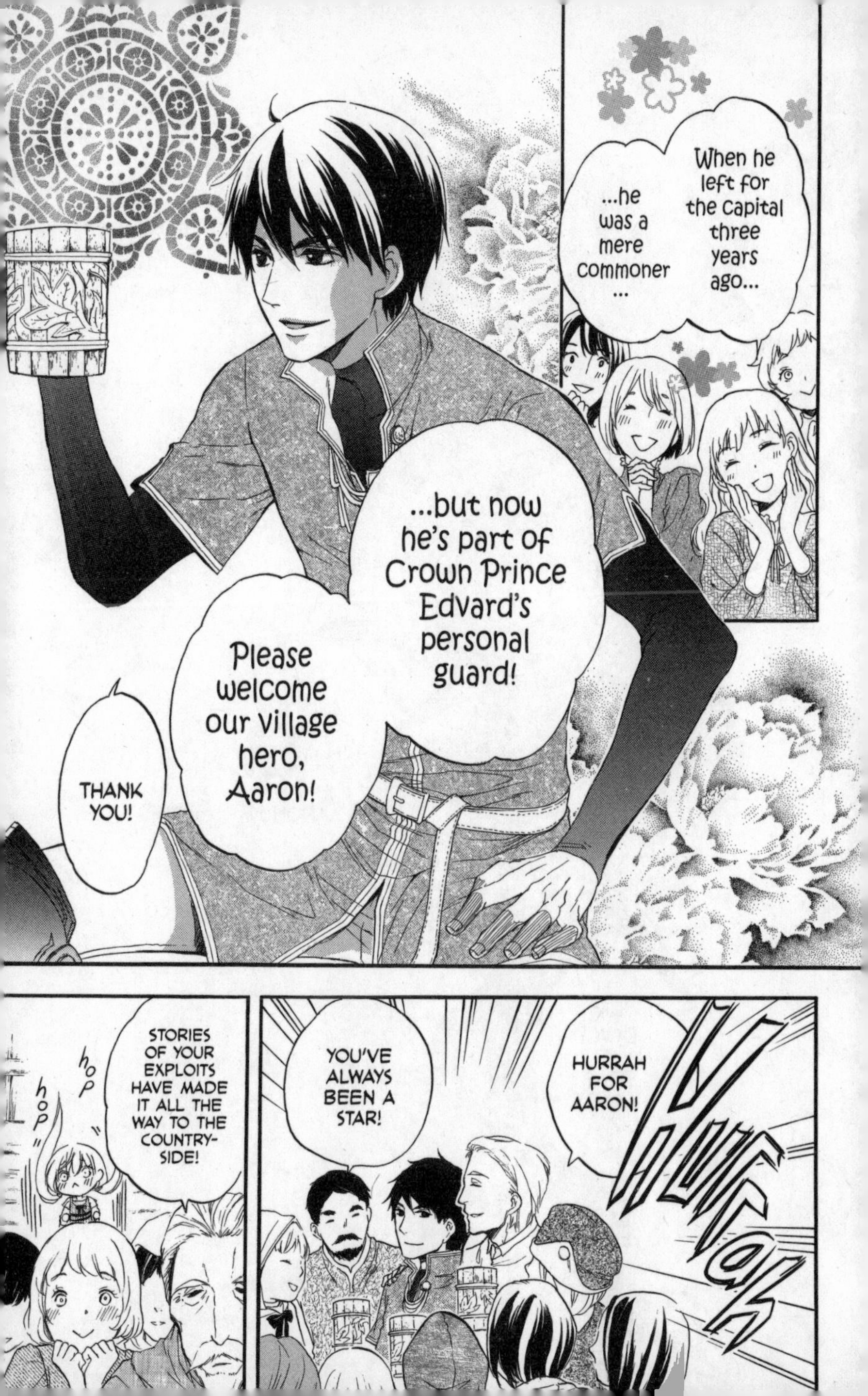
When he left for the capital three years ago...
...he was a mere commoner...
...but now he's part of Crown Prince Edvard's personal guard!
Please welcome our village hero, Aaron!
THANK YOU!
HURRAH FOR AARON!
Hurrah
YOU'VE ALWAYS BEEN A STAR!
STORIES OF YOUR EXPLOITS HAVE MADE IT ALL THE WAY TO THE COUNTRY-SIDE!
hop
hop

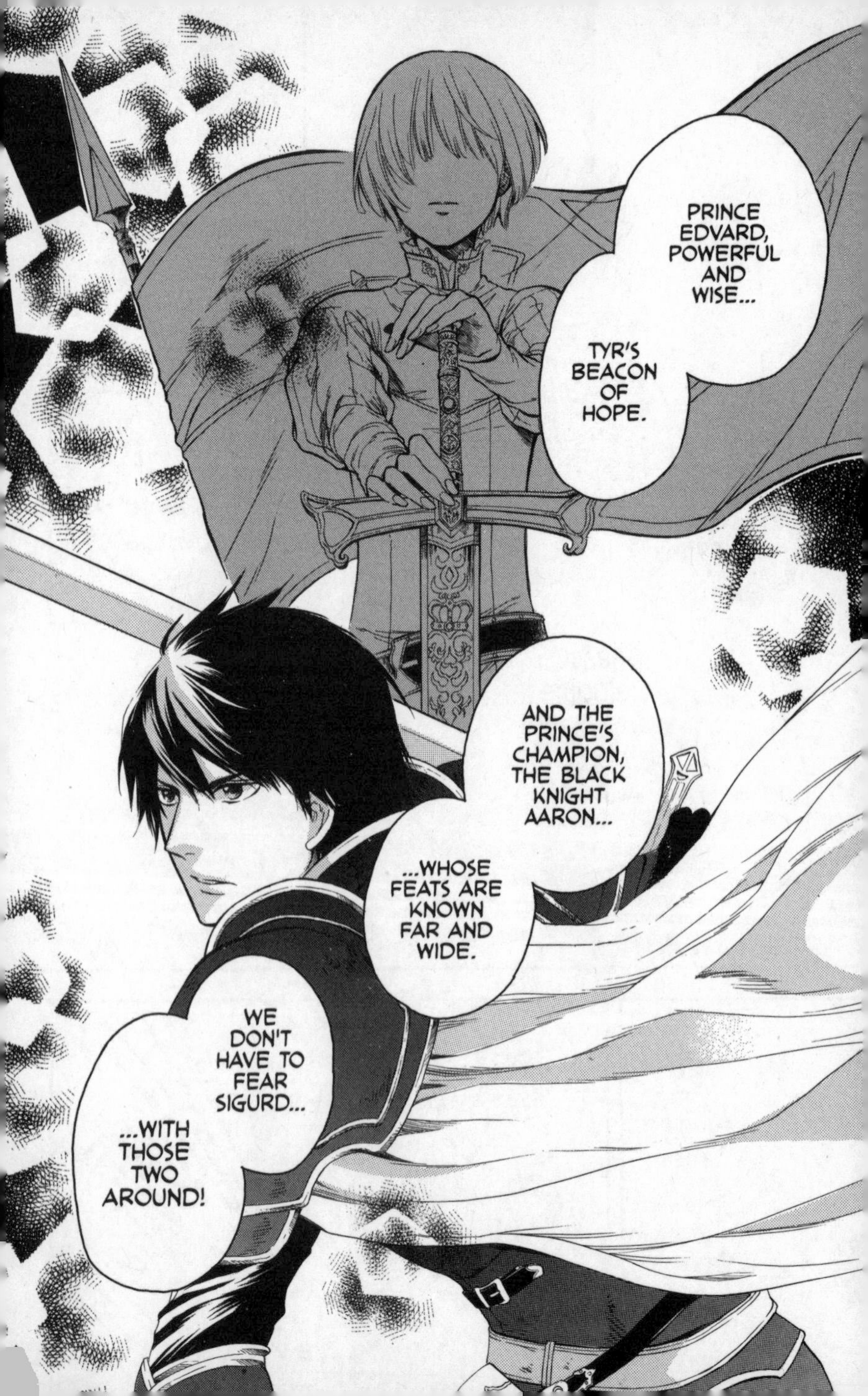
PRINCE EDVARD, POWERFUL AND WISE...
TYR'S BEACON OF HOPE.
AND THE PRINCE'S CHAMPION, THE BLACK KNIGHT AARON...
...WHOSE FEATS ARE KNOWN FAR AND WIDE.
WE DON'T HAVE TO FEAR SIGURD...
...WITH THOSE TWO AROUND!

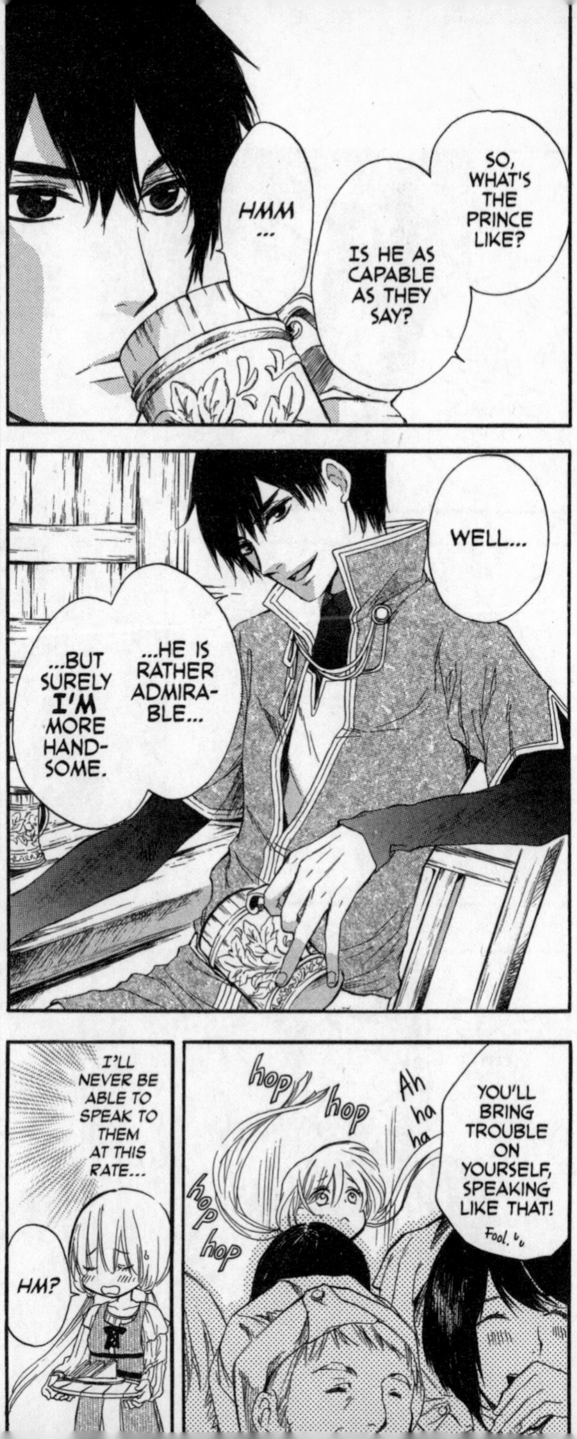
SO, WHAT'S THE PRINCE LIKE?
IS HE AS CAPABLE AS THEY SAY?
HMM...
WELL...
...HE IS RATHER ADMIRABLE...
...BUT SURELY I'M MORE HANDSOME.
YOU'LL BRING TROUBLE ON YOURSELF, SPEAKING LIKE THAT!
Fool.
Ah ha ha
hop hop
hop hop
I'LL NEVER BE ABLE TO SPEAK TO THEM AT THIS RATE...
HM?

Thank you for picking up a copy of *Prince Freya*, volume 1.

I've always been drawn to medieval European fantasies, but I've never attempted to create one because I thought it would be more than I could manage.

But somehow luck came my way and I got a chance to work on one.

While I still feel like I have a lot more to learn, working on this story is so exciting!

I hope the series continues long enough that I can transform Freya from a crybaby into someone admirable.

Let's watch over her together.

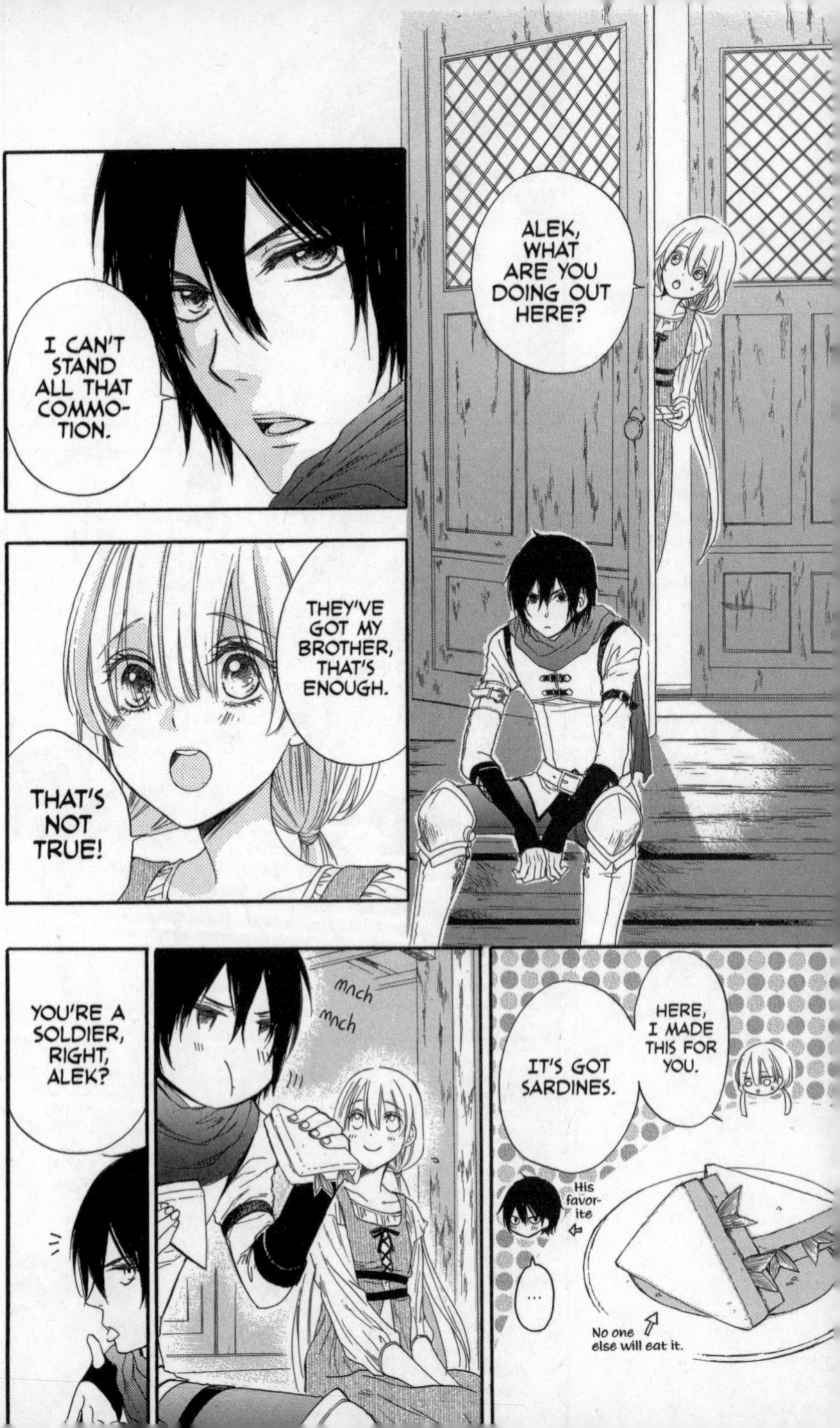
ALEK, WHAT ARE YOU DOING OUT HERE?
I CAN'T STAND ALL THAT COMMOTION.
THEY'VE GOT MY BROTHER, THAT'S ENOUGH.
THAT'S NOT TRUE!
HERE, I MADE THIS FOR YOU.
IT'S GOT SARDINES.
His favorite
...
No one else will eat it.
mnch
mnch
YOU'RE A SOLDIER, RIGHT, ALEK?

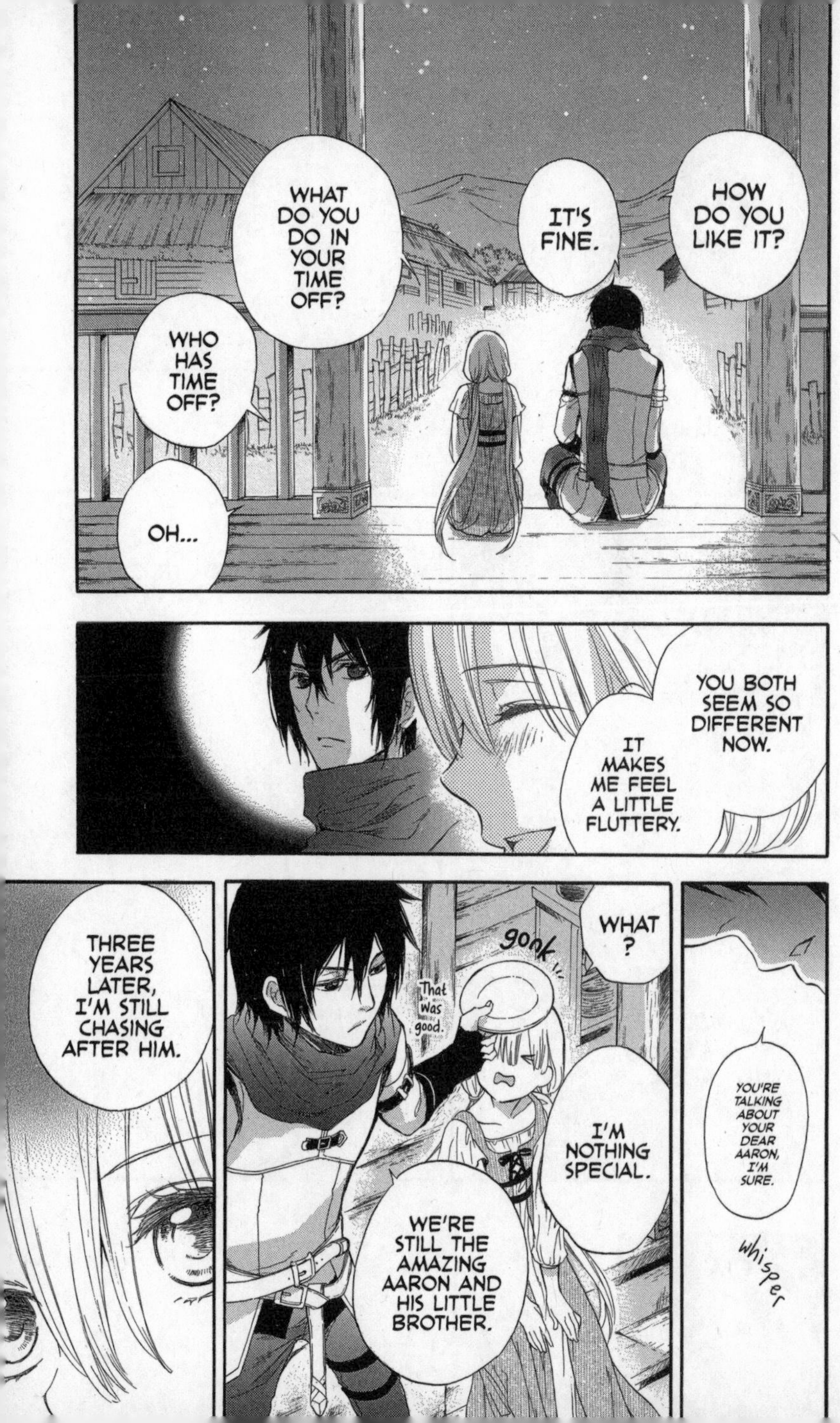
HOW DO YOU LIKE IT?
IT'S FINE.
WHAT DO YOU DO IN YOUR TIME OFF?
WHO HAS TIME OFF?
OH...
YOU BOTH SEEM SO DIFFERENT NOW.
IT MAKES ME FEEL A LITTLE FLUTTERY.
YOU'RE TALKING ABOUT YOUR DEAR AARON, I'M SURE.
whisper
WHAT?
gonk
That was good.
I'M NOTHING SPECIAL.
WE'RE STILL THE AMAZING AARON AND HIS LITTLE BROTHER.
THREE YEARS LATER, I'M STILL CHASING AFTER HIM.

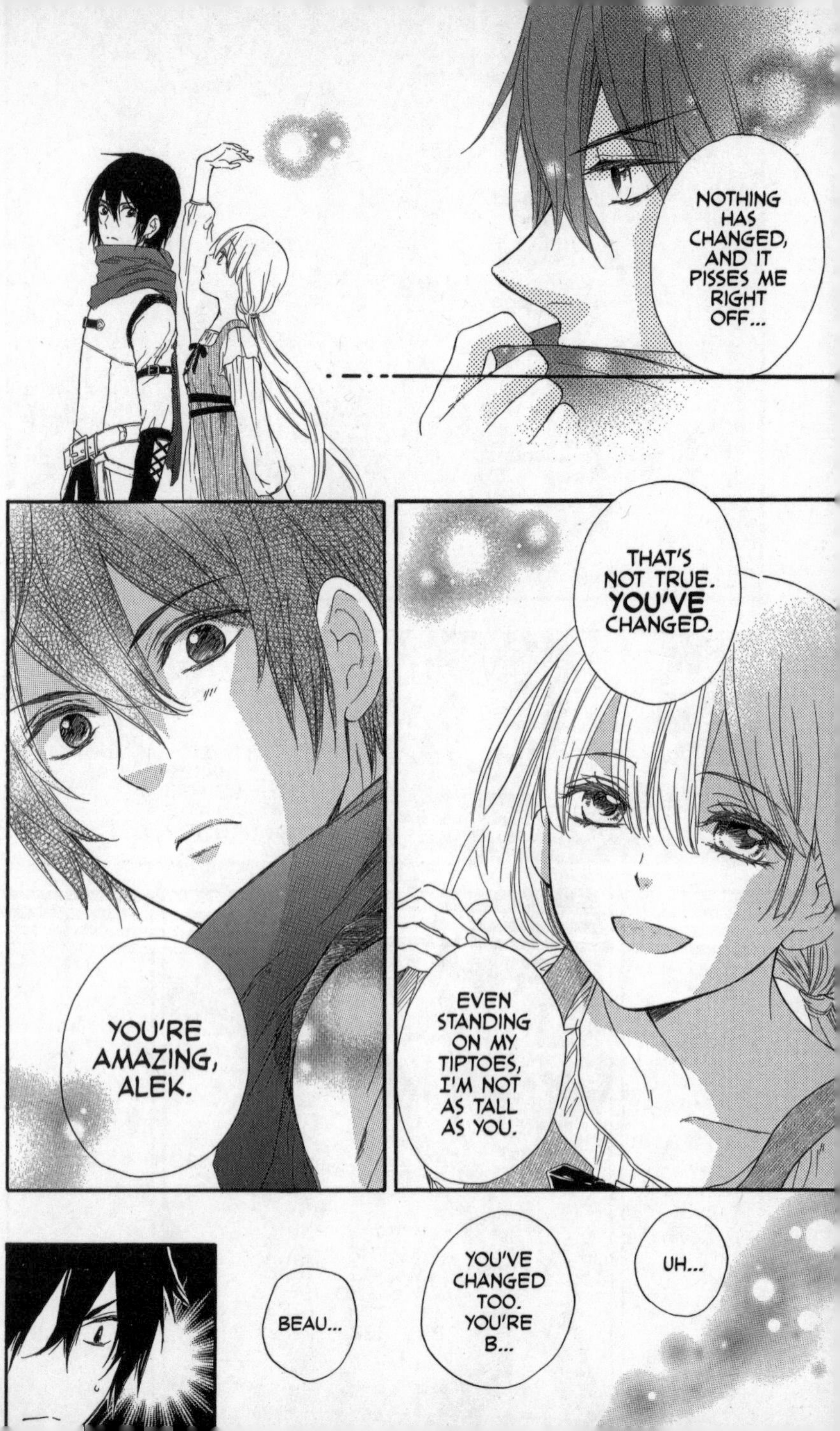
NOTHING HAS CHANGED, AND IT PISSES ME RIGHT OFF...
THAT'S NOT TRUE. **YOU'VE** CHANGED.
EVEN STANDING ON MY TIPTOES, I'M NOT AS TALL AS YOU.
YOU'RE AMAZING, ALEK.
UH...
YOU'VE CHANGED TOO. YOU'RE B...
BEAU...

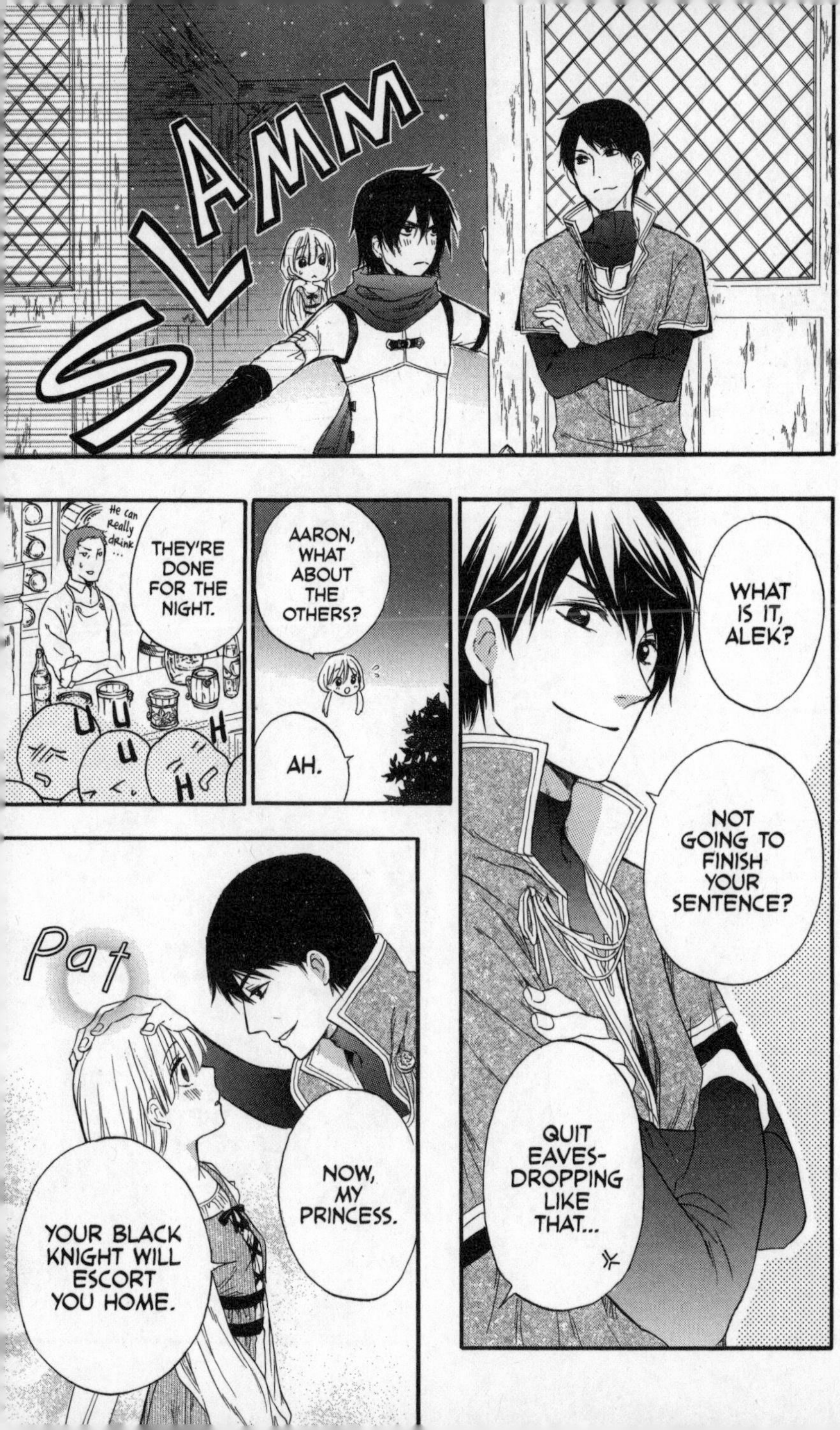
SLAMM
WHAT IS IT, ALEK?
NOT GOING TO FINISH YOUR SENTENCE?
QUIT EAVES-DROPPING LIKE THAT...
AARON, WHAT ABOUT THE OTHERS?
AH.
THEY'RE DONE FOR THE NIGHT.
He can really drink...
UUUHH
Pat
NOW, MY PRINCESS.
YOUR BLACK KNIGHT WILL ESCORT YOU HOME.

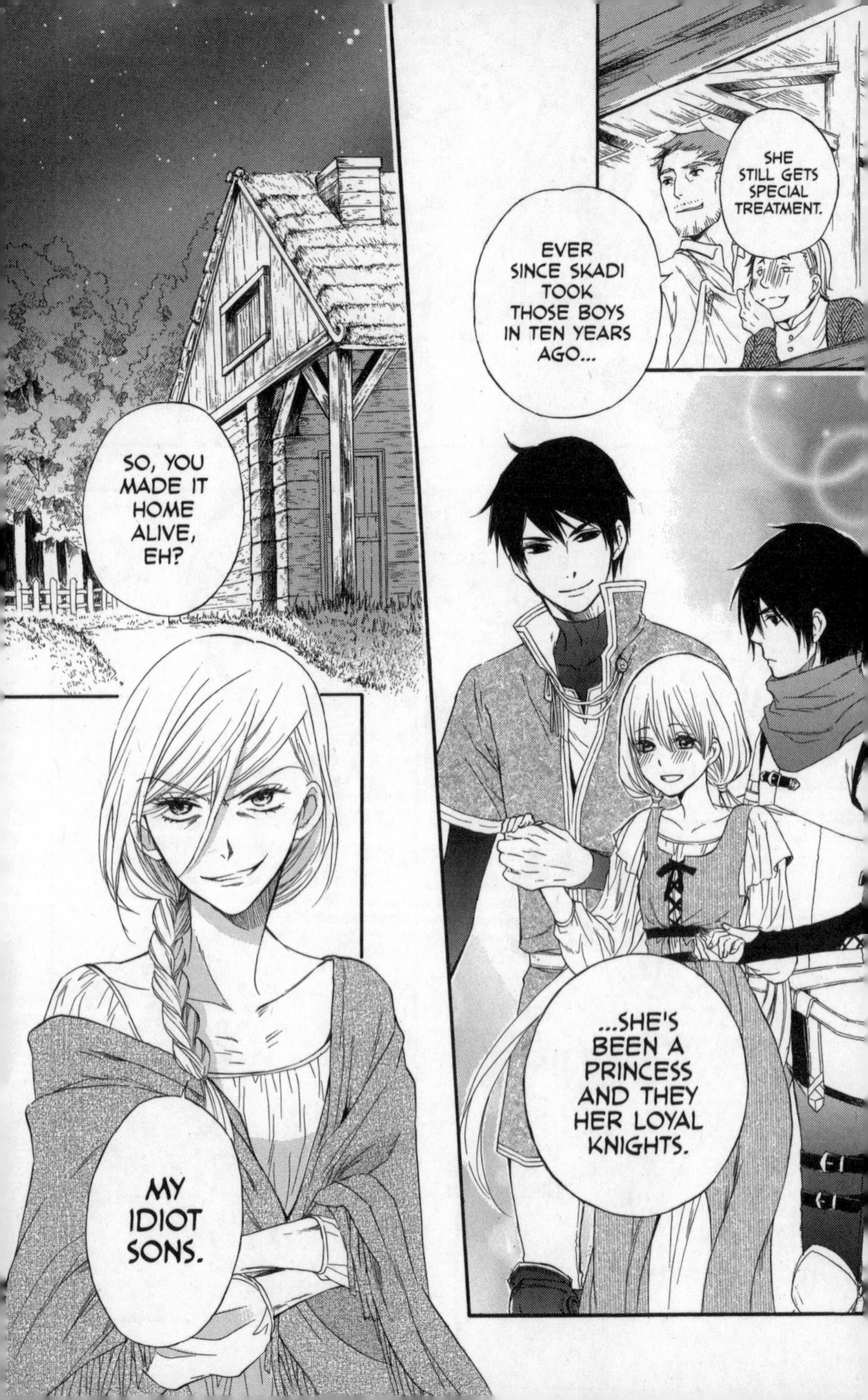
SHE STILL GETS SPECIAL TREATMENT.
EVER SINCE SKADI TOOK THOSE BOYS IN TEN YEARS AGO...
...SHE'S BEEN A PRINCESS AND THEY HER LOYAL KNIGHTS.
SO, YOU MADE IT HOME ALIVE, EH?
MY IDIOT SONS.

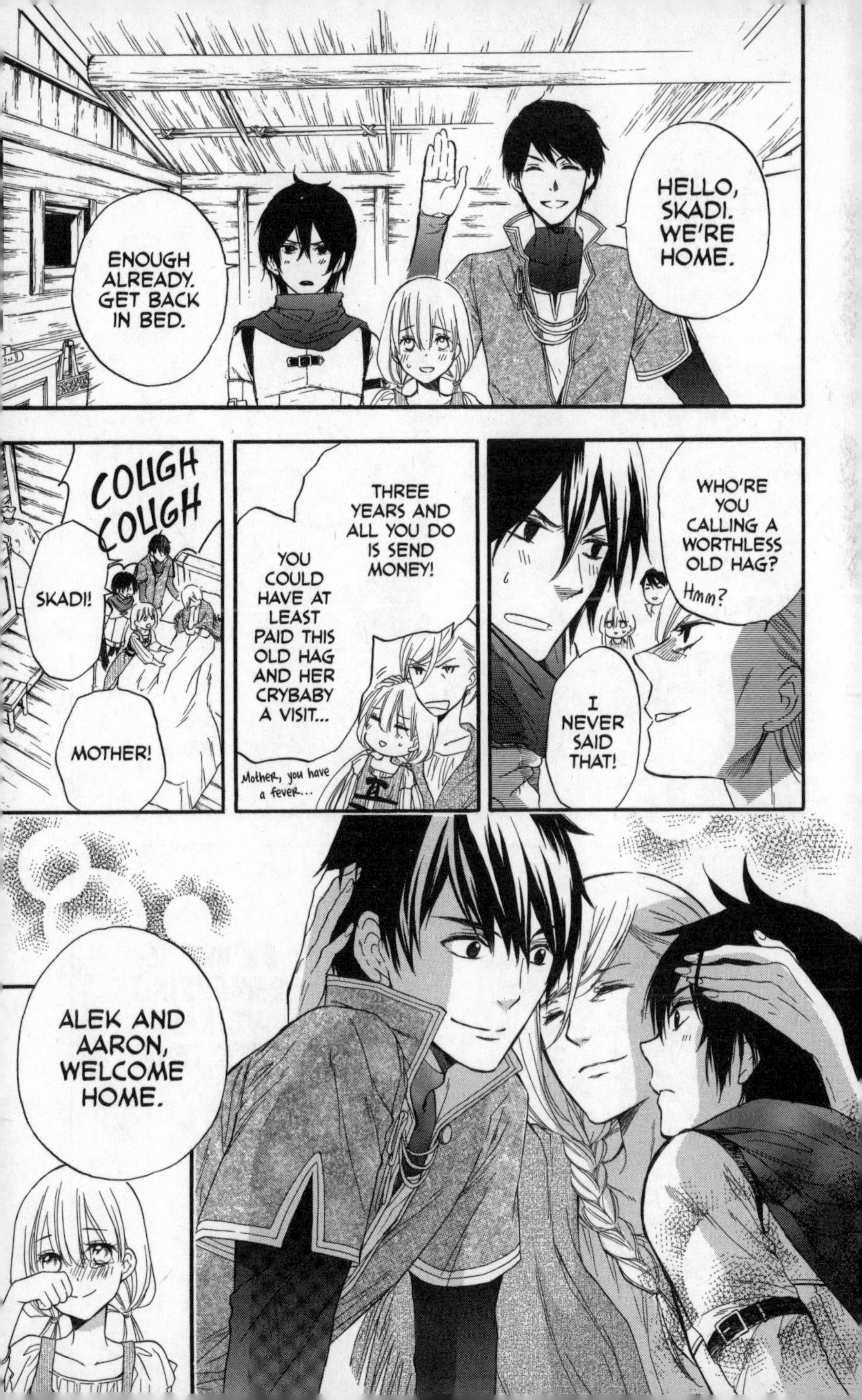
HELLO, SKADI. WE'RE HOME.
ENOUGH ALREADY. GET BACK IN BED.
WHO'RE YOU CALLING A WORTHLESS OLD HAG?
Hmm?
I NEVER SAID THAT!
THREE YEARS AND ALL YOU DO IS SEND MONEY!
YOU COULD HAVE AT LEAST PAID THIS OLD HAG AND HER CRYBABY A VISIT...
Mother, you have a fever...
COUGH COUGH
SKADI!
MOTHER!
ALEK AND AARON, WELCOME HOME.

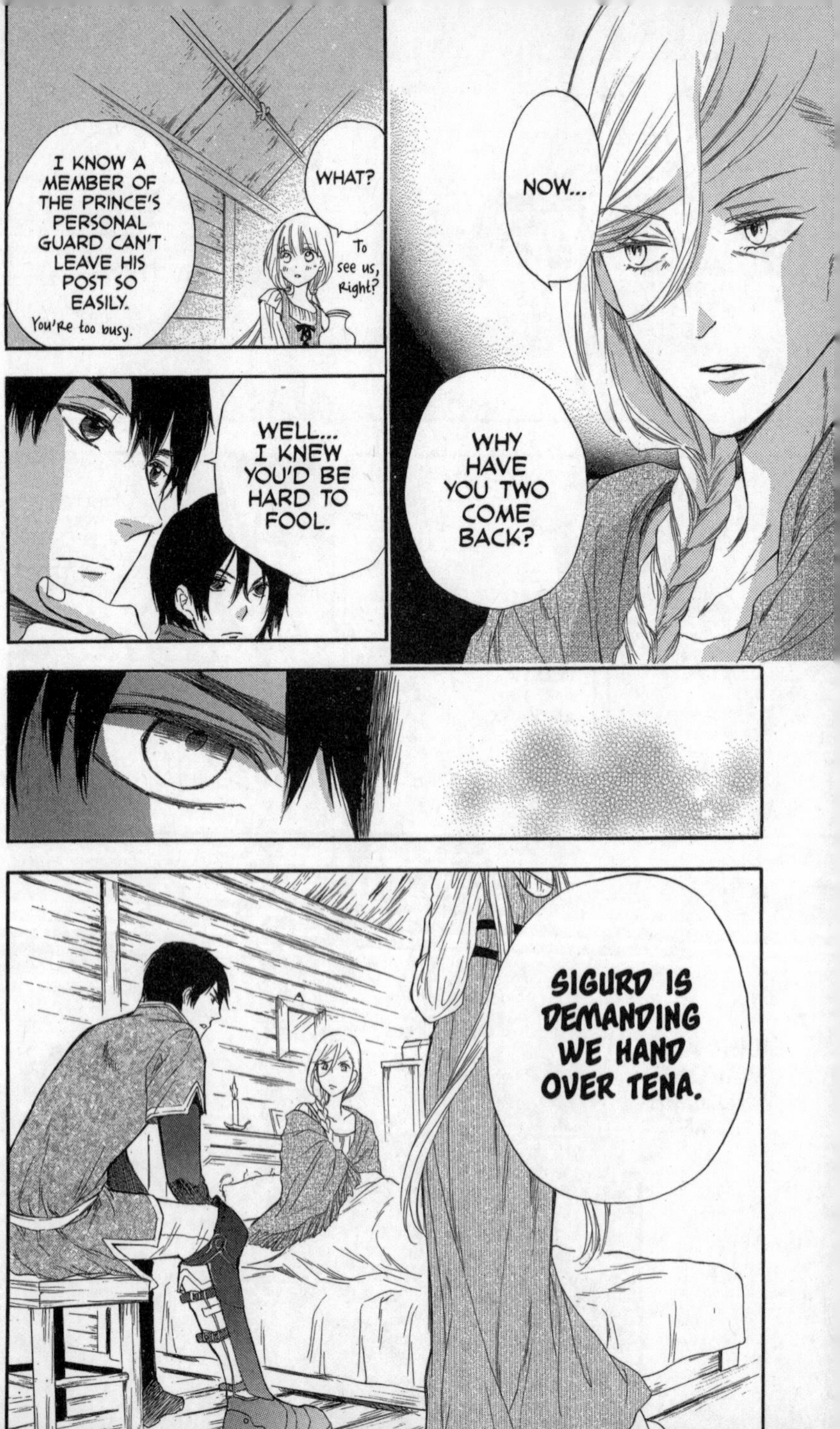
NOW...
WHY HAVE YOU TWO COME BACK?
WHAT?
To see us, Right?
I KNOW A MEMBER OF THE PRINCE'S PERSONAL GUARD CAN'T LEAVE HIS POST SO EASILY.
You're too busy.
WELL... I KNEW YOU'D BE HARD TO FOOL.
SIGURD IS DEMANDING WE HAND OVER TENA.

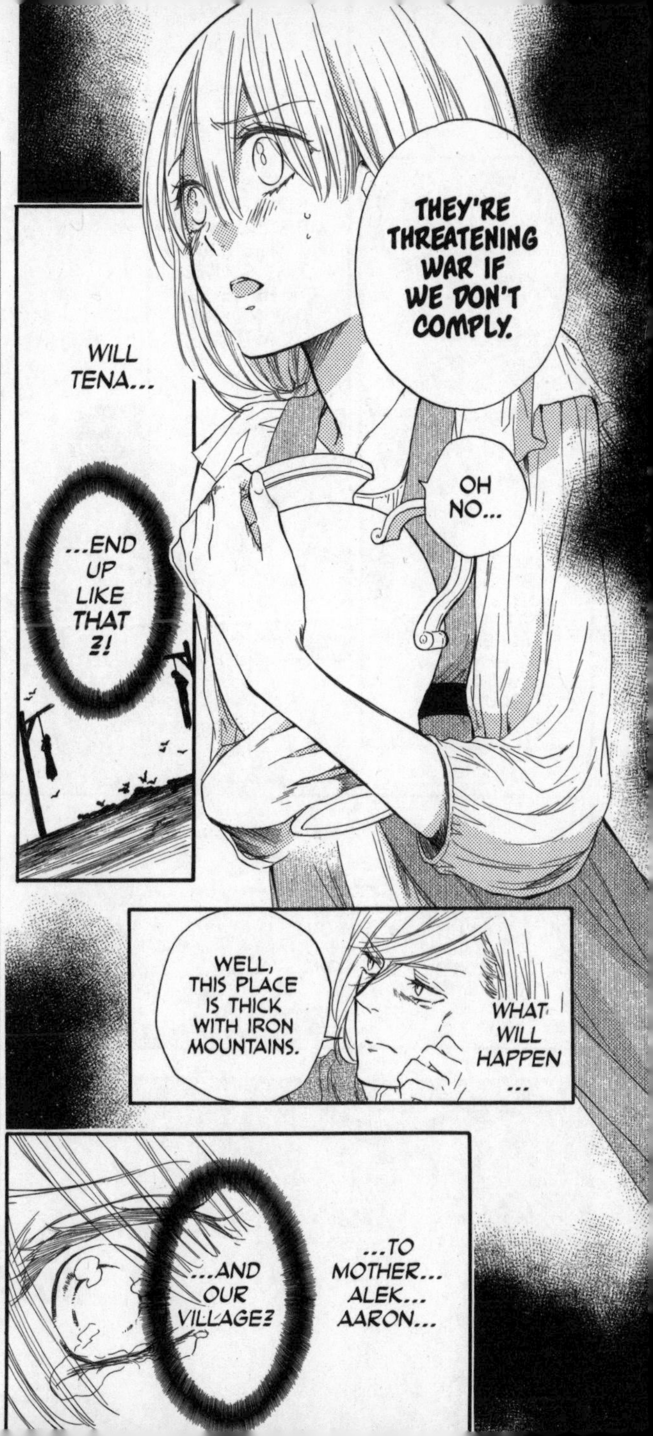
THEY'RE THREATENING WAR IF WE DON'T COMPLY.
OH NO...
WILL TENA...
...END UP LIKE THAT?!
WELL, THIS PLACE IS THICK WITH IRON MOUNTAINS.
WHAT WILL HAPPEN...
...TO MOTHER... ALEK... AARON...
...AND OUR VILLAGE?

F

"The heroine should be an ordinary girl."

Freya's character was born after much discussion.

Until now, my heroines have tended to be rather gutsy and dignified, reflecting my personal preferences.

In comparison, Freya is quite wimpy and weak.

I'll have to work diligently to polish her into a bright and shining woman.

Although I have to say that leaping off a cliff is not exactly ordinary.

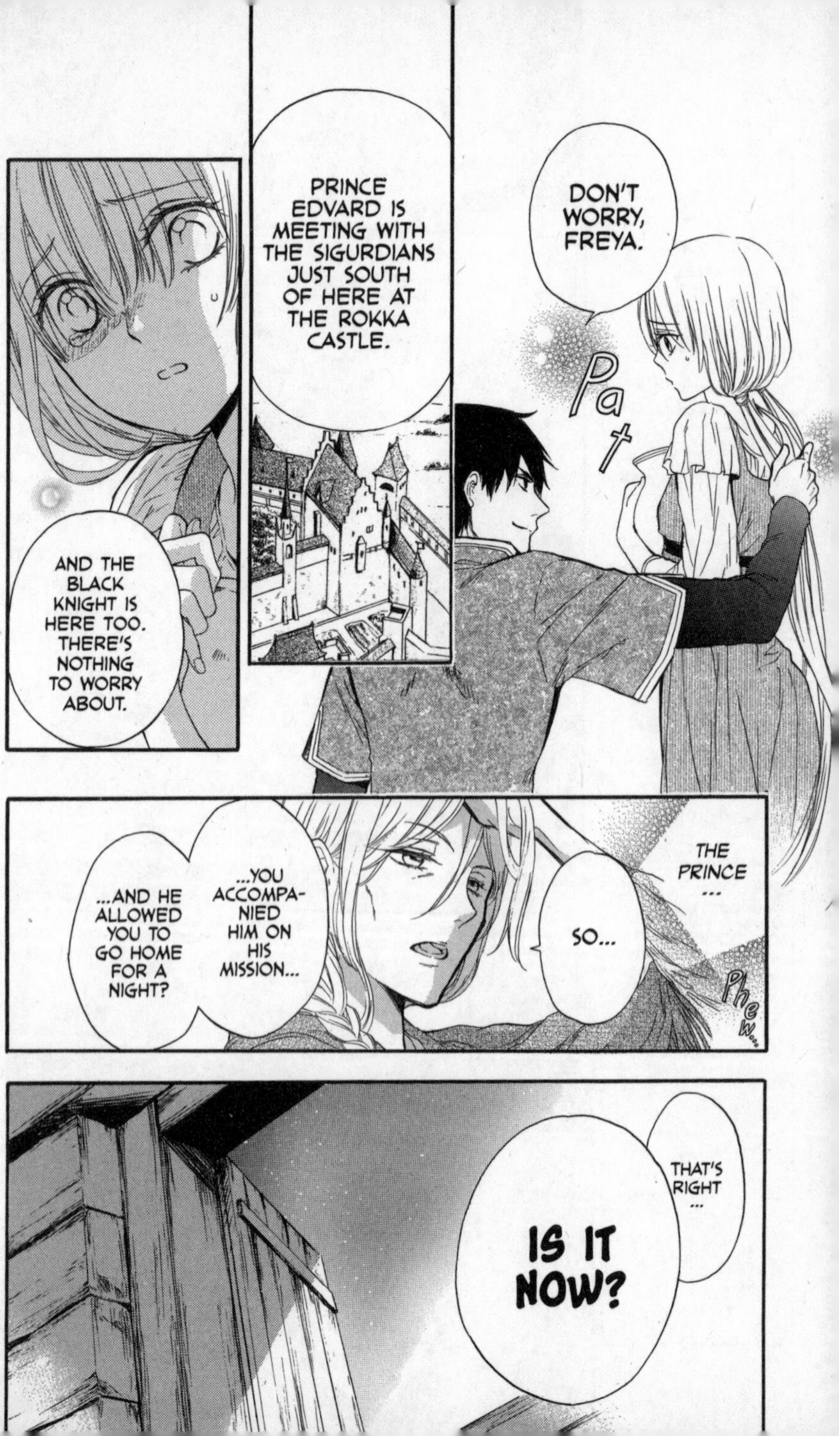
DON'T WORRY, FREYA.
Pat
PRINCE EDVARD IS MEETING WITH THE SIGURDIANS JUST SOUTH OF HERE AT THE ROKKA CASTLE.
AND THE BLACK KNIGHT IS HERE TOO. THERE'S NOTHING TO WORRY ABOUT.
THE PRINCE...
Phew...
SO...
...YOU ACCOMPANIED HIM ON HIS MISSION...
...AND HE ALLOWED YOU TO GO HOME FOR A NIGHT?
THAT'S RIGHT...
IS IT NOW?

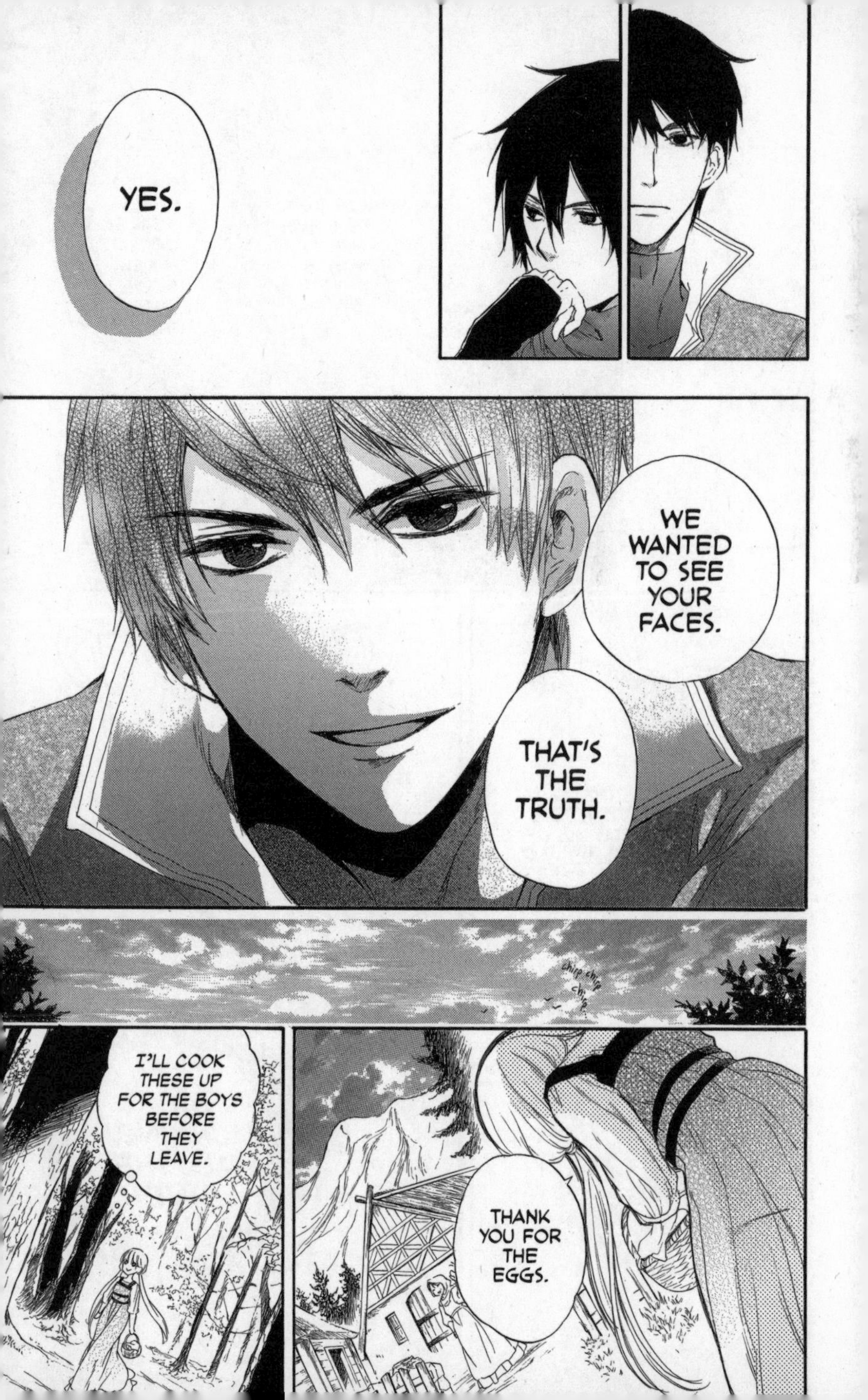
YES.
WE WANTED TO SEE YOUR FACES.
THAT'S THE TRUTH.
chirp chirp chirp
THANK YOU FOR THE EGGS.
I'LL COOK THESE UP FOR THE BOYS BEFORE THEY LEAVE.

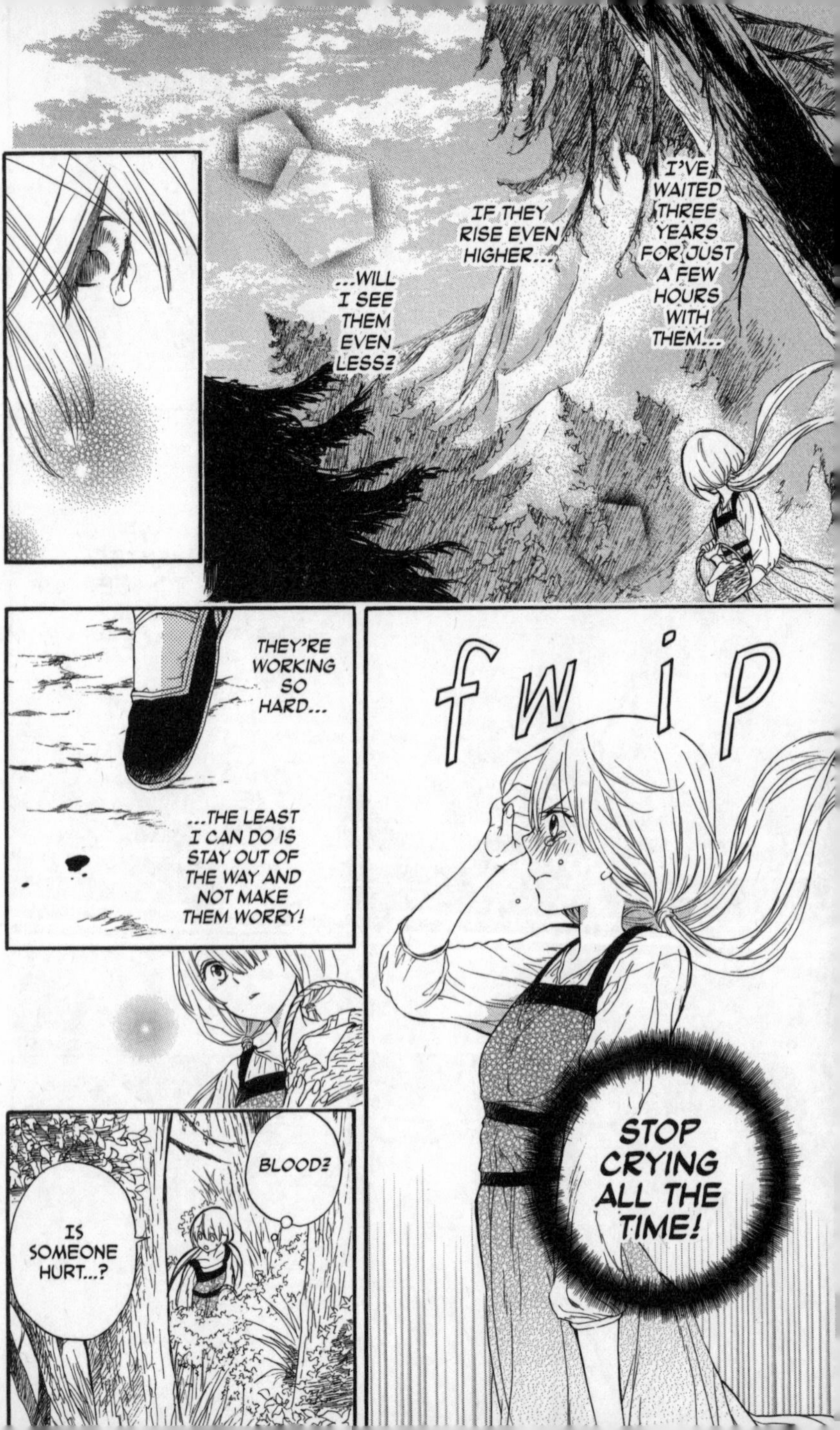
I'VE WAITED THREE YEARS FOR JUST A FEW HOURS WITH THEM...
IF THEY RISE EVEN HIGHER...
...WILL I SEE THEM EVEN LESS?
fwip
STOP CRYING ALL THE TIME!
THEY'RE WORKING SO HARD...
...THE LEAST I CAN DO IS STAY OUT OF THE WAY AND NOT MAKE THEM WORRY!
BLOOD?
IS SOMEONE HURT...?

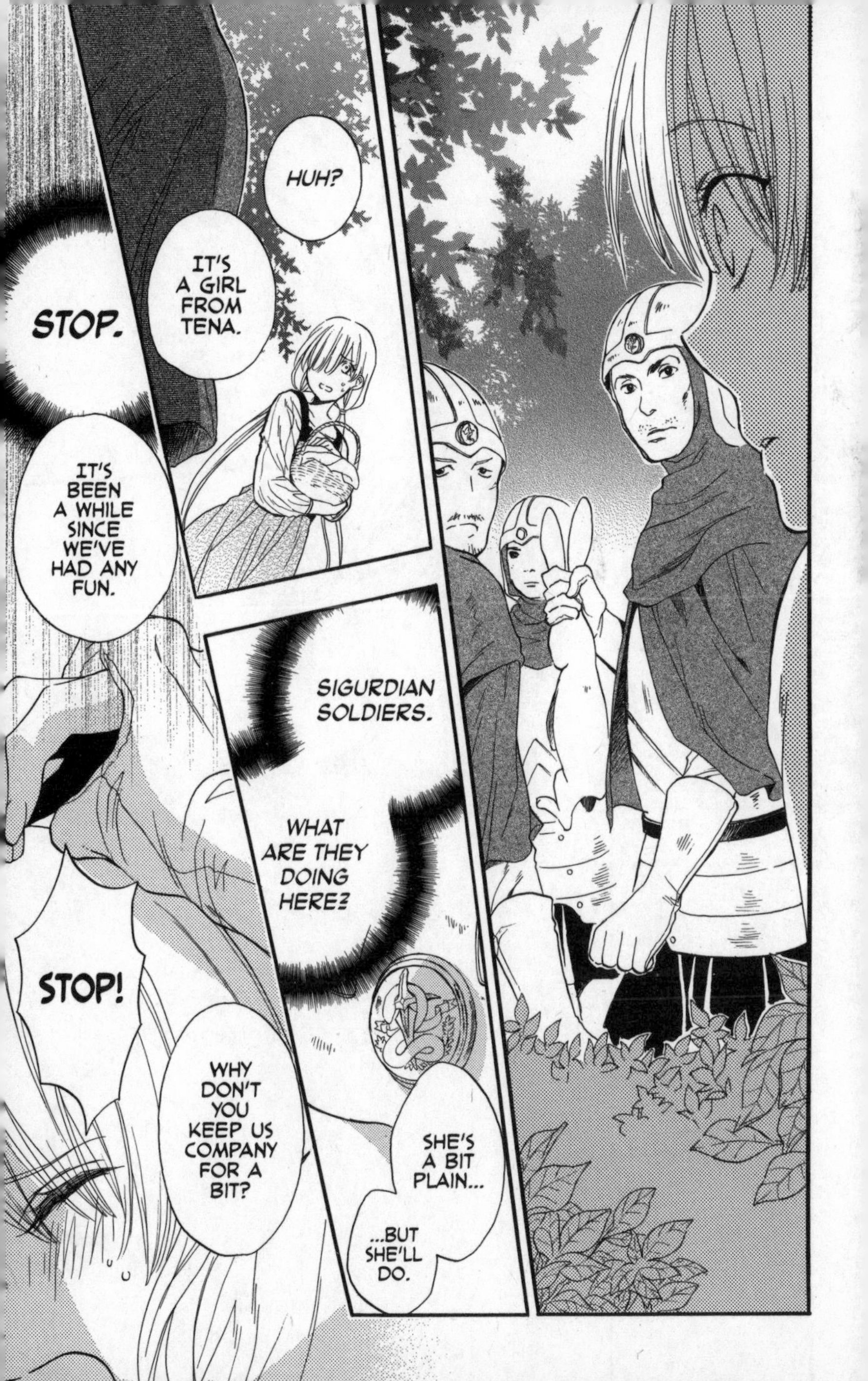
HUH?
IT'S A GIRL FROM TENA.
SIGURDIAN SOLDIERS.
WHAT ARE THEY DOING HERE?
SHE'S A BIT PLAIN...
...BUT SHE'LL DO.
STOP.
IT'S BEEN A WHILE SINCE WE'VE HAD ANY FUN.
STOP!
WHY DON'T YOU KEEP US COMPANY FOR A BIT?

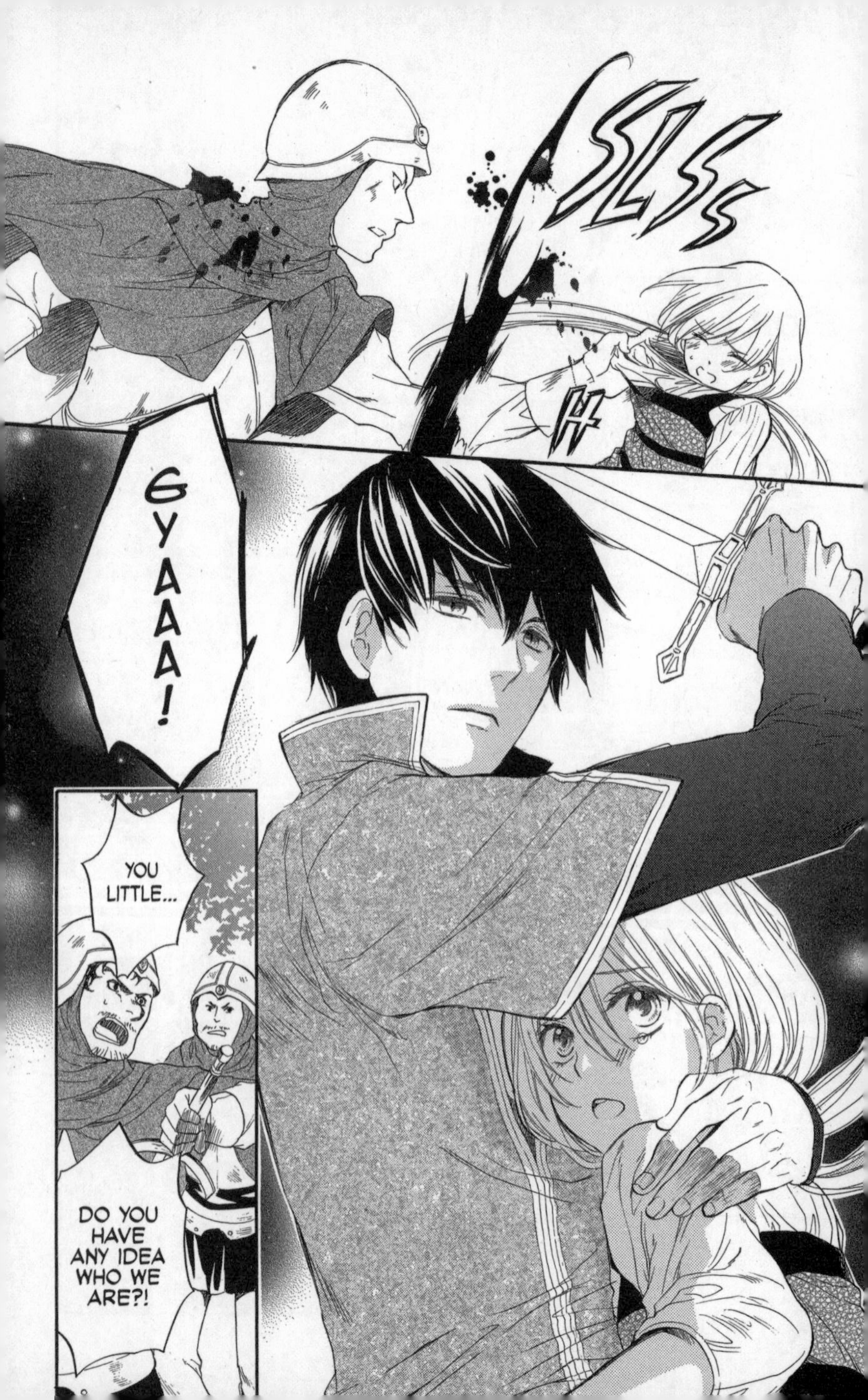
SLISS
H
GYAAAA!
YOU LITTLE...
DO YOU HAVE ANY IDEA WHO WE ARE?!

A

Aaron, the older brother you can count on.

The hero in my last story was rather delicate, so I'm really enjoying drawing a well-built man this time.

That said, when I was developing the story, I repeatedly received feedback that my character design wasn't very attractive, which left me stumped.

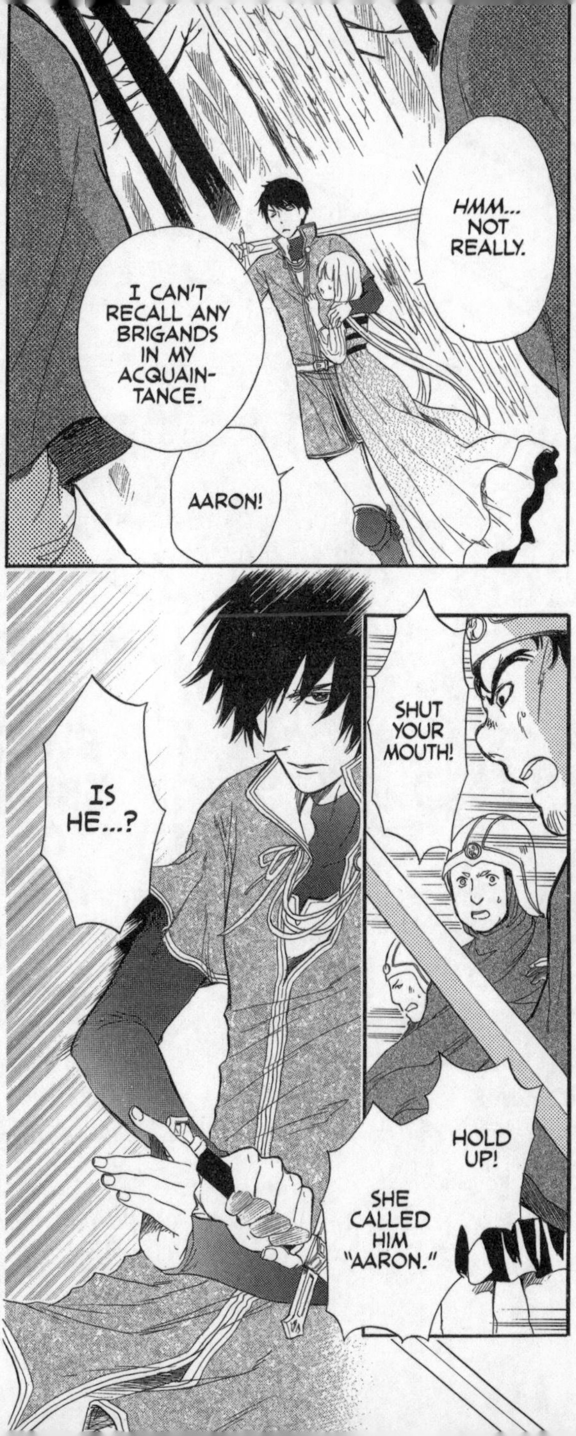

HMM... NOT REALLY.
I CAN'T RECALL ANY BRIGANDS IN MY ACQUAIN-TANCE.
AARON!
SHUT YOUR MOUTH!
HOLD UP!
SHE CALLED HIM "AARON."
IS HE...?

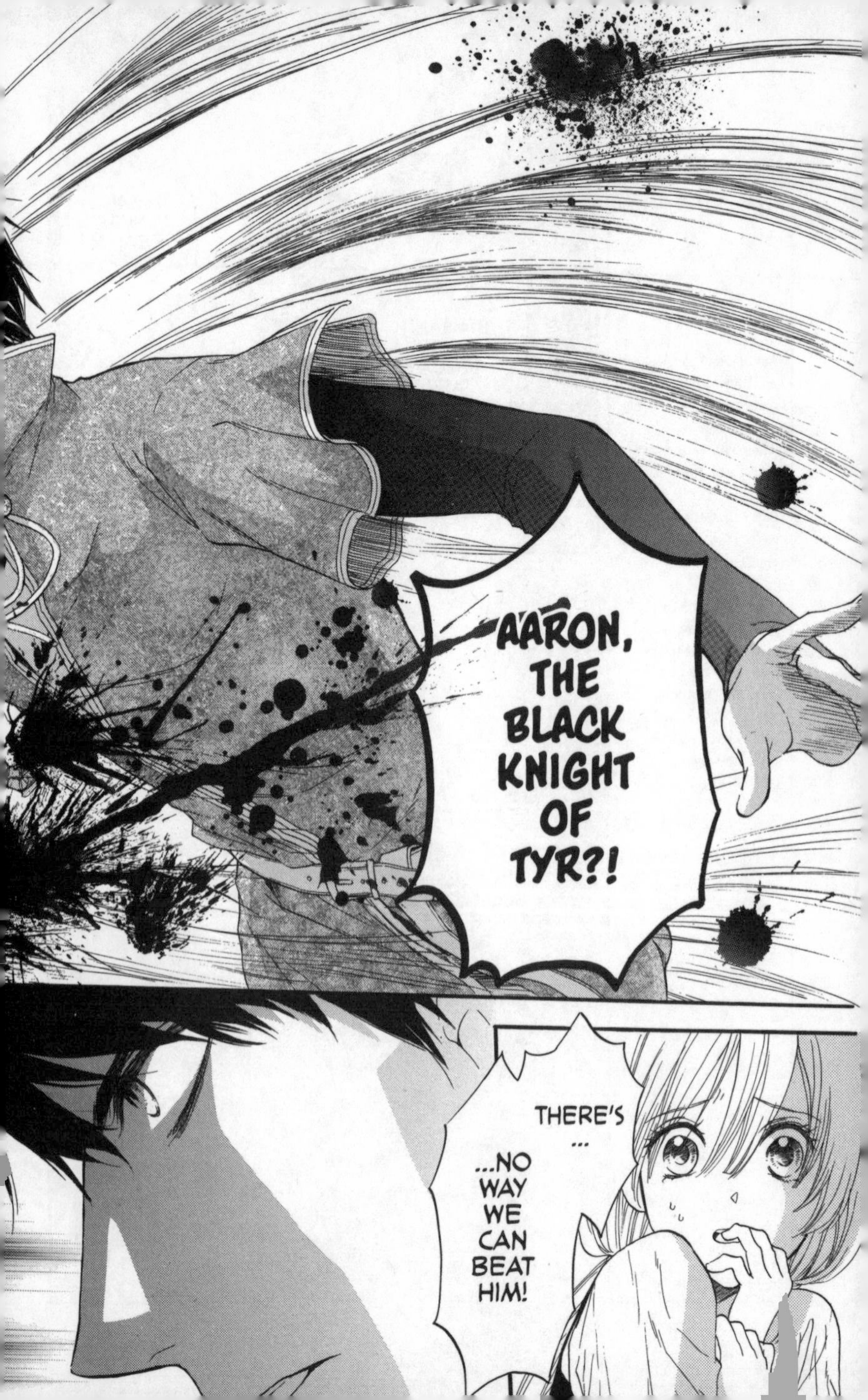
AARON, THE BLACK KNIGHT OF TYR?!
THERE'S ...
...NO WAY WE CAN BEAT HIM!

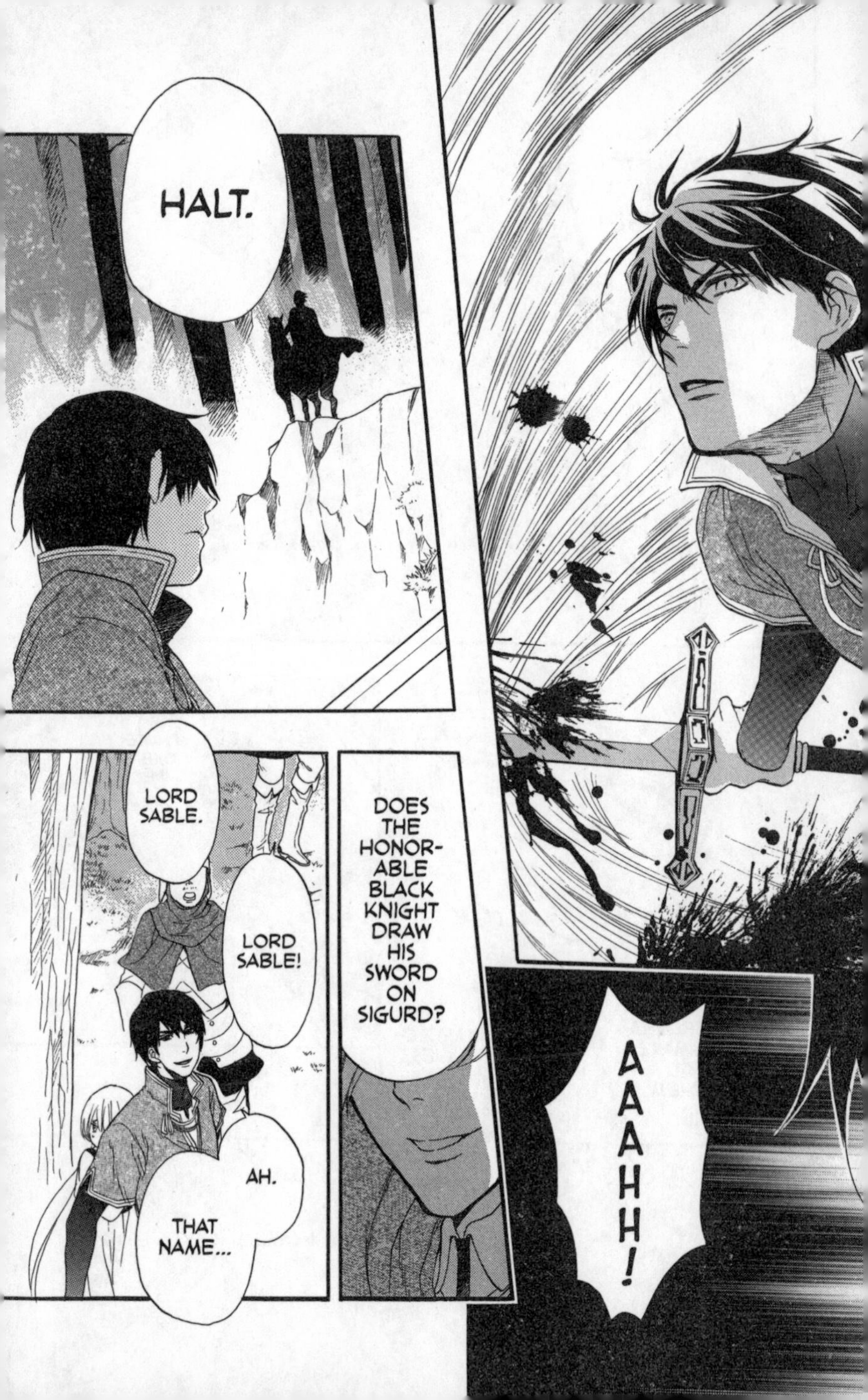
HALT.
DOES THE HONORABLE BLACK KNIGHT DRAW HIS SWORD ON SIGURD?
LORD SABLE.
LORD SABLE!
AH.
THAT NAME...
AAAAHH!

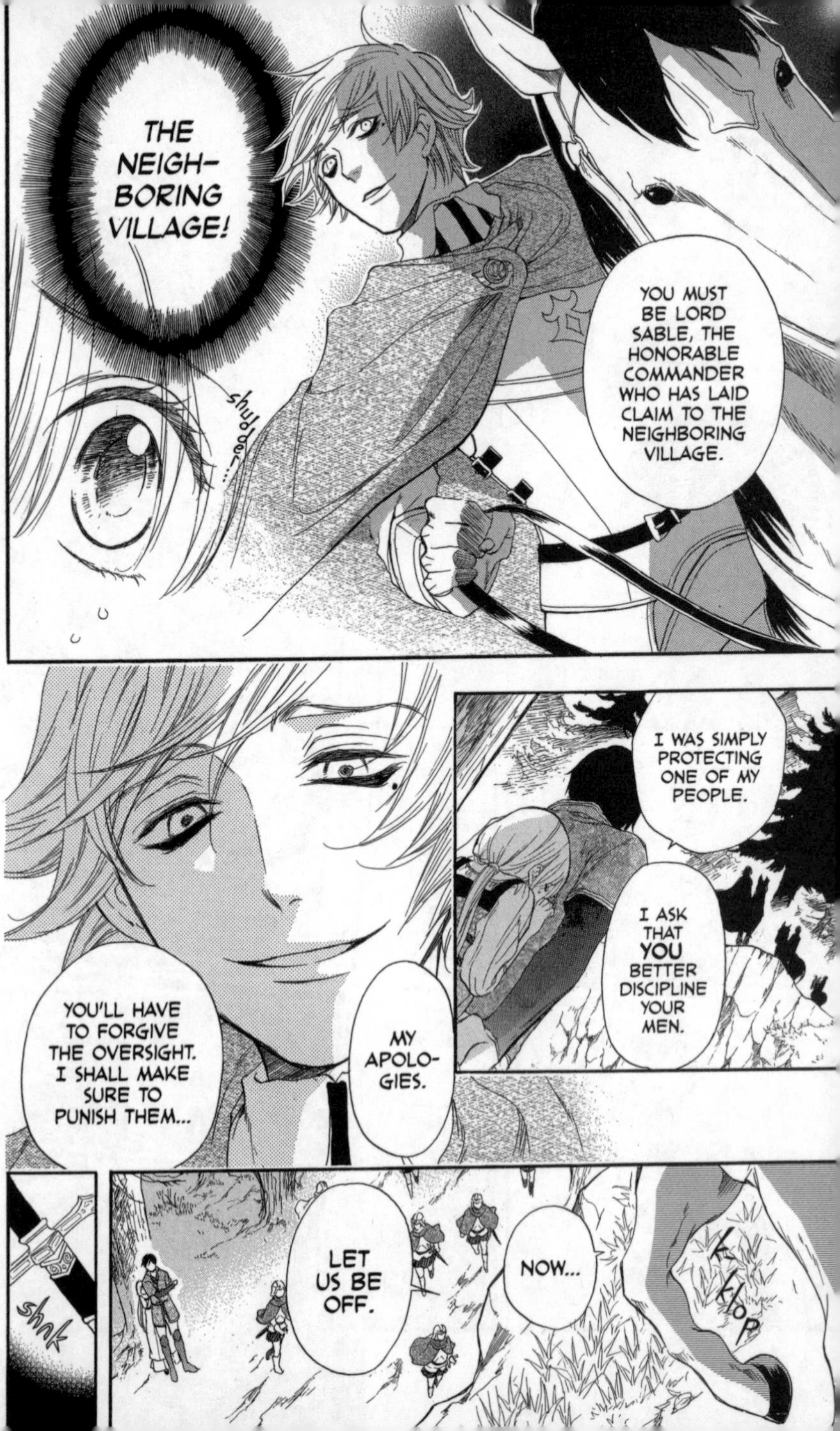
YOU MUST BE LORD SABLE, THE HONORABLE COMMANDER WHO HAS LAID CLAIM TO THE NEIGHBORING VILLAGE.
THE NEIGH-BORING VILLAGE!
shudder...
I WAS SIMPLY PROTECTING ONE OF MY PEOPLE.
I ASK THAT **YOU** BETTER DISCIPLINE YOUR MEN.
MY APOLO-GIES.
YOU'LL HAVE TO FORGIVE THE OVERSIGHT. I SHALL MAKE SURE TO PUNISH THEM...
klop
NOW...
LET US BE OFF.
shnk

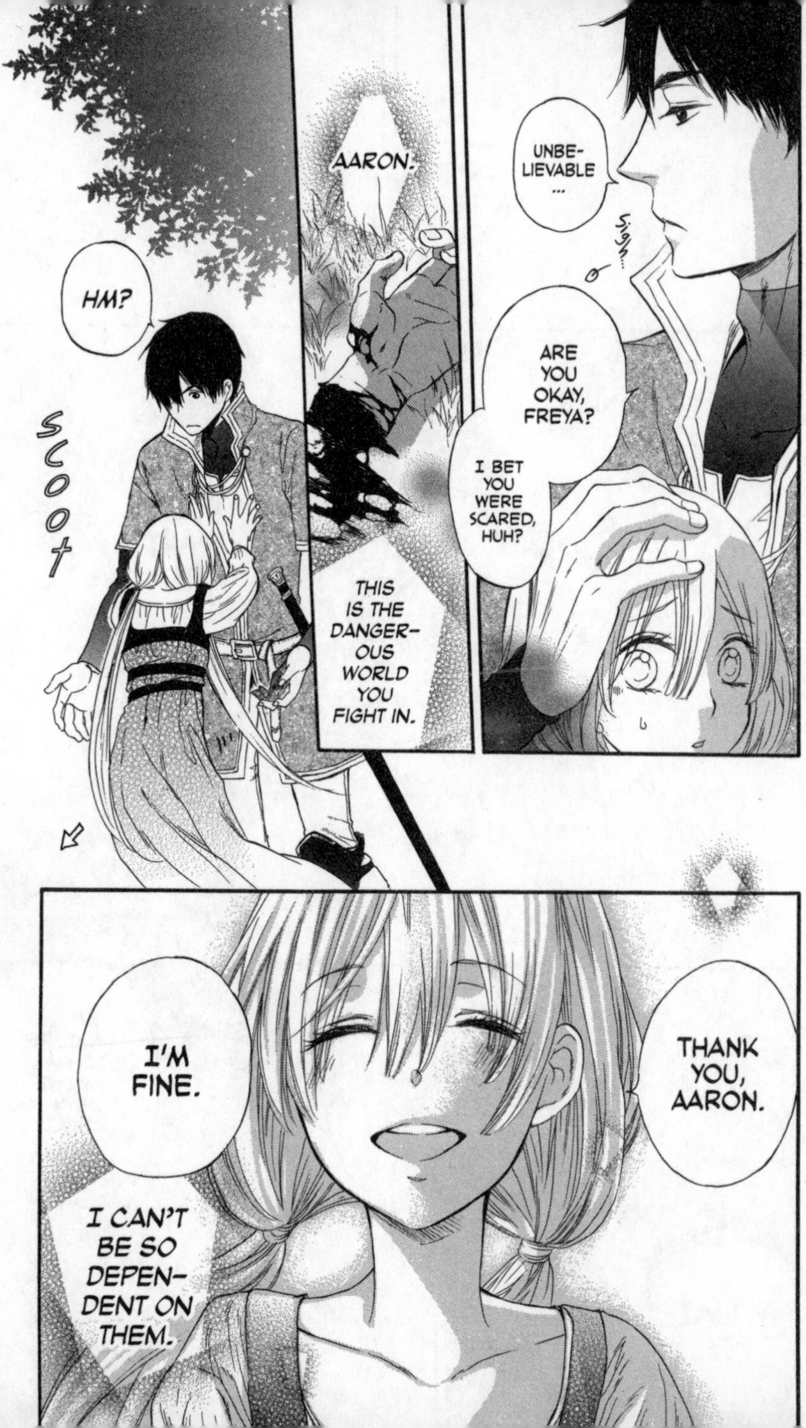
UNBE-LIEVABLE...
Sigh...
ARE YOU OKAY, FREYA?
I BET YOU WERE SCARED, HUH?
AARON.
THIS IS THE DANGER-OUS WORLD YOU FIGHT IN.
HM?
SCOOT
THANK YOU, AARON.
I'M FINE.
I CAN'T BE SO DEPEN-DENT ON THEM.

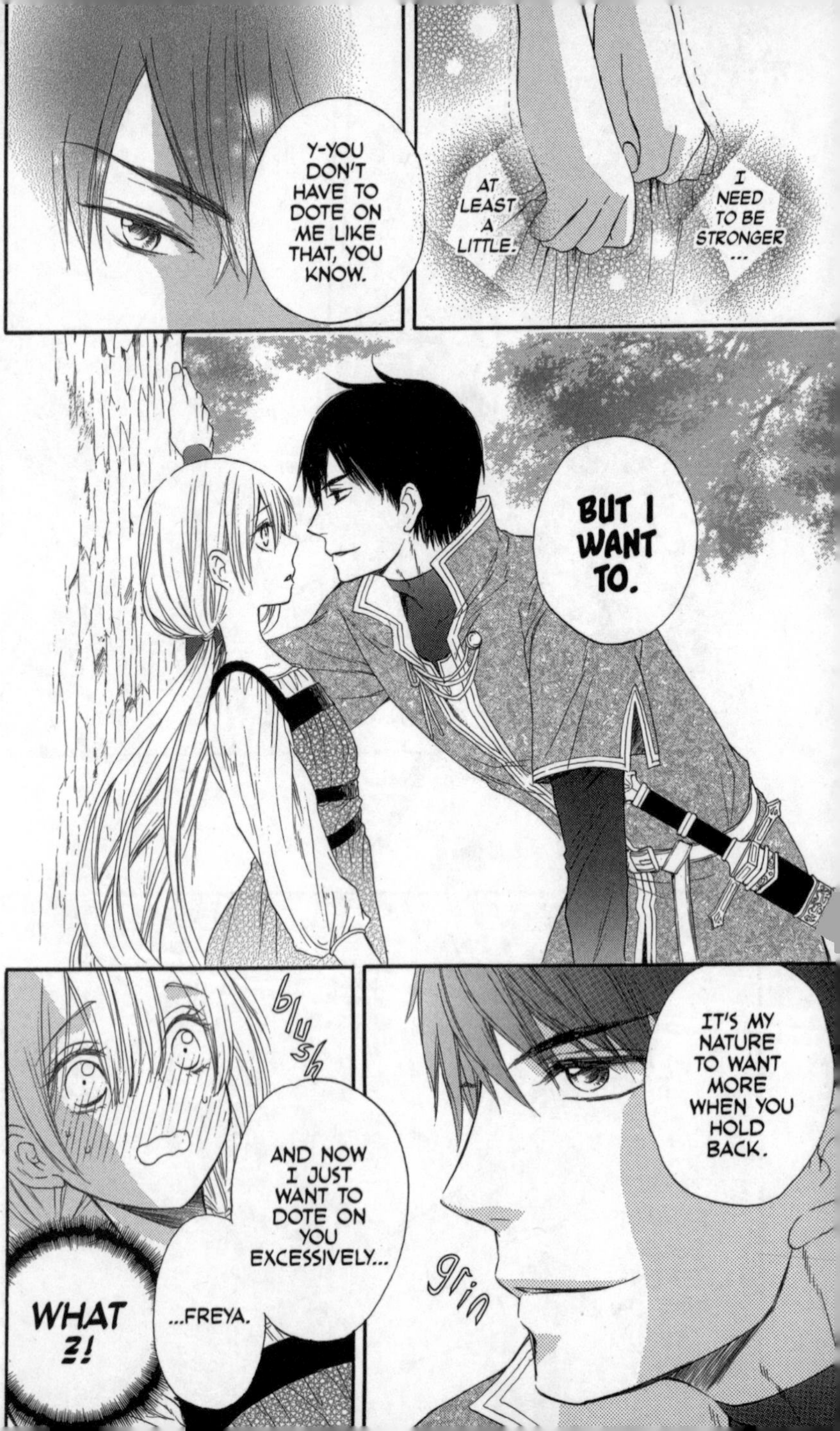

I NEED TO BE STRONGER...
AT LEAST A LITTLE.
Y-YOU DON'T HAVE TO DOTE ON ME LIKE THAT, YOU KNOW.
BUT I WANT TO.
IT'S MY NATURE TO WANT MORE WHEN YOU HOLD BACK.
grin
AND NOW I JUST WANT TO DOTE ON YOU EXCESSIVELY...
...FREYA.
blush
WHAT?!

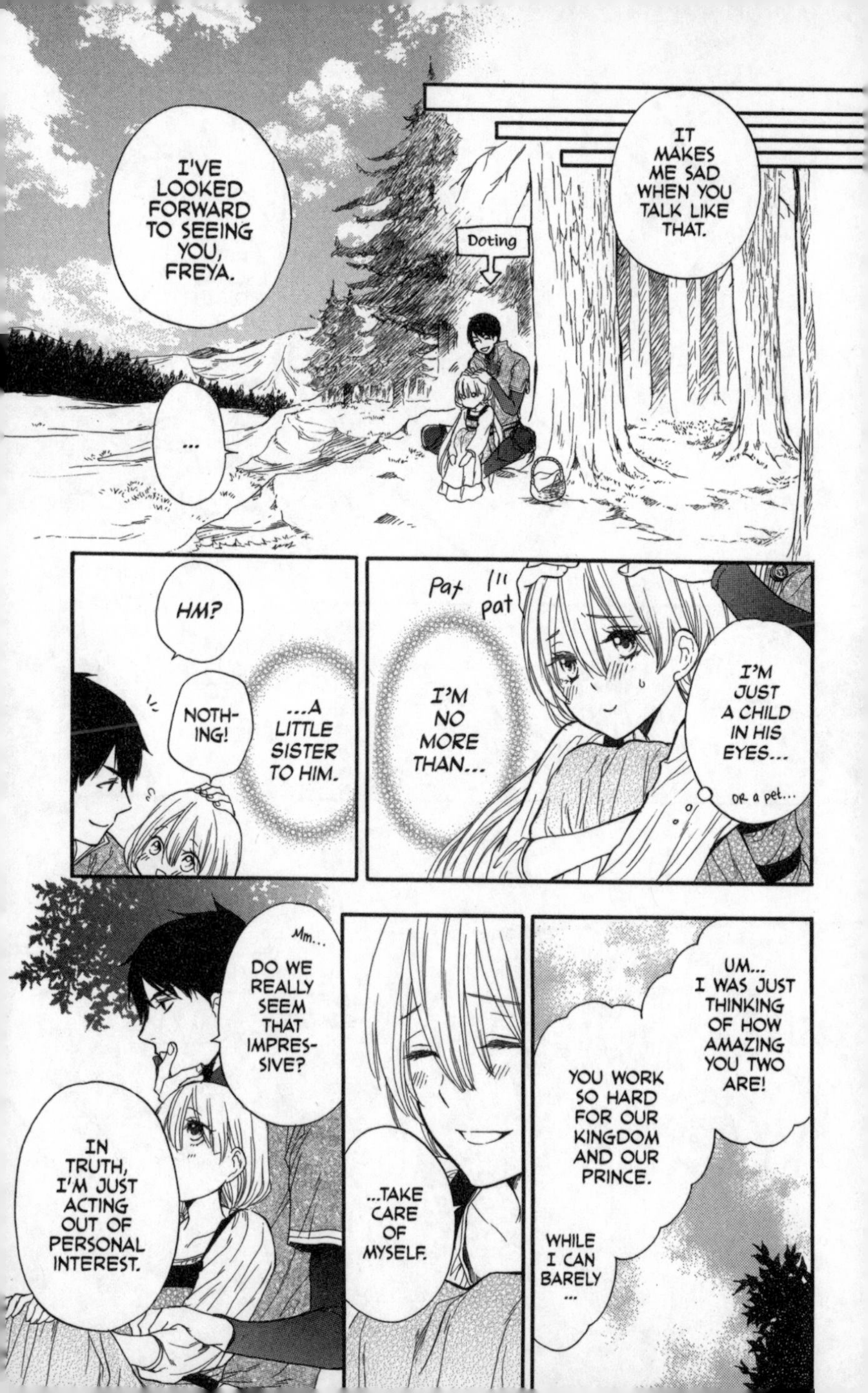
IT MAKES ME SAD WHEN YOU TALK LIKE THAT.
Doting
I'VE LOOKED FORWARD TO SEEING YOU, FREYA.
...
Pat pat
I'M JUST A CHILD IN HIS EYES...
OR a pet...
I'M NO MORE THAN...
...A LITTLE SISTER TO HIM.
HM?
NOTH-ING!
UM... I WAS JUST THINKING OF HOW AMAZING YOU TWO ARE!
YOU WORK SO HARD FOR OUR KINGDOM AND OUR PRINCE.
WHILE I CAN BARELY ...
...TAKE CARE OF MYSELF.
Mm...
DO WE REALLY SEEM THAT IMPRESSIVE?
IN TRUTH, I'M JUST ACTING OUT OF PERSONAL INTEREST.

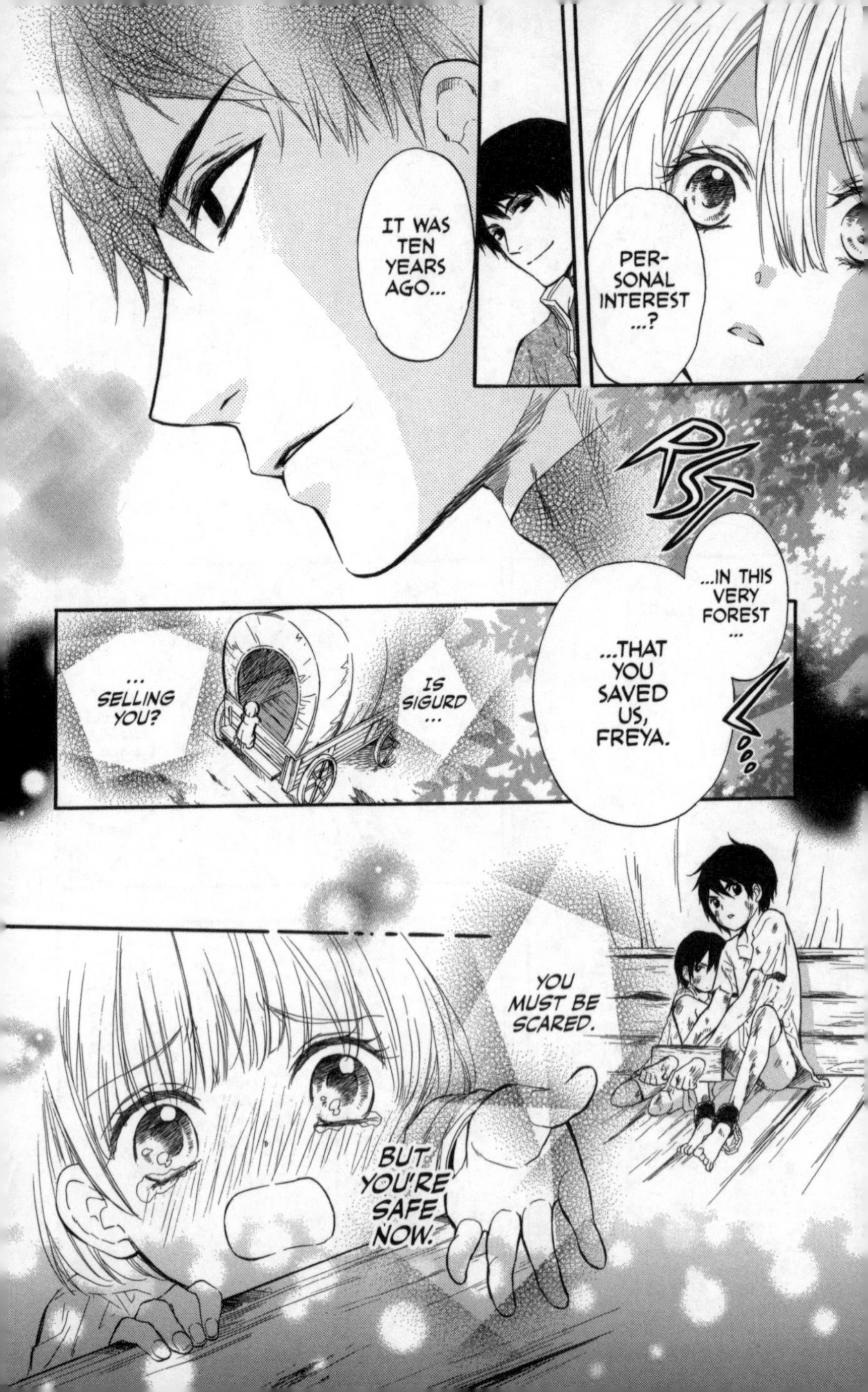
PER-
SONAL
INTEREST
...?
IT WAS
TEN
YEARS
AGO...
RST
...IN THIS
VERY
FOREST
...
...THAT
YOU
SAVED
US,
FREYA.
Looo
IS
SIGURD
...
...
SELLING
YOU?
YOU
MUST BE
SCARED.
BUT
YOU'RE
SAFE
NOW.

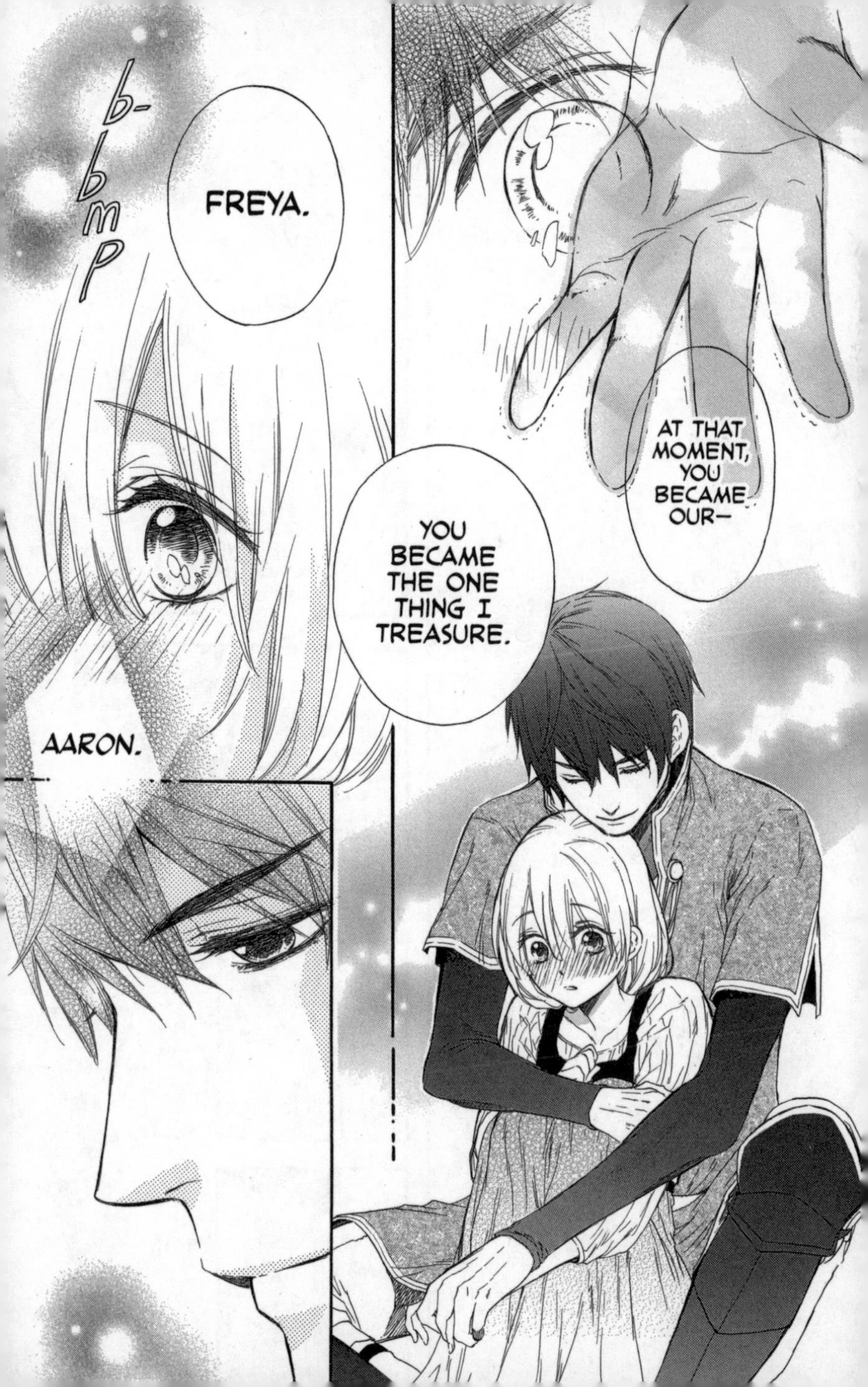
AT THAT MOMENT, YOU BECAME OUR—
YOU BECAME THE ONE THING I TREASURE.
b-bmp
FREYA.
AARON.

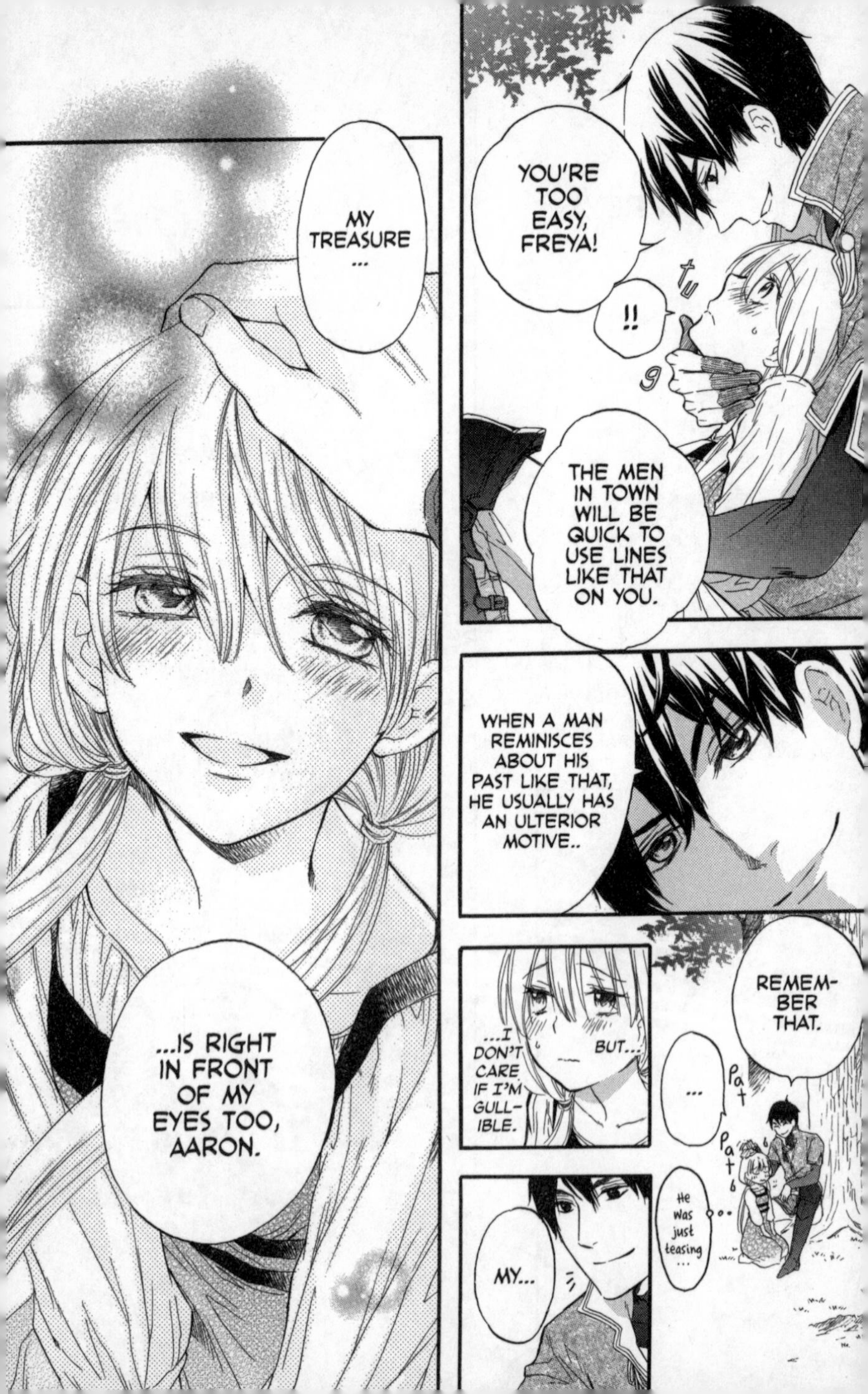
YOU'RE TOO EASY, FREYA!
tu
!!
g
THE MEN IN TOWN WILL BE QUICK TO USE LINES LIKE THAT ON YOU.
WHEN A MAN REMINISCES ABOUT HIS PAST LIKE THAT, HE USUALLY HAS AN ULTERIOR MOTIVE..
REMEMBER THAT.
Pat
Pat
...
He was just teasing...
BUT...
...I DON'T CARE IF I'M GULLIBLE.
MY...
MY TREASURE...
...IS RIGHT IN FRONT OF MY EYES TOO, AARON.

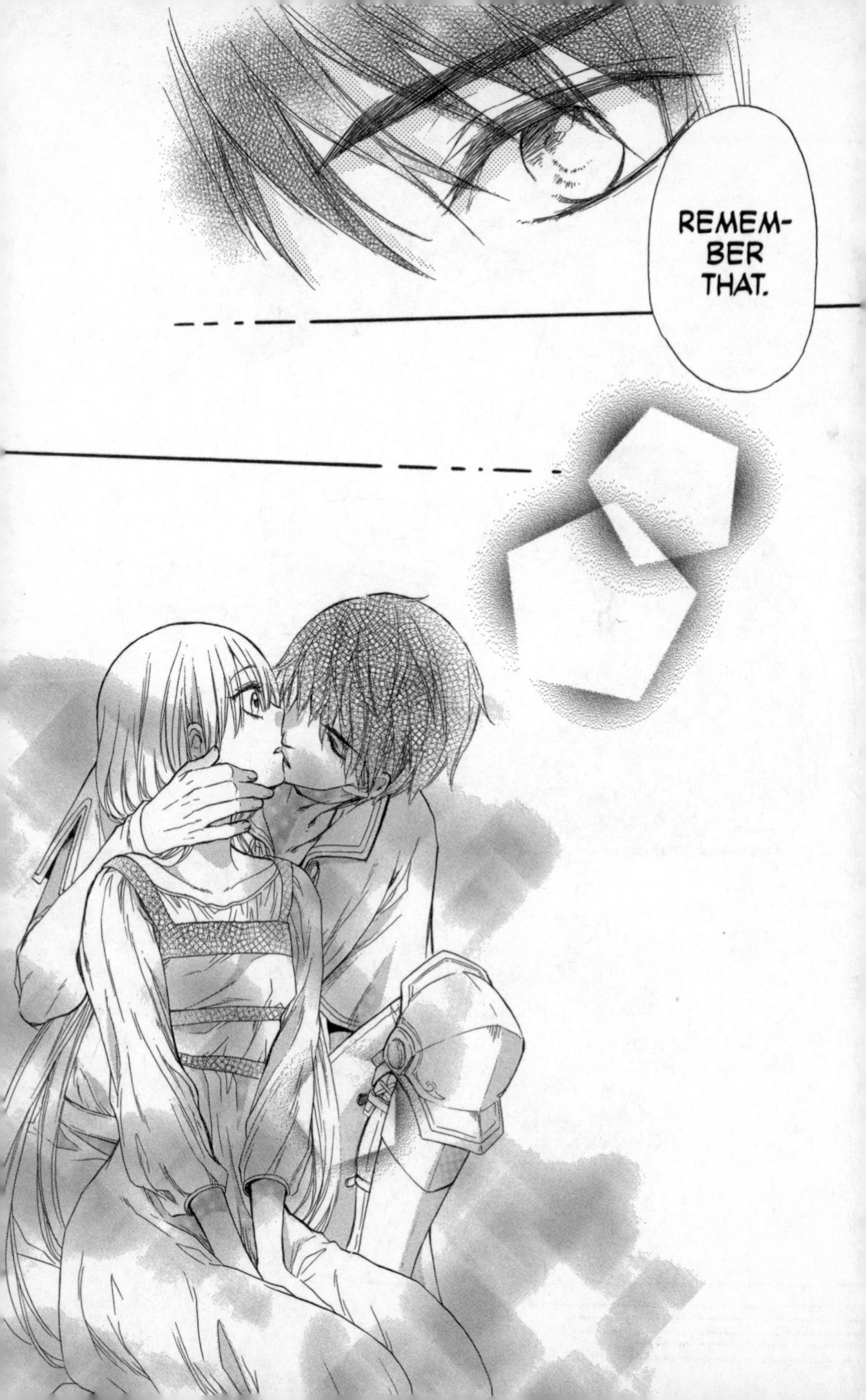
REMEM-
BER
THAT.

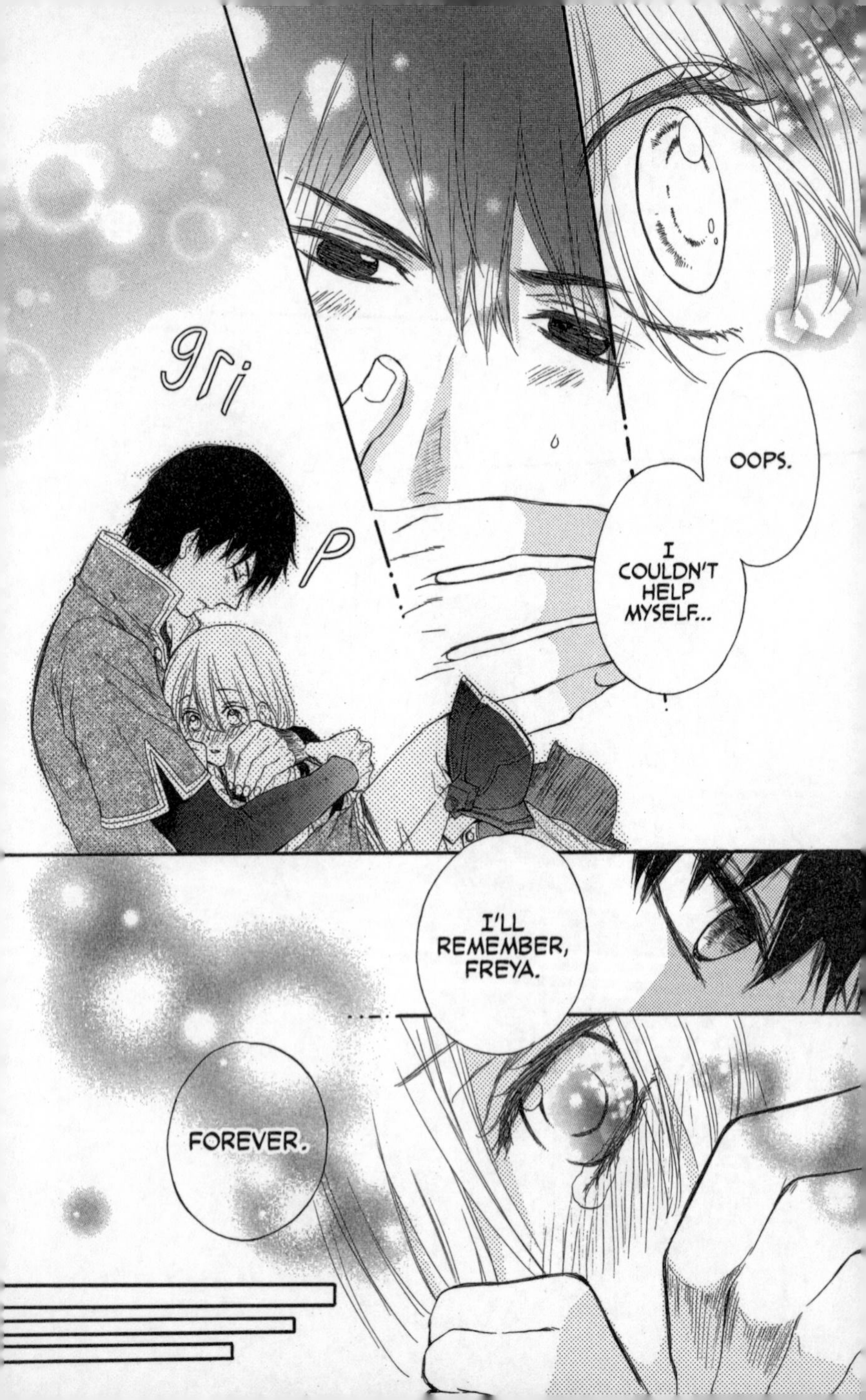
OOPS.
I COULDN'T HELP MYSELF...
grip
I'LL REMEMBER, FREYA.
FOREVER.

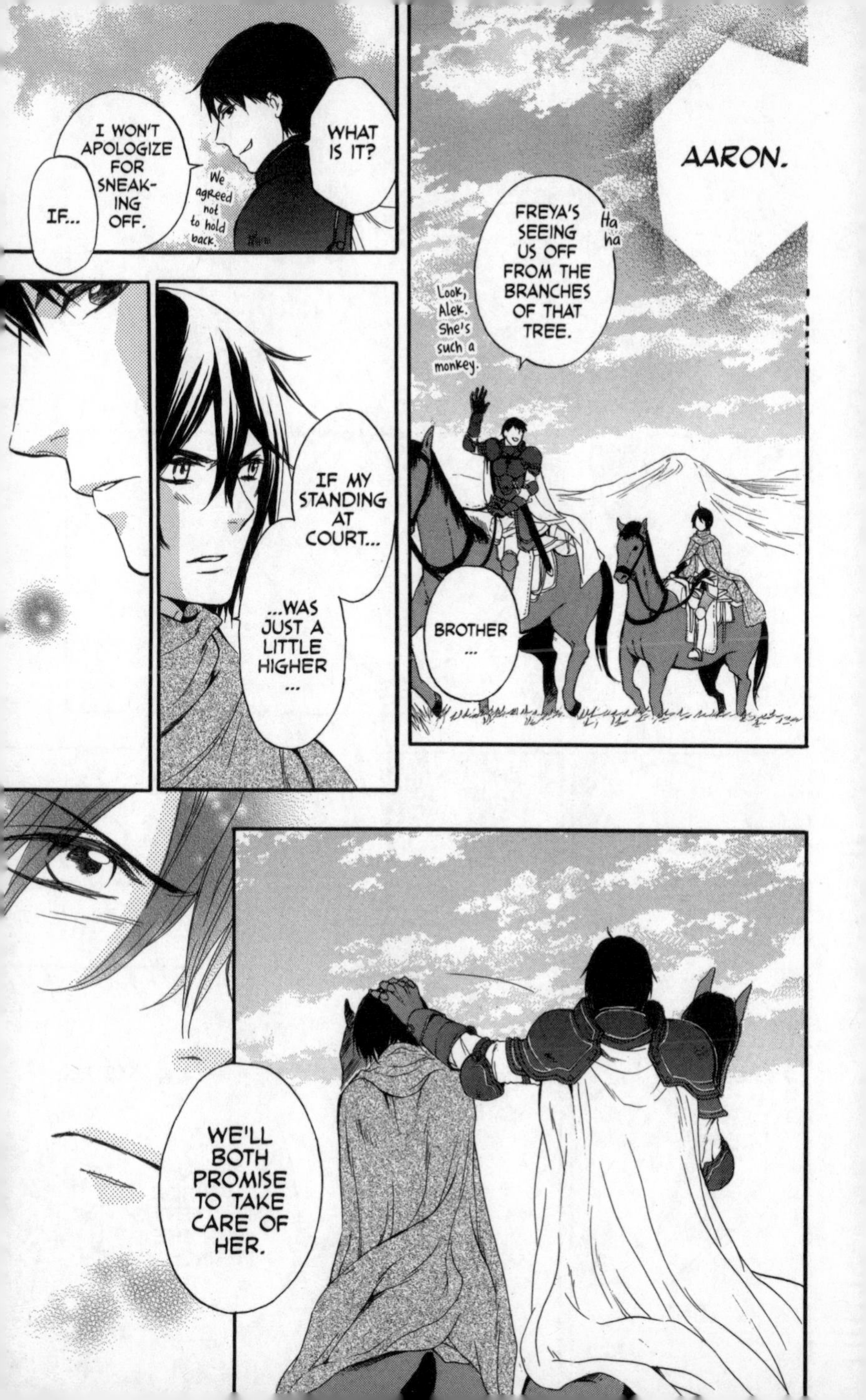
AARON.
FREYA'S SEEING US OFF FROM THE BRANCHES OF THAT TREE.
Ha ha
Look, Alek. She's such a monkey.
BROTHER...
WHAT IS IT?
We agreed not to hold back.
I WON'T APOLOGIZE FOR SNEAKING OFF.
IF...
IF MY STANDING AT COURT...
...WAS JUST A LITTLE HIGHER...
WE'LL BOTH PROMISE TO TAKE CARE OF HER.

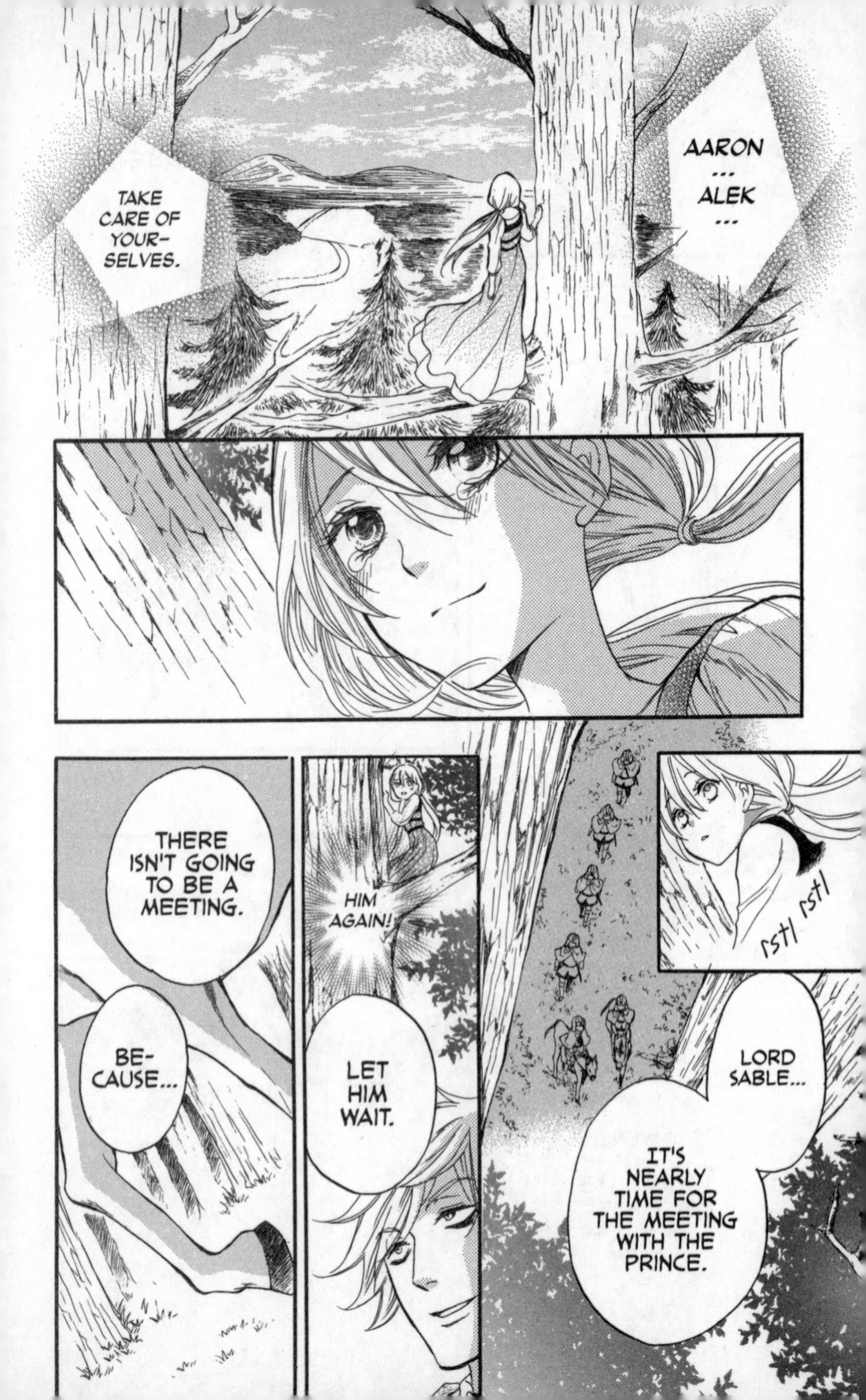
AARON ... ALEK ...
TAKE CARE OF YOURSELVES.
rstl rstl
LORD SABLE...
IT'S NEARLY TIME FOR THE MEETING WITH THE PRINCE.
HIM AGAIN!
LET HIM WAIT.
THERE ISN'T GOING TO BE A MEETING.
BE-CAUSE...

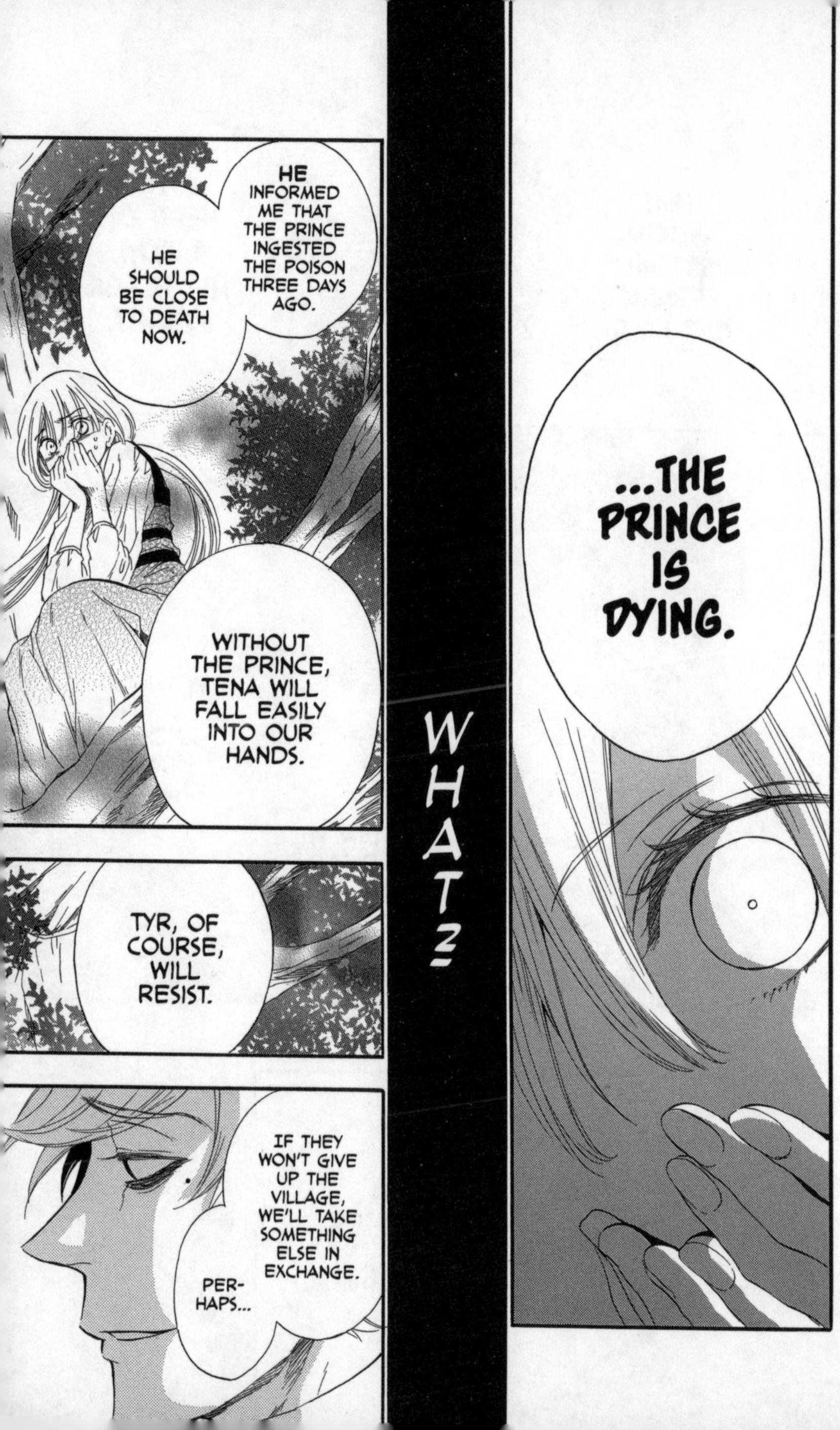
...THE PRINCE IS DYING.
WHAT?!
HE INFORMED ME THAT THE PRINCE INGESTED THE POISON THREE DAYS AGO.
HE SHOULD BE CLOSE TO DEATH NOW.
WITHOUT THE PRINCE, TENA WILL FALL EASILY INTO OUR HANDS.
TYR, OF COURSE, WILL RESIST.
IF THEY WON'T GIVE UP THE VILLAGE, WE'LL TAKE SOMETHING ELSE IN EXCHANGE.
PER-HAPS...

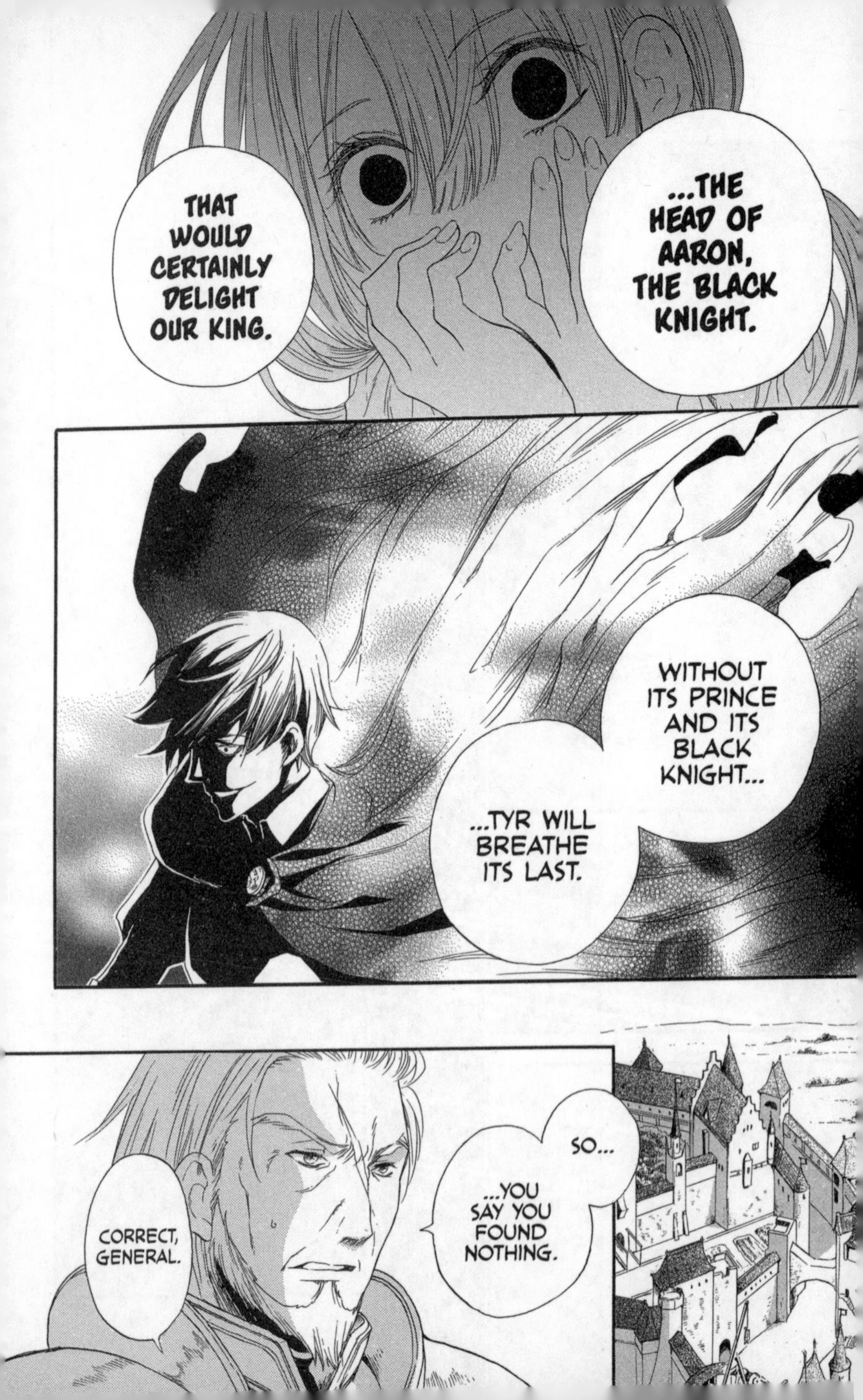
...THE HEAD OF AARON, THE BLACK KNIGHT.
THAT WOULD CERTAINLY DELIGHT OUR KING.
WITHOUT ITS PRINCE AND ITS BLACK KNIGHT...
...TYR WILL BREATHE ITS LAST.
SO...
...YOU SAY YOU FOUND NOTHING.
CORRECT, GENERAL.

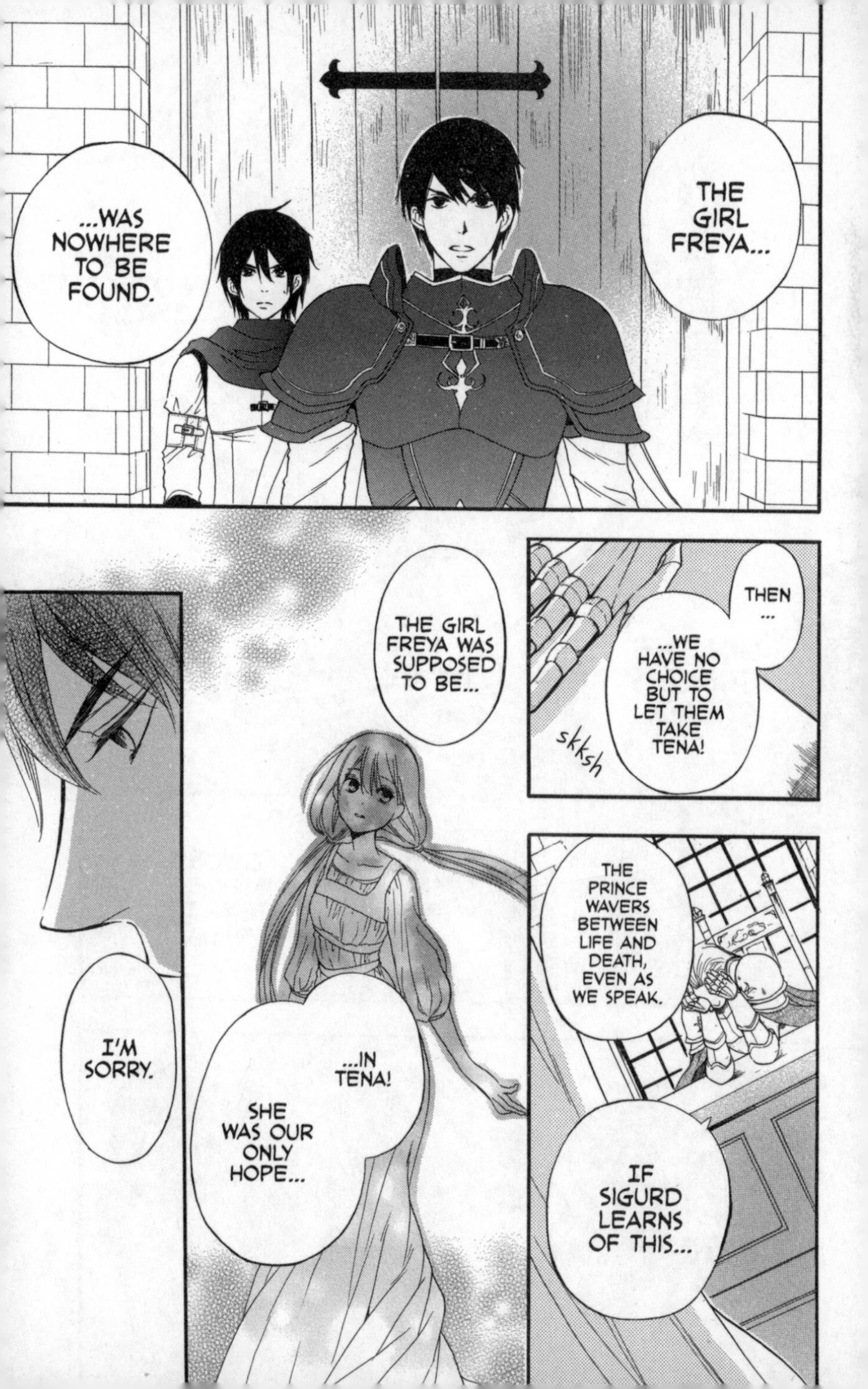
THE GIRL FREYA...
...WAS NOWHERE TO BE FOUND.
THEN...
...WE HAVE NO CHOICE BUT TO LET THEM TAKE TENA!
skksh
THE PRINCE WAVERS BETWEEN LIFE AND DEATH, EVEN AS WE SPEAK.
IF SIGURD LEARNS OF THIS...
THE GIRL FREYA WAS SUPPOSED TO BE...
...IN TENA!
SHE WAS OUR ONLY HOPE...
I'M SORRY.

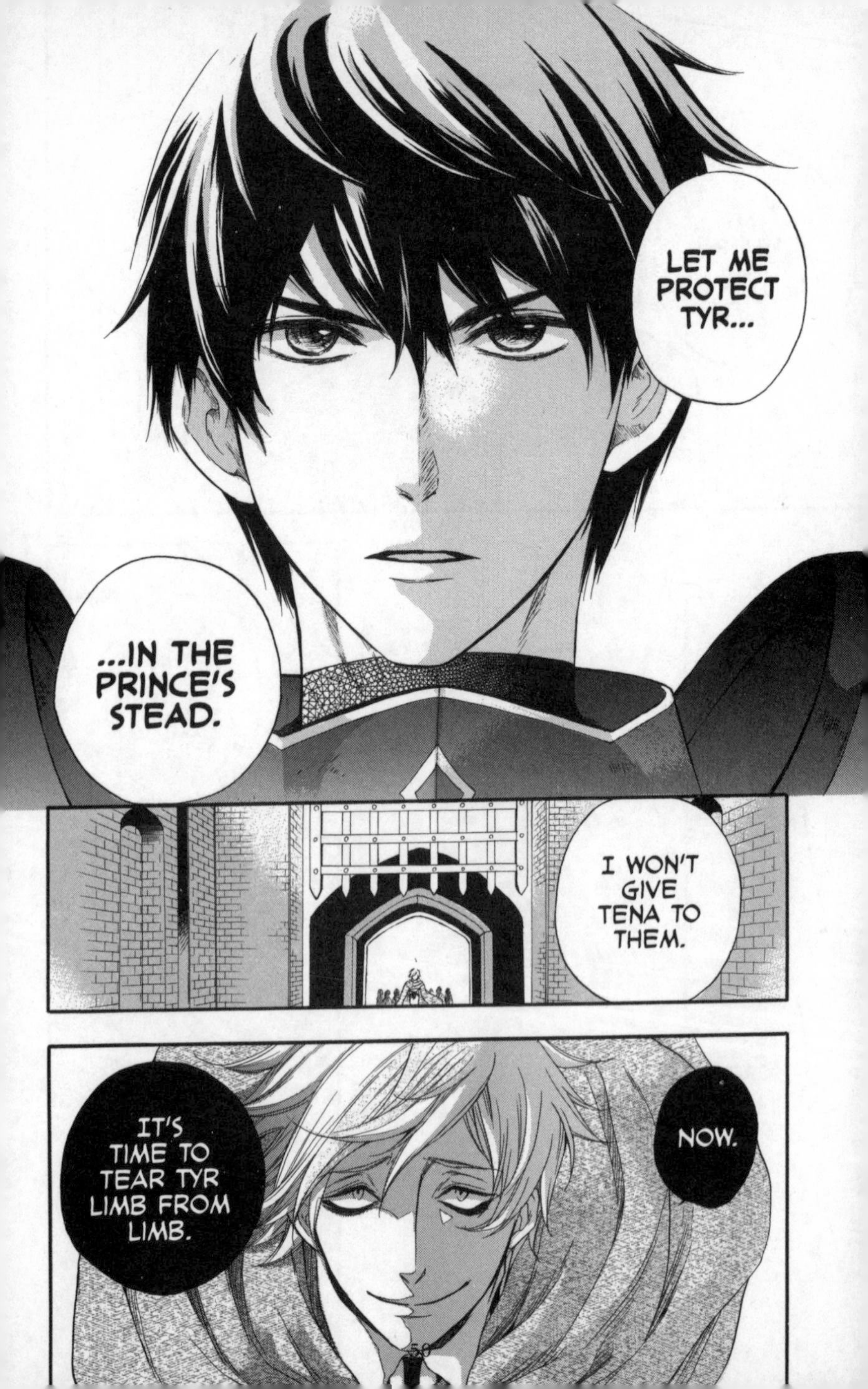
LET ME PROTECT TYR...
...IN THE PRINCE'S STEAD.
I WON'T GIVE TENA TO THEM.
NOW.
IT'S TIME TO TEAR TYR LIMB FROM LIMB.

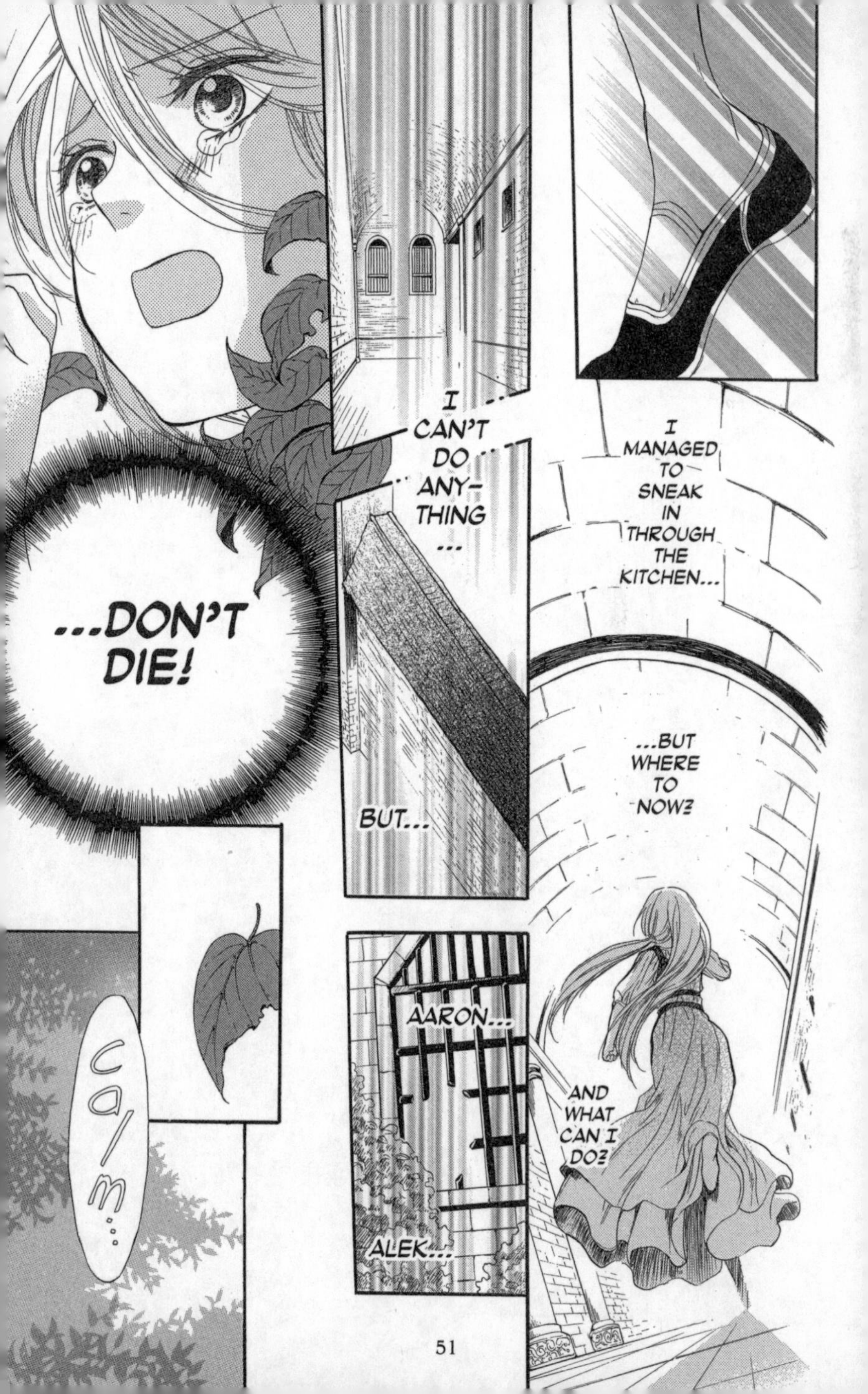
I MANAGED TO SNEAK IN THROUGH THE KITCHEN...
...BUT WHERE TO NOW?
AND WHAT CAN I DO?
I CAN'T DO ANY-THING...
BUT...
AARON...
ALEK...
...DON'T DIE!
Calm...

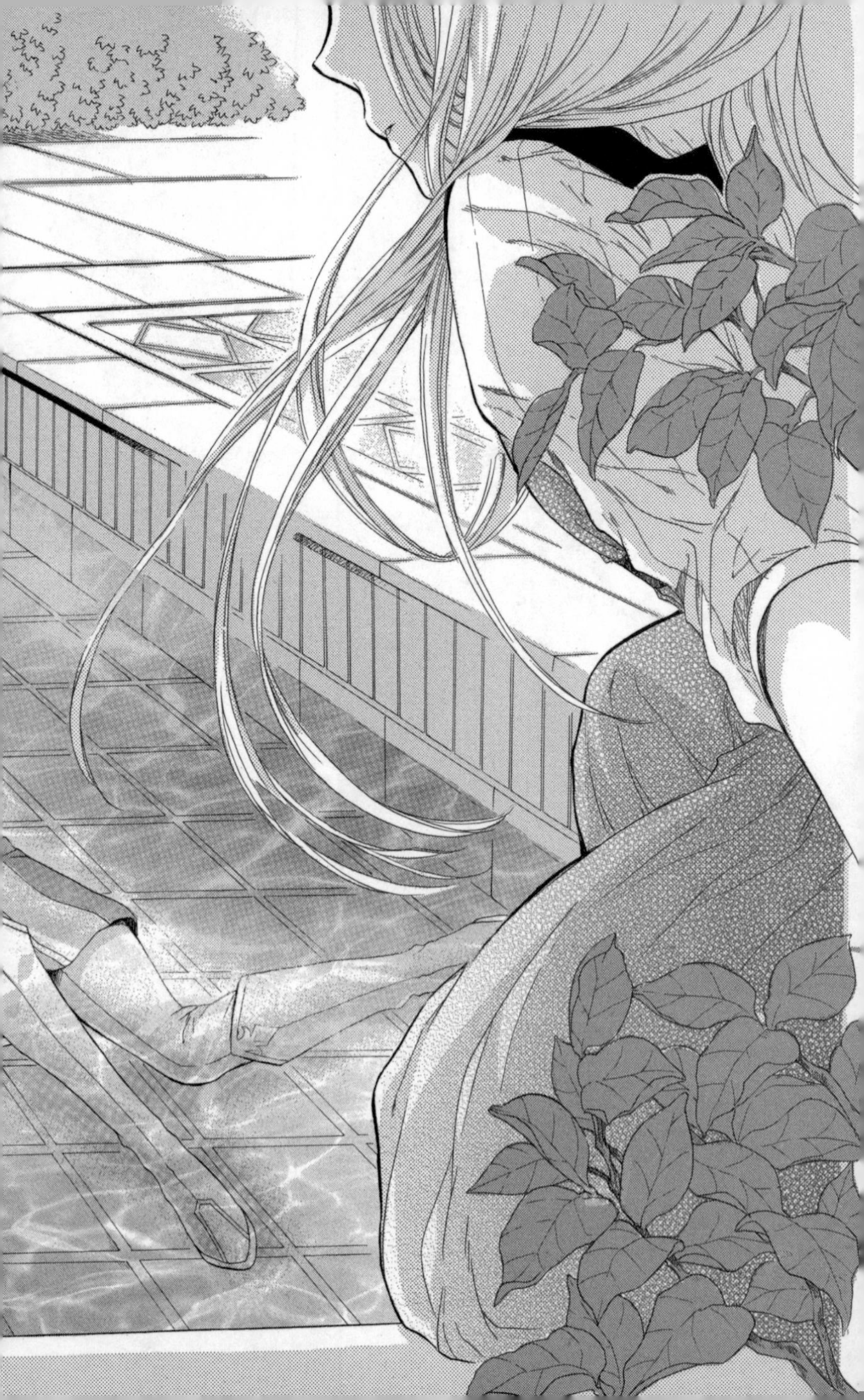

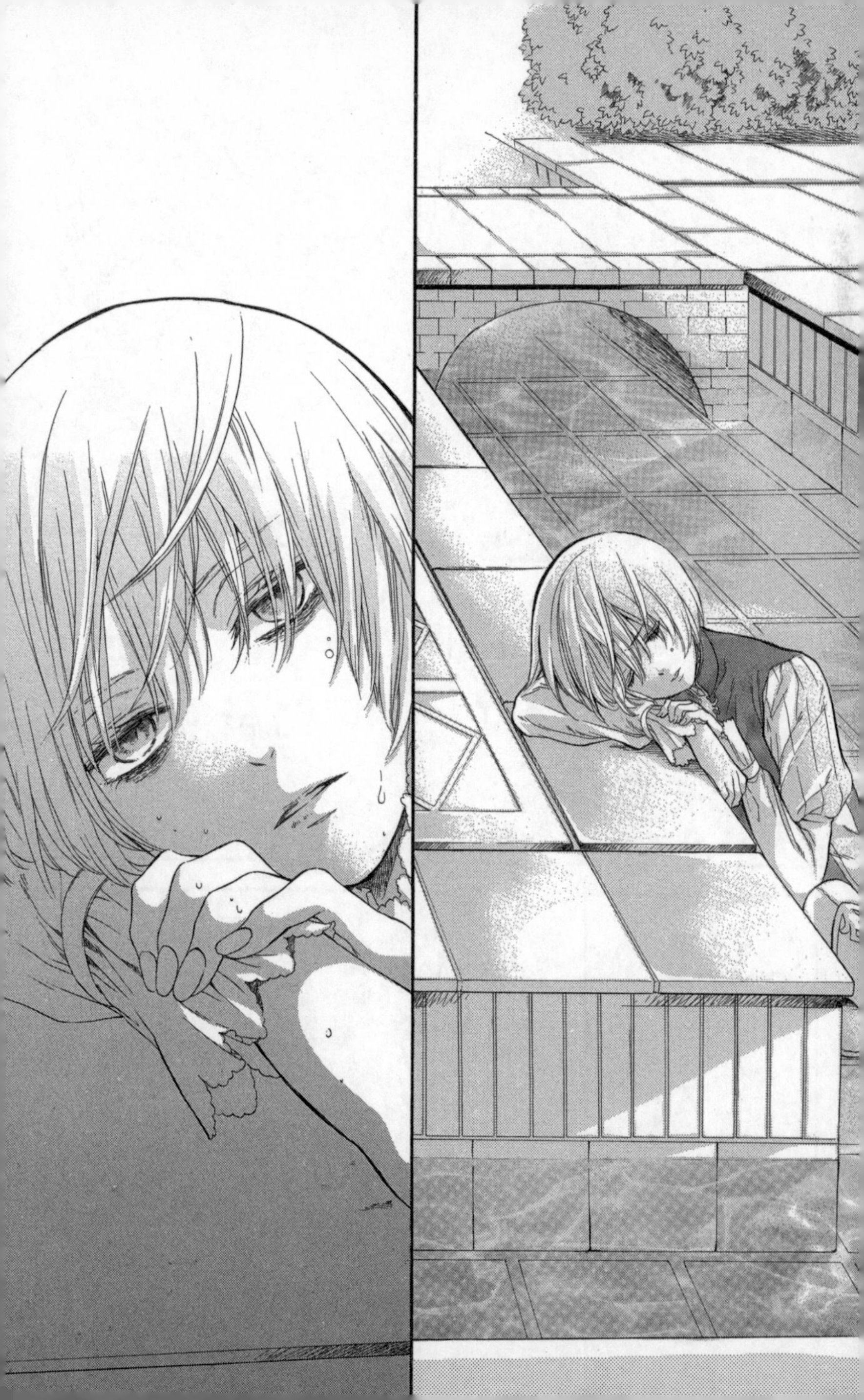

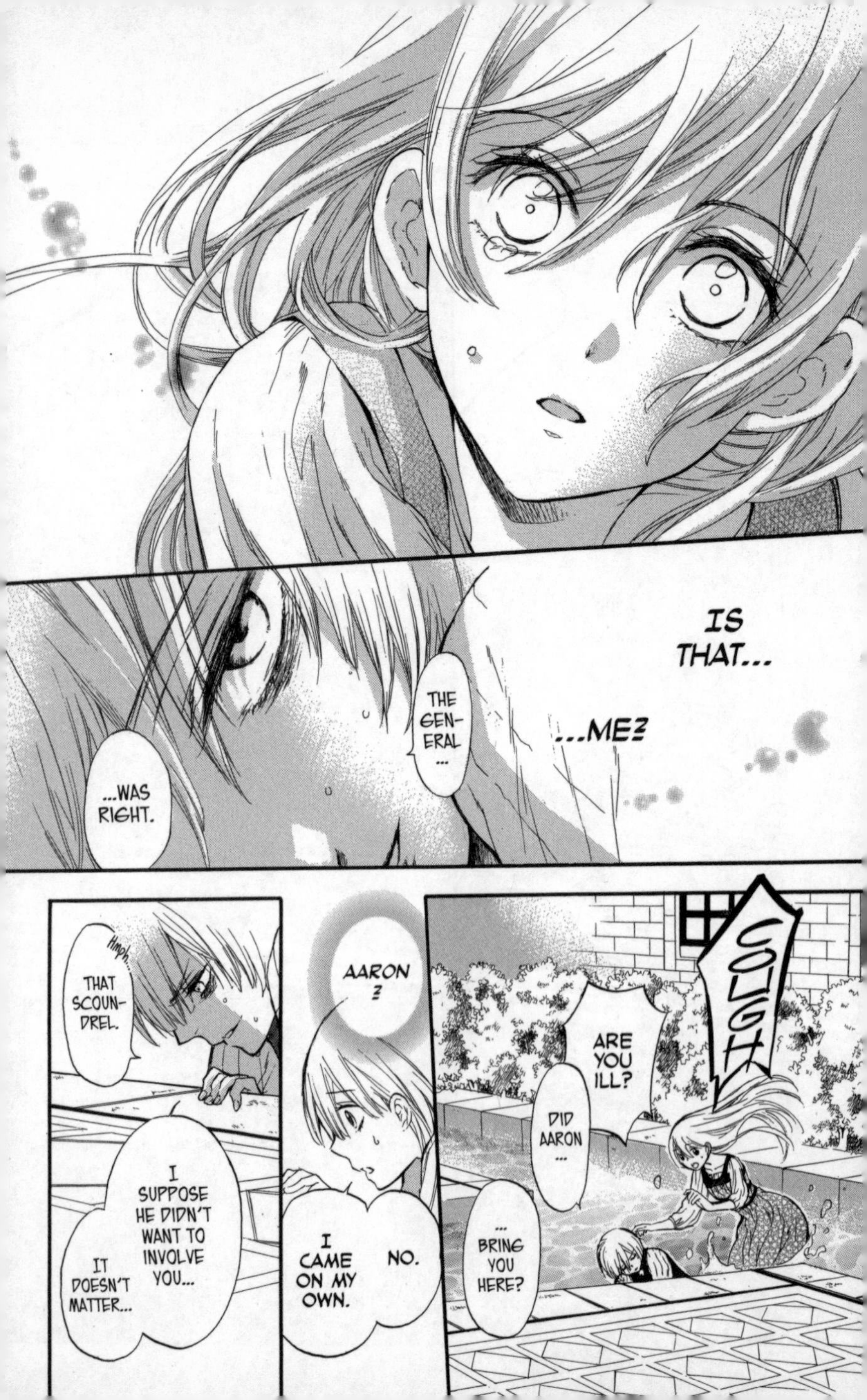
IS THAT...
...ME?
THE GENERAL...
...WAS RIGHT.
COUGH
ARE YOU ILL?
DID AARON...
...BRING YOU HERE?
AARON?
NO.
I CAME ON MY OWN.
Hmph.
THAT SCOUNDREL.
I SUPPOSE HE DIDN'T WANT TO INVOLVE YOU...
IT DOESN'T MATTER...

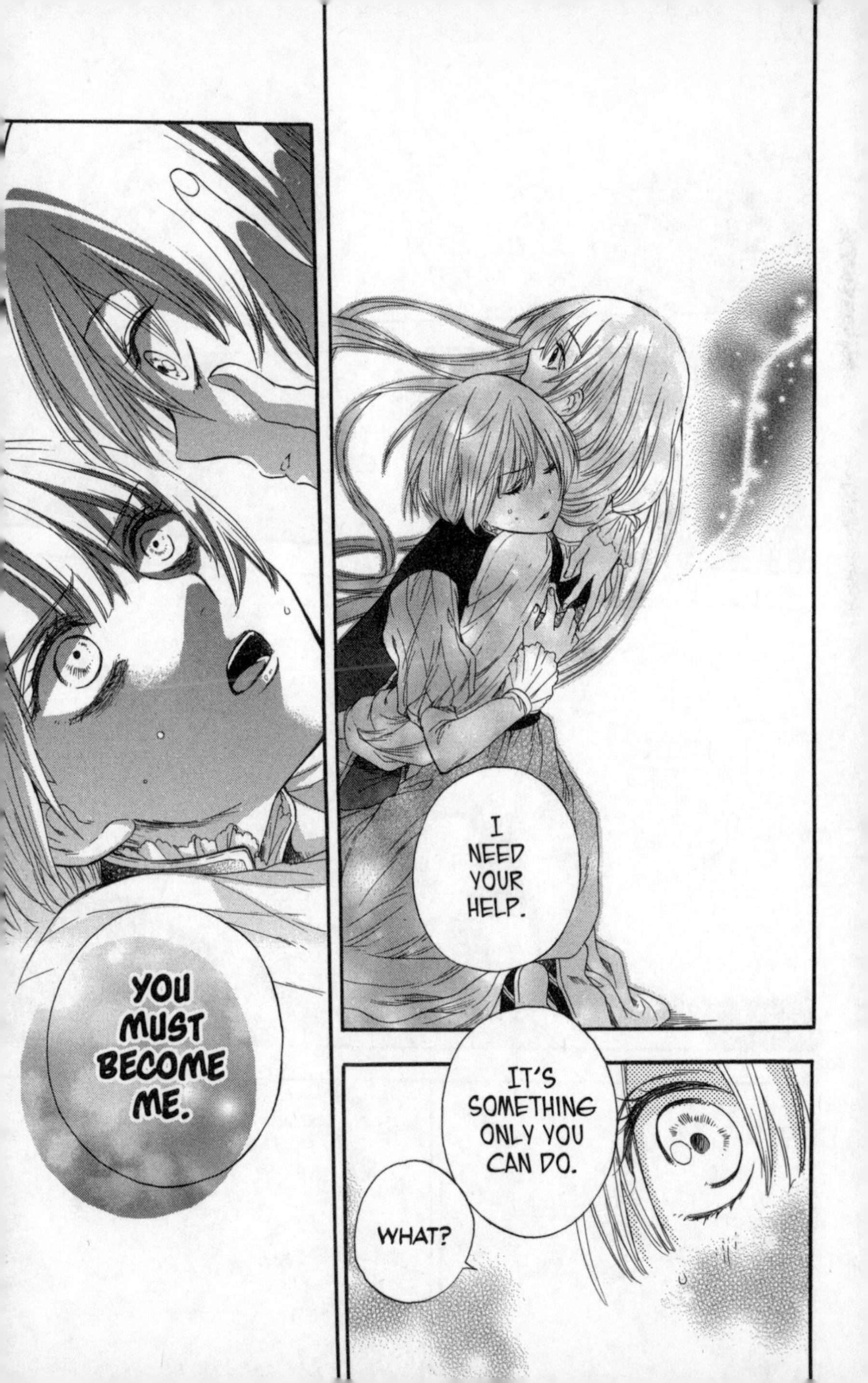
I NEED YOUR HELP.
IT'S SOMETHING ONLY YOU CAN DO.
WHAT?
YOU MUST BECOME ME.

IS...

HOW CAN I...?!

WHAT ?!

ONLY YOU CAN DO THIS.

YOU MUST.

YOU CAN.

...HE...?

PROTECT TYR.

PLEASE.

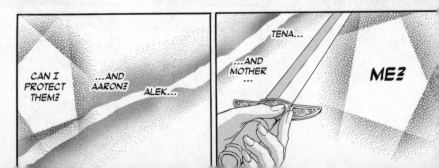

CAN I PROTECT THEM?

...AND AARON?

ALEK...

TENA...

...AND MOTHER ...

ME?

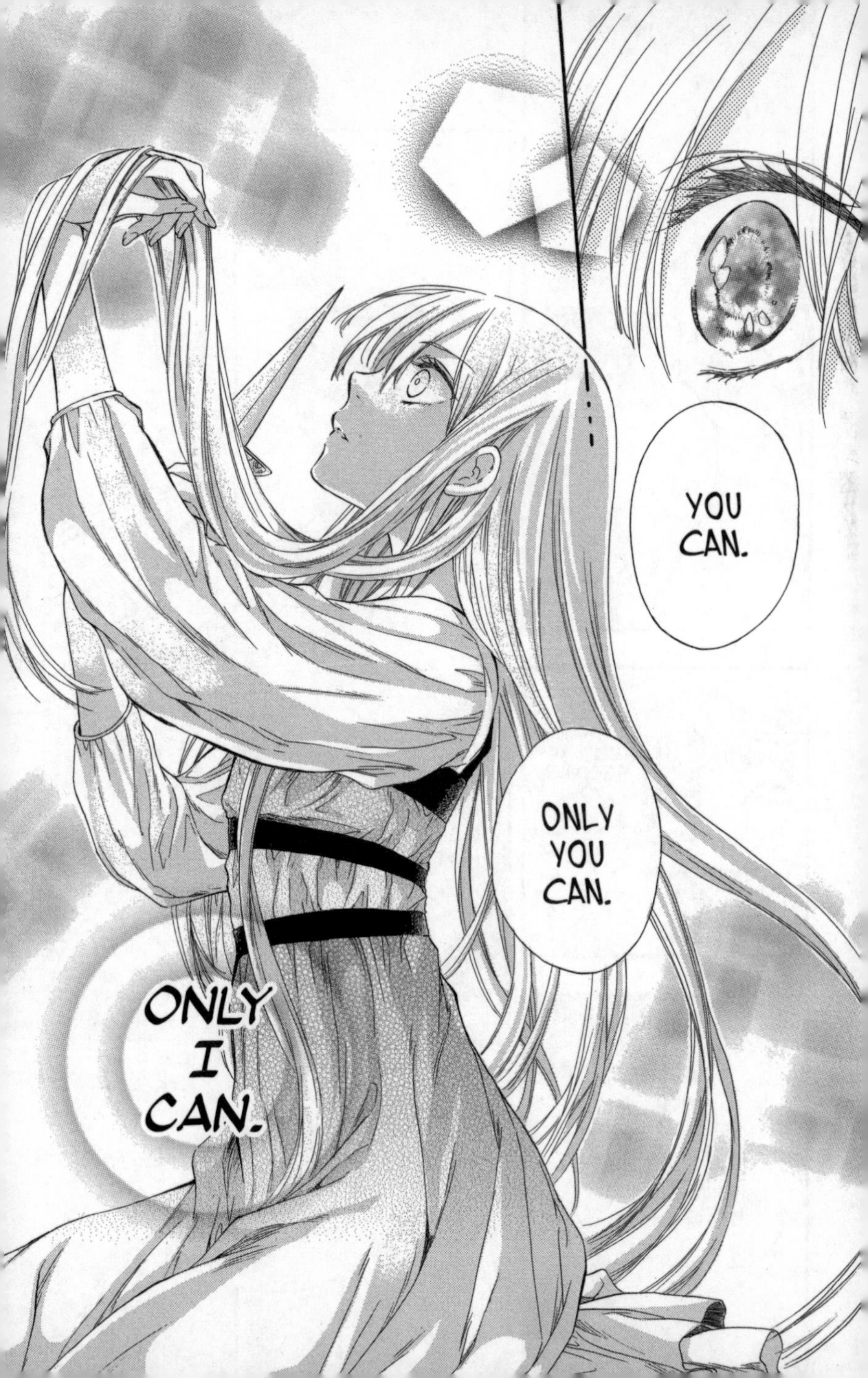
...
YOU CAN.
ONLY YOU CAN.
ONLY I CAN.

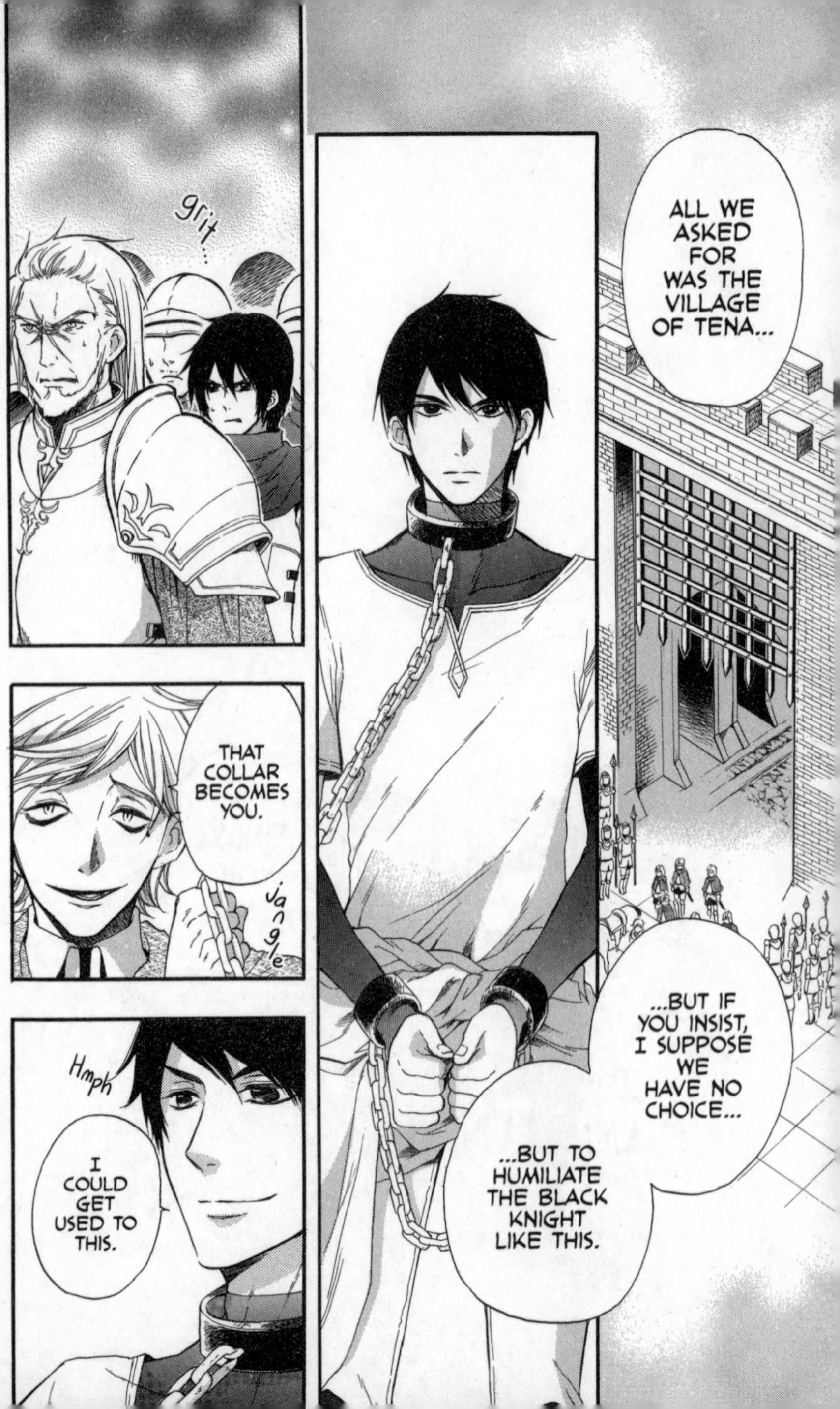
ALL WE ASKED FOR WAS THE VILLAGE OF TENA...
...BUT IF YOU INSIST, I SUPPOSE WE HAVE NO CHOICE...
...BUT TO HUMILIATE THE BLACK KNIGHT LIKE THIS.
grit...
THAT COLLAR BECOMES YOU.
jangle
Hmph
I COULD GET USED TO THIS.

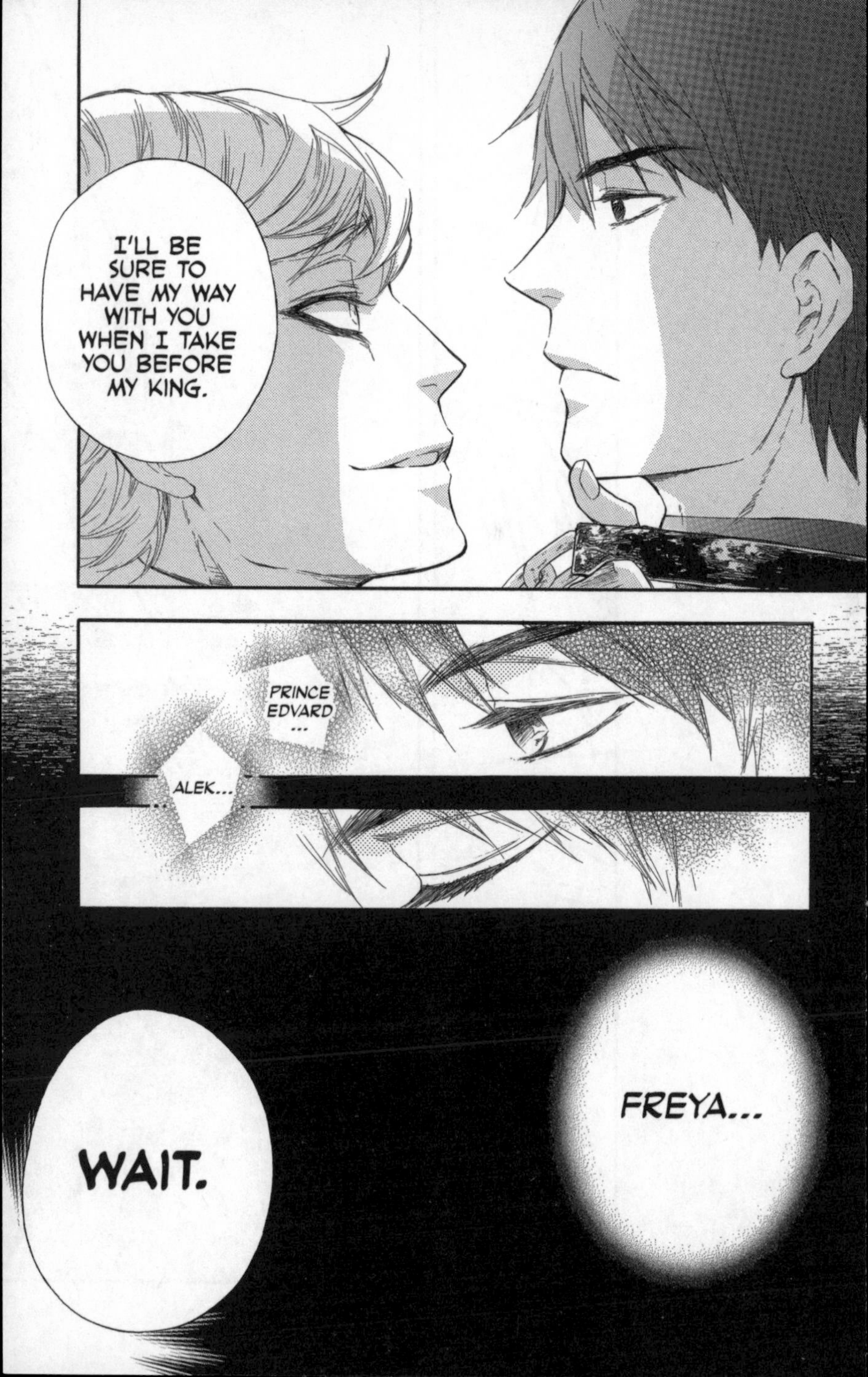
I'LL BE SURE TO HAVE MY WAY WITH YOU WHEN I TAKE YOU BEFORE MY KING.
PRINCE EDVARD ...
ALEK...
FREYA...
WAIT.

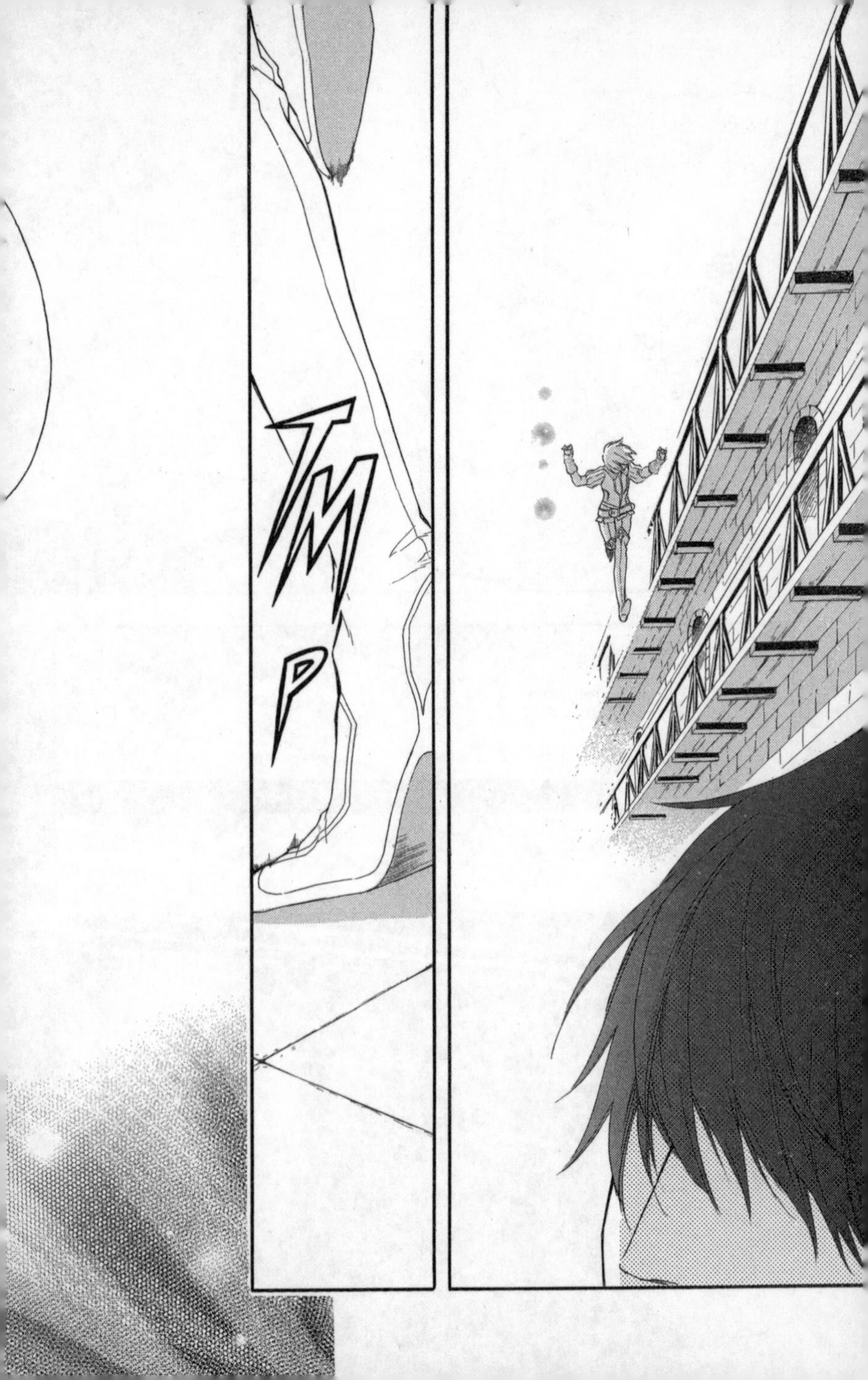
TMP

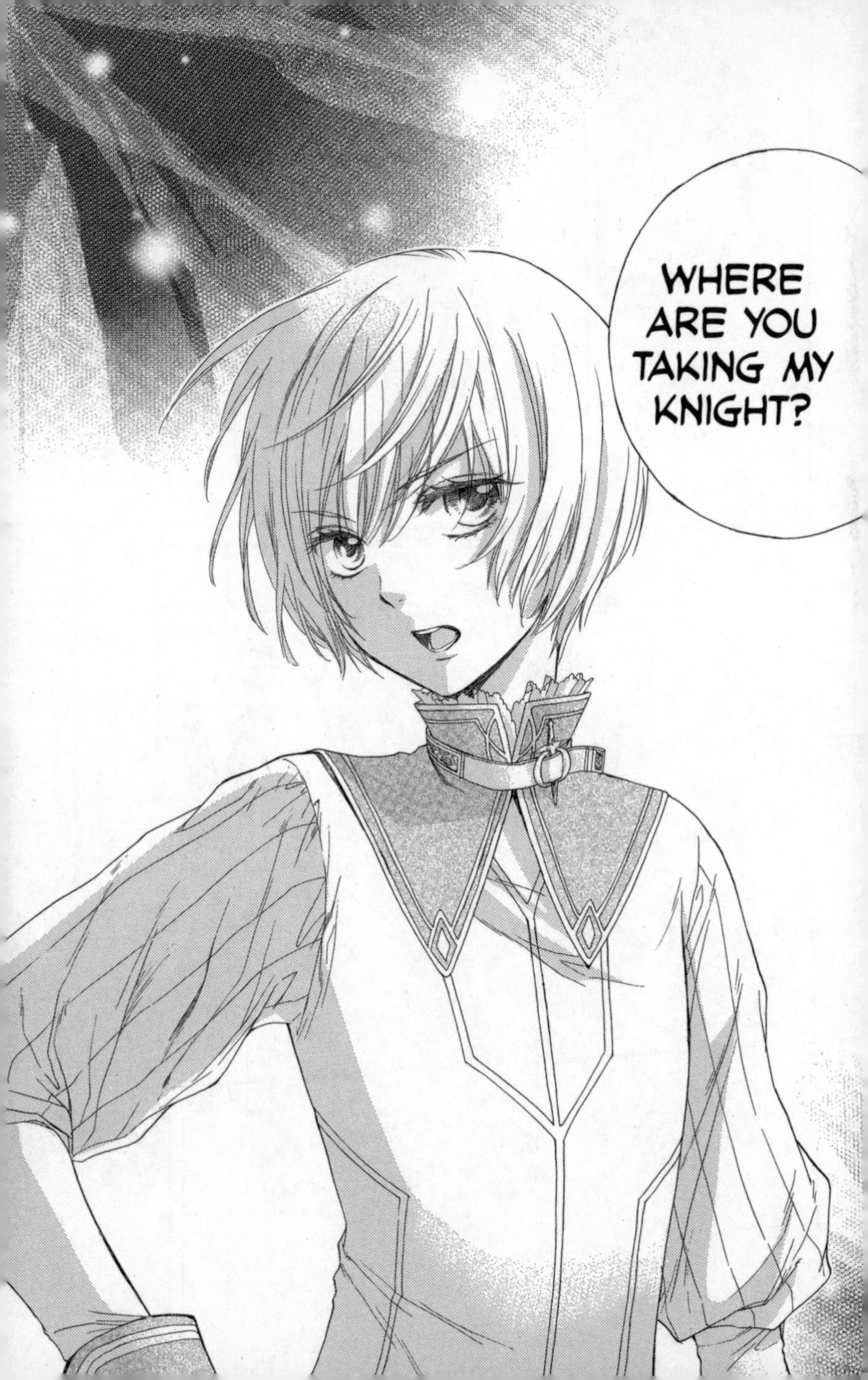
WHERE ARE YOU TAKING MY KNIGHT?

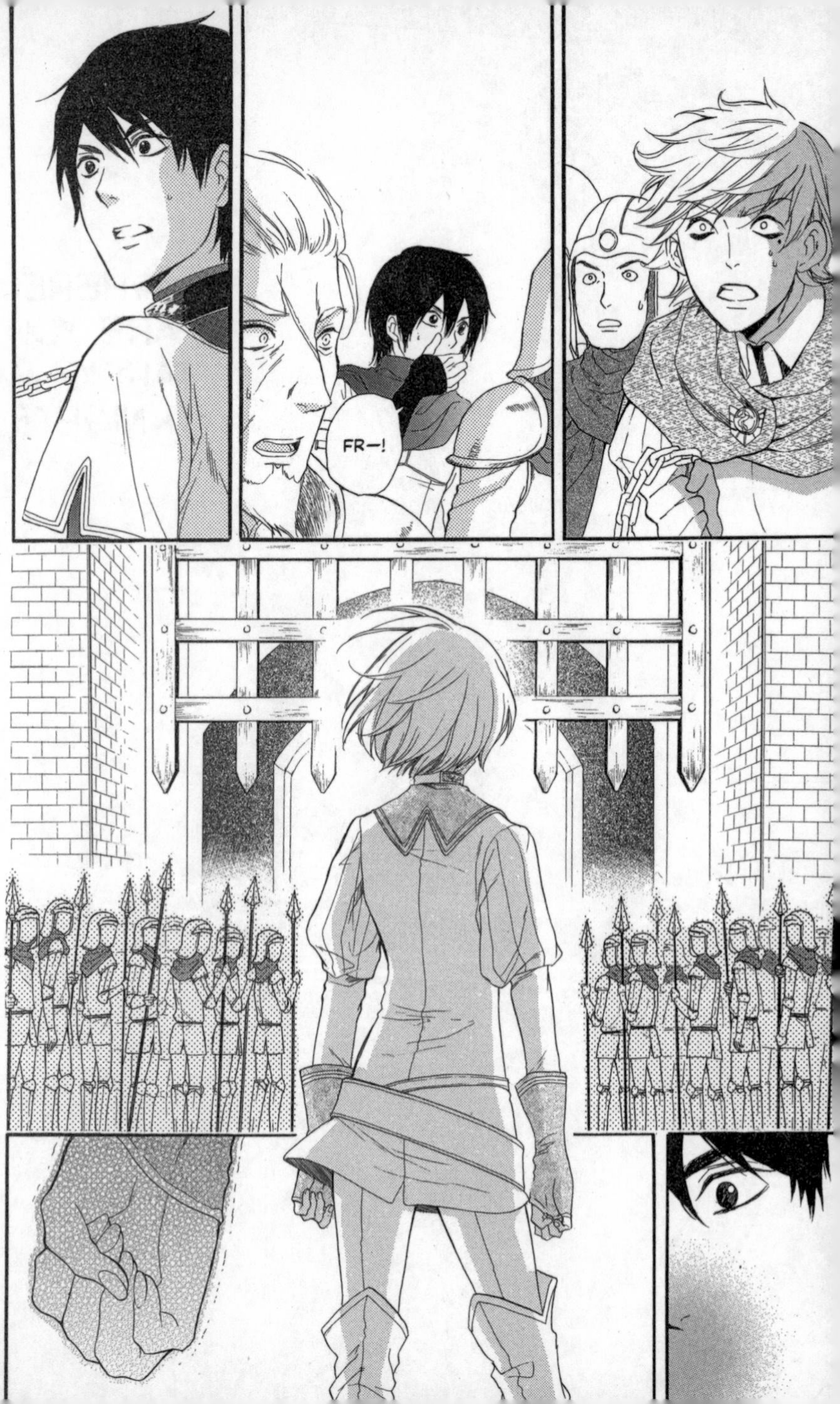
FR—!

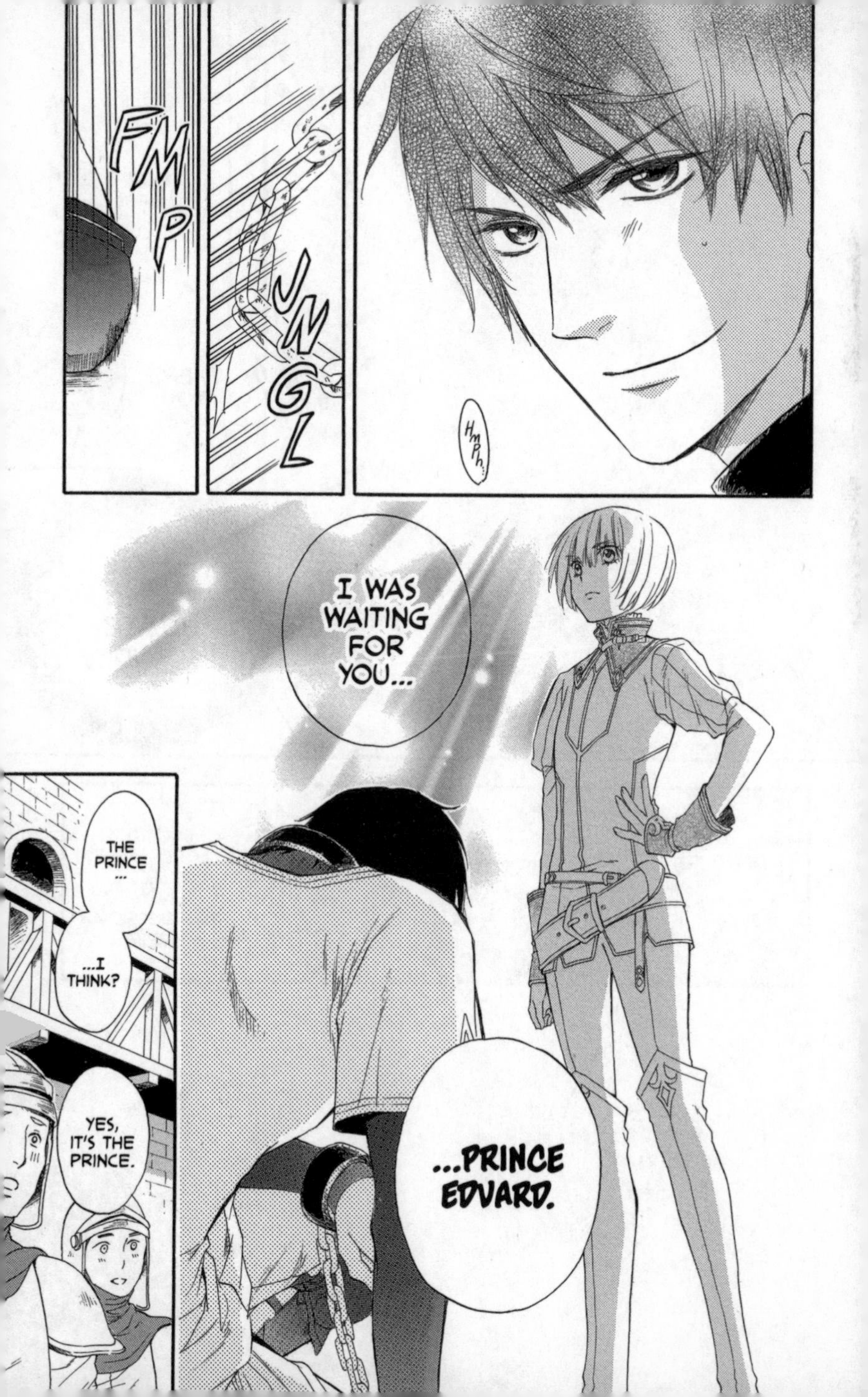
Hmph...
JNGL
FMP
I WAS WAITING FOR YOU...
...PRINCE EDVARD.
THE PRINCE...
...I THINK?
YES, IT'S THE PRINCE.

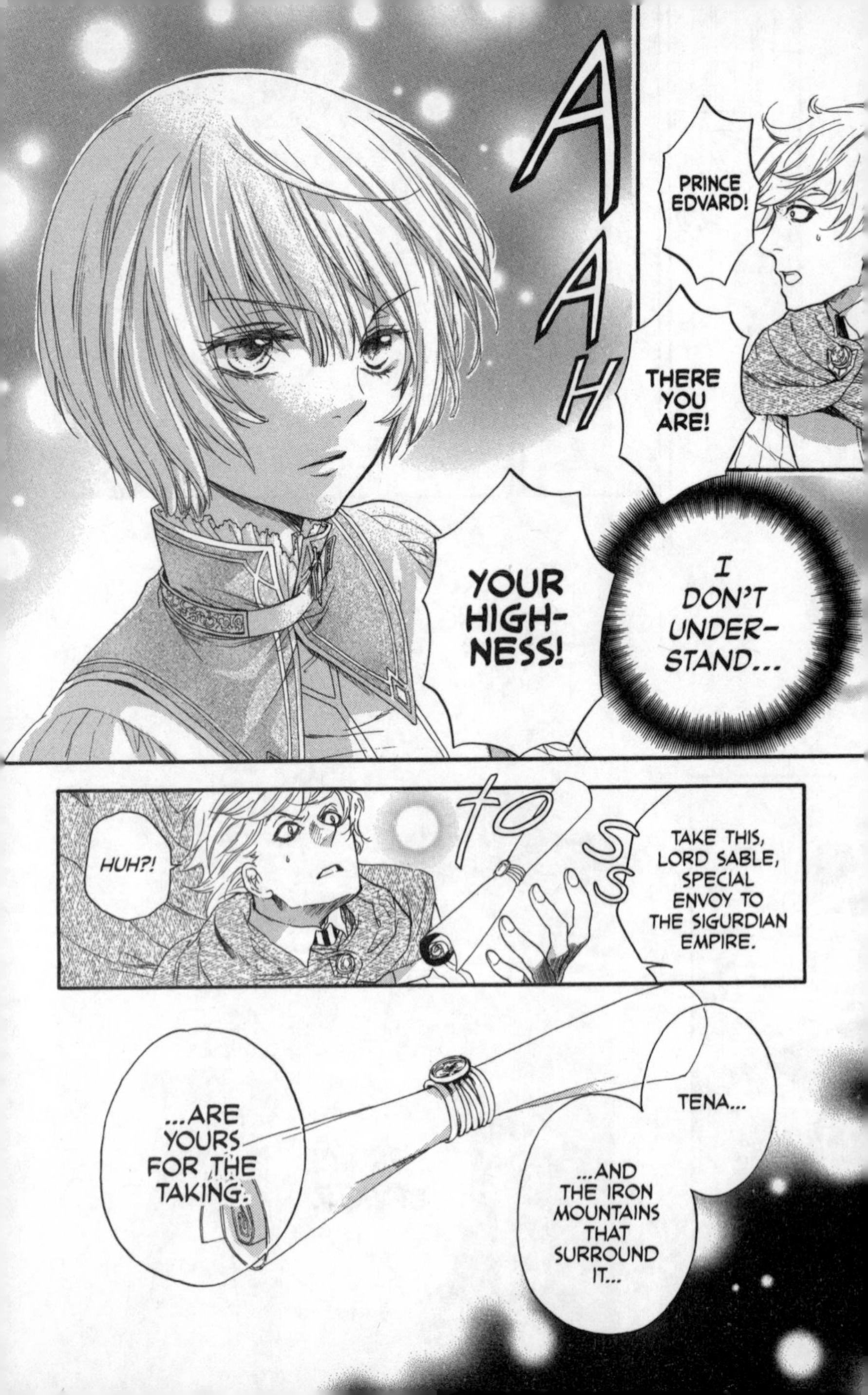
PRINCE EDVARD!
THERE YOU ARE!
YOUR HIGH-NESS!
AAAH
I DON'T UNDER-STAND...
TAKE THIS, LORD SABLE, SPECIAL ENVOY TO THE SIGURDIAN EMPIRE.
toss
HUH?!
TENA...
...AND THE IRON MOUNTAINS THAT SURROUND IT...
...ARE YOURS FOR THE TAKING.

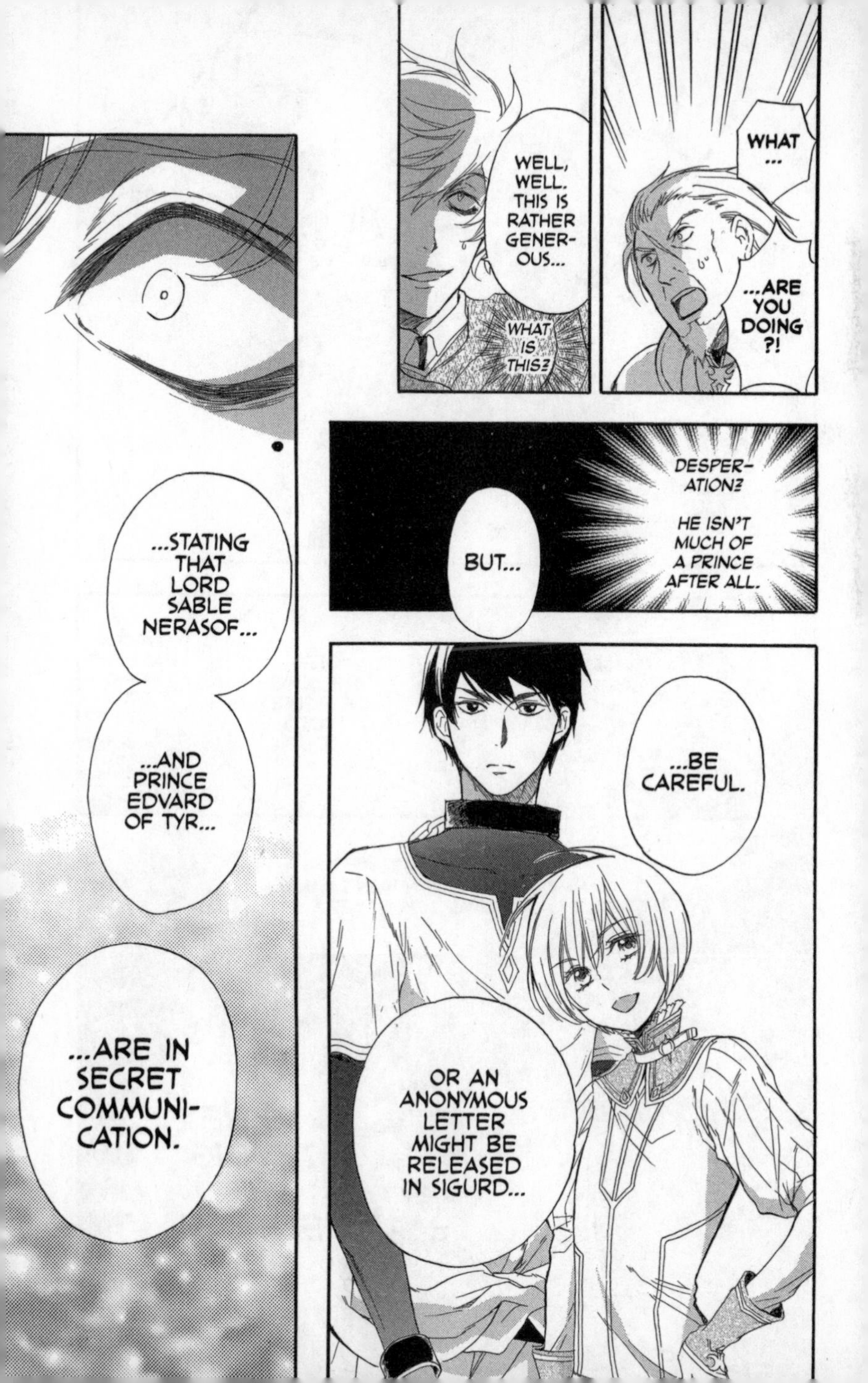
WHAT...
...ARE YOU DOING?!
WELL, WELL. THIS IS RATHER GENER-OUS...
WHAT IS THIS?
DESPER-ATION?
HE ISN'T MUCH OF A PRINCE AFTER ALL.
BUT...
...BE CAREFUL.
OR AN ANONYMOUS LETTER MIGHT BE RELEASED IN SIGURD...
...STATING THAT LORD SABLE NERASOF...
...AND PRINCE EDVARD OF TYR...
...ARE IN SECRET COMMUNI-CATION.

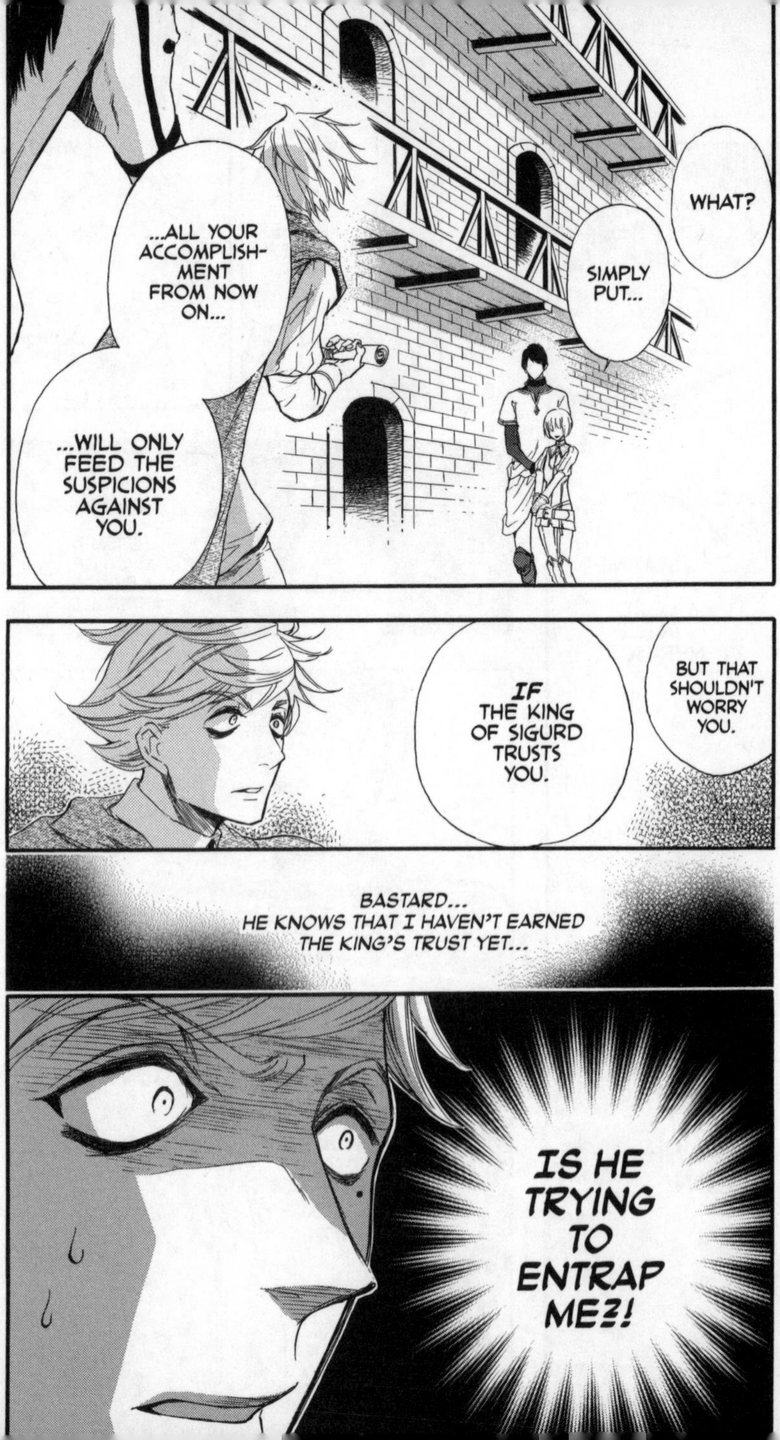
WHAT?
SIMPLY PUT...
...ALL YOUR ACCOMPLISHMENT FROM NOW ON...
...WILL ONLY FEED THE SUSPICIONS AGAINST YOU.
BUT THAT SHOULDN'T WORRY YOU.
IF THE KING OF SIGURD TRUSTS YOU.
BASTARD... HE KNOWS THAT I HAVEN'T EARNED THE KING'S TRUST YET...
IS HE TRYING TO ENTRAP ME?!

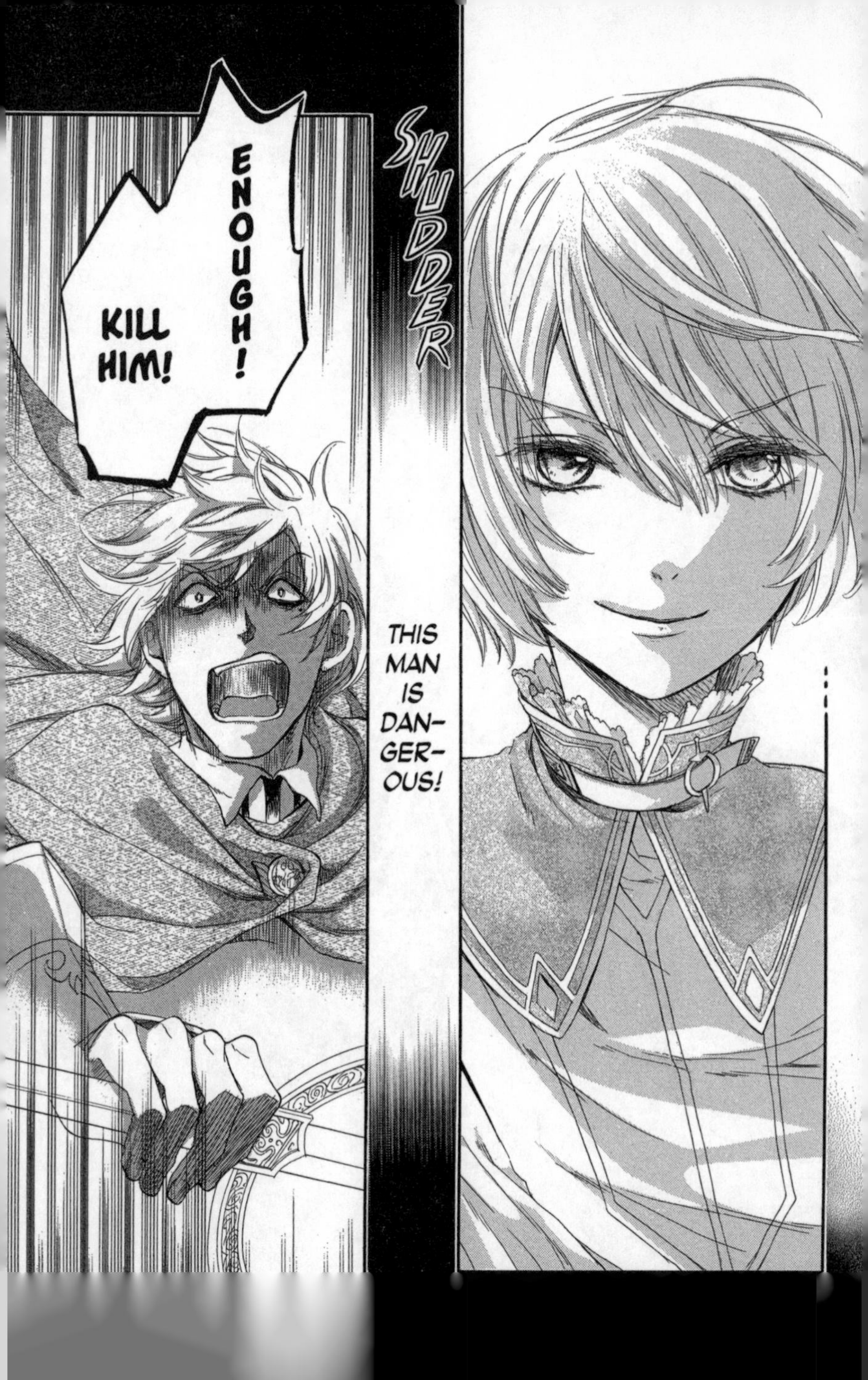
...
THIS MAN IS DAN-GER-OUS!
SHUDDER
ENOUGH!
KILL HIM!

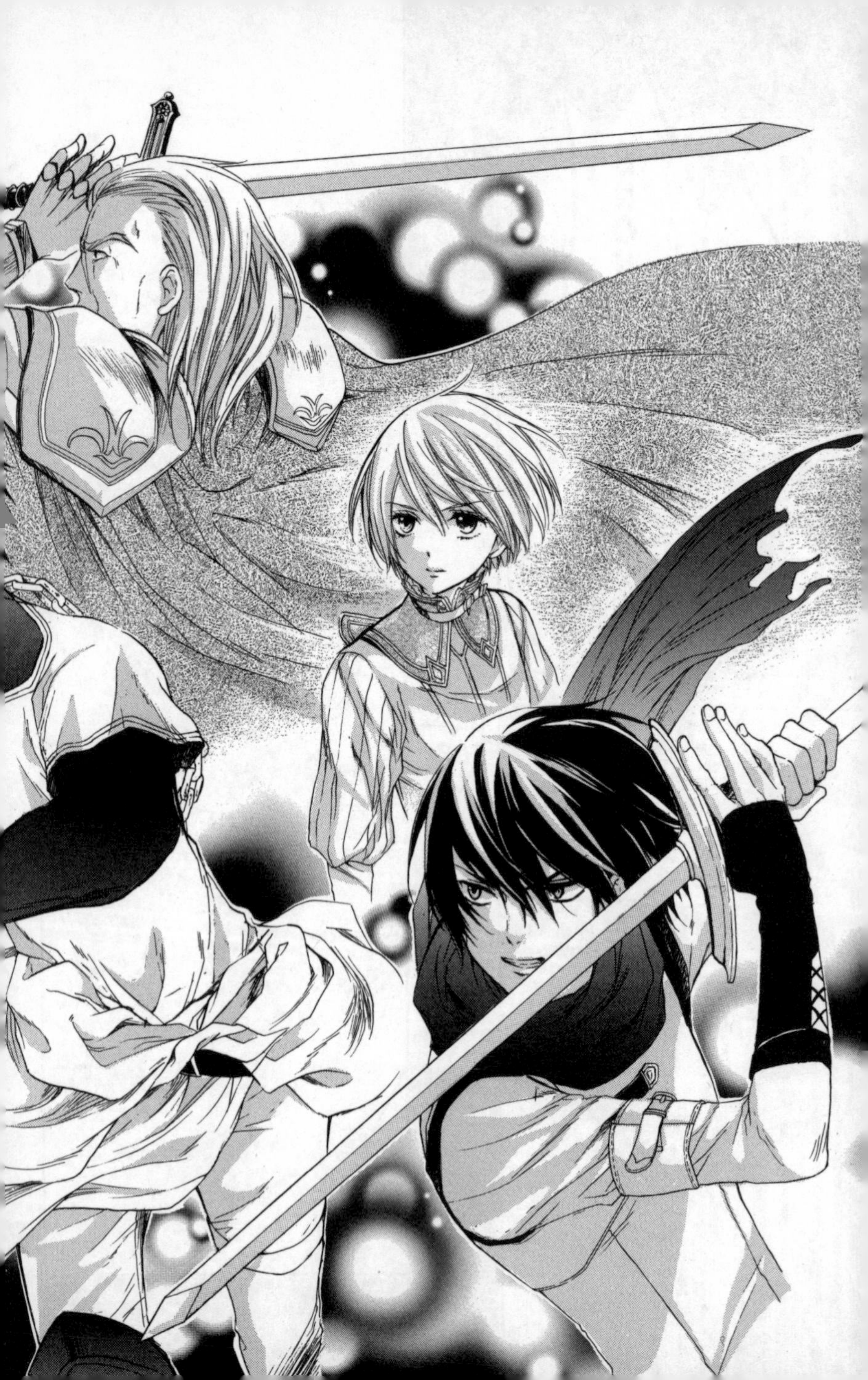

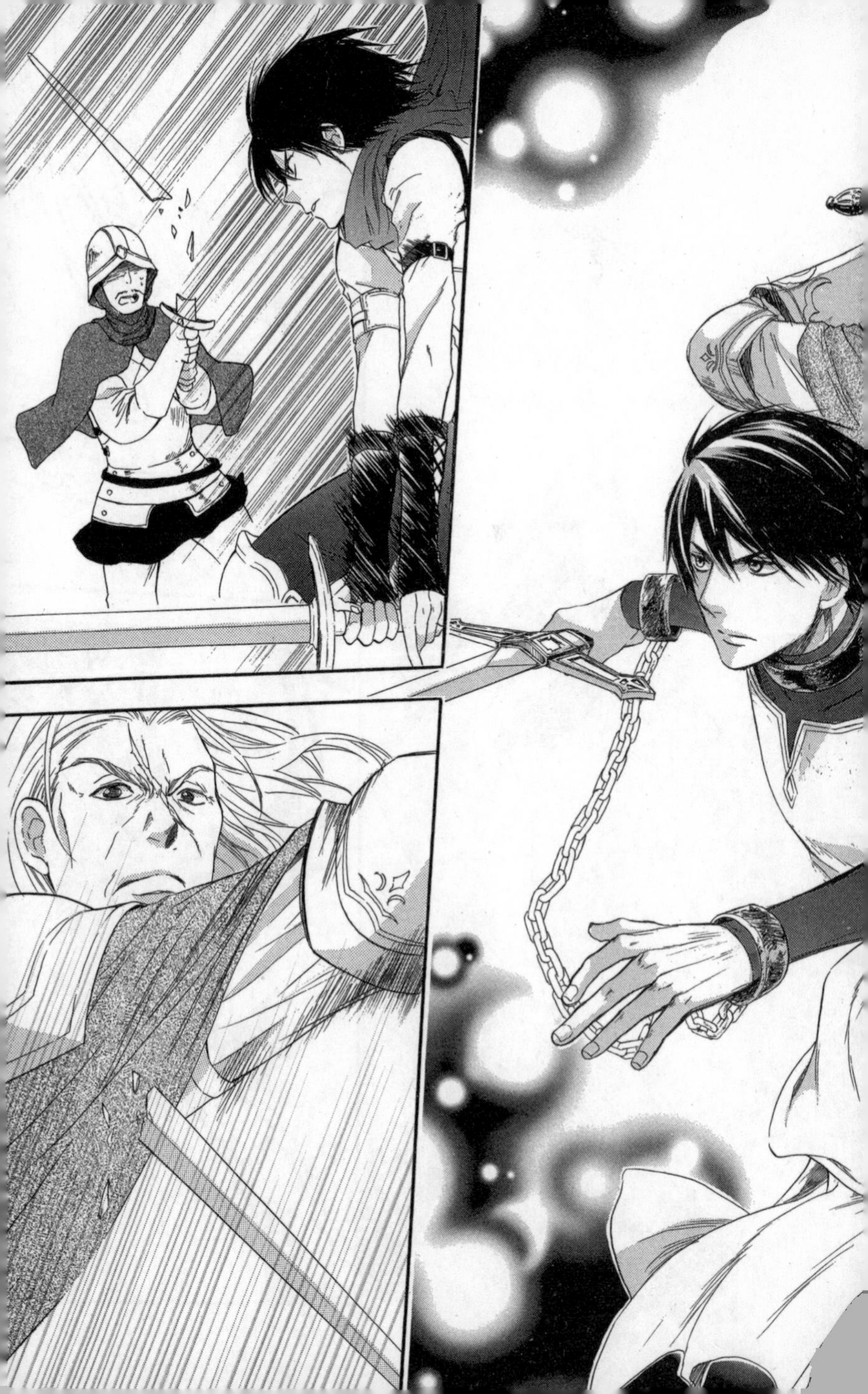

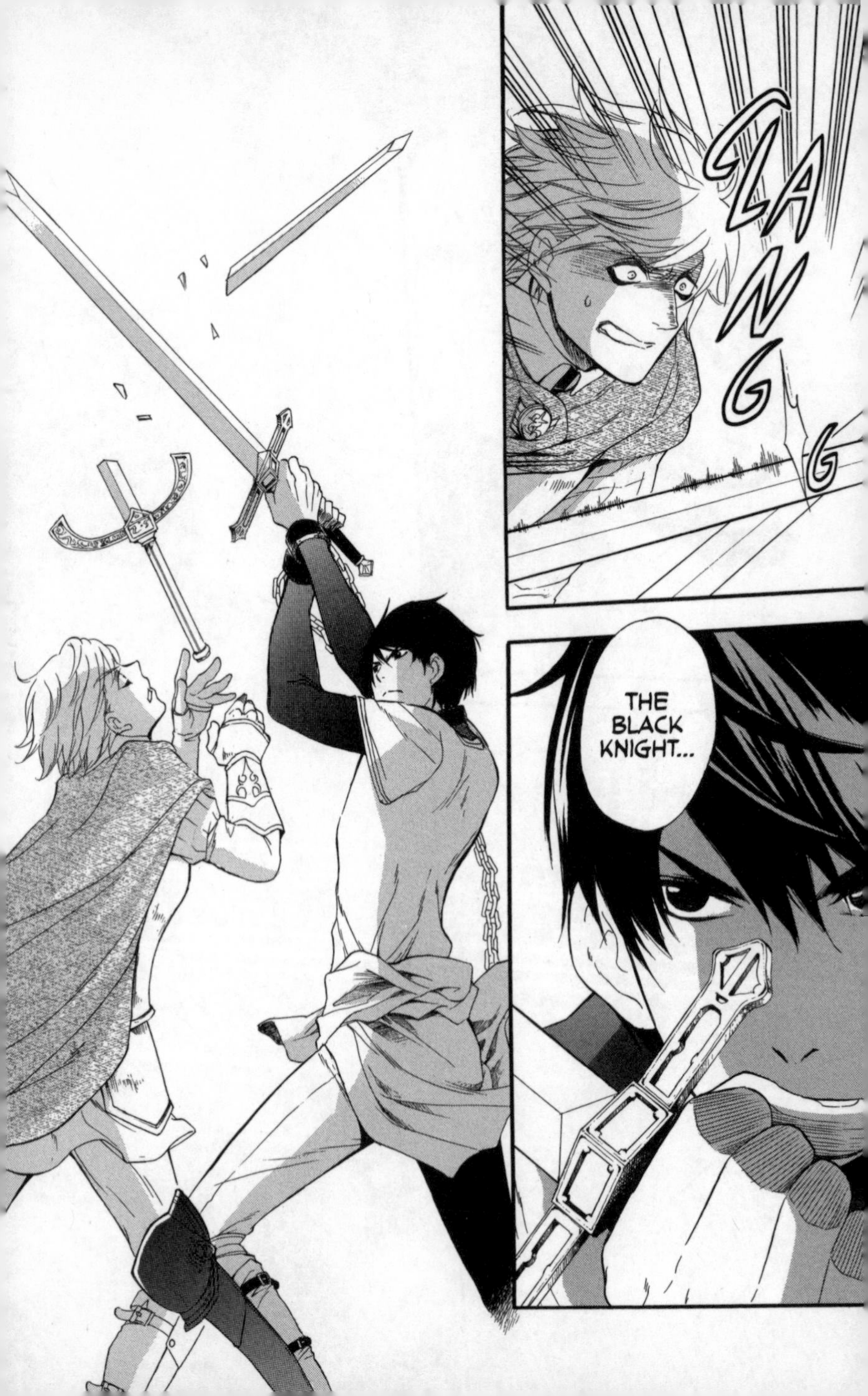
CLANGG
THE BLACK KNIGHT...

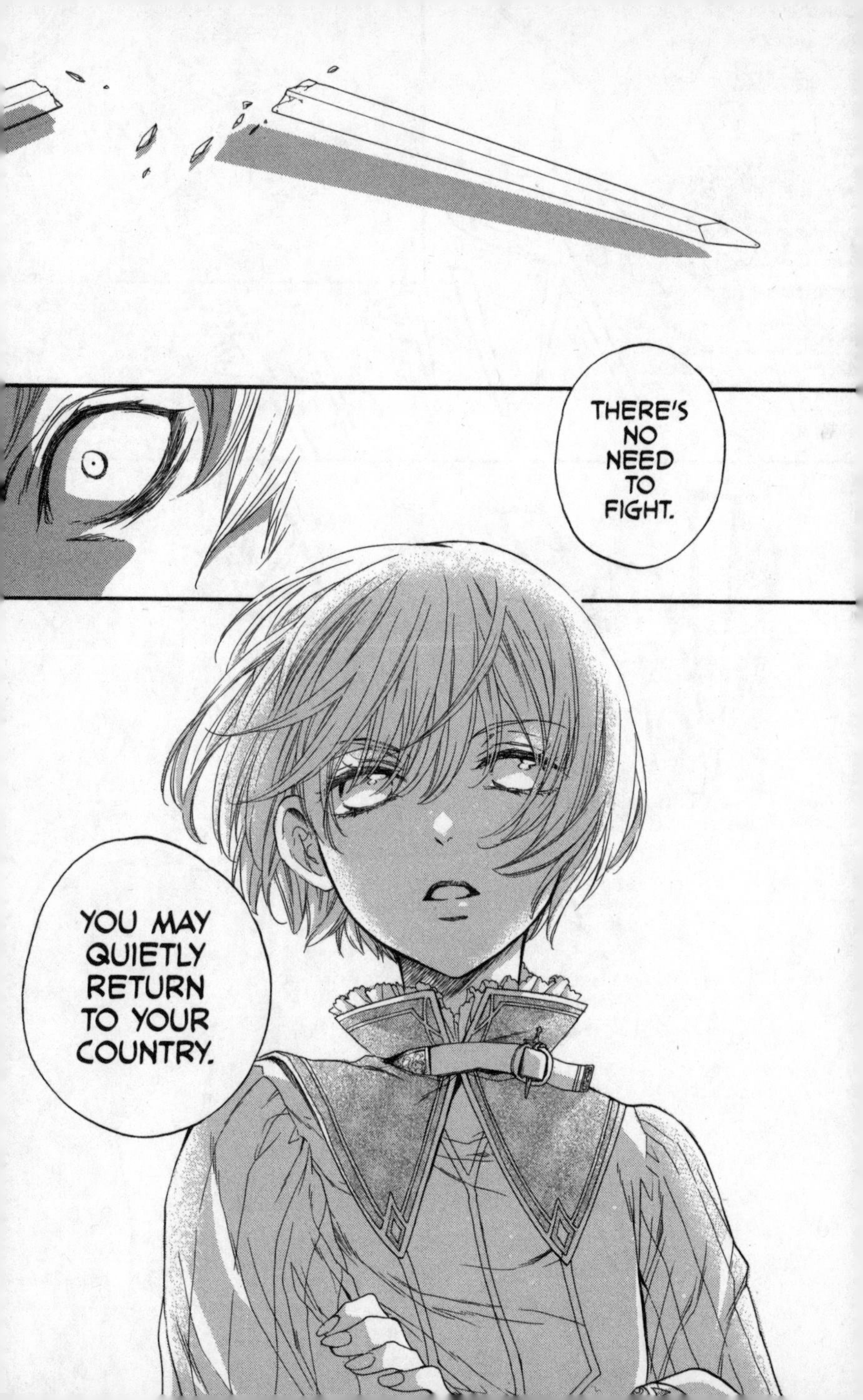
THERE'S NO NEED TO FIGHT.
YOU MAY QUIETLY RETURN TO YOUR COUNTRY.

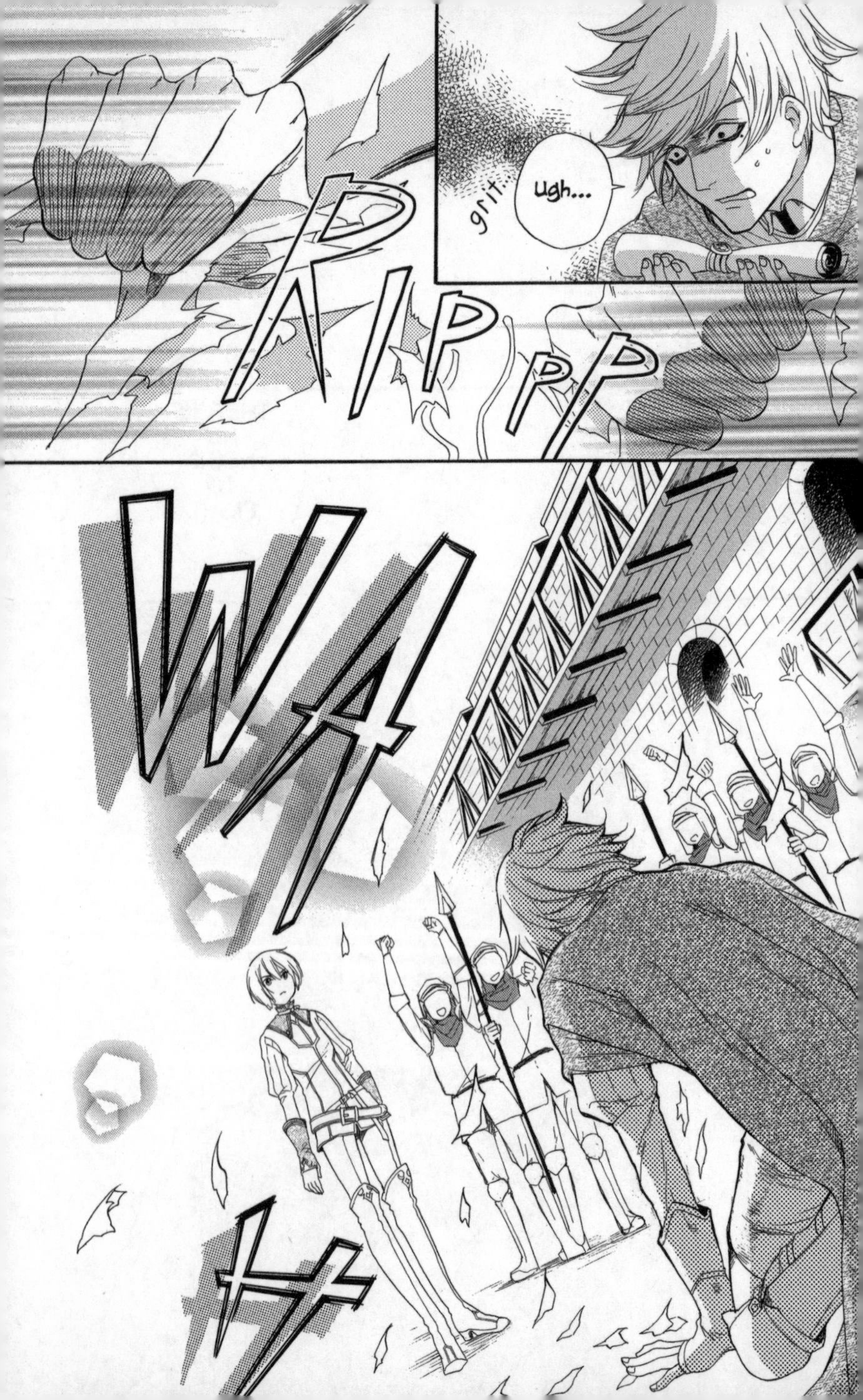
grit...
ugh...
DAPPP
WA

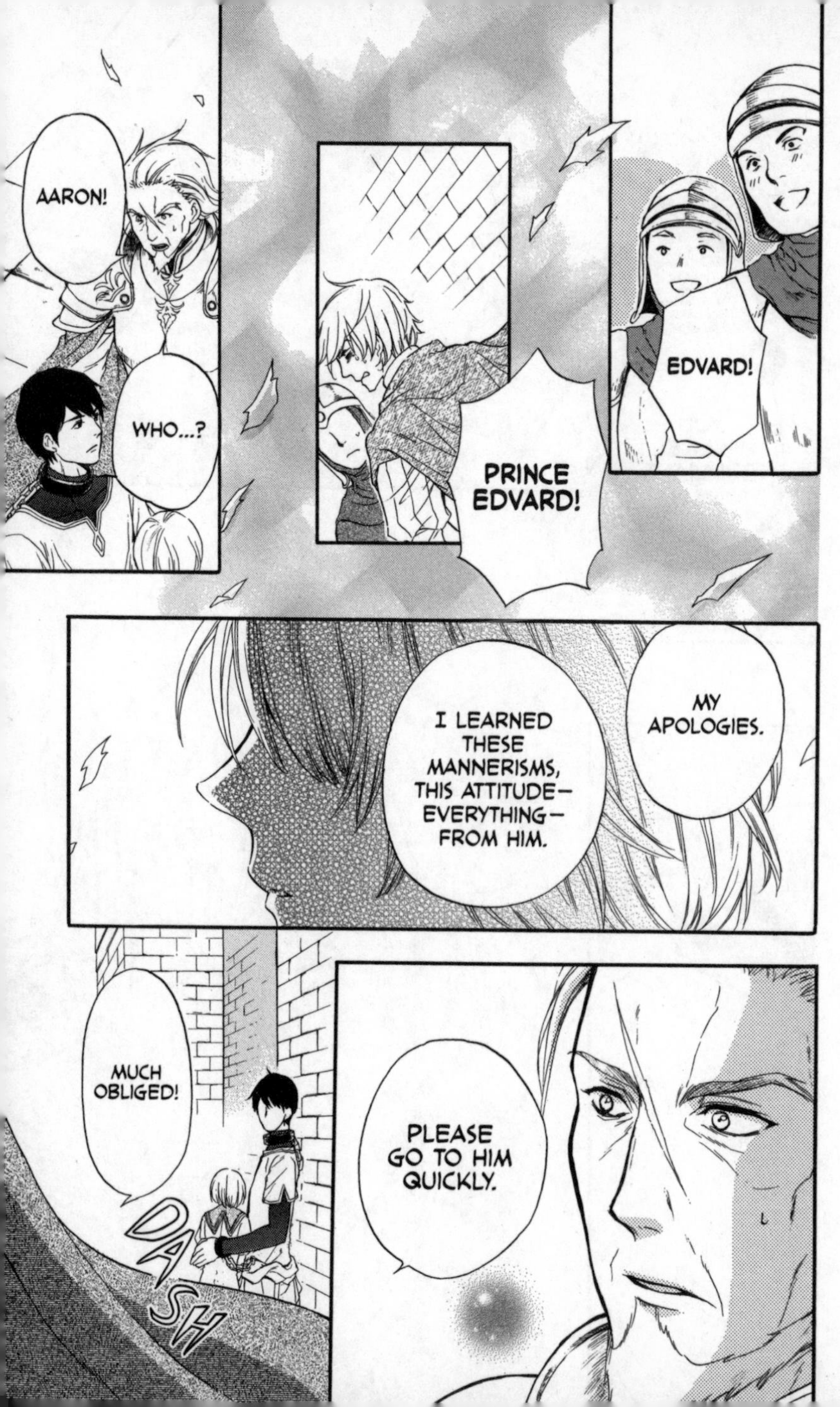
EDVARD!
PRINCE EDVARD!
AARON!
WHO...?
MY APOLOGIES.
I LEARNED THESE MANNERISMS, THIS ATTITUDE— EVERYTHING— FROM HIM.
PLEASE GO TO HIM QUICKLY.
MUCH OBLIGED!
DASH

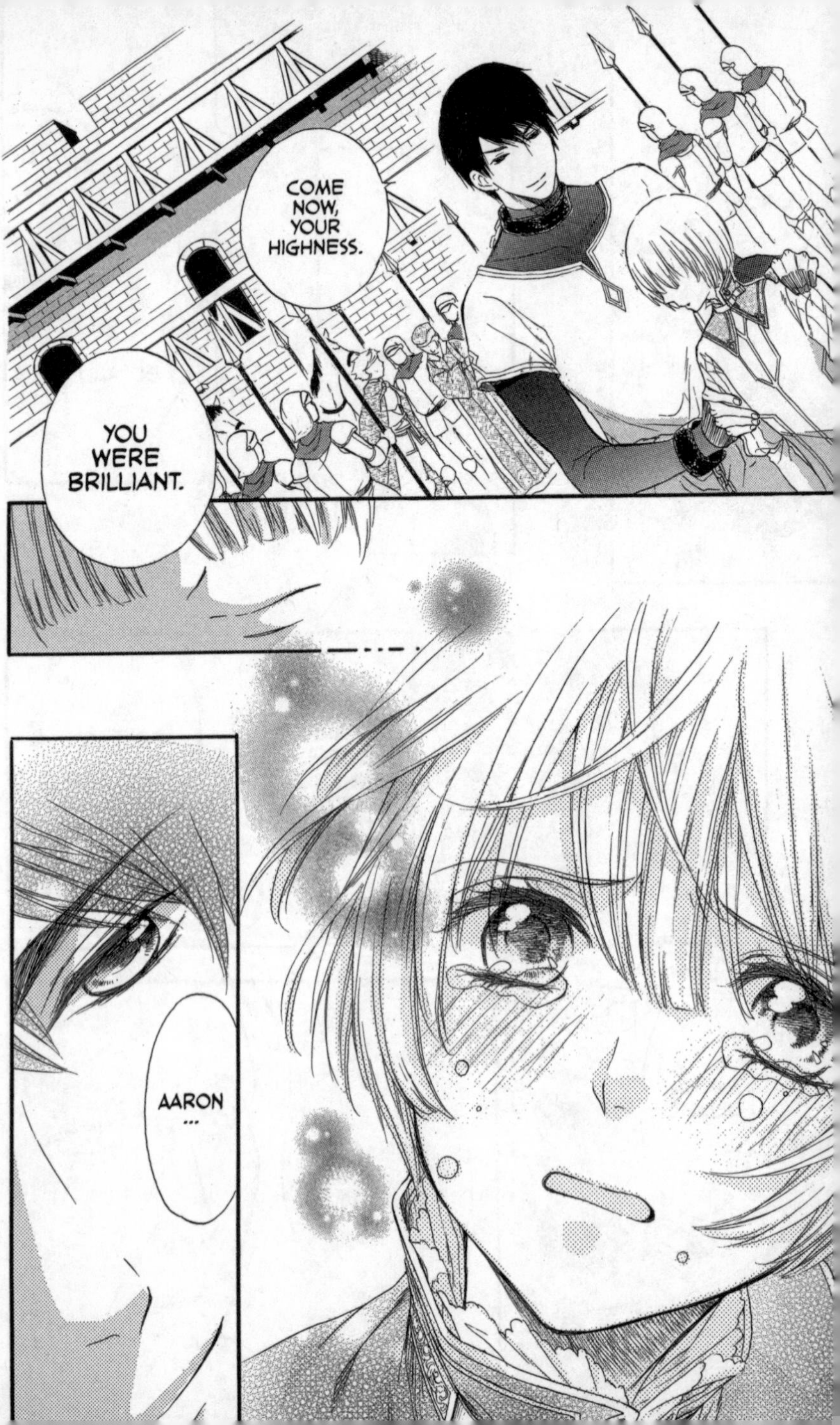
COME NOW, YOUR HIGHNESS.
YOU WERE BRILLIANT.
AARON ...

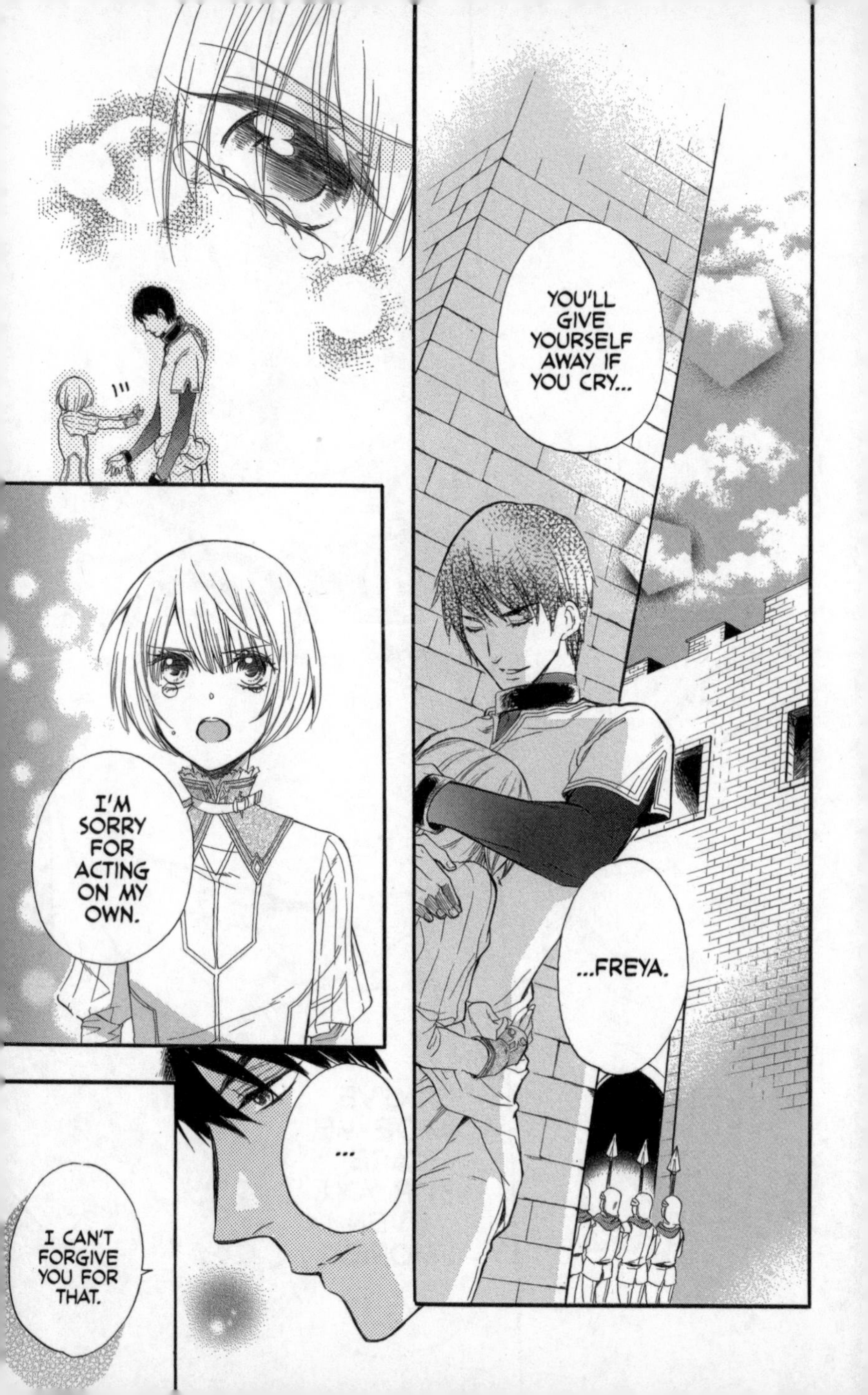
YOU'LL GIVE YOURSELF AWAY IF YOU CRY...
...FREYA.
I'M SORRY FOR ACTING ON MY OWN.
...
I CAN'T FORGIVE YOU FOR THAT.

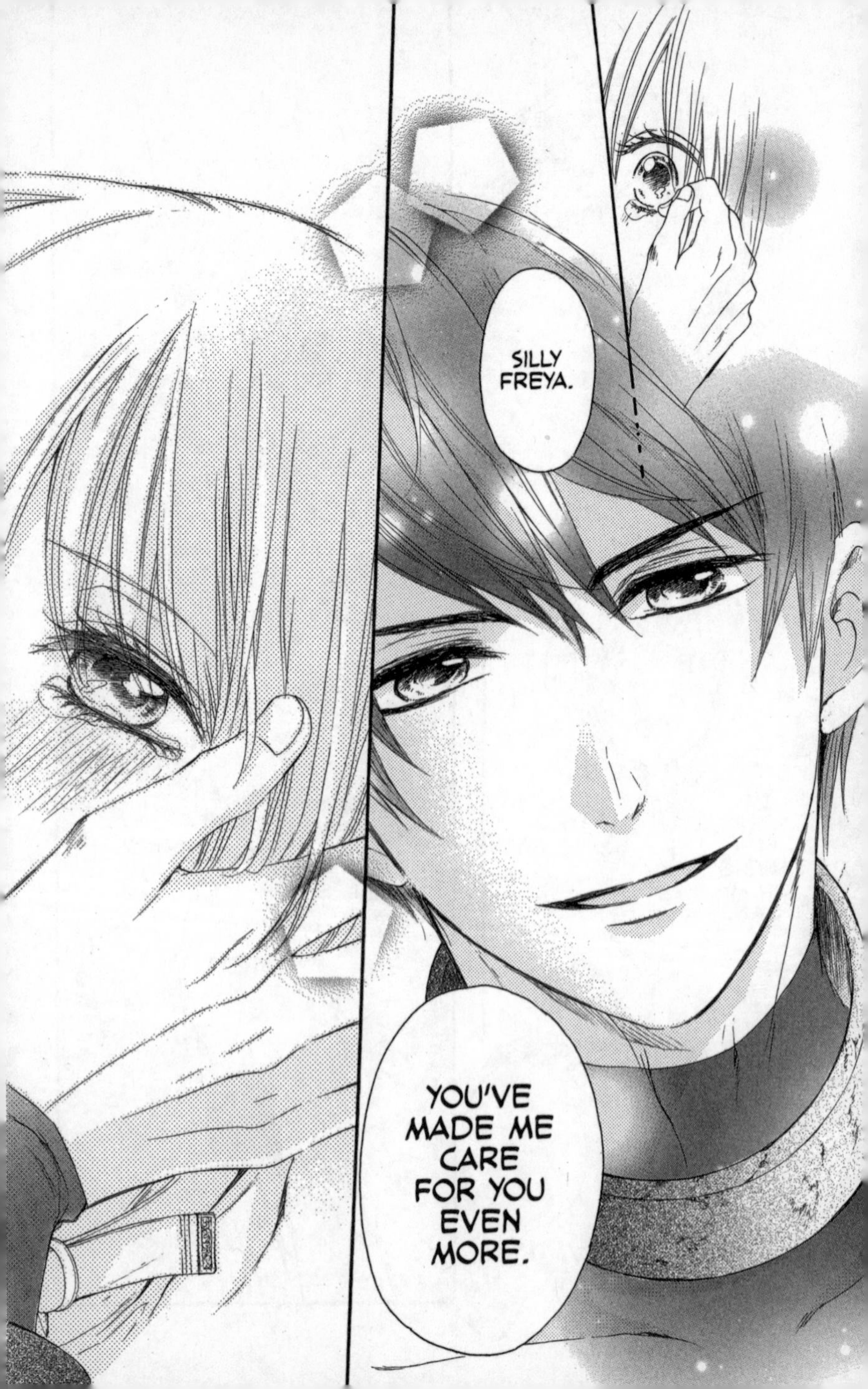
SILLY FREYA.
YOU'VE MADE ME CARE FOR YOU EVEN MORE.

EVEN THOUGH I HAVE NOTHING...

...AND I STILL CRY ALL THE TIME...

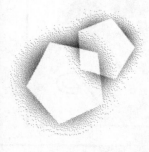

...I WANTED TO PROTECT HIM.

I'M GLAD I COULD PROTECT HIM.

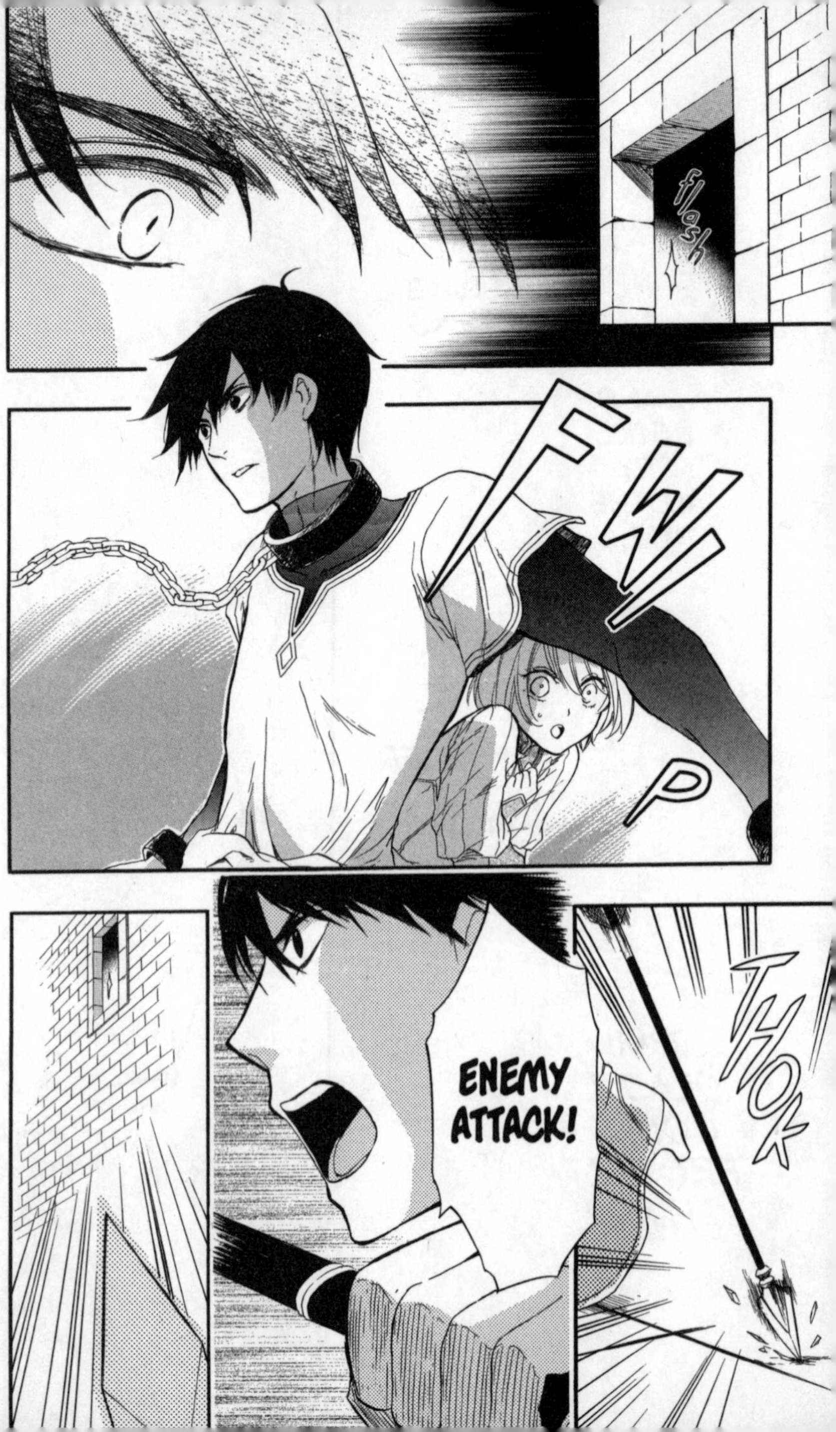
flash
FWIP
THOK
ENEMY ATTACK!

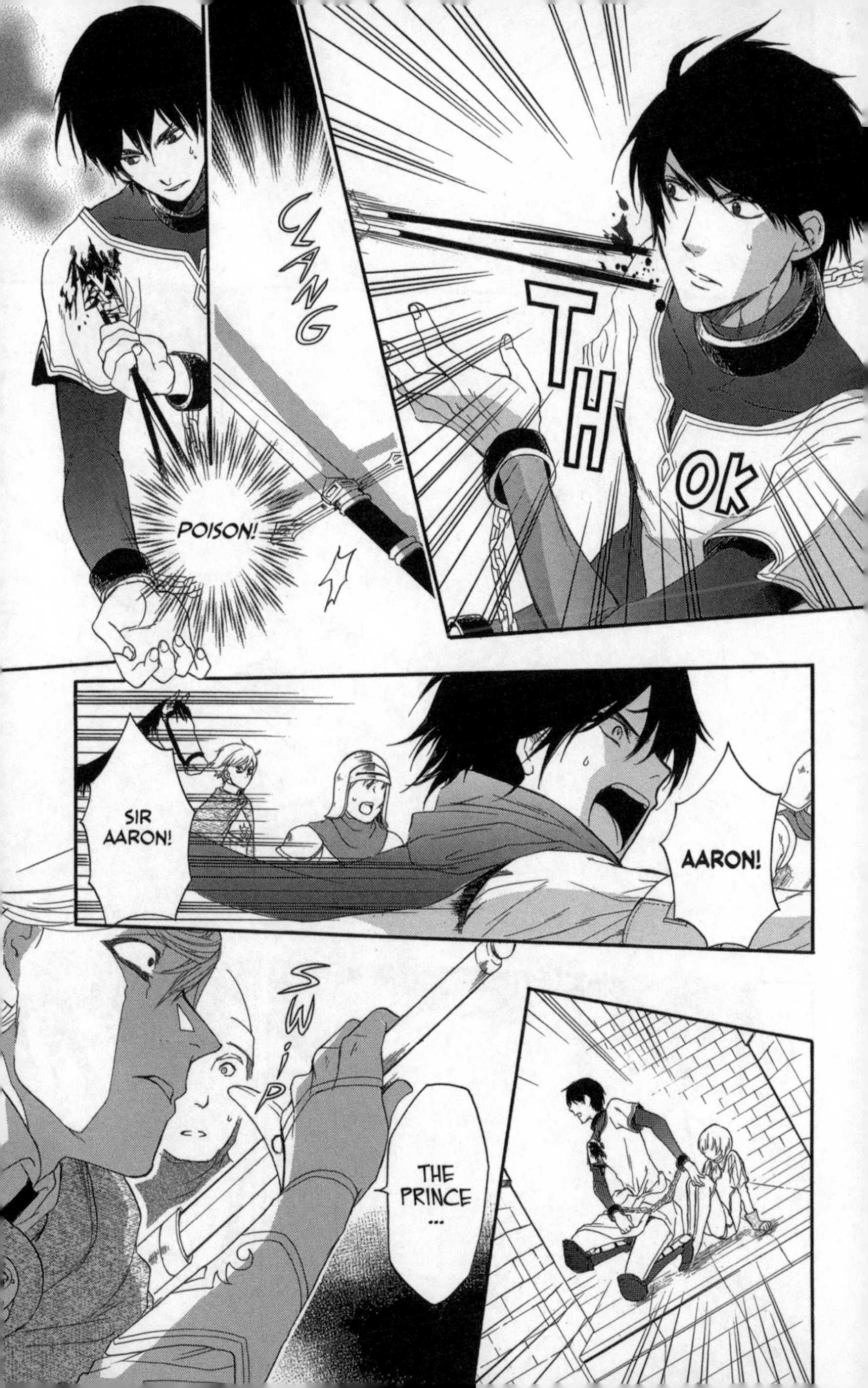
THOK
CLANG
POISON!
AARON!
SIR AARON!
SWIP
THE PRINCE ...

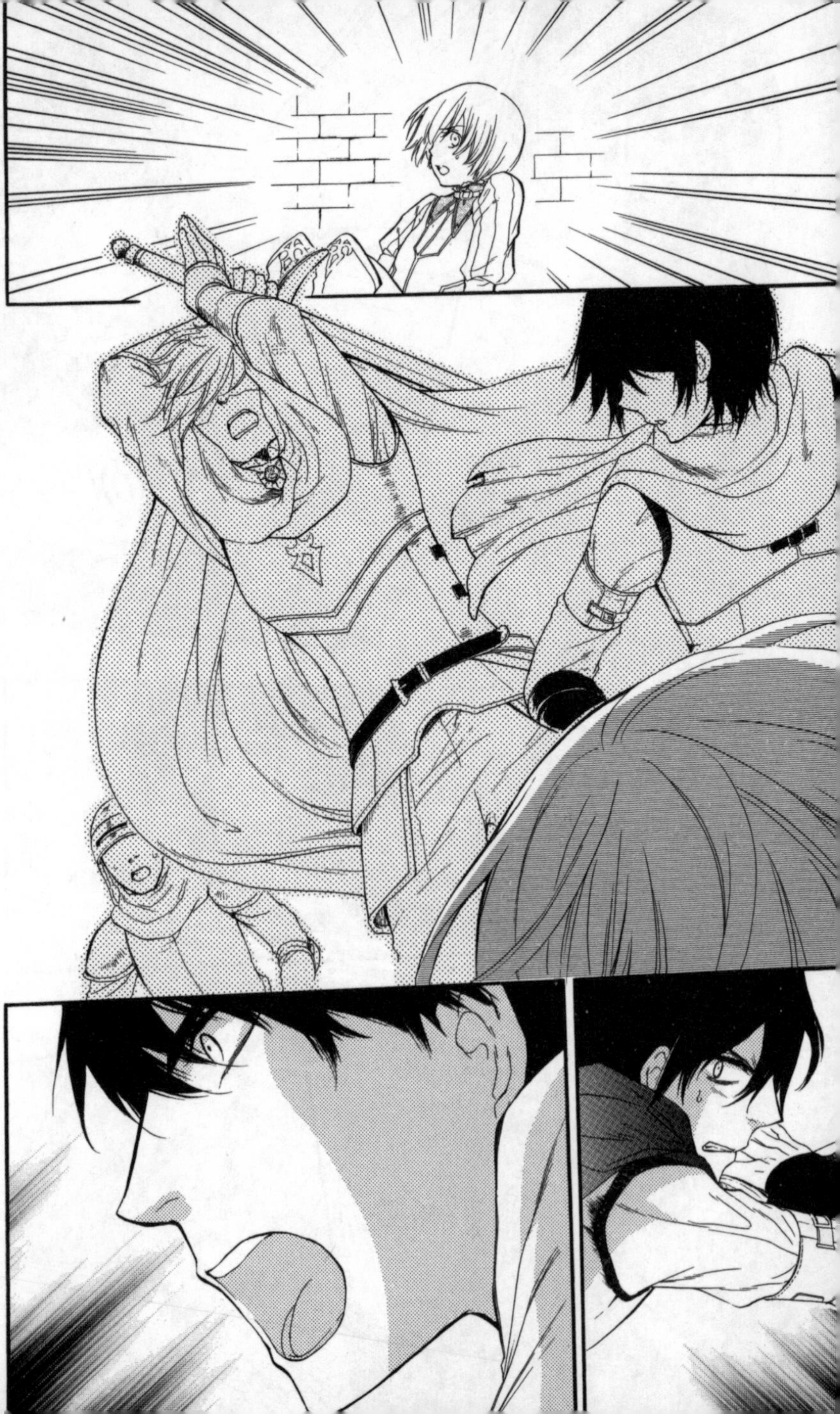

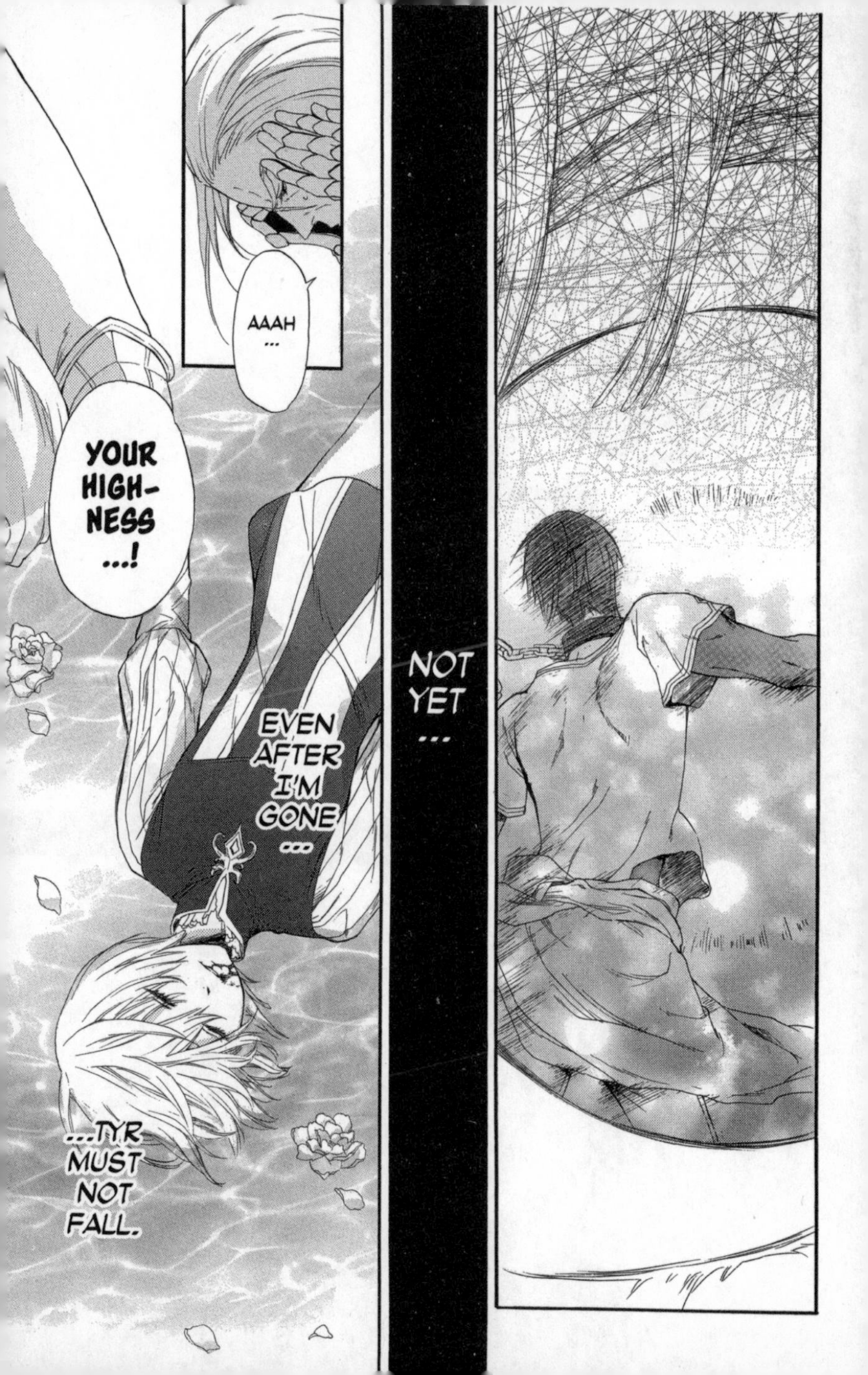
NOT YET ...
AAAH ...
YOUR HIGH-NESS ...!
EVEN AFTER I'M GONE ...
...TYR MUST NOT FALL.

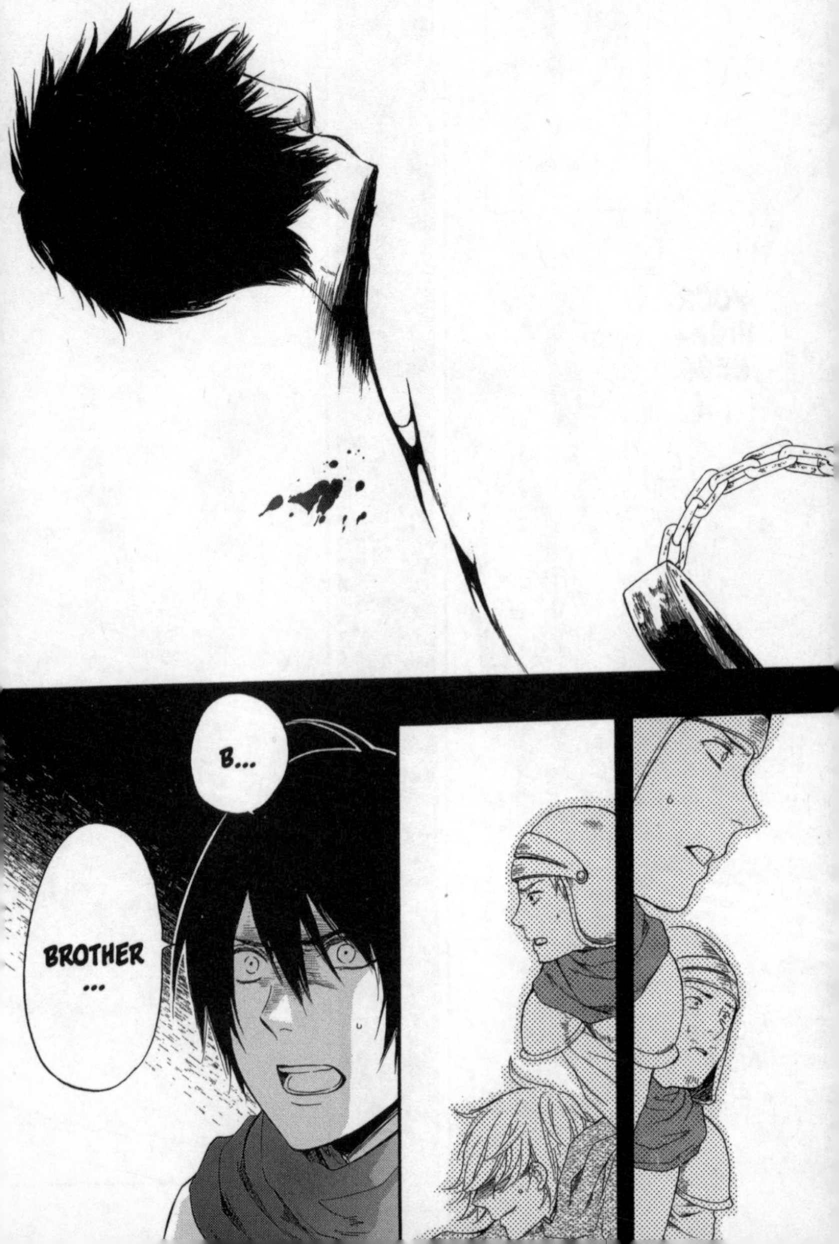
B...
BROTHER ...

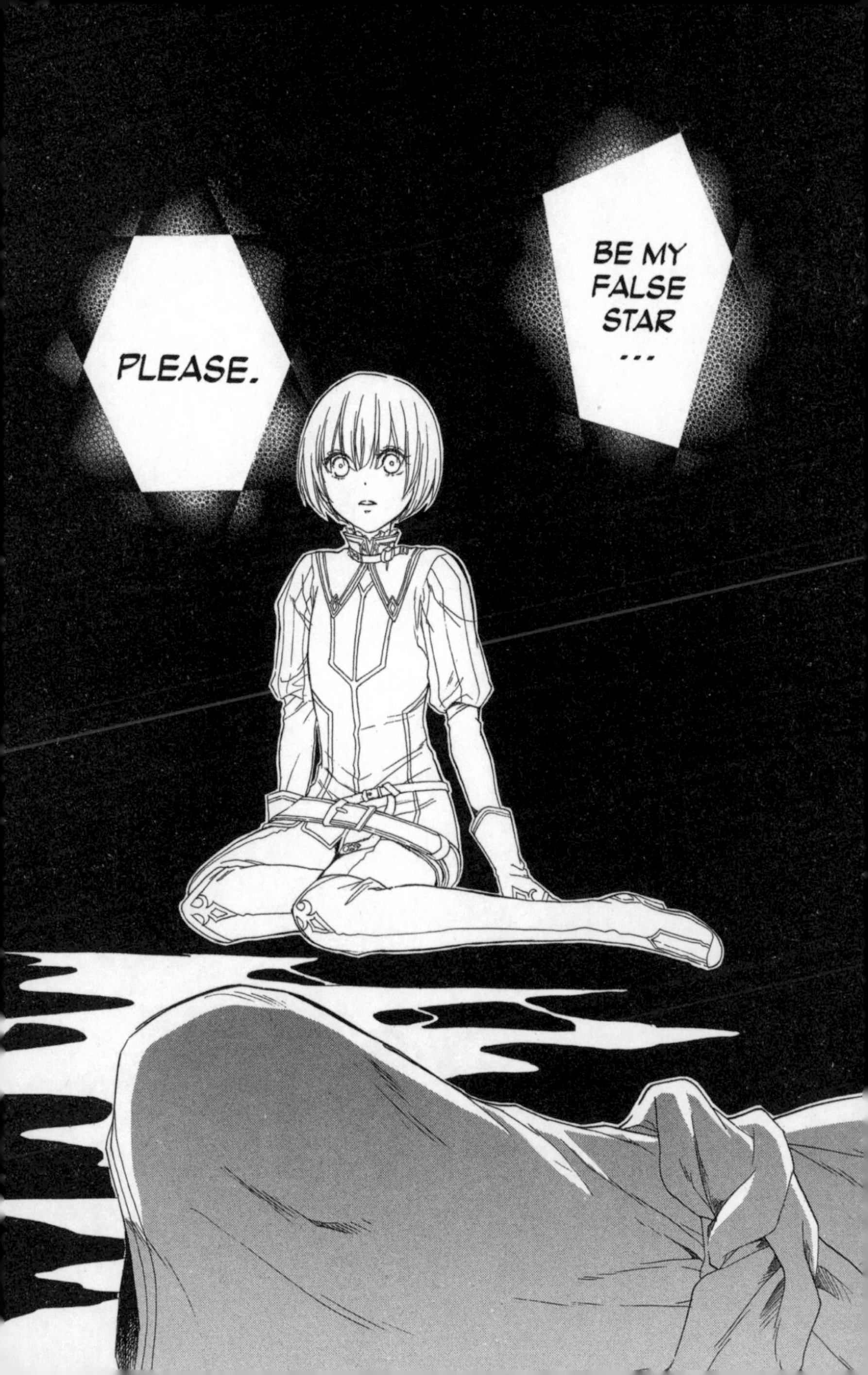
BE MY FALSE STAR ...
PLEASE.

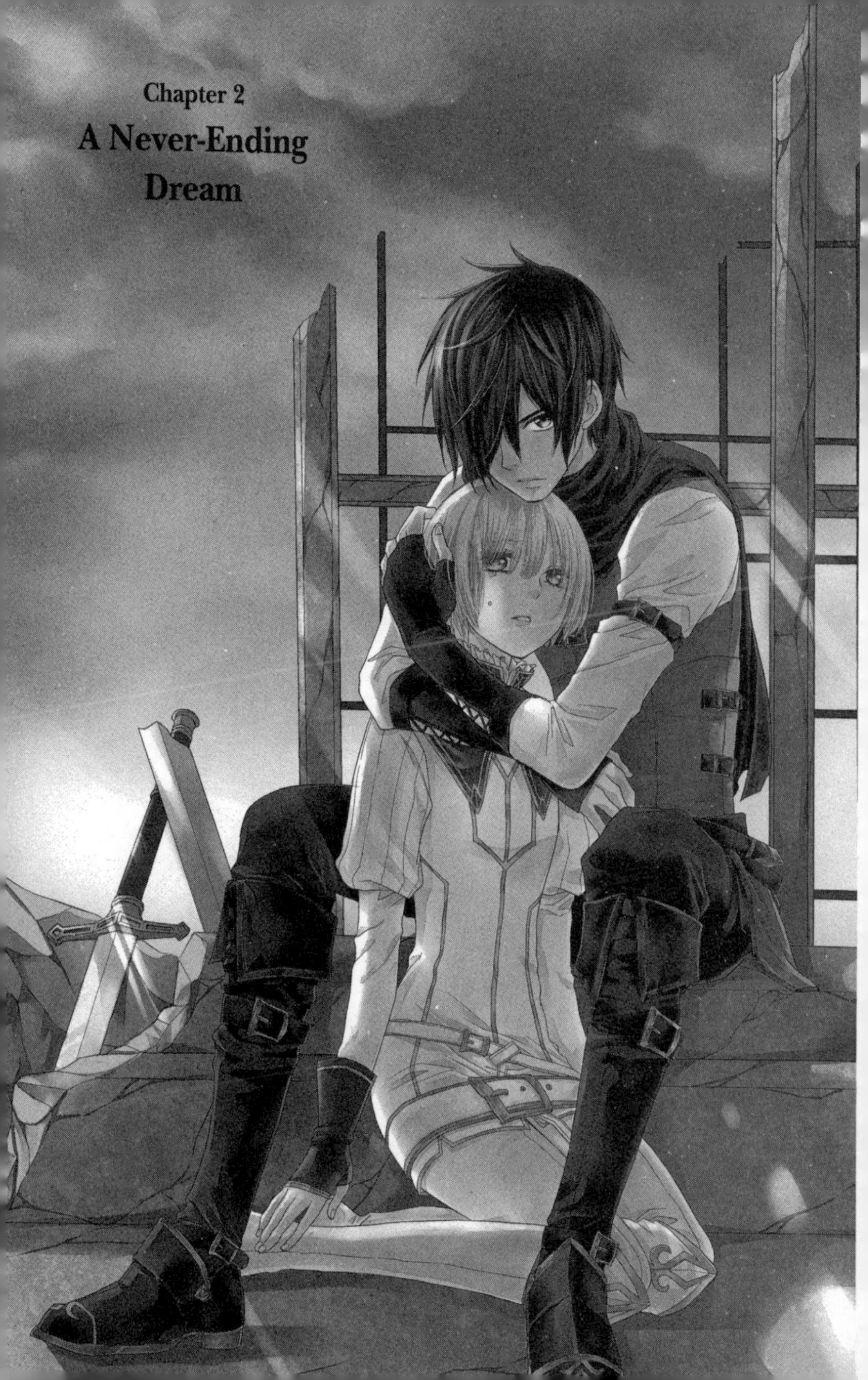
Chapter 2
A Never-Ending Dream

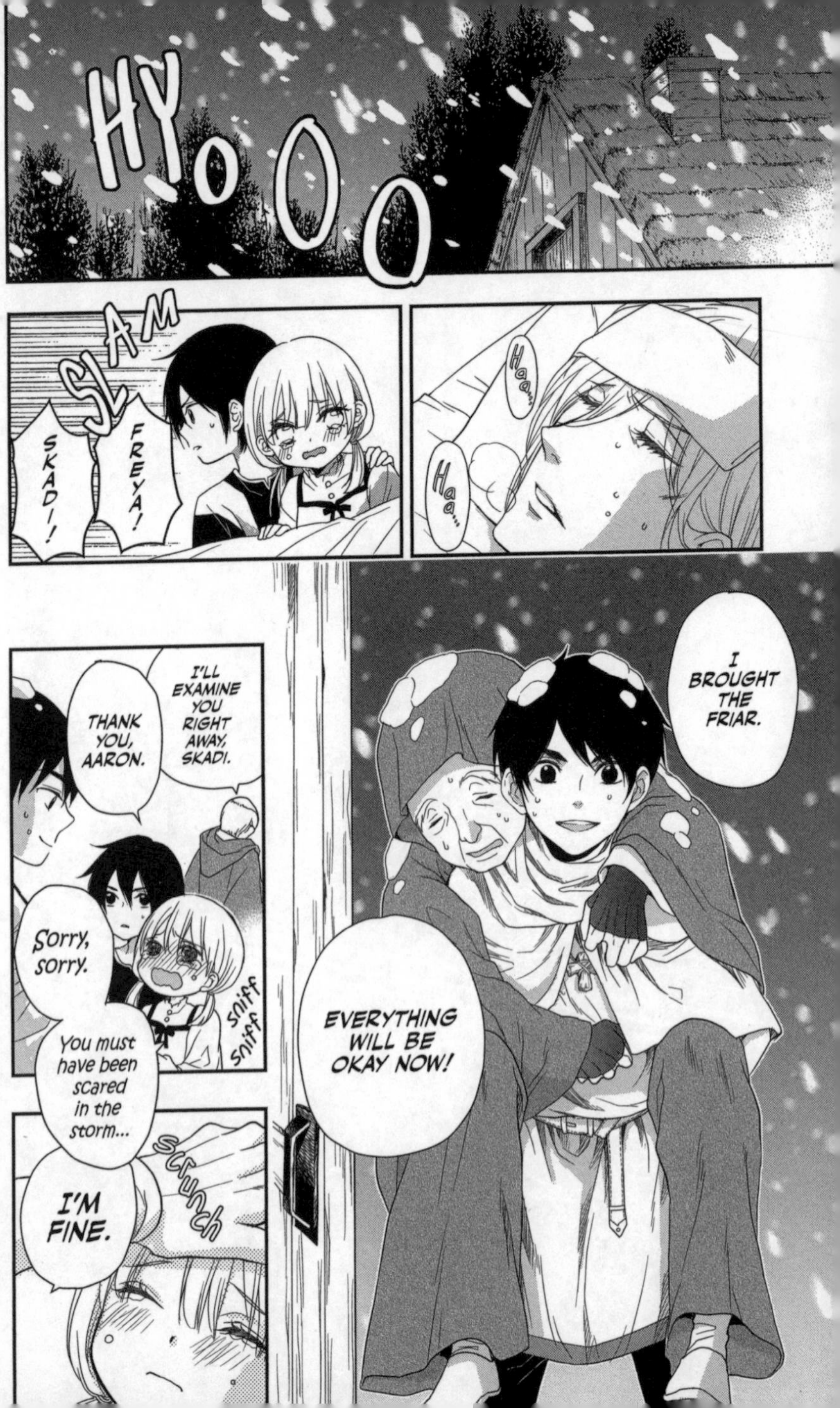
HYOOO
Haa...
Haa...
SLAM
FREYA!
SKADI!
I BROUGHT THE FRIAR.
EVERYTHING WILL BE OKAY NOW!
I'LL EXAMINE YOU RIGHT AWAY, SKADI.
THANK YOU, AARON.
Sorry, sorry.
sniff sniff
You must have been scared in the storm...
scrunch
I'M FINE.

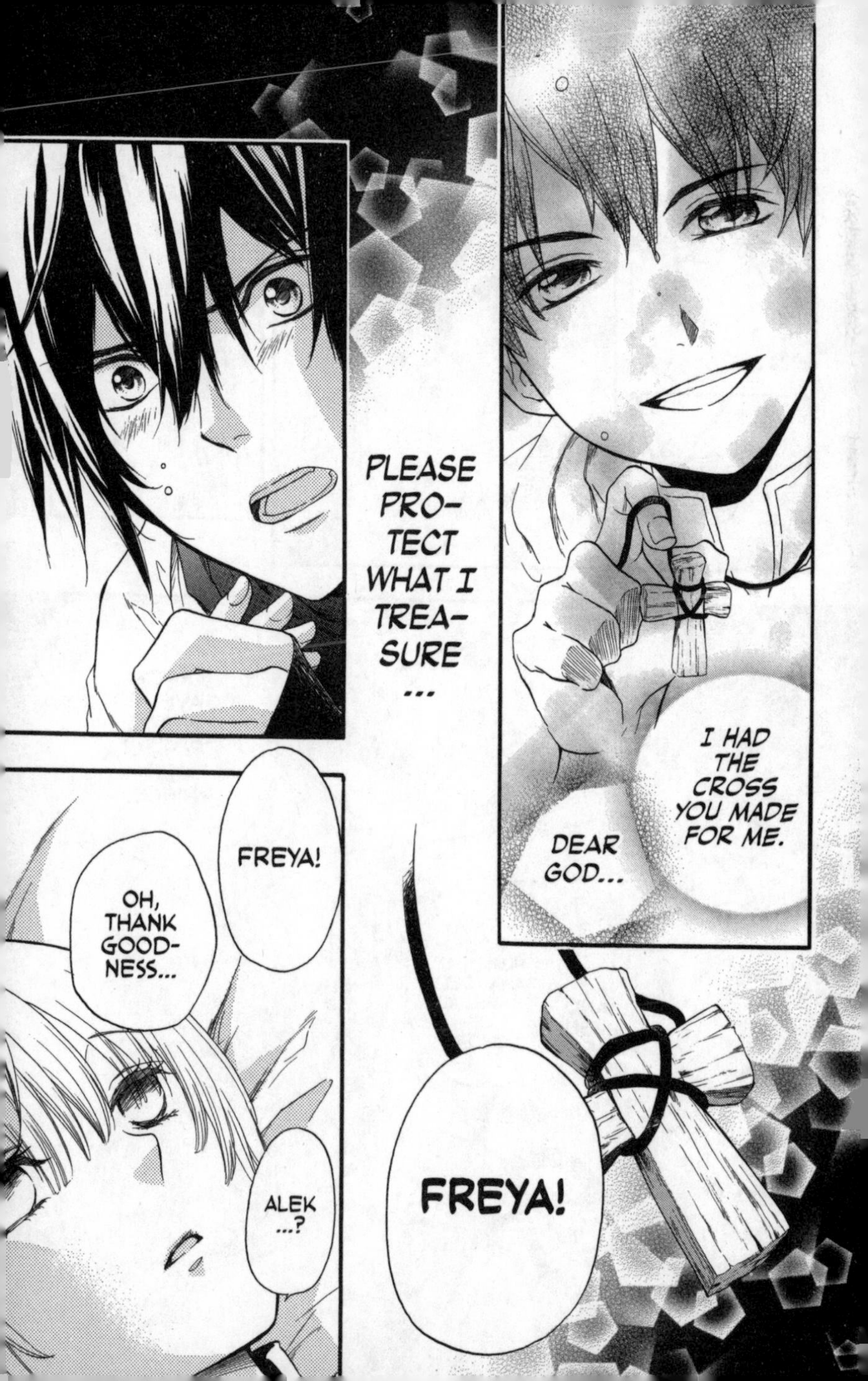
I HAD THE CROSS YOU MADE FOR ME.
DEAR GOD...
PLEASE PROTECT WHAT I TREASURE...
FREYA!
FREYA!
OH, THANK GOODNESS...
ALEK ...?

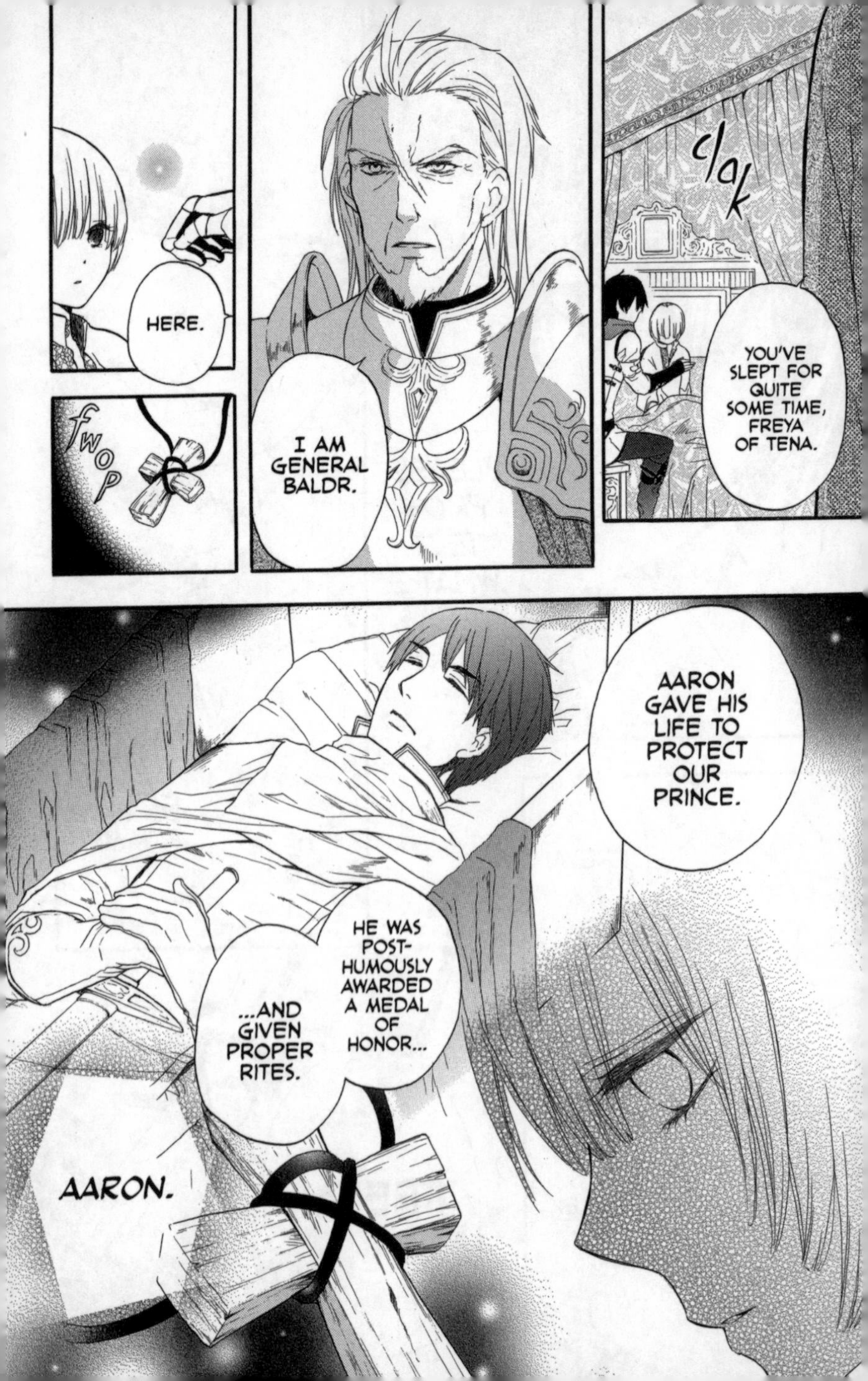
clak
YOU'VE SLEPT FOR QUITE SOME TIME, FREYA OF TENA.
I AM GENERAL BALDR.
HERE.
fwop
AARON GAVE HIS LIFE TO PROTECT OUR PRINCE.
HE WAS POST-HUMOUSLY AWARDED A MEDAL OF HONOR...
...AND GIVEN PROPER RITES.
AARON.

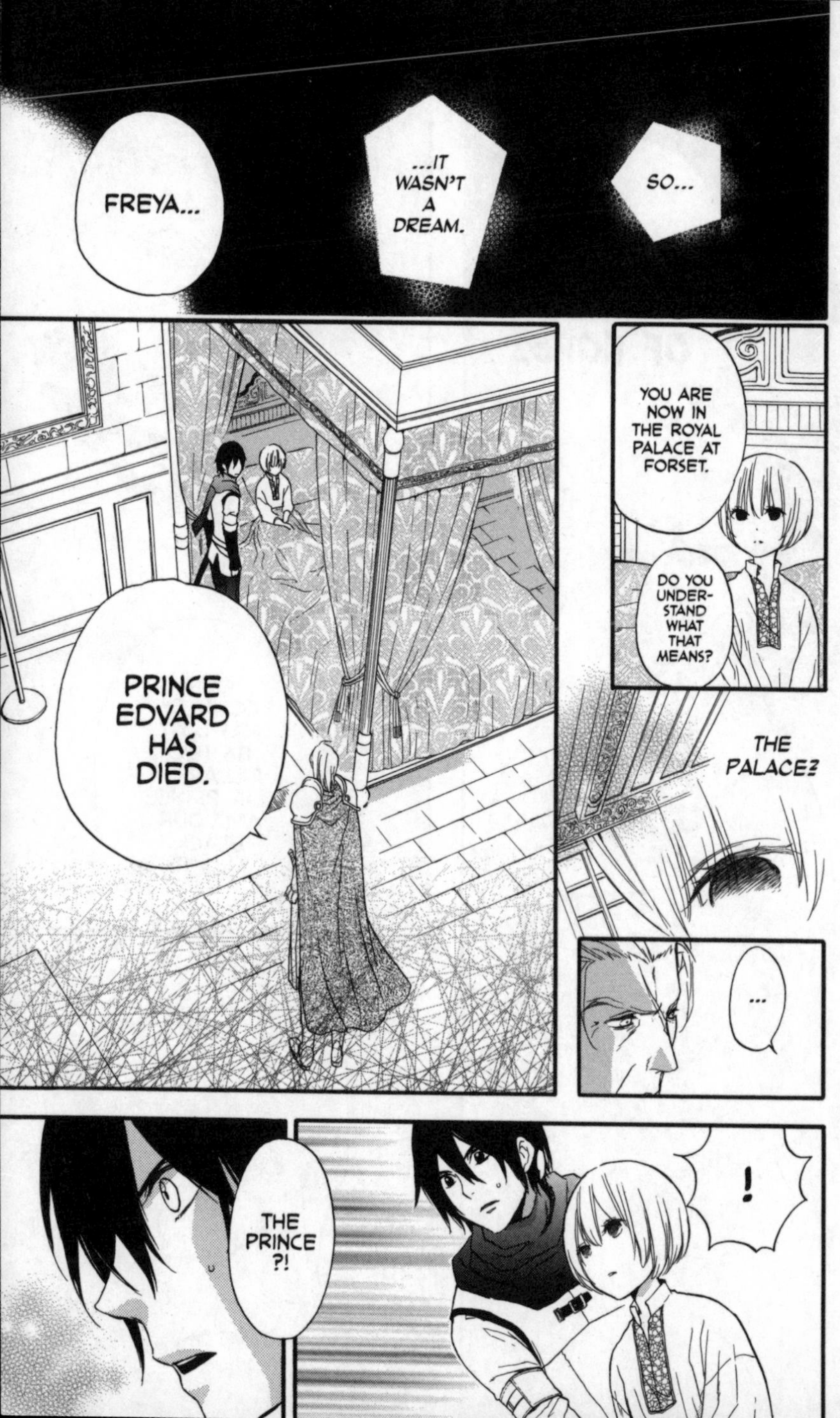
SO...
...IT WASN'T A DREAM.
FREYA...
YOU ARE NOW IN THE ROYAL PALACE AT FORSET.
DO YOU UNDER-STAND WHAT THAT MEANS?
THE PALACE?
...
PRINCE EDVARD HAS DIED.
!
THE PRINCE ?!

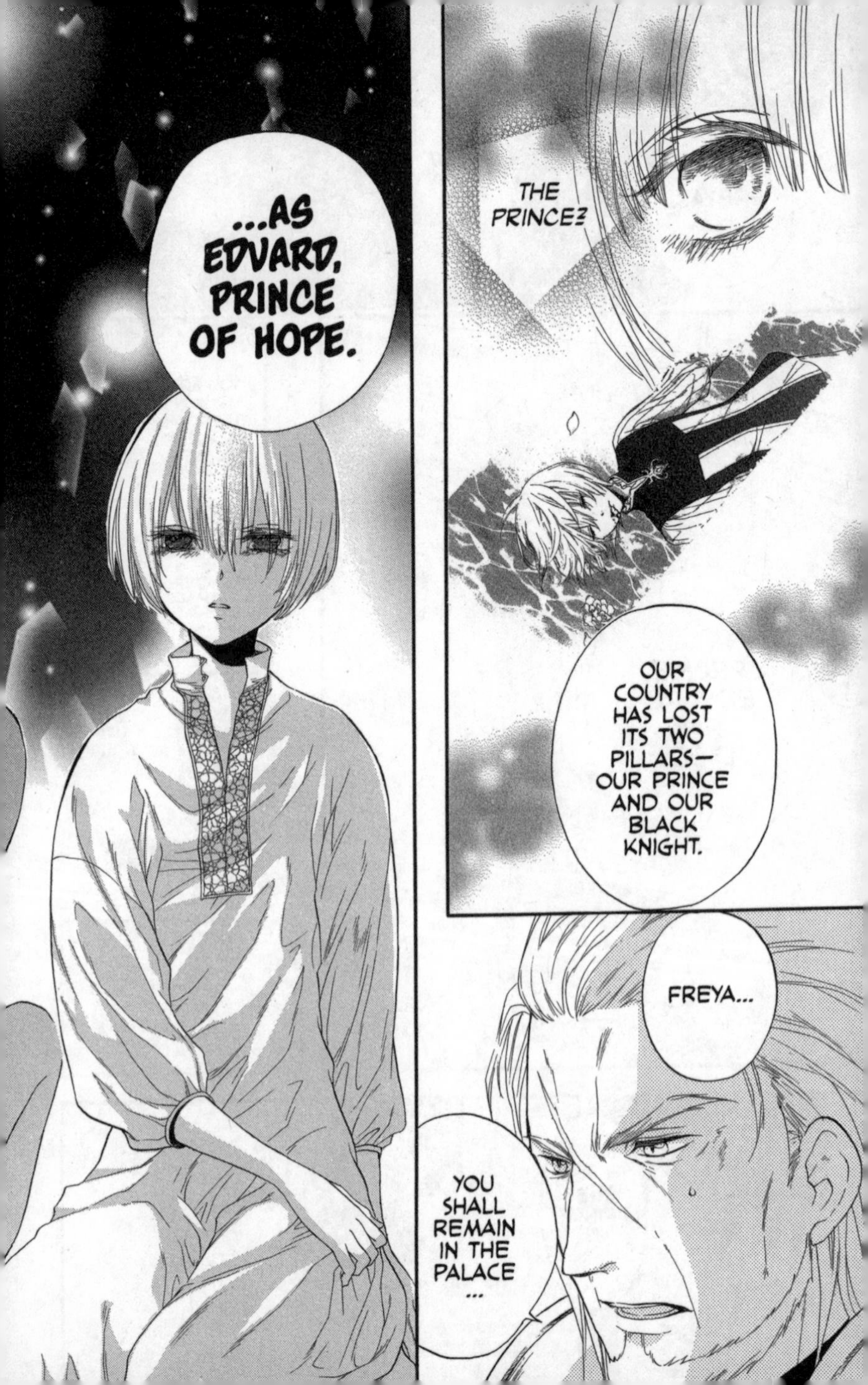
THE PRINCE?
OUR COUNTRY HAS LOST ITS TWO PILLARS—OUR PRINCE AND OUR BLACK KNIGHT.
FREYA...
YOU SHALL REMAIN IN THE PALACE...
...AS EDVARD, PRINCE OF HOPE.

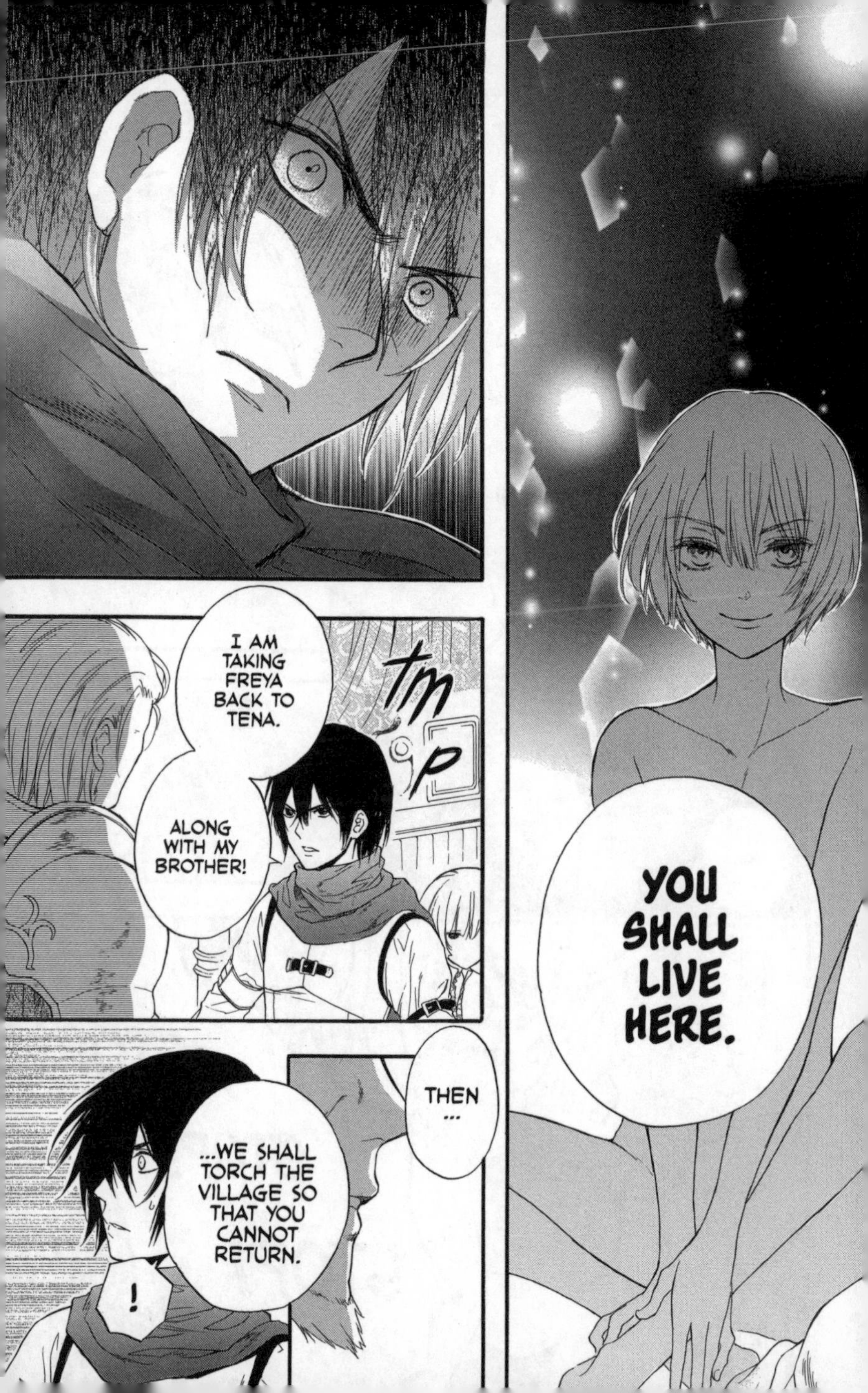
YOU SHALL LIVE HERE.
I AM TAKING FREYA BACK TO TENA.
tmp
ALONG WITH MY BROTHER!
THEN ...
...WE SHALL TORCH THE VILLAGE SO THAT YOU CANNOT RETURN.
!

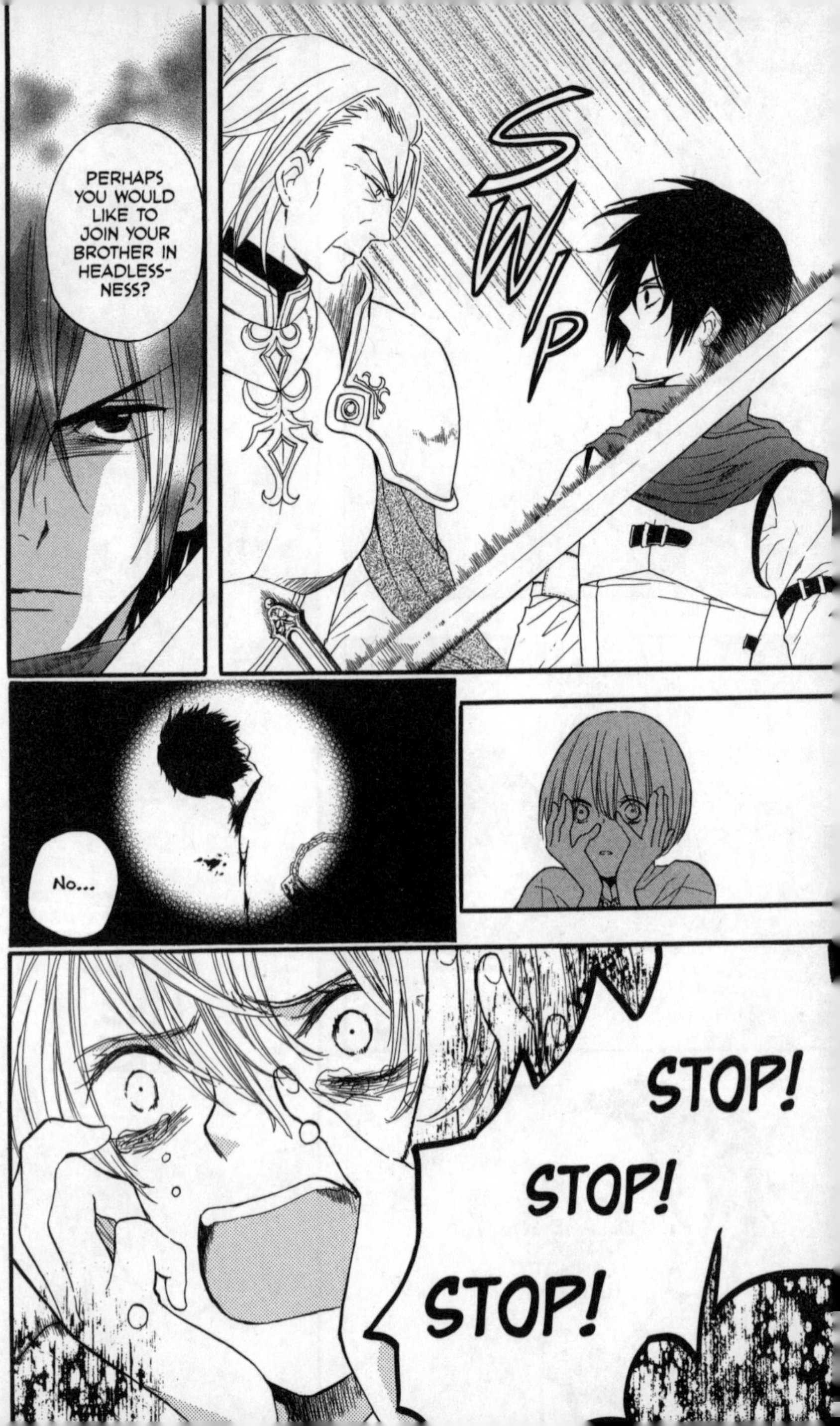
SWIP
PERHAPS YOU WOULD LIKE TO JOIN YOUR BROTHER IN HEADLESS-NESS?
No...
STOP!
STOP!
STOP!

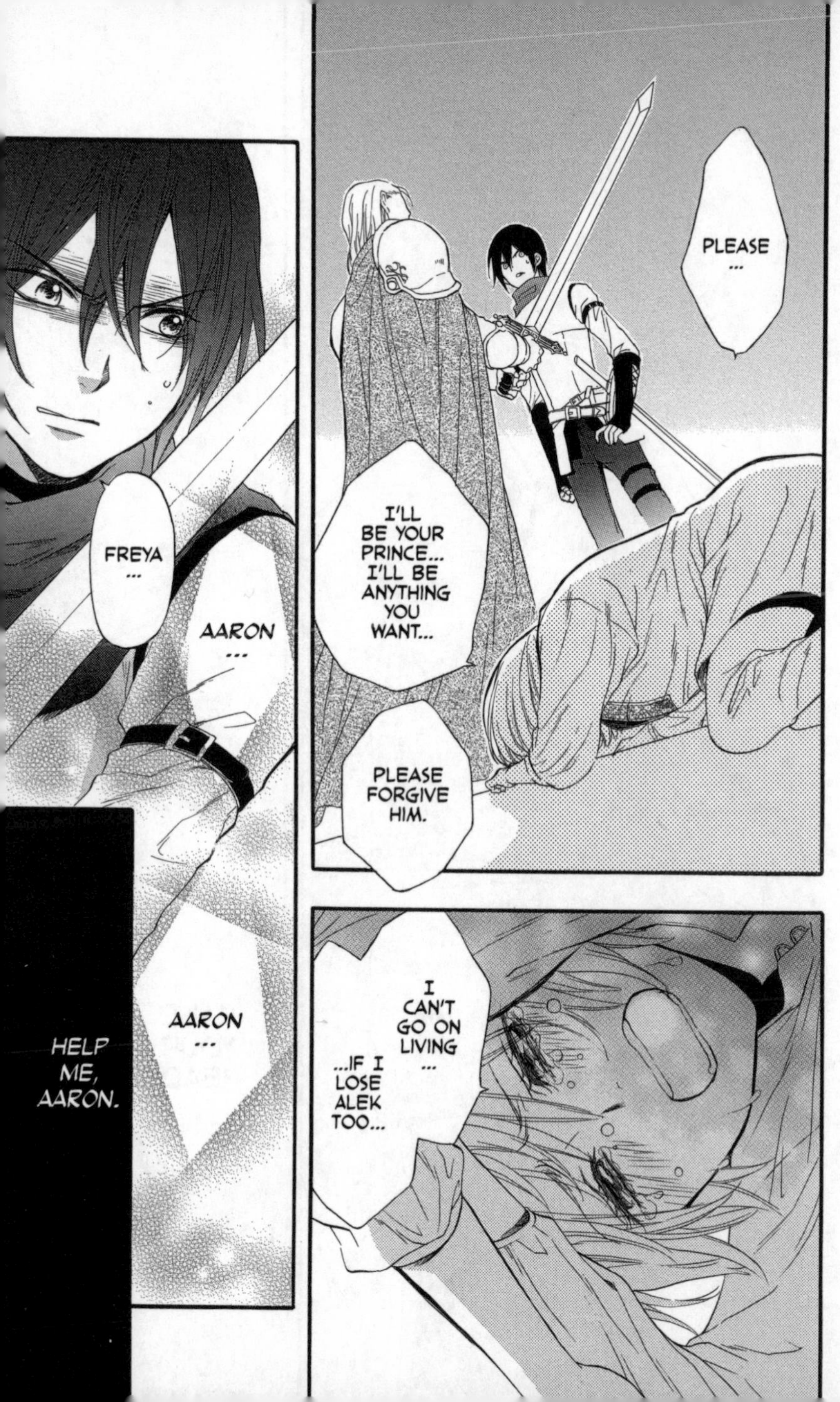
PLEASE ...
I'LL BE YOUR PRINCE... I'LL BE ANYTHING YOU WANT...
PLEASE FORGIVE HIM.
I CAN'T GO ON LIVING ...
...IF I LOSE ALEK TOO...
FREYA ...
AARON ...
AARON ...
HELP ME, AARON.

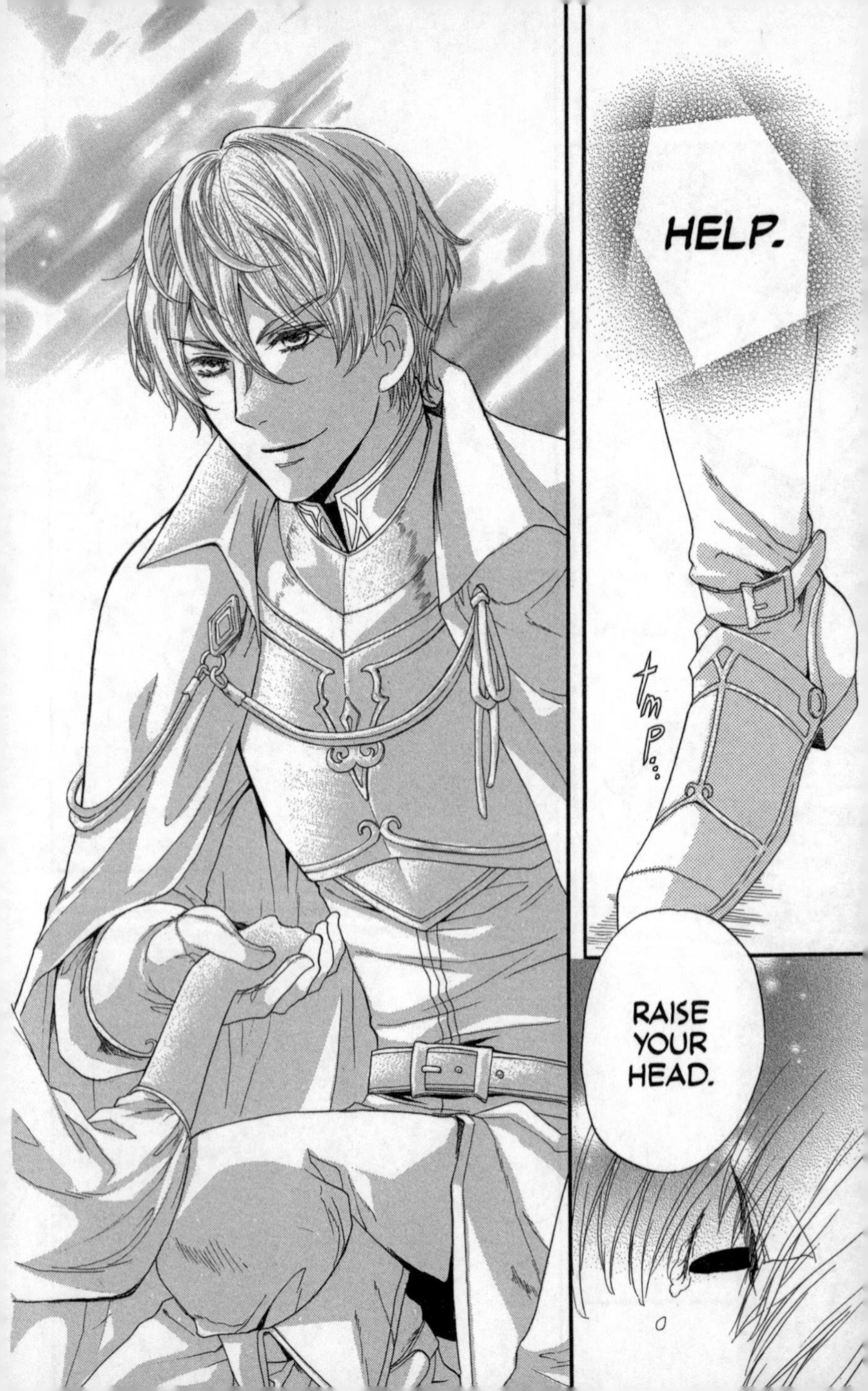
HELP.
tmp...
RAISE YOUR HEAD.

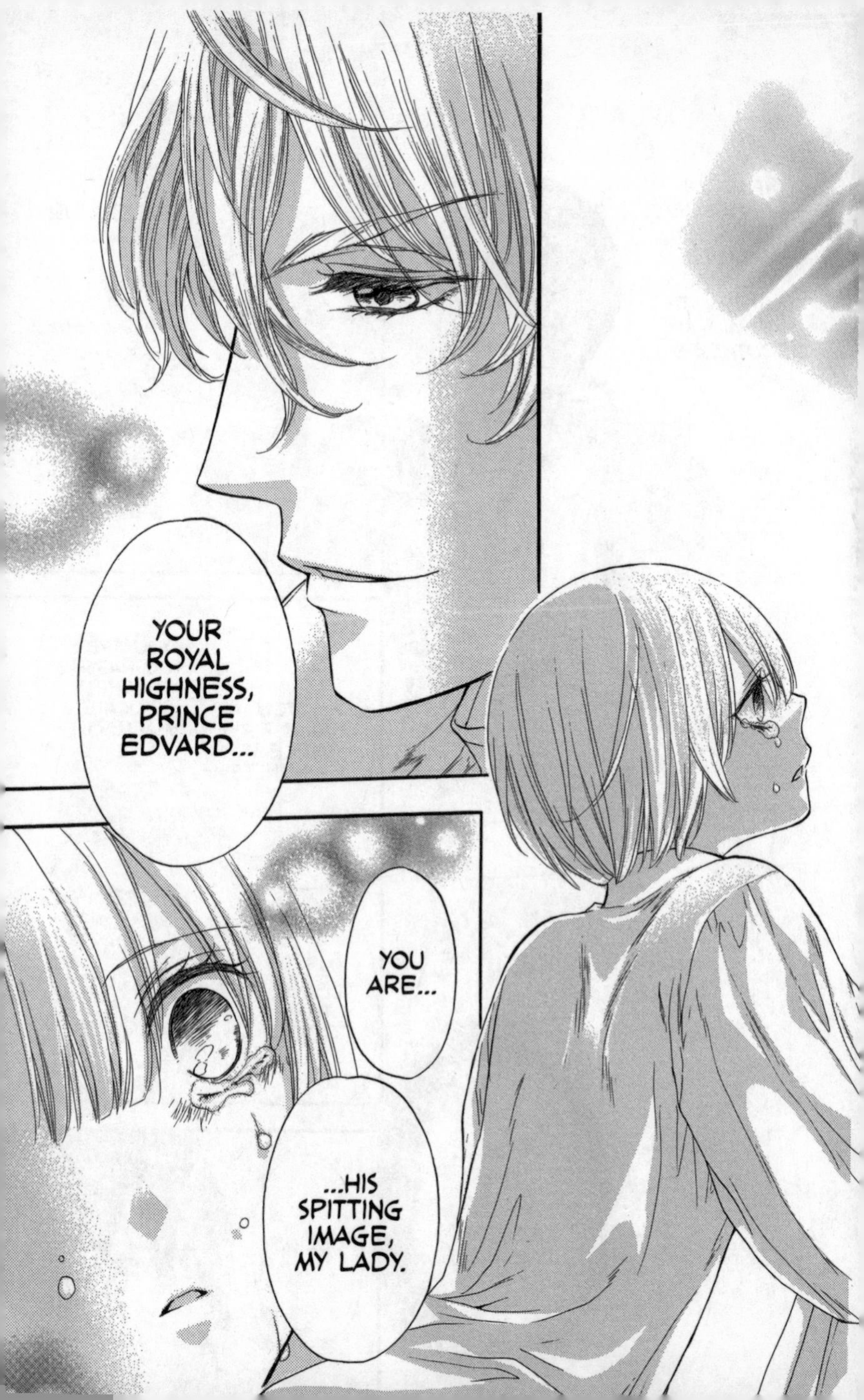
YOUR ROYAL HIGHNESS, PRINCE EDVARD...
YOU ARE...
...HIS SPITTING IMAGE, MY LADY.

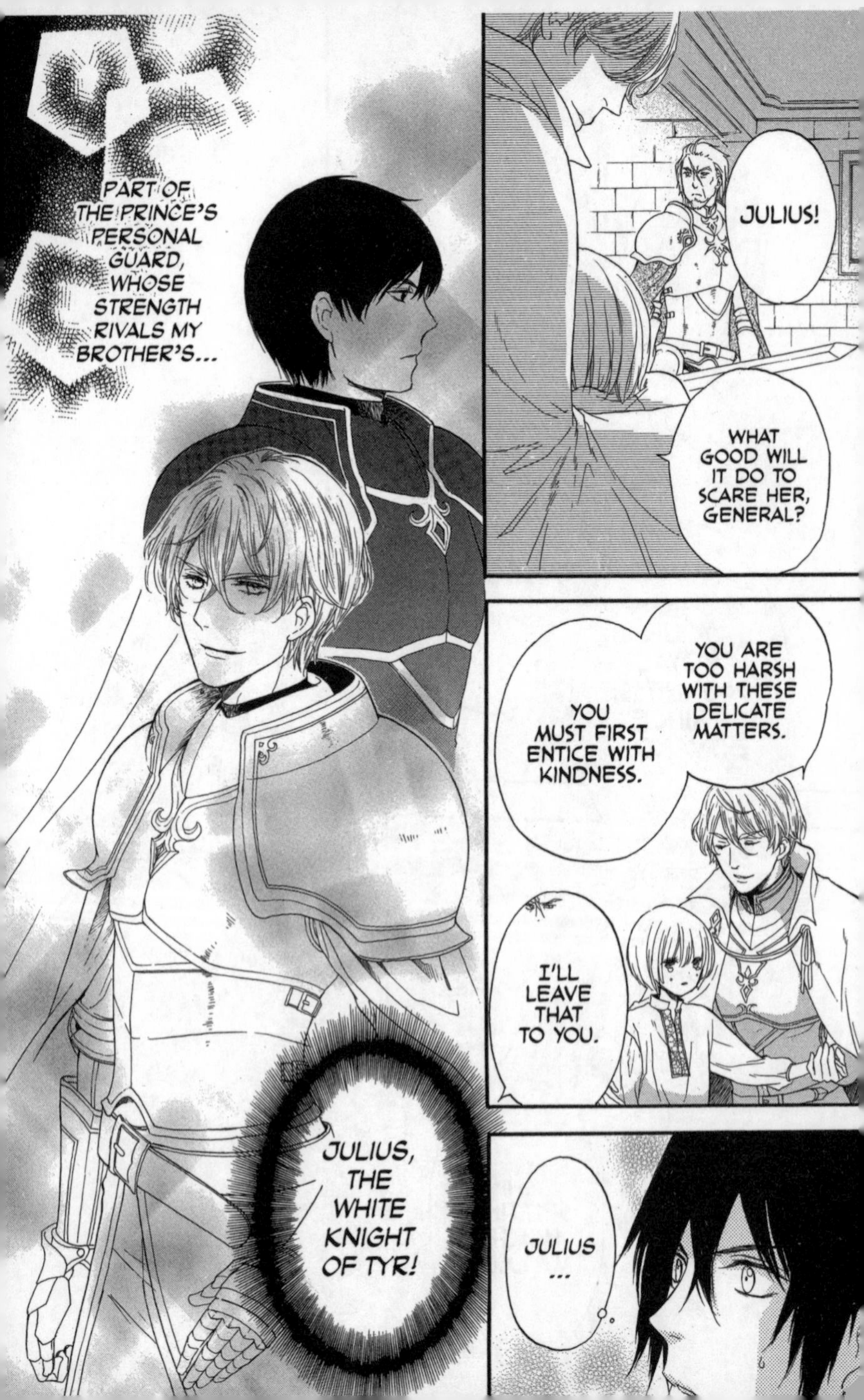
JULIUS!
WHAT GOOD WILL IT DO TO SCARE HER, GENERAL?
YOU ARE TOO HARSH WITH THESE DELICATE MATTERS.
YOU MUST FIRST ENTICE WITH KINDNESS.
I'LL LEAVE THAT TO YOU.
JULIUS ...
PART OF THE PRINCE'S PERSONAL GUARD, WHOSE STRENGTH RIVALS MY BROTHER'S...
JULIUS, THE WHITE KNIGHT OF TYR!

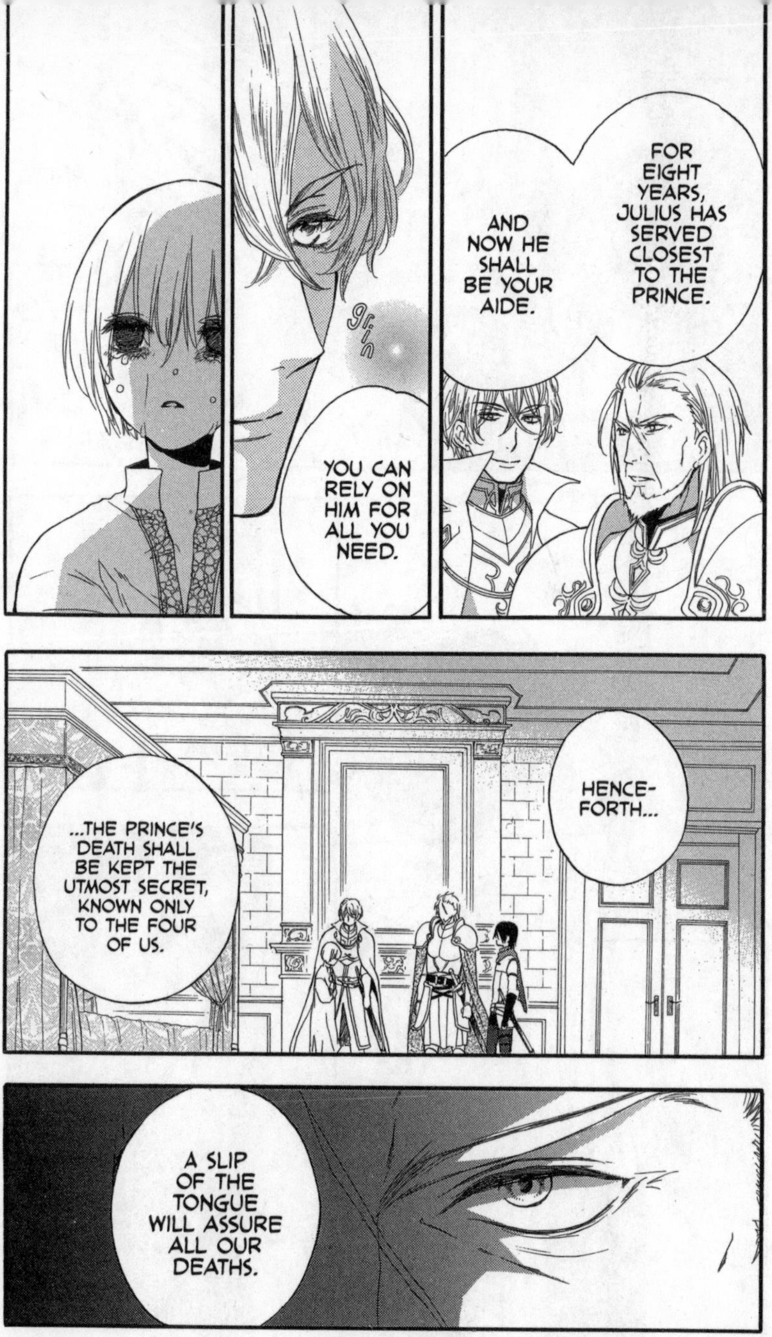
FOR EIGHT YEARS, JULIUS HAS SERVED CLOSEST TO THE PRINCE.
AND NOW HE SHALL BE YOUR AIDE.
grin
YOU CAN RELY ON HIM FOR ALL YOU NEED.
HENCE-FORTH...
...THE PRINCE'S DEATH SHALL BE KEPT THE UTMOST SECRET, KNOWN ONLY TO THE FOUR OF US.
A SLIP OF THE TONGUE WILL ASSURE ALL OUR DEATHS.

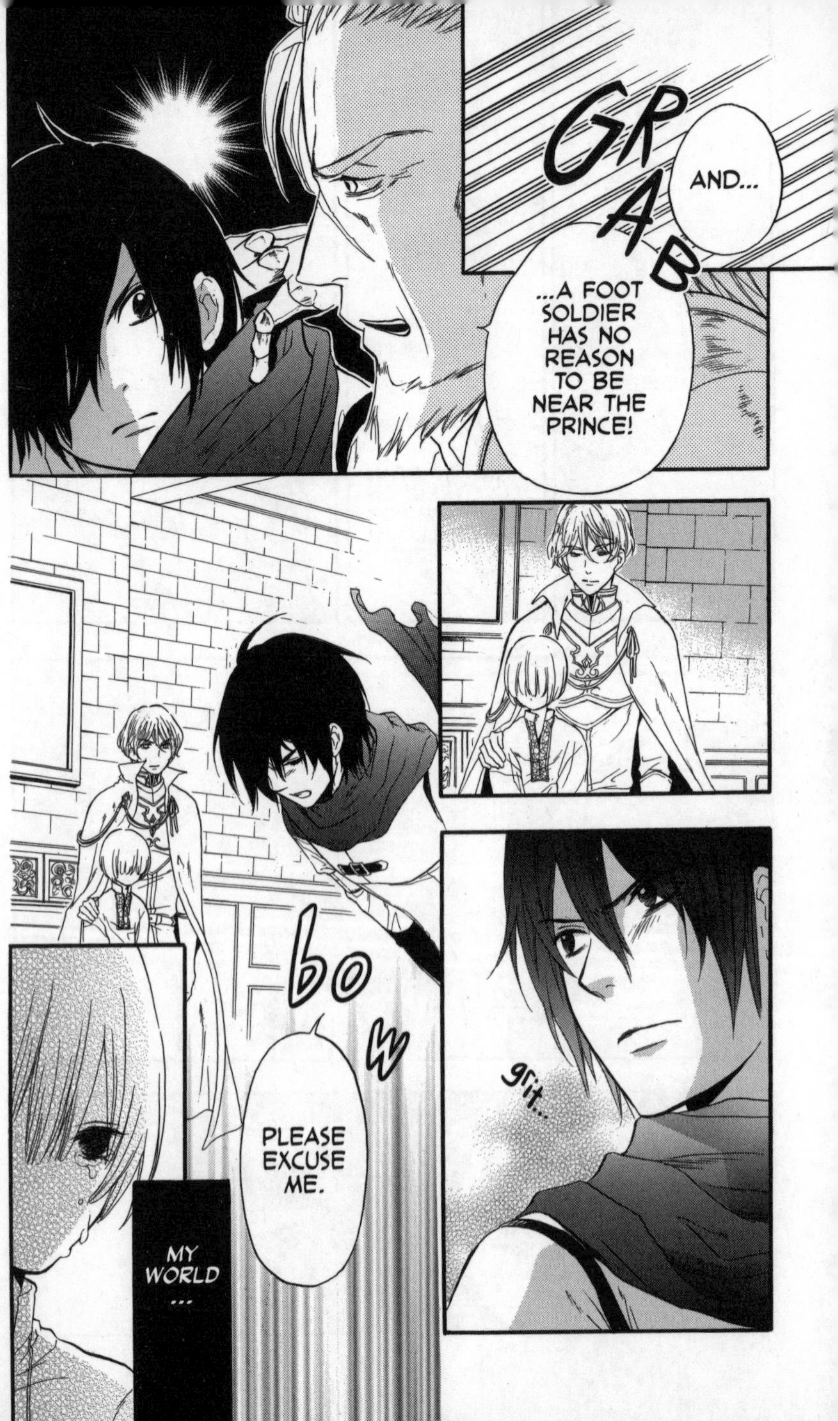
GRAB
AND...
...A FOOT SOLDIER HAS NO REASON TO BE NEAR THE PRINCE!
grit...
bow
PLEASE EXCUSE ME.
MY WORLD ...

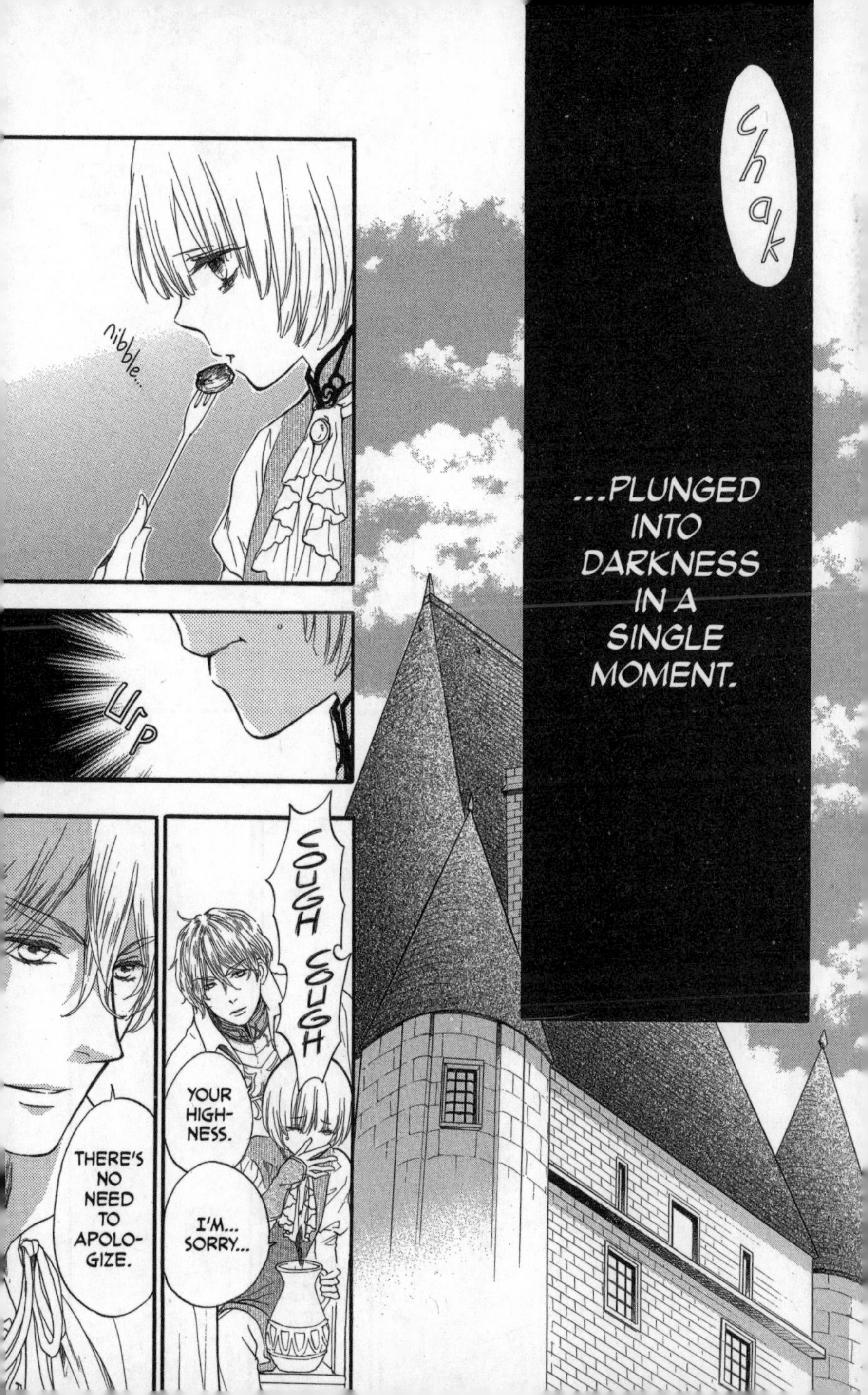
Chak
...PLUNGED INTO DARKNESS IN A SINGLE MOMENT.
nibble...
Urp
COUGH COUGH COUGH
YOUR HIGH-NESS.
I'M... SORRY...
THERE'S NO NEED TO APOLO-GIZE.

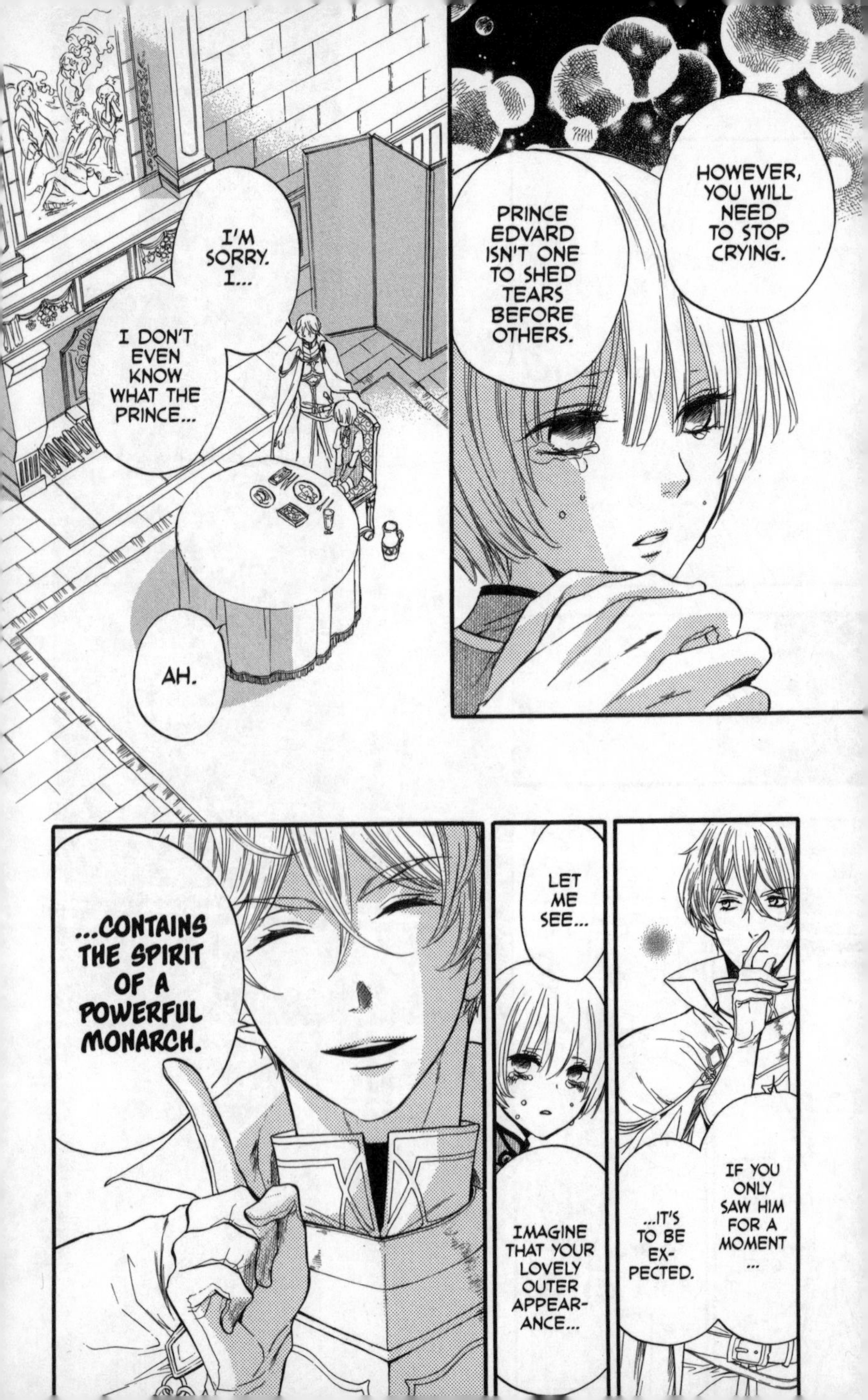
HOWEVER, YOU WILL NEED TO STOP CRYING.
PRINCE EDVARD ISN'T ONE TO SHED TEARS BEFORE OTHERS.
I'M SORRY. I...
I DON'T EVEN KNOW WHAT THE PRINCE...
AH.
IF YOU ONLY SAW HIM FOR A MOMENT ...
...IT'S TO BE EX-PECTED.
LET ME SEE...
IMAGINE THAT YOUR LOVELY OUTER APPEAR-ANCE...
...CONTAINS THE SPIRIT OF A POWERFUL MONARCH.

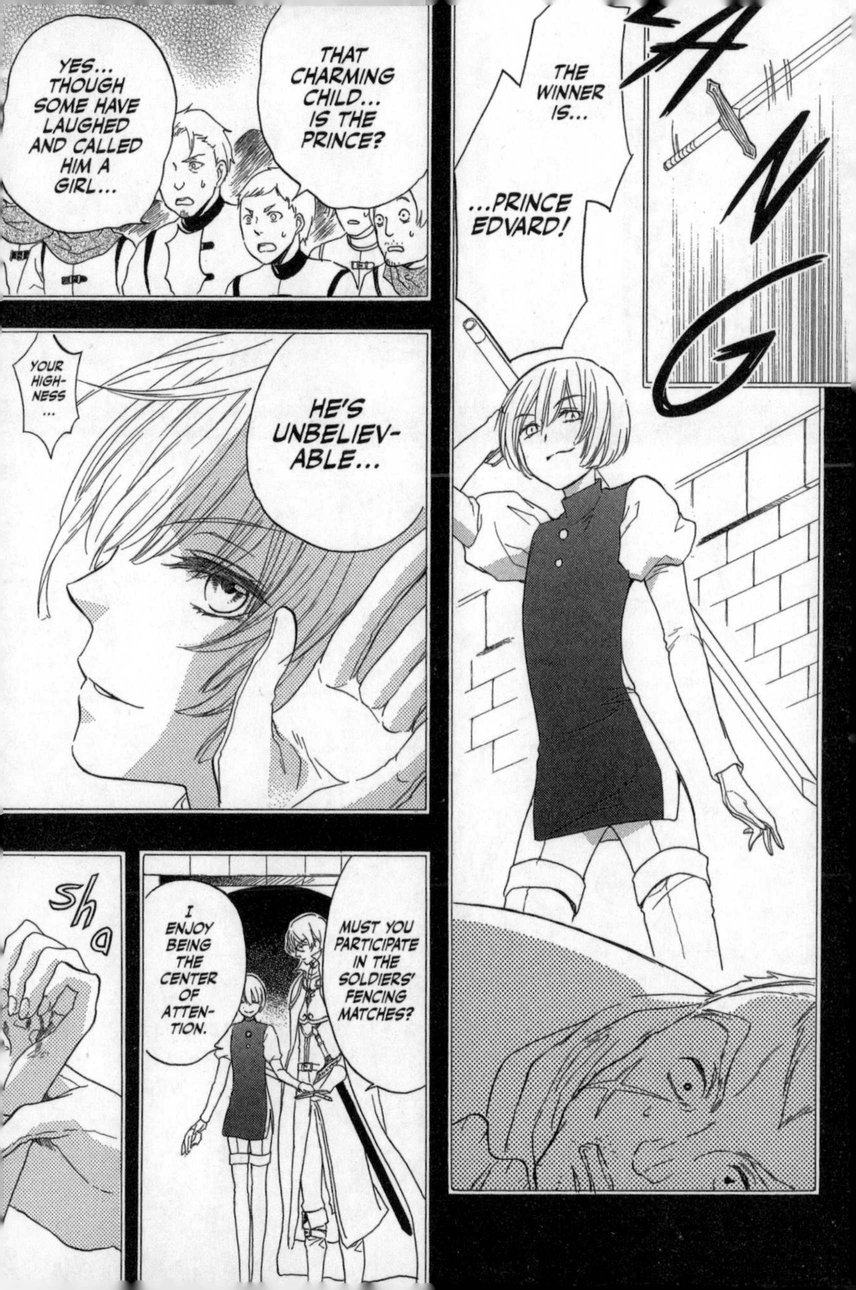
CLANG
THE WINNER IS...
...PRINCE EDVARD!
THAT CHARMING CHILD... IS THE PRINCE?
YES... THOUGH SOME HAVE LAUGHED AND CALLED HIM A GIRL...
HE'S UNBELIEVABLE...
YOUR HIGHNESS...
MUST YOU PARTICIPATE IN THE SOLDIERS' FENCING MATCHES?
I ENJOY BEING THE CENTER OF ATTENTION.
sha

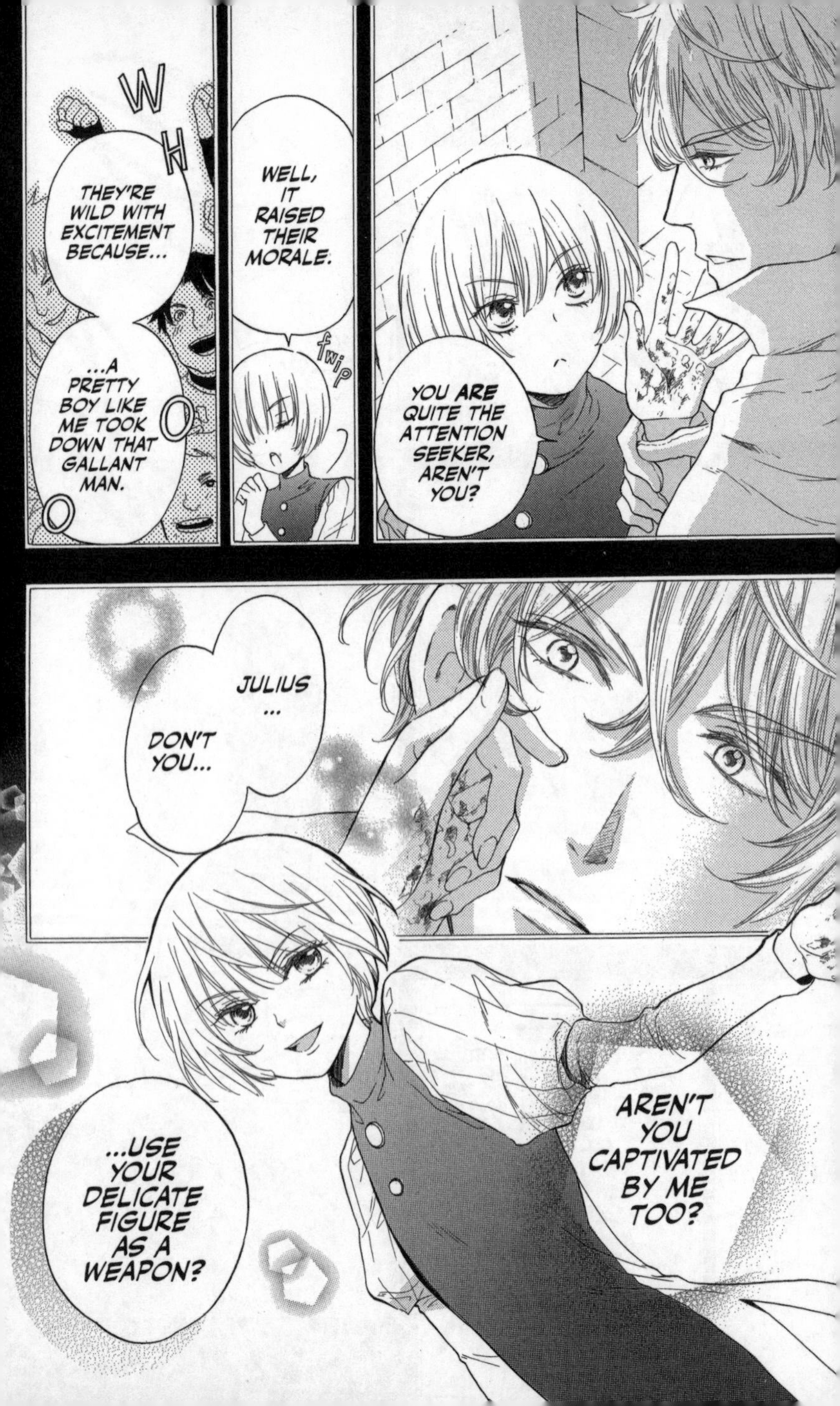
YOU ARE QUITE THE ATTENTION SEEKER, AREN'T YOU?
WELL, IT RAISED THEIR MORALE.
fwip
THEY'RE WILD WITH EXCITEMENT BECAUSE...
...A PRETTY BOY LIKE ME TOOK DOWN THAT GALLANT MAN.
WHOO
JULIUS...
DON'T YOU...
...USE YOUR DELICATE FIGURE AS A WEAPON?
AREN'T YOU CAPTIVATED BY ME TOO?

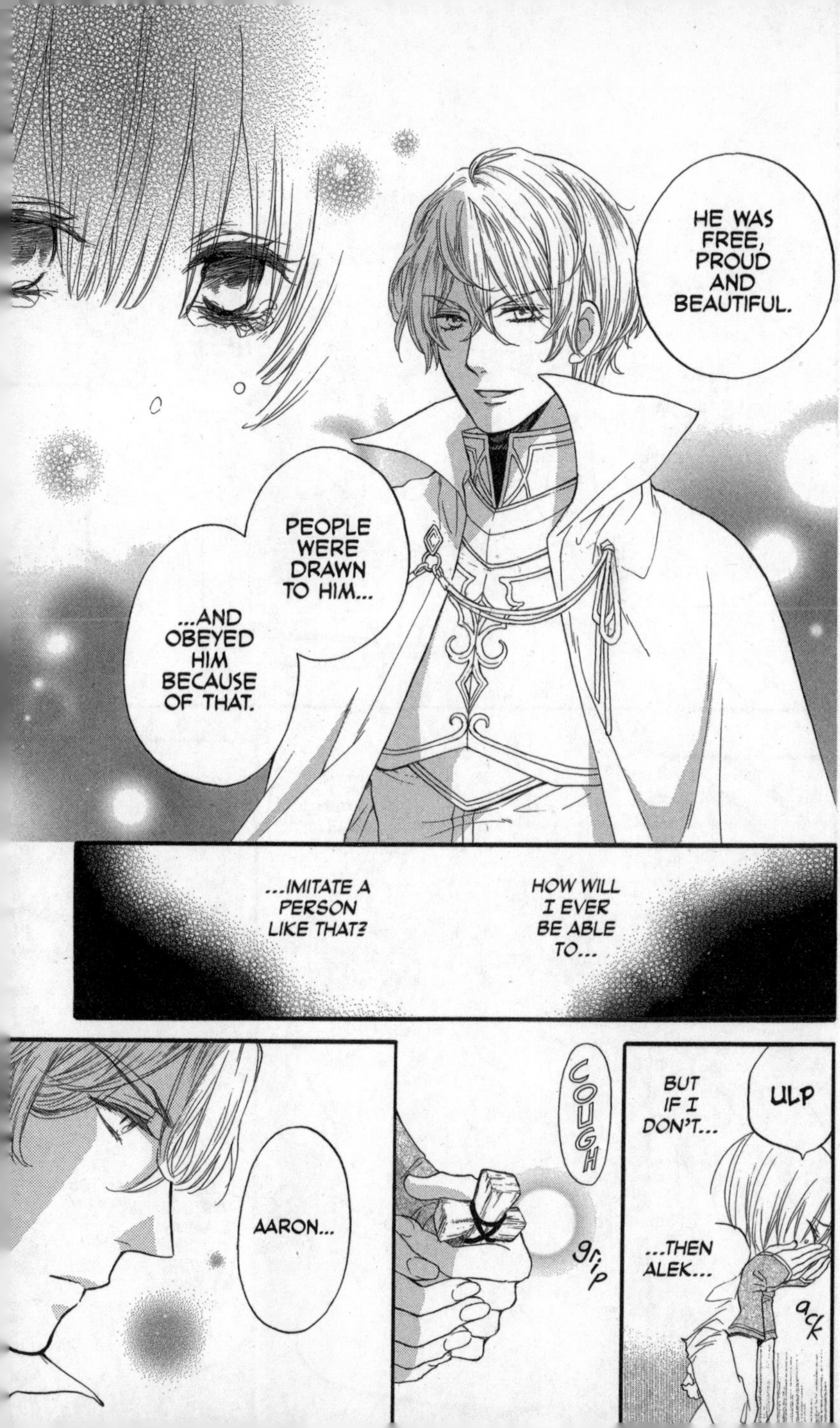
HE WAS FREE, PROUD AND BEAUTIFUL.
PEOPLE WERE DRAWN TO HIM...
...AND OBEYED HIM BECAUSE OF THAT.
HOW WILL I EVER BE ABLE TO...
...IMITATE A PERSON LIKE THAT?
ULP
BUT IF I DON'T...
...THEN ALEK...
ack
COUGH
grip
AARON...

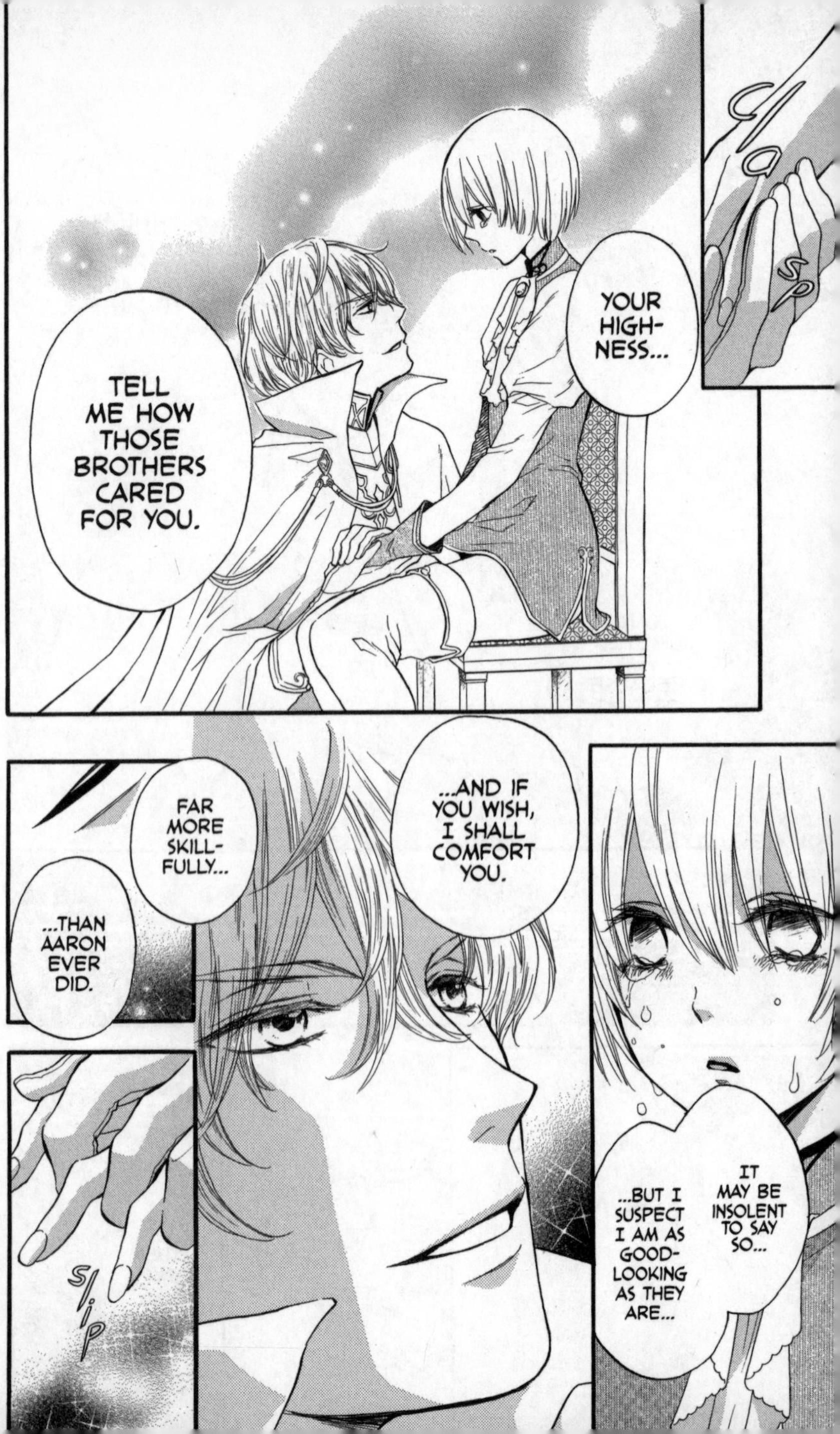
clasp
YOUR HIGHNESS...
TELL ME HOW THOSE BROTHERS CARED FOR YOU.
IT MAY BE INSOLENT TO SAY SO...
...BUT I SUSPECT I AM AS GOOD-LOOKING AS THEY ARE...
...AND IF YOU WISH, I SHALL COMFORT YOU.
FAR MORE SKILLFULLY...
...THAN AARON EVER DID.
slip

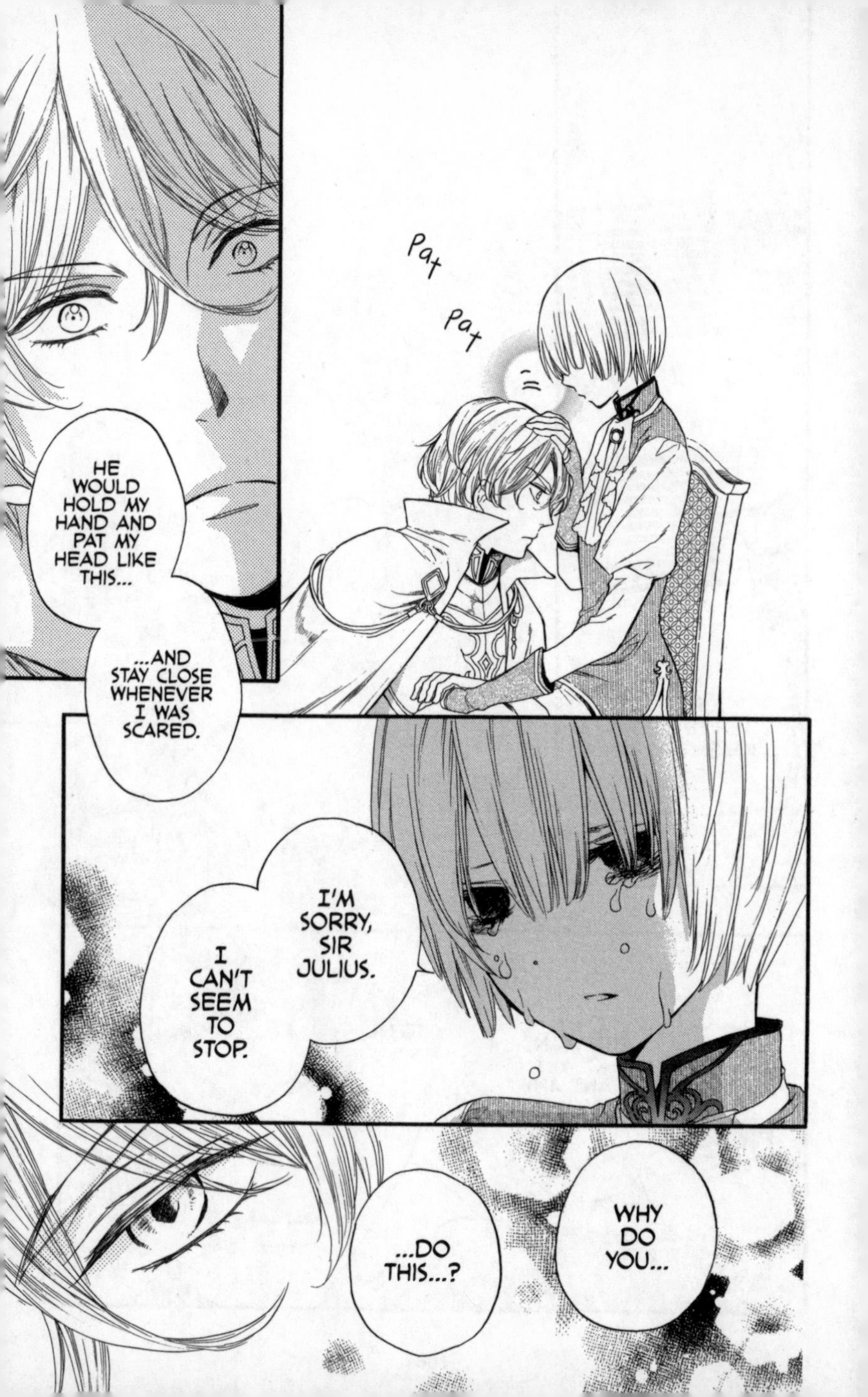
Pat
Pat
HE WOULD HOLD MY HAND AND PAT MY HEAD LIKE THIS...
...AND STAY CLOSE WHENEVER I WAS SCARED.
I'M SORRY, SIR JULIUS.
I CAN'T SEEM TO STOP.
WHY DO YOU...
...DO THIS...?

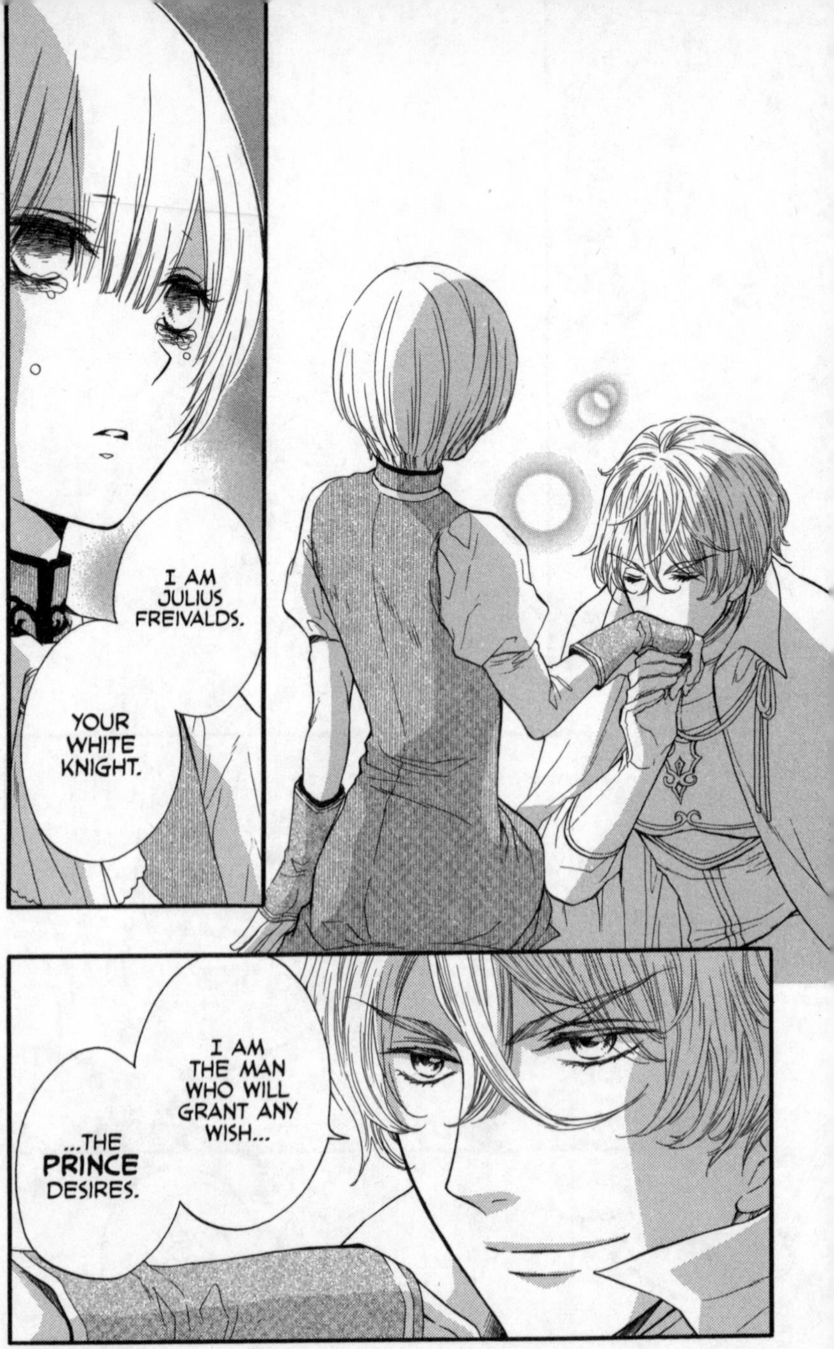
I AM JULIUS FREIVALDS.
YOUR WHITE KNIGHT.
I AM THE MAN WHO WILL GRANT ANY WISH...
...THE **PRINCE** DESIRES.

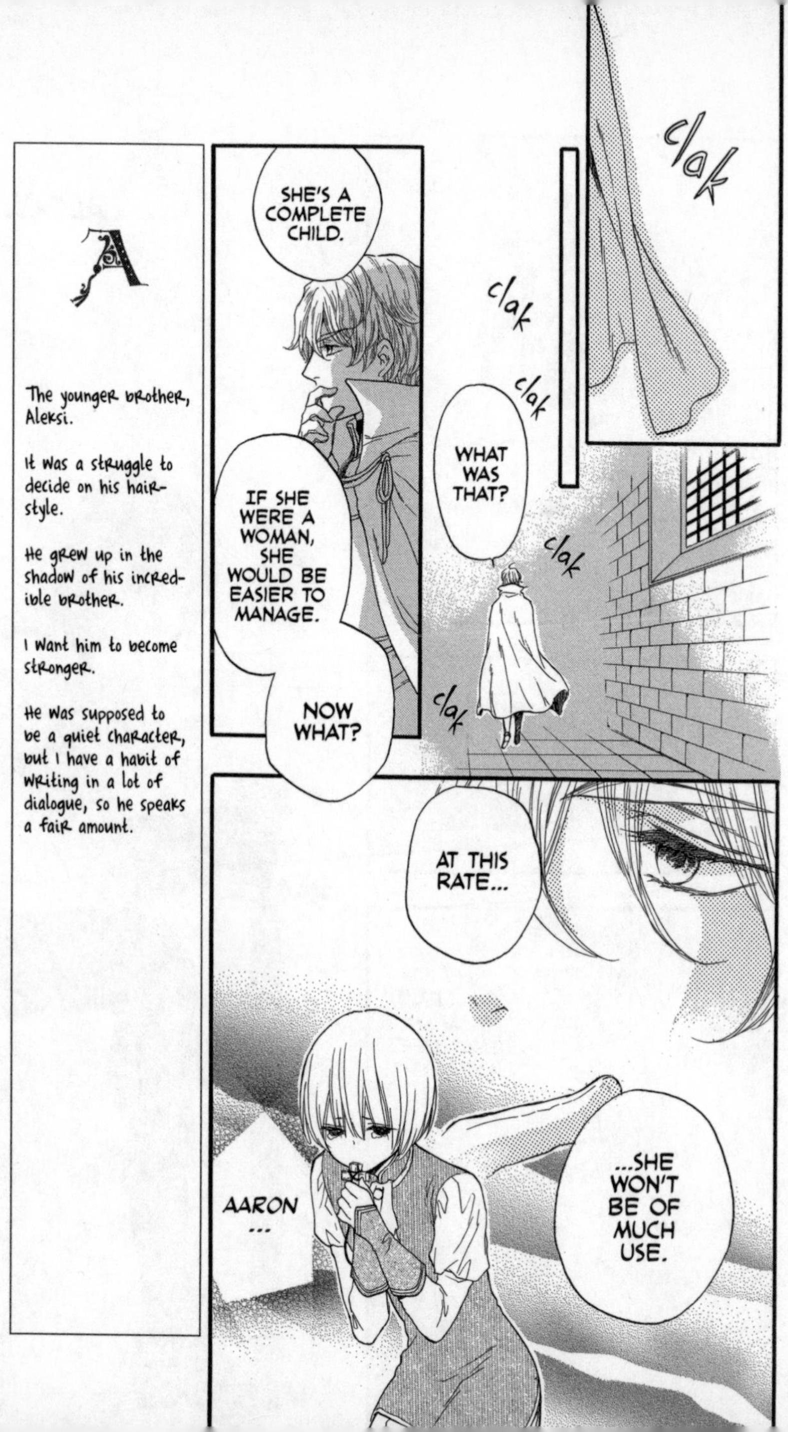
clak
clak
clak
WHAT WAS THAT?
clak
clak
SHE'S A COMPLETE CHILD.
IF SHE WERE A WOMAN, SHE WOULD BE EASIER TO MANAGE.
NOW WHAT?
AT THIS RATE...
...SHE WON'T BE OF MUCH USE.
AARON...

A

The younger brother, Aleksi.

It was a struggle to decide on his hair-style.

He grew up in the shadow of his incred-ible brother.

I want him to become stronger.

He was supposed to be a quiet character, but I have a habit of writing in a lot of dialogue, so he speaks a fair amount.

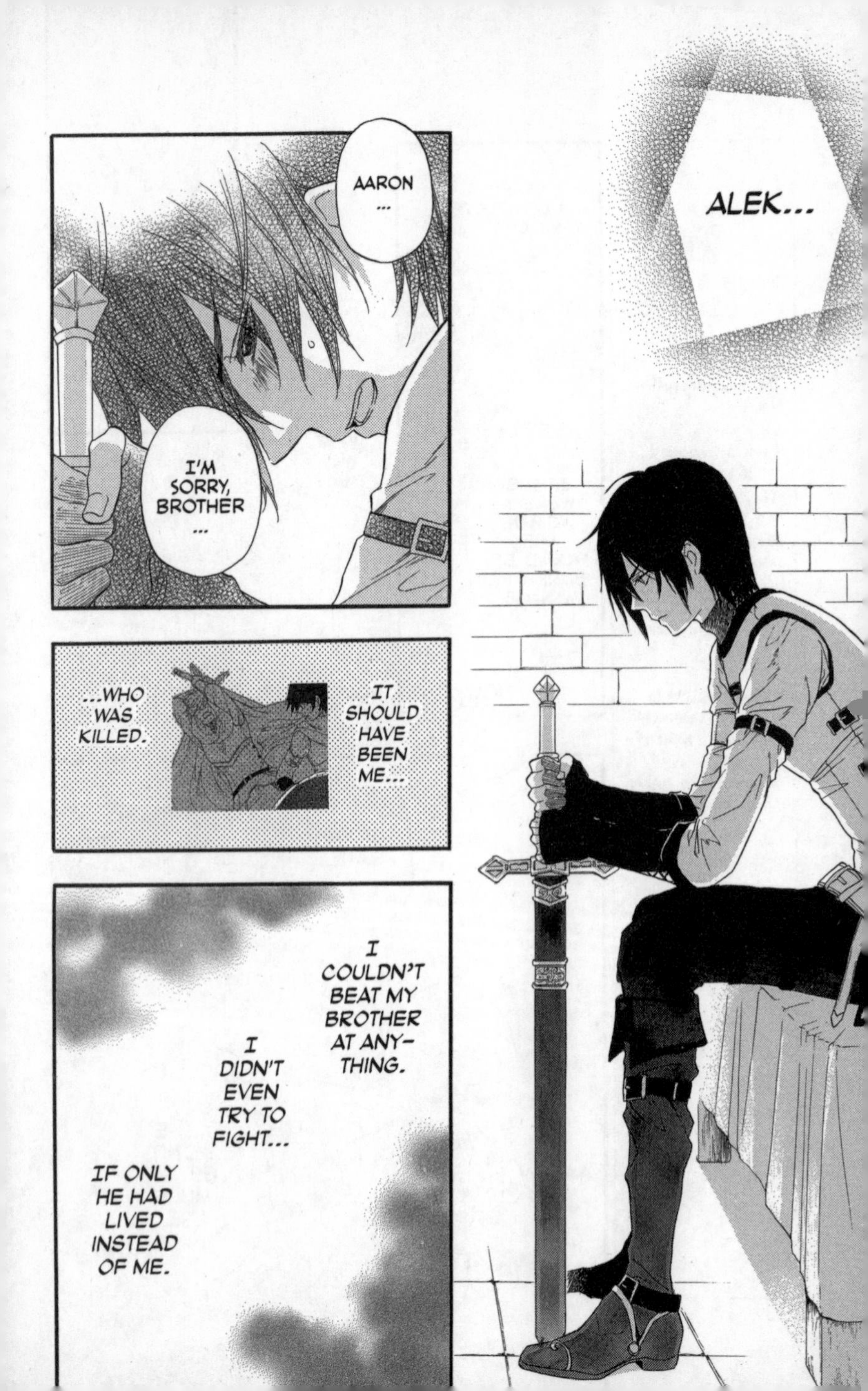
ALEK...
AARON ...
I'M SORRY, BROTHER ...
IT SHOULD HAVE BEEN ME...
...WHO WAS KILLED.
I COULDN'T BEAT MY BROTHER AT ANYTHING.
I DIDN'T EVEN TRY TO FIGHT...
IF ONLY HE HAD LIVED INSTEAD OF ME.

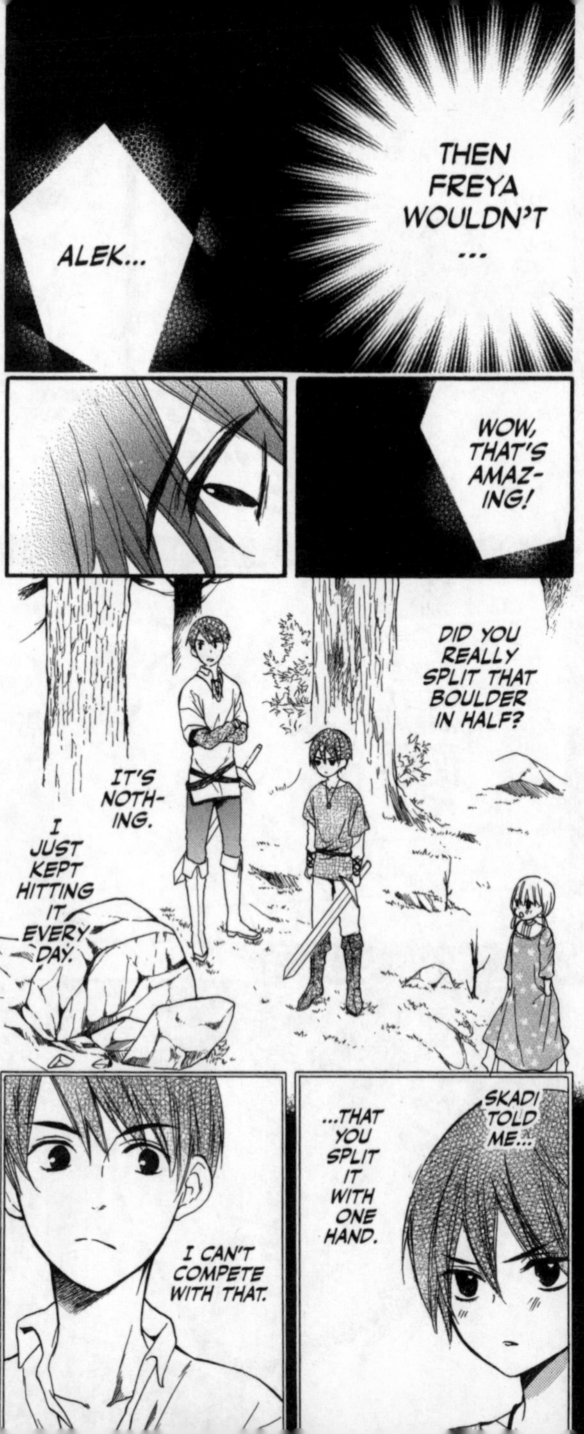
THEN FREYA WOULDN'T ...
ALEK...
WOW, THAT'S AMAZ-ING!
DID YOU REALLY SPLIT THAT BOULDER IN HALF?
IT'S NOTH-ING.
I JUST KEPT HITTING IT EVERY DAY.
SKADI TOLD ME...
...THAT YOU SPLIT IT WITH ONE HAND.
I CAN'T COMPETE WITH THAT.

Prince Edvard is the most fun to draw.

I'm a sucker for charismatic types who march to their own drummer.

I wish he could appear more often, but the setup is what it is...

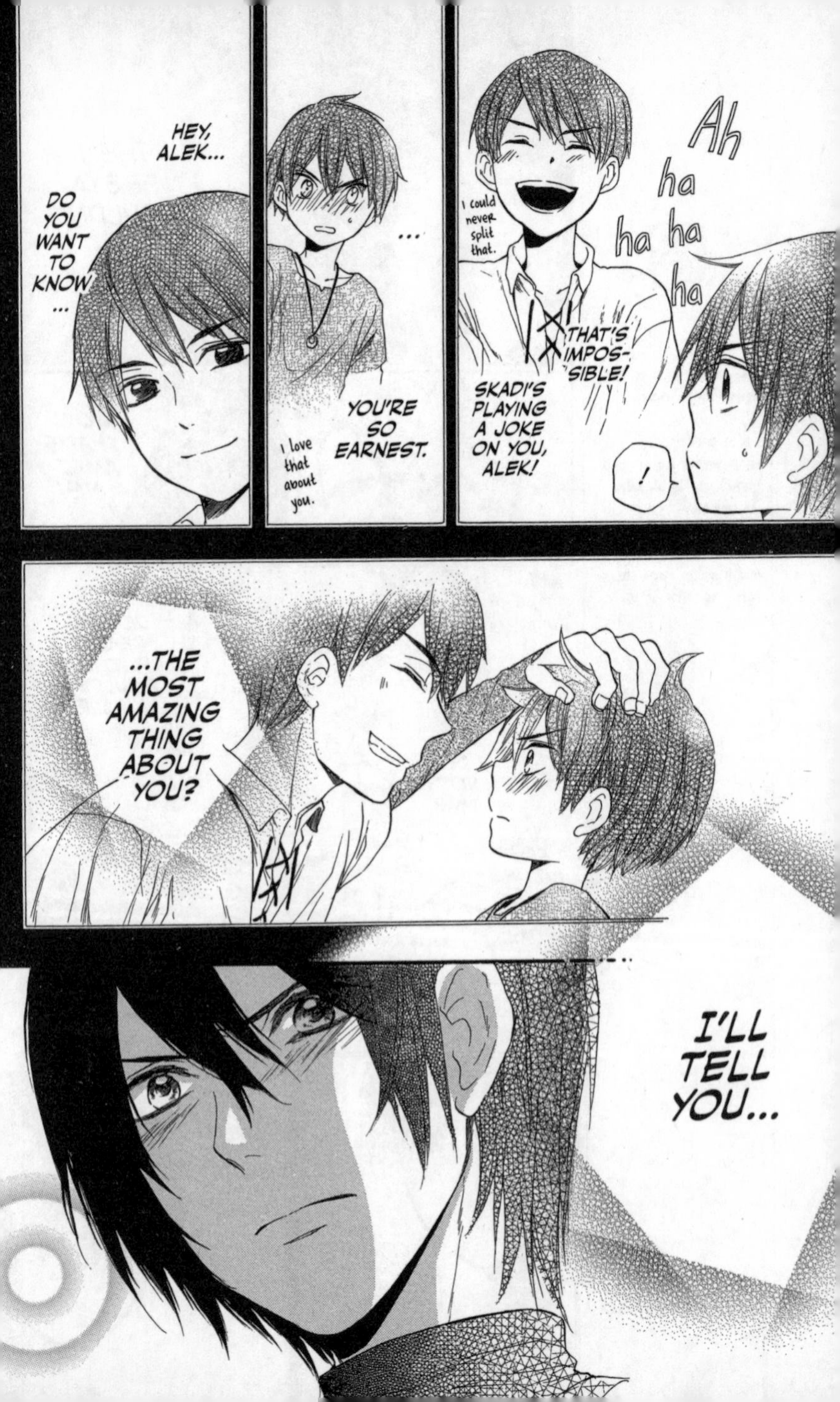
Ah ha ha ha ha
I could never split that.
THAT'S IMPOSSIBLE!
SKADI'S PLAYING A JOKE ON YOU, ALEK!
!
...
YOU'RE SO EARNEST.
I love that about you.
HEY, ALEK...
DO YOU WANT TO KNOW...
...THE MOST AMAZING THING ABOUT YOU?
I'LL TELL YOU...

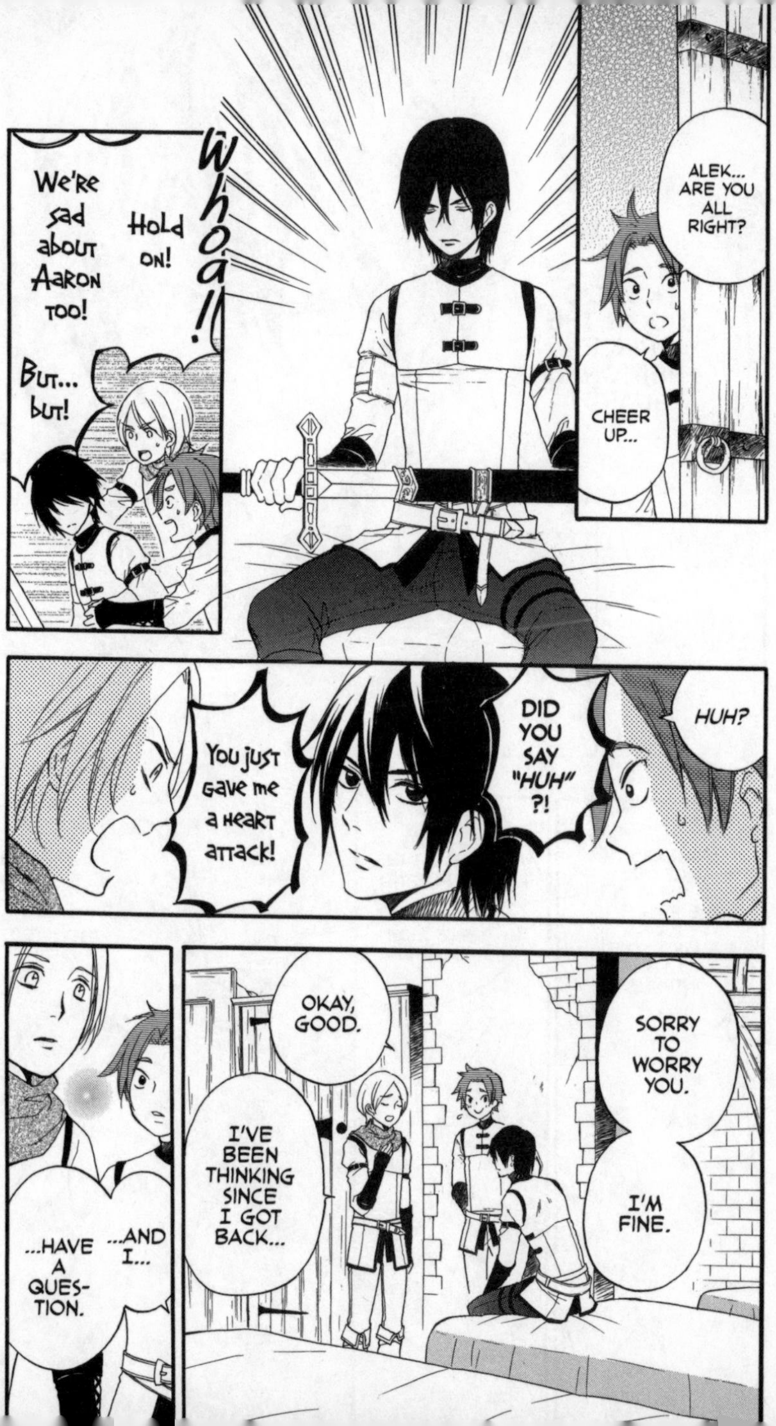
ALEK... ARE YOU ALL RIGHT?
CHEER UP...
Whoa!!
Hold on!
We're sad about Aaron too!
But... but!
HUH?
DID YOU SAY "HUH"?!
You just gave me a heart attack!
SORRY TO WORRY YOU.
I'M FINE.
OKAY, GOOD.
I'VE BEEN THINKING SINCE I GOT BACK...
...AND I...
...HAVE A QUESTION.

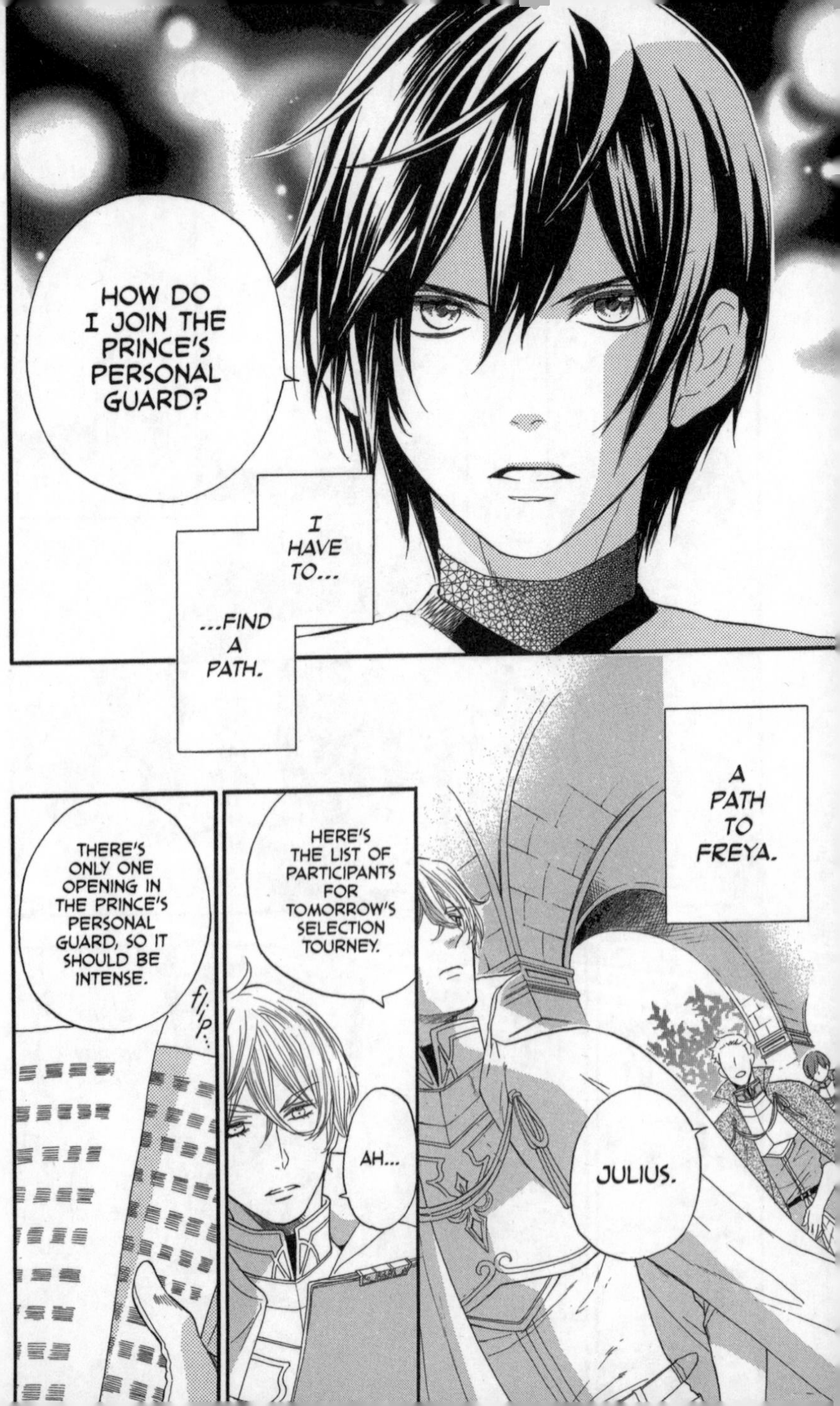
HOW DO I JOIN THE PRINCE'S PERSONAL GUARD?
I HAVE TO...
...FIND A PATH.
A PATH TO FREYA.
JULIUS.
HERE'S THE LIST OF PARTICIPANTS FOR TOMORROW'S SELECTION TOURNEY.
AH...
THERE'S ONLY ONE OPENING IN THE PRINCE'S PERSONAL GUARD, SO IT SHOULD BE INTENSE.
flip...

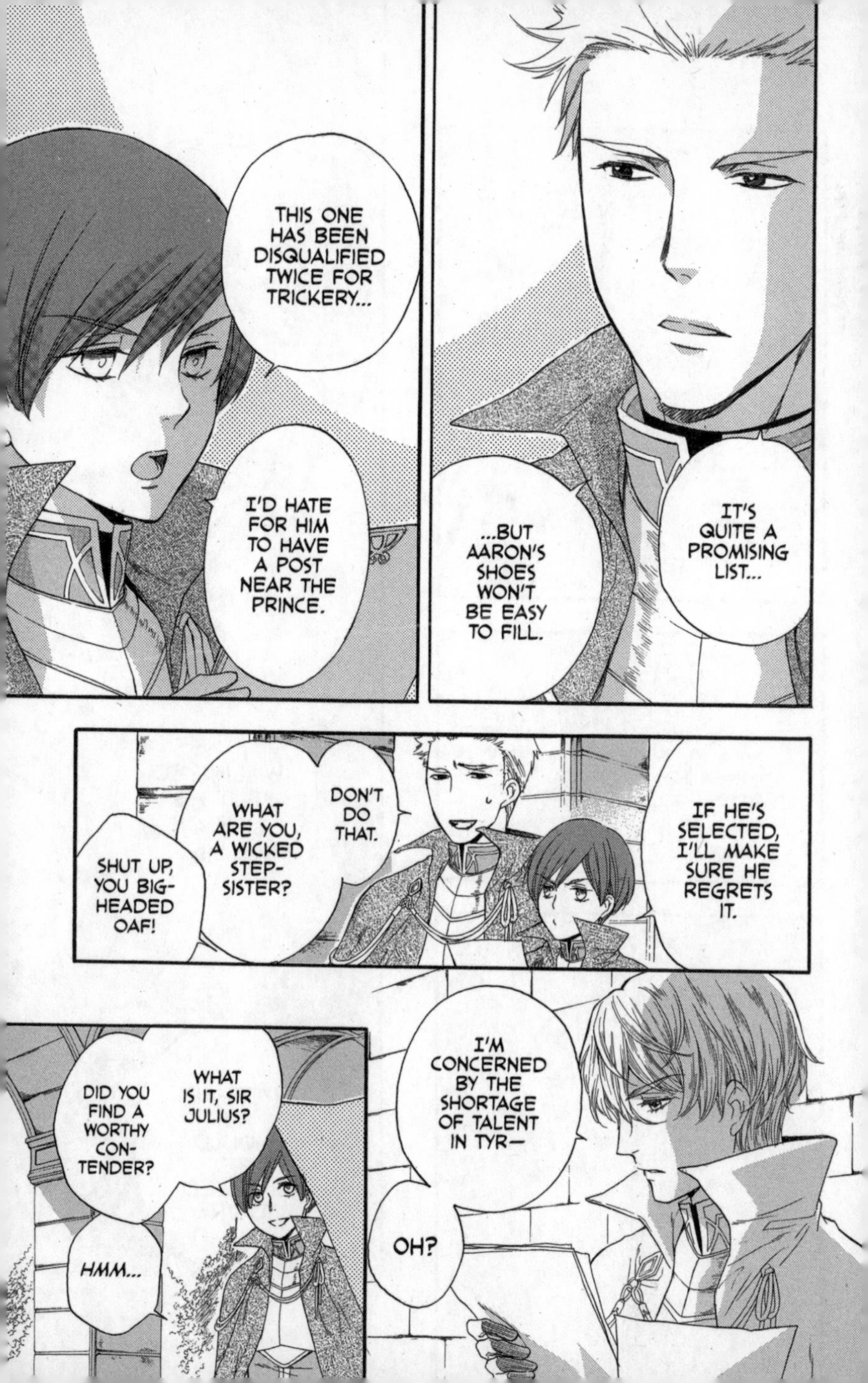
IT'S QUITE A PROMISING LIST...
...BUT AARON'S SHOES WON'T BE EASY TO FILL.
THIS ONE HAS BEEN DISQUALIFIED TWICE FOR TRICKERY...
I'D HATE FOR HIM TO HAVE A POST NEAR THE PRINCE.
IF HE'S SELECTED, I'LL MAKE SURE HE REGRETS IT.
DON'T DO THAT.
WHAT ARE YOU, A WICKED STEP-SISTER?
SHUT UP, YOU BIG-HEADED OAF!
I'M CONCERNED BY THE SHORTAGE OF TALENT IN TYR—
OH?
WHAT IS IT, SIR JULIUS?
DID YOU FIND A WORTHY CONTENDER?
HMM...

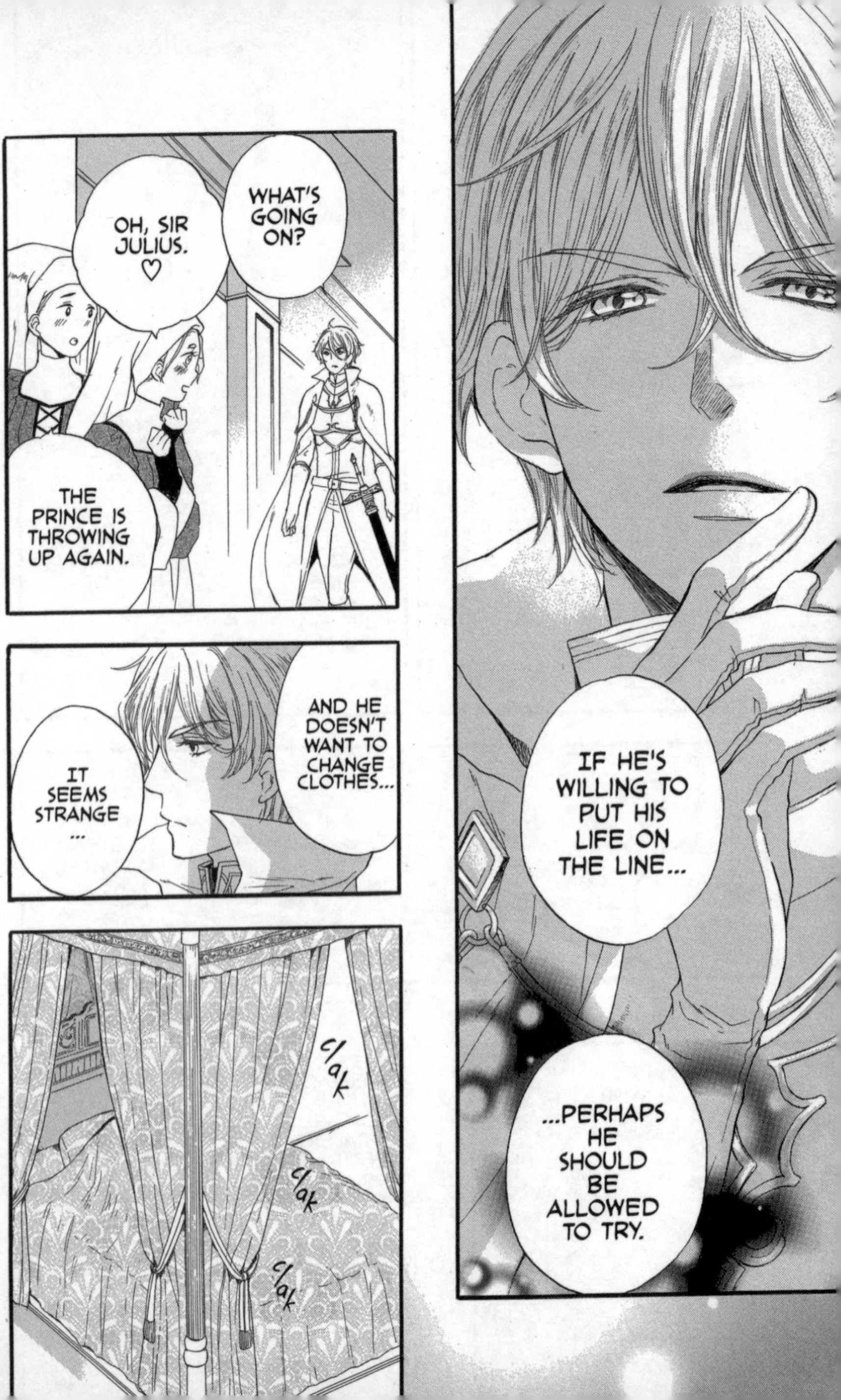
IF HE'S WILLING TO PUT HIS LIFE ON THE LINE...
...PERHAPS HE SHOULD BE ALLOWED TO TRY.
WHAT'S GOING ON?
OH, SIR JULIUS. ♡
THE PRINCE IS THROWING UP AGAIN.
AND HE DOESN'T WANT TO CHANGE CLOTHES...
IT SEEMS STRANGE...
clak
clak
clak

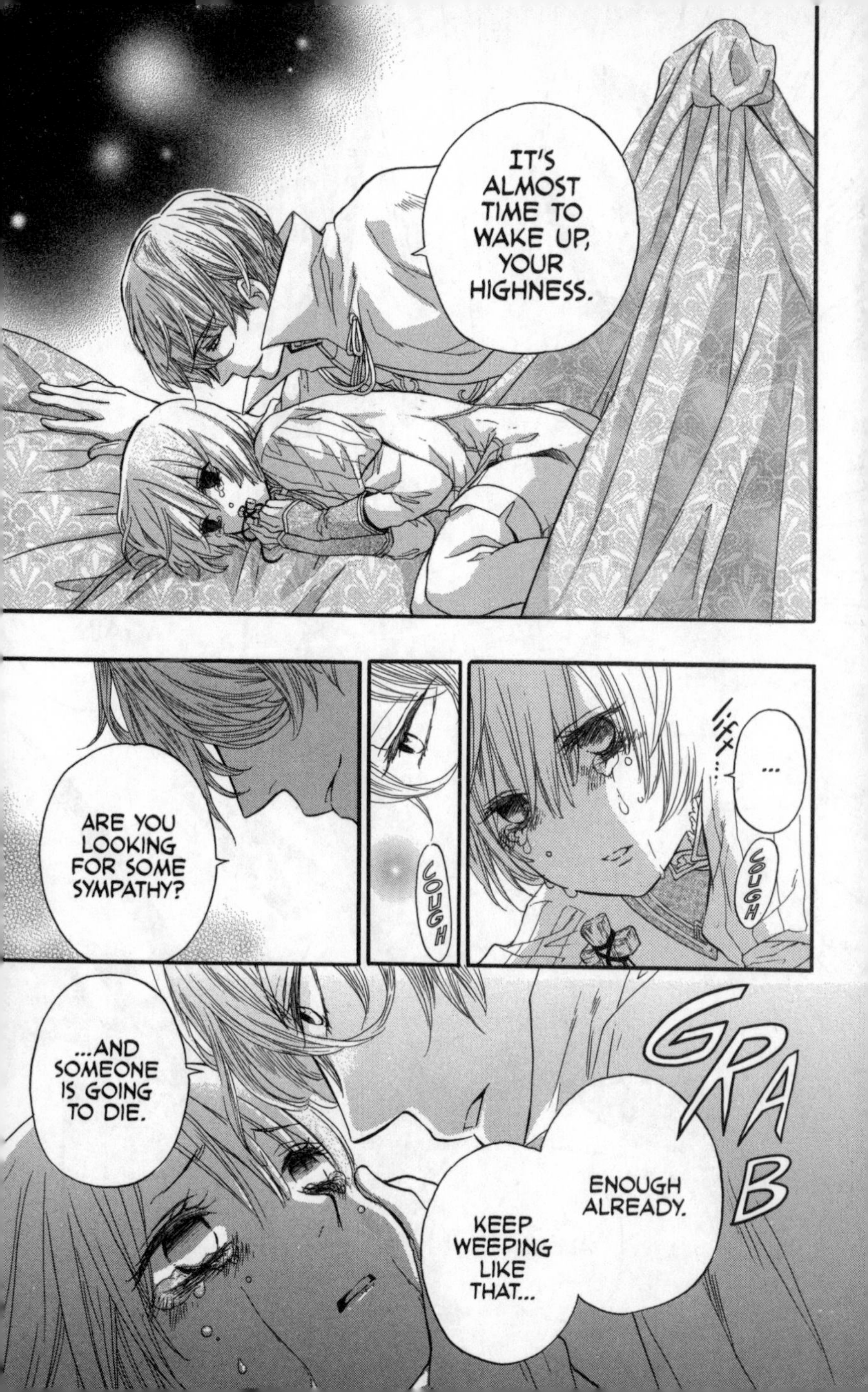
IT'S ALMOST TIME TO WAKE UP, YOUR HIGHNESS.
lift...
...
COUGH
COUGH
ARE YOU LOOKING FOR SOME SYMPATHY?
GRAB
ENOUGH ALREADY.
KEEP WEEPING LIKE THAT...
...AND SOMEONE IS GOING TO DIE.

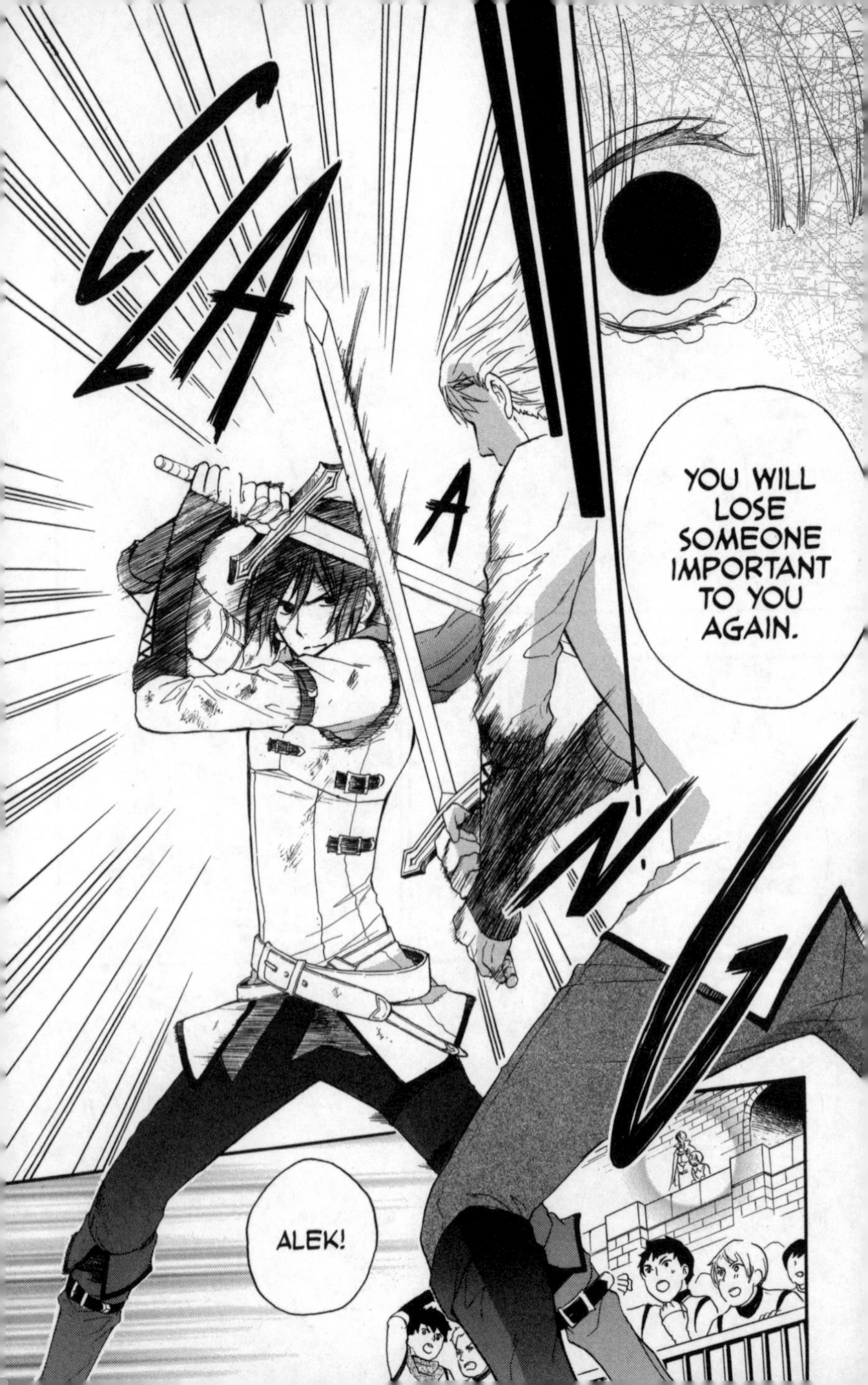
YOU WILL LOSE SOMEONE IMPORTANT TO YOU AGAIN.
CA
A
N
G
ALEK!

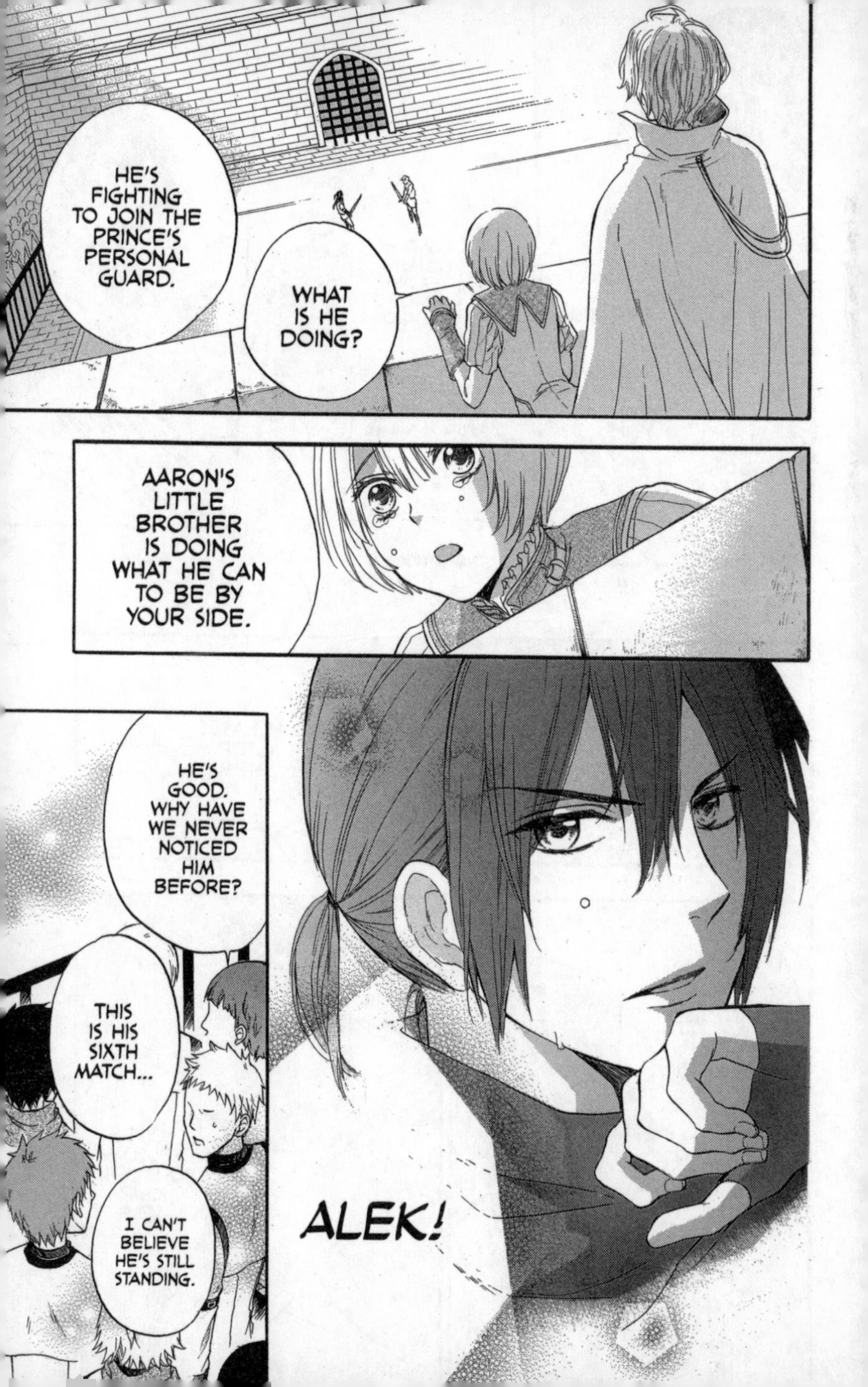
WHAT IS HE DOING?
HE'S FIGHTING TO JOIN THE PRINCE'S PERSONAL GUARD.
AARON'S LITTLE BROTHER IS DOING WHAT HE CAN TO BE BY YOUR SIDE.
ALEK!
HE'S GOOD. WHY HAVE WE NEVER NOTICED HIM BEFORE?
THIS IS HIS SIXTH MATCH...
I CAN'T BELIEVE HE'S STILL STANDING.

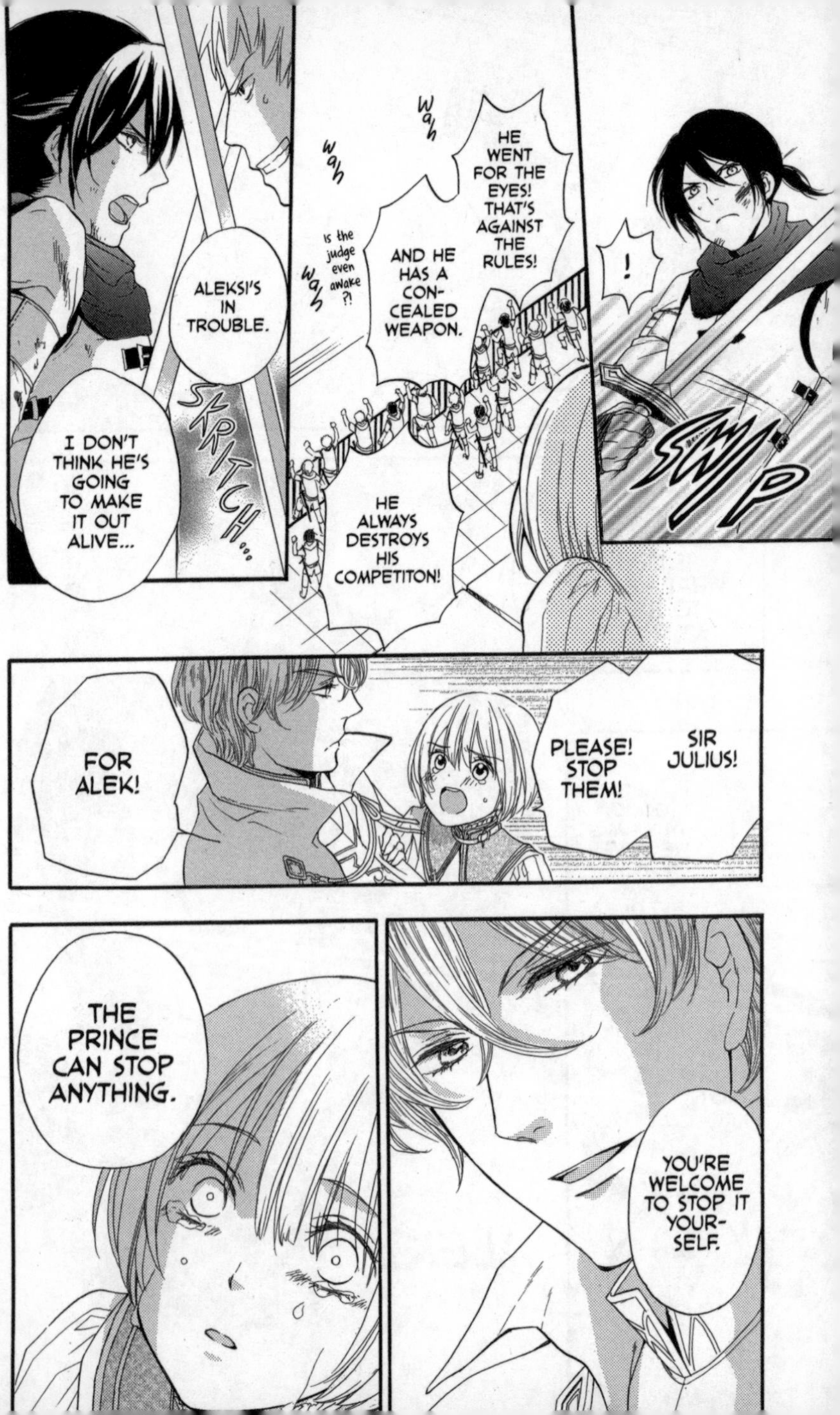
!
SWIP
HE WENT FOR THE EYES! THAT'S AGAINST THE RULES!
Wah
Wah
AND HE HAS A CON-CEALED WEAPON.
is the judge even awake ?!
Wah
HE ALWAYS DESTROYS HIS COMPETITON!
ALEKSI'S IN TROUBLE.
I DON'T THINK HE'S GOING TO MAKE IT OUT ALIVE...
SKRITCH...
SIR JULIUS!
PLEASE! STOP THEM!
FOR ALEK!
YOU'RE WELCOME TO STOP IT YOUR-SELF.
THE PRINCE CAN STOP ANYTHING.

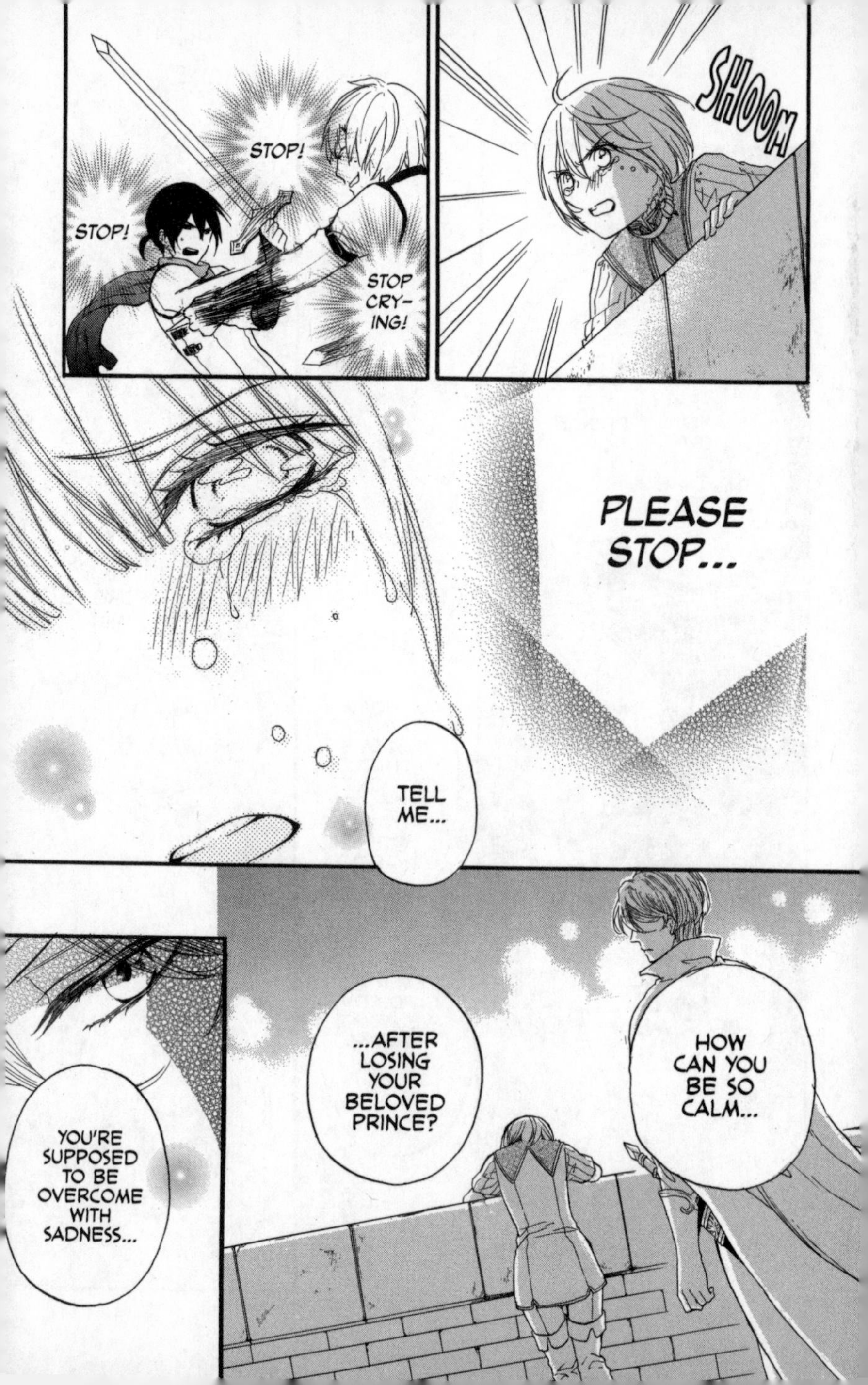
SHOOM
STOP!
STOP CRY-ING!
STOP!
PLEASE STOP...
TELL ME...
HOW CAN YOU BE SO CALM...
...AFTER LOSING YOUR BELOVED PRINCE?
YOU'RE SUPPOSED TO BE OVERCOME WITH SADNESS...

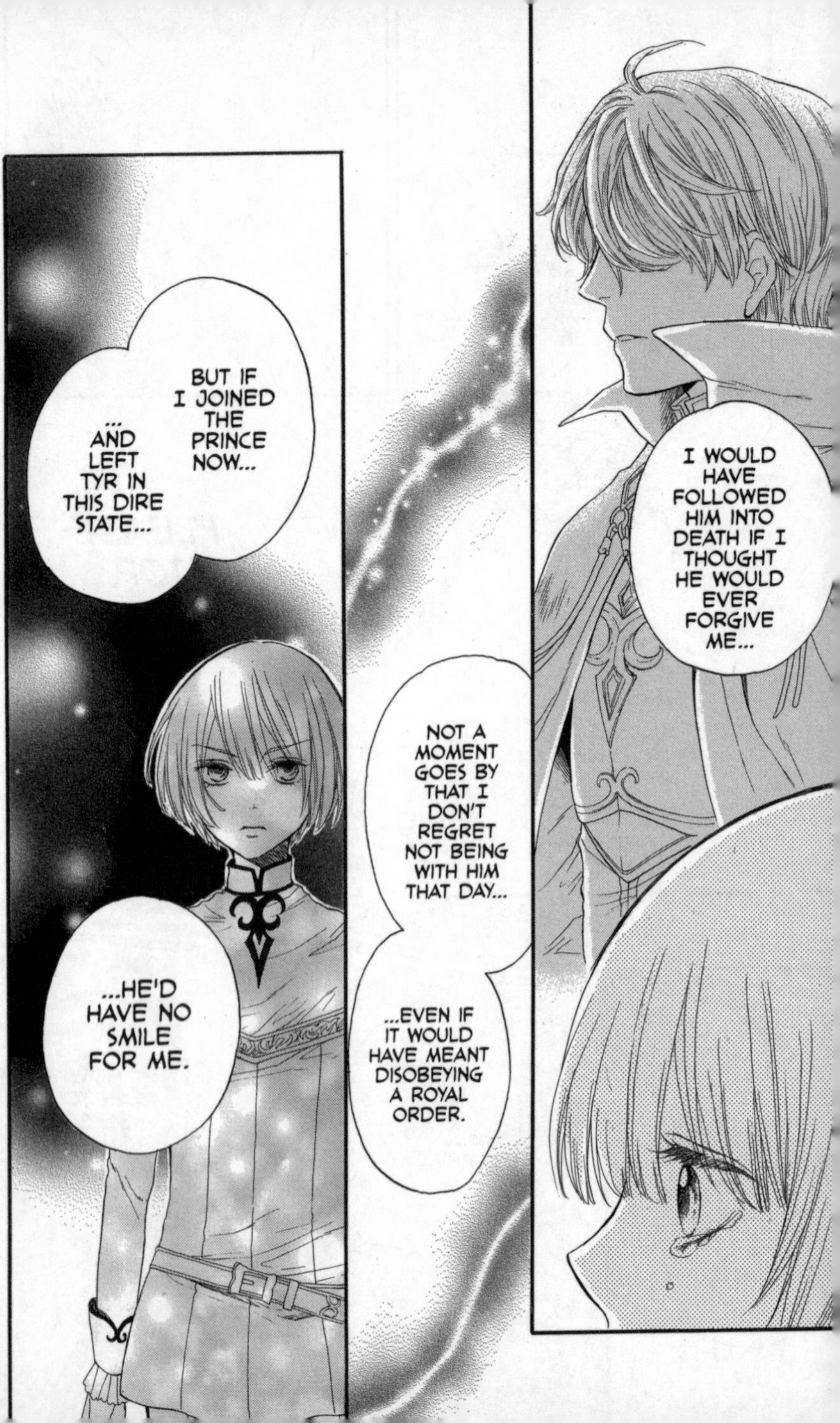
I WOULD HAVE FOLLOWED HIM INTO DEATH IF I THOUGHT HE WOULD EVER FORGIVE ME...
NOT A MOMENT GOES BY THAT I DON'T REGRET NOT BEING WITH HIM THAT DAY...
...EVEN IF IT WOULD HAVE MEANT DISOBEYING A ROYAL ORDER.
BUT IF I JOINED THE PRINCE NOW...
...AND LEFT TYR IN THIS DIRE STATE...
...HE'D HAVE NO SMILE FOR ME.

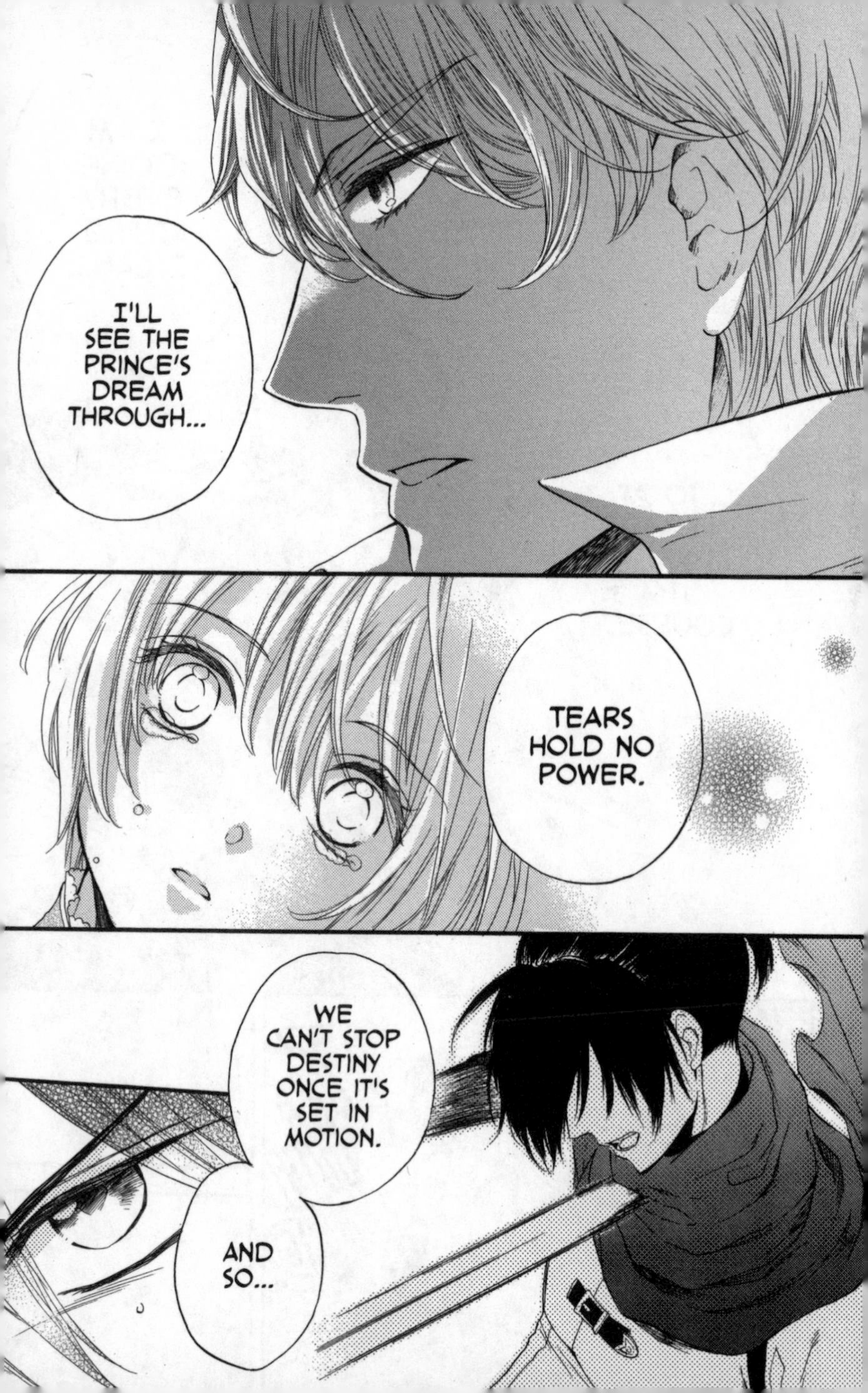
I'LL SEE THE PRINCE'S DREAM THROUGH...
TEARS HOLD NO POWER.
WE CAN'T STOP DESTINY ONCE IT'S SET IN MOTION.
AND SO...

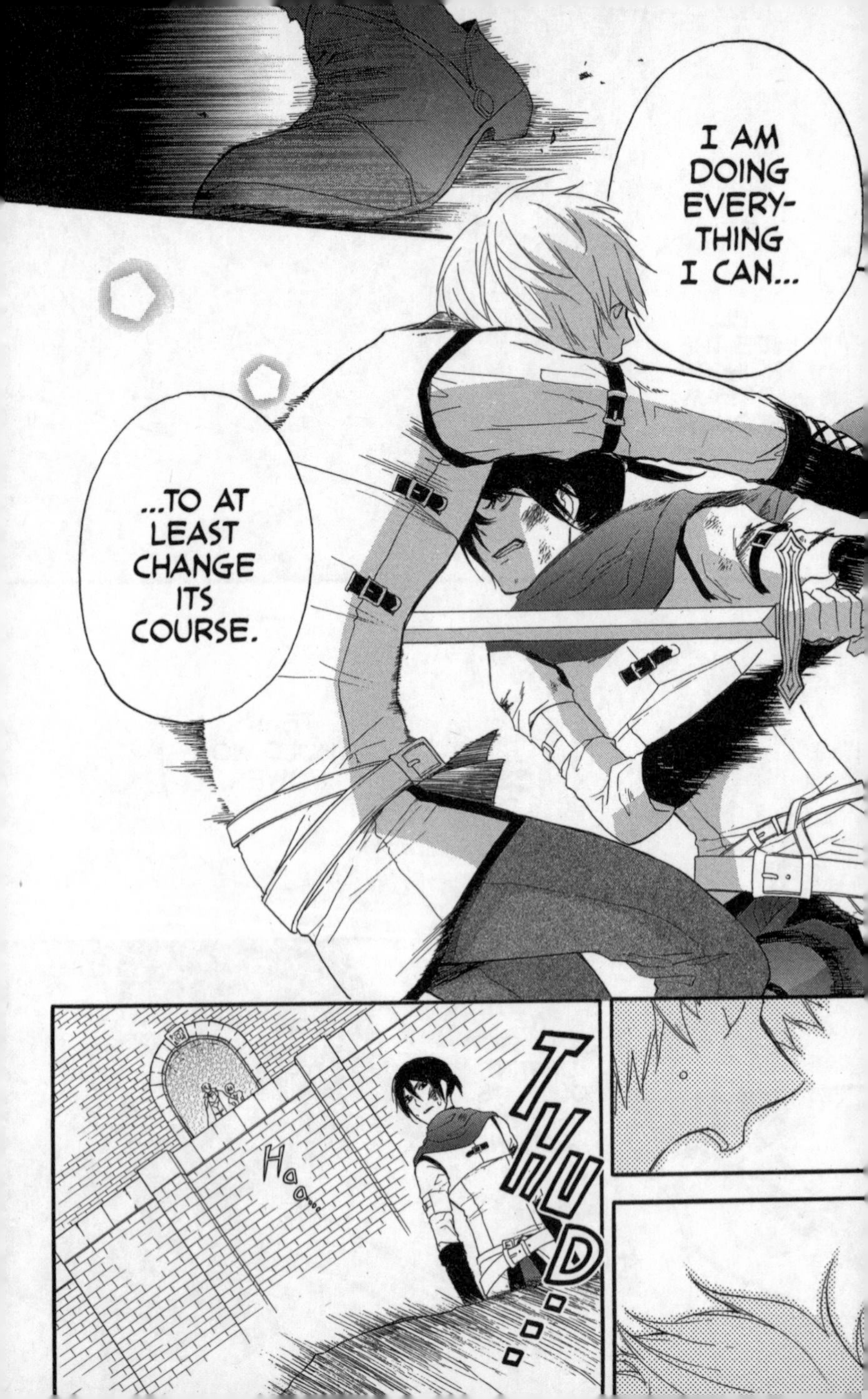
I AM DOING EVERY-THING I CAN...
...TO AT LEAST CHANGE ITS COURSE.
THUD...
Haa...

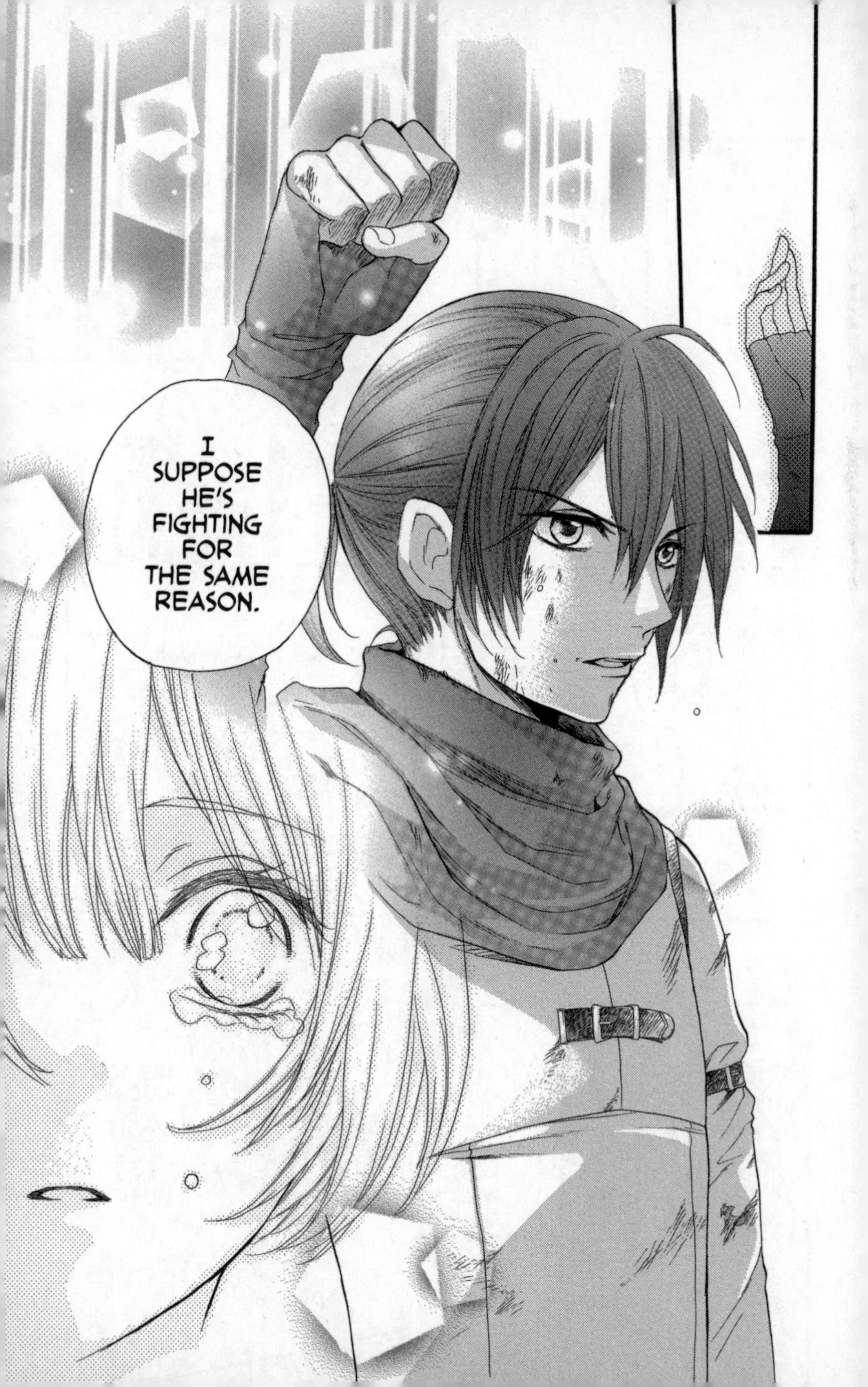
I SUPPOSE HE'S FIGHTING FOR THE SAME REASON.

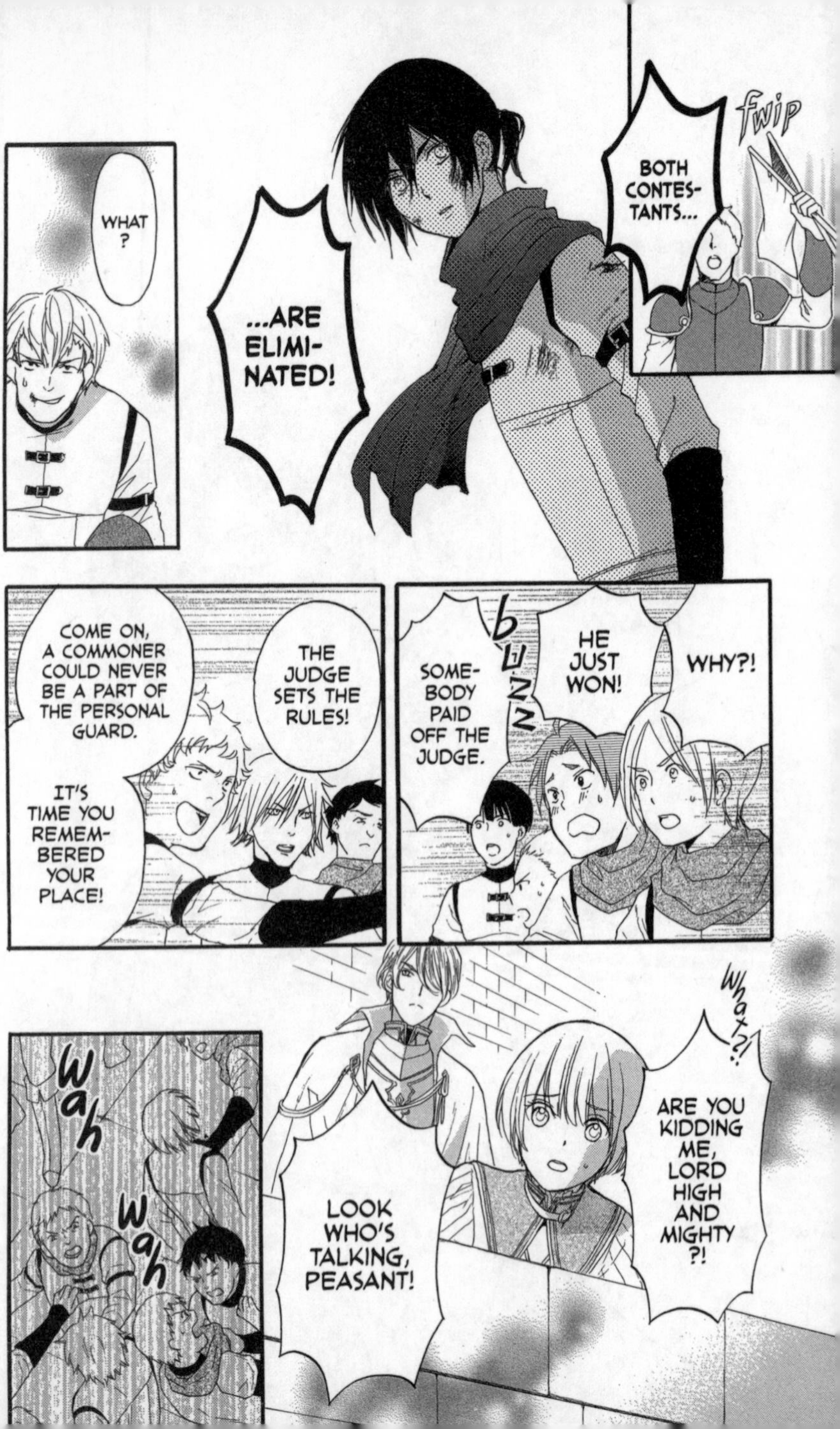
fwip
BOTH CONTESTANTS...
...ARE ELIMINATED!
WHAT?
WHY?!
HE JUST WON!
buzz
SOMEBODY PAID OFF THE JUDGE.
THE JUDGE SETS THE RULES!
COME ON, A COMMONER COULD NEVER BE A PART OF THE PERSONAL GUARD.
IT'S TIME YOU REMEMBERED YOUR PLACE!
What?!
ARE YOU KIDDING ME, LORD HIGH AND MIGHTY?!
LOOK WHO'S TALKING, PEASANT!
Wah
Wah

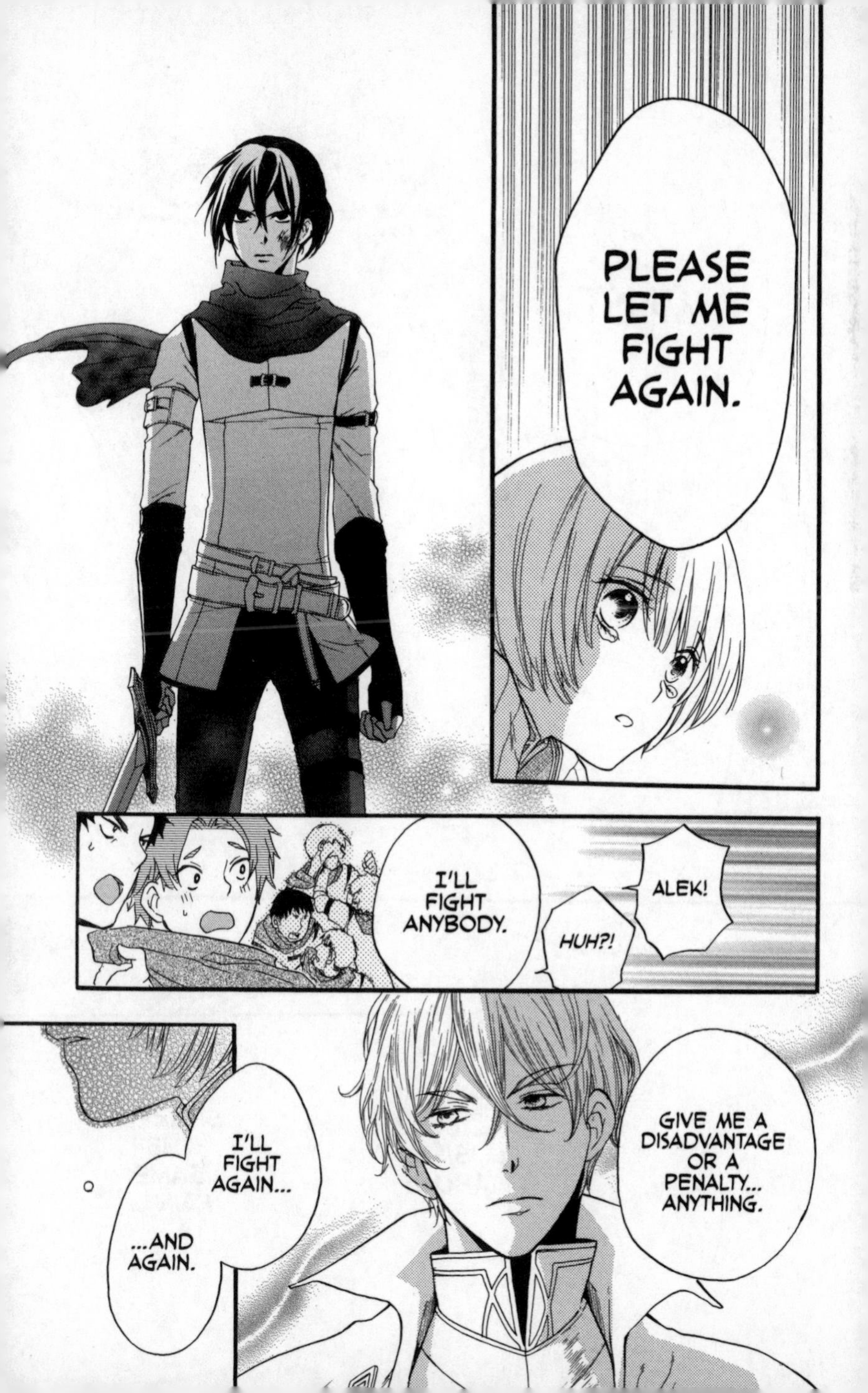
PLEASE LET ME FIGHT AGAIN.
ALEK!
HUH?!
I'LL FIGHT ANYBODY.
GIVE ME A DISADVANTAGE OR A PENALTY... ANYTHING.
I'LL FIGHT AGAIN...
...AND AGAIN.

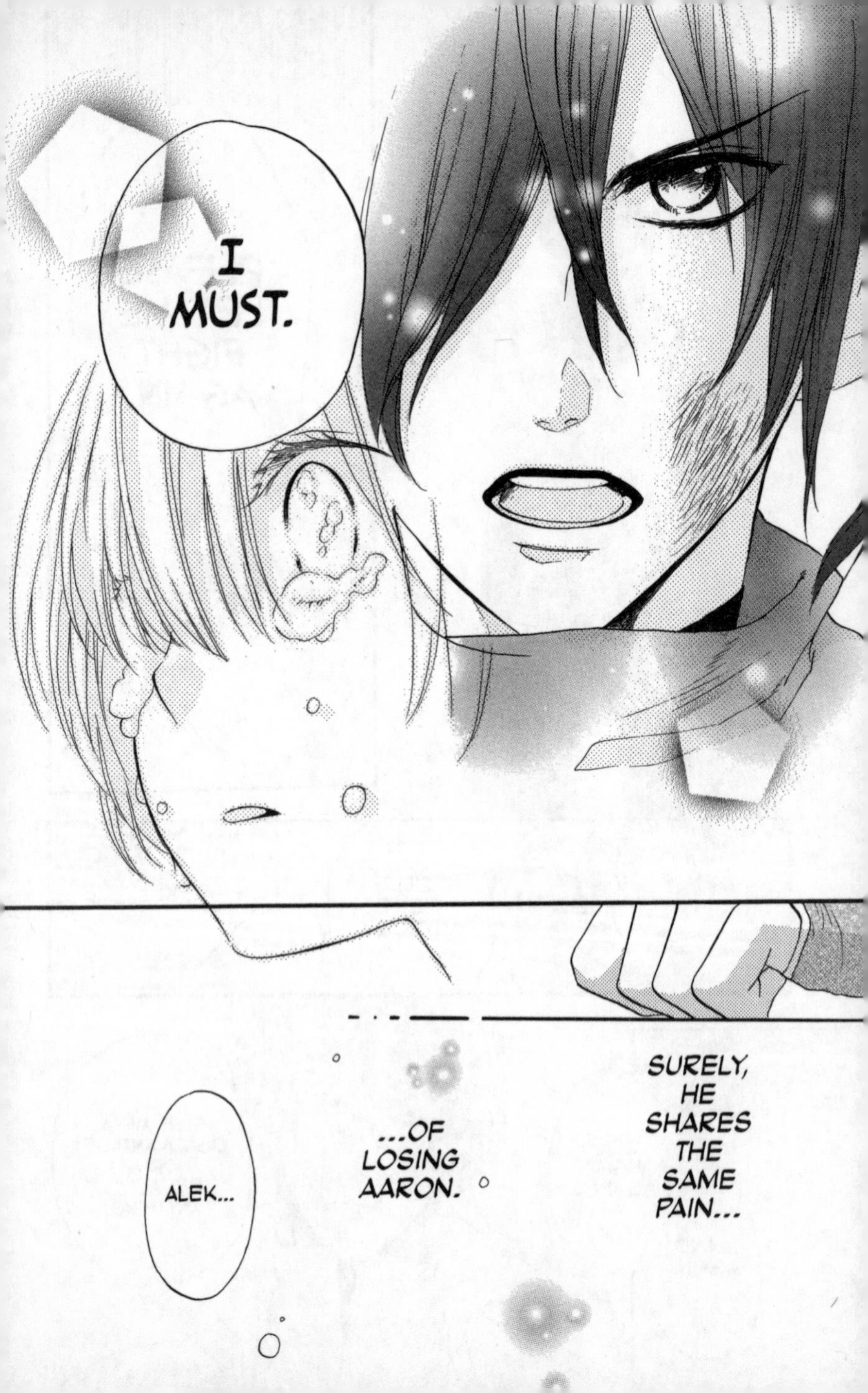
I MUST.
SURELY, HE SHARES THE SAME PAIN...
...OF LOSING AARON.
ALEK...

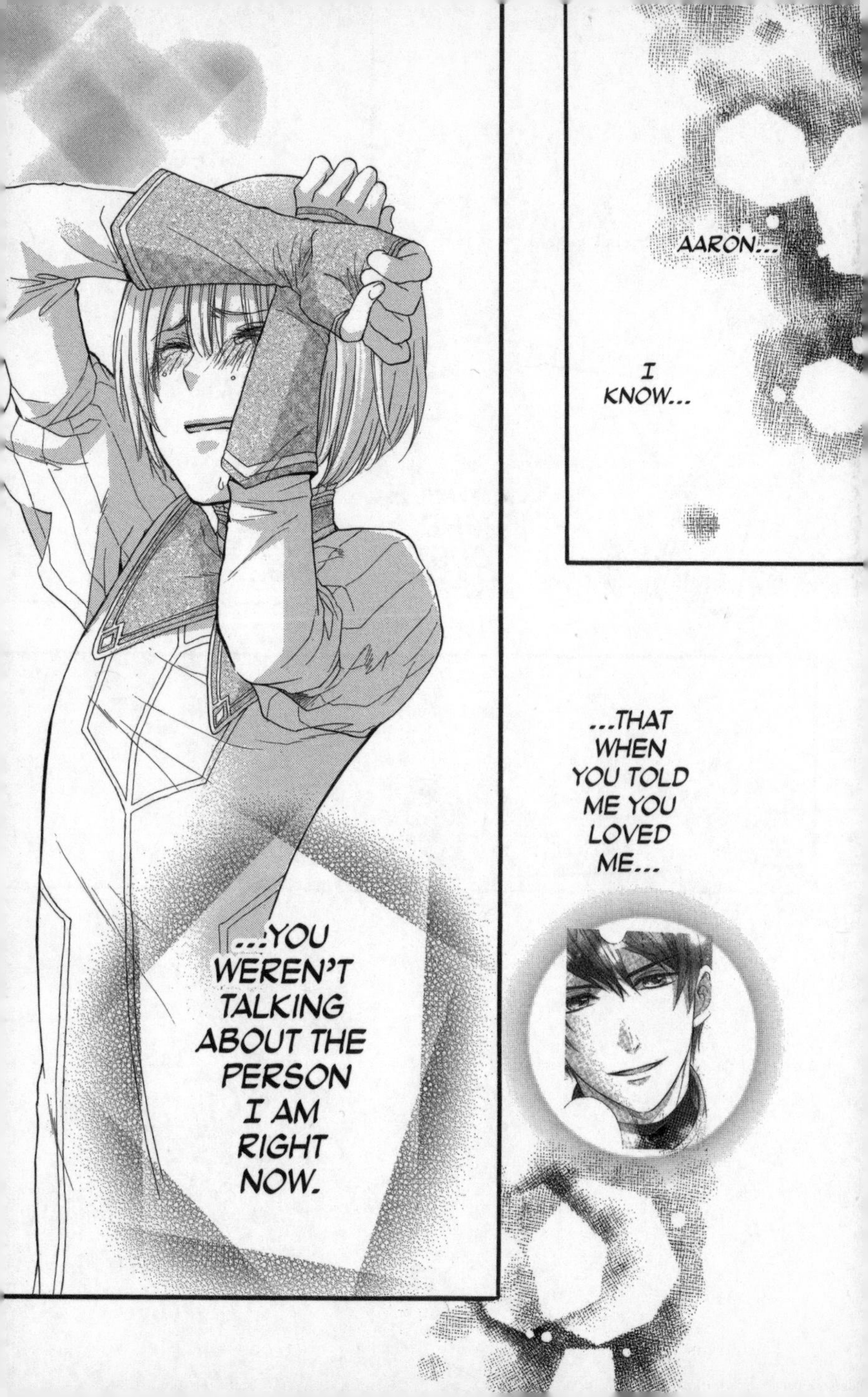
AARON...
I KNOW...
...THAT WHEN YOU TOLD ME YOU LOVED ME...
...YOU WEREN'T TALKING ABOUT THE PERSON I AM RIGHT NOW.

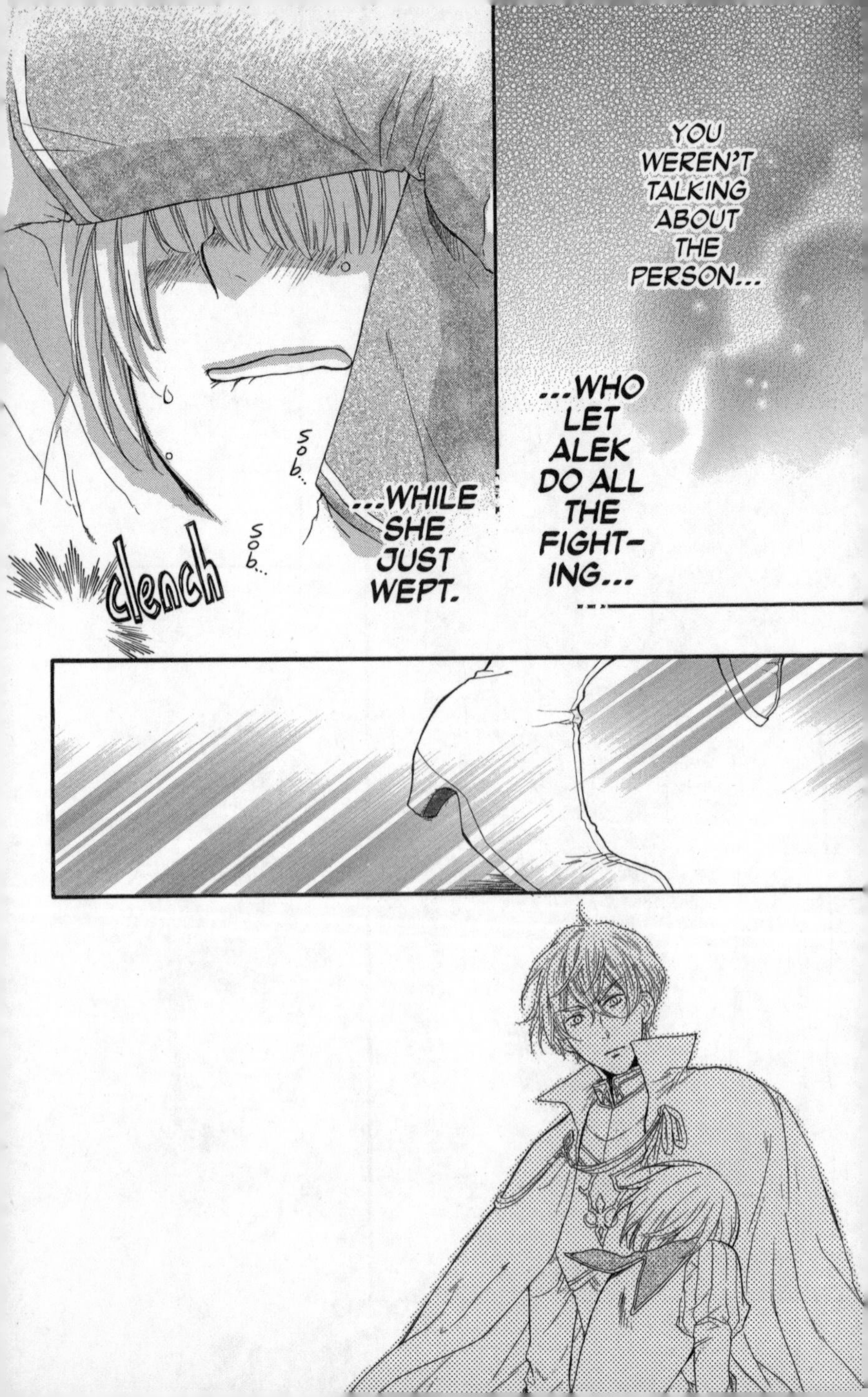
YOU WEREN'T TALKING ABOUT THE PERSON...
...WHO LET ALEK DO ALL THE FIGHTING...
...WHILE SHE JUST WEPT.
sob...
sob...
clench

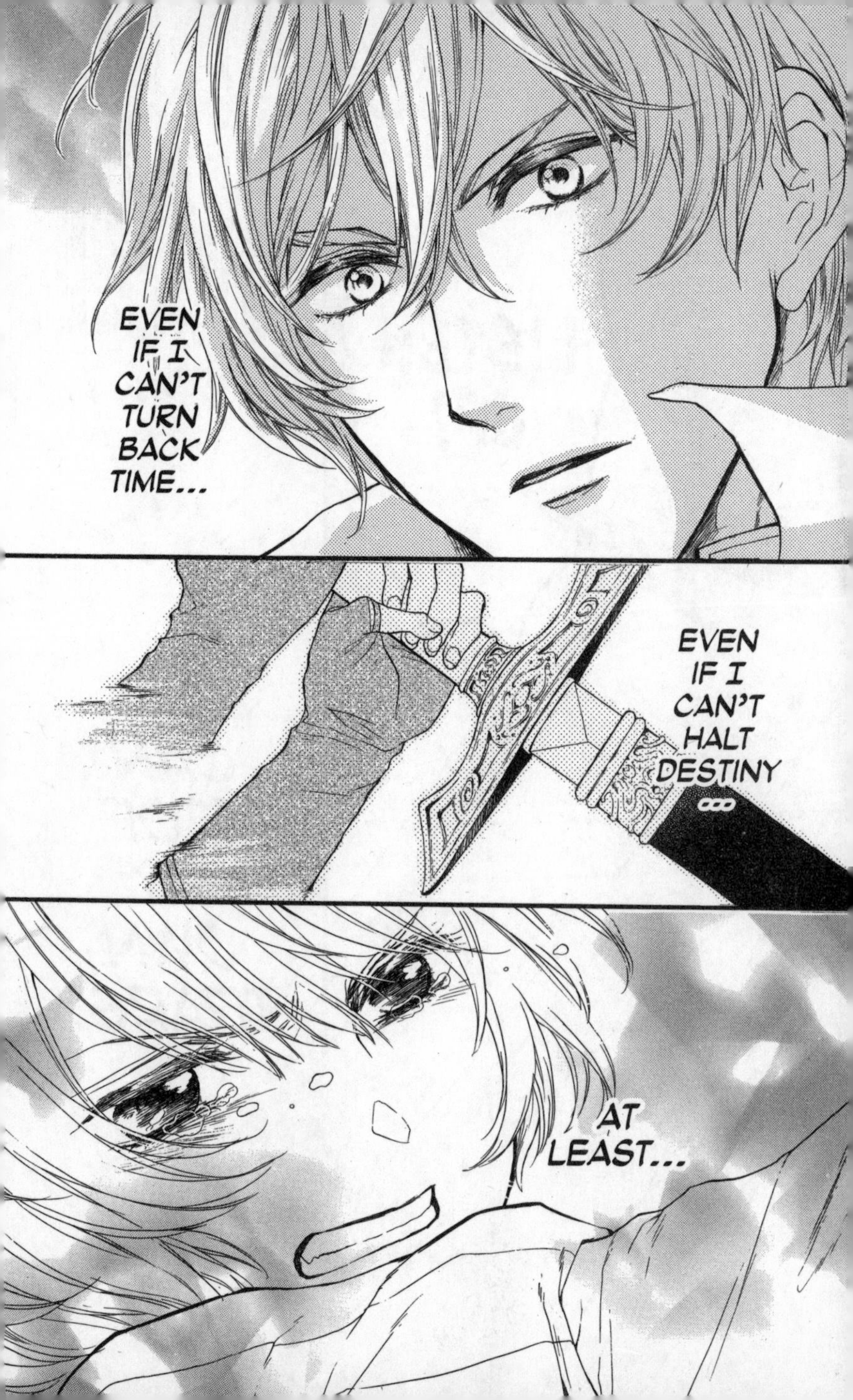
EVEN IF I CAN'T TURN BACK TIME...
EVEN IF I CAN'T HALT DESTINY ...
AT LEAST...

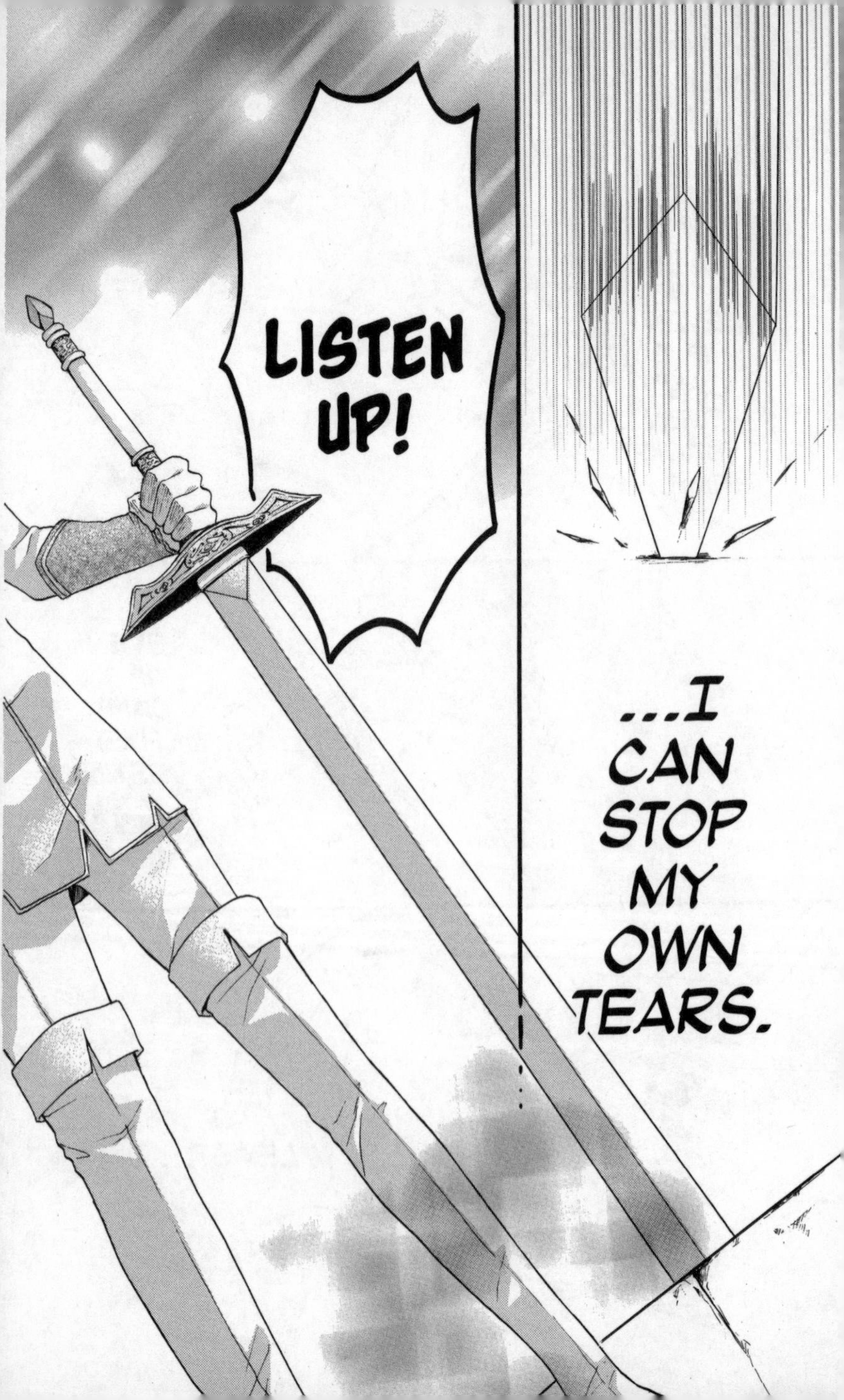
...I CAN STOP MY OWN TEARS.
LISTEN UP!

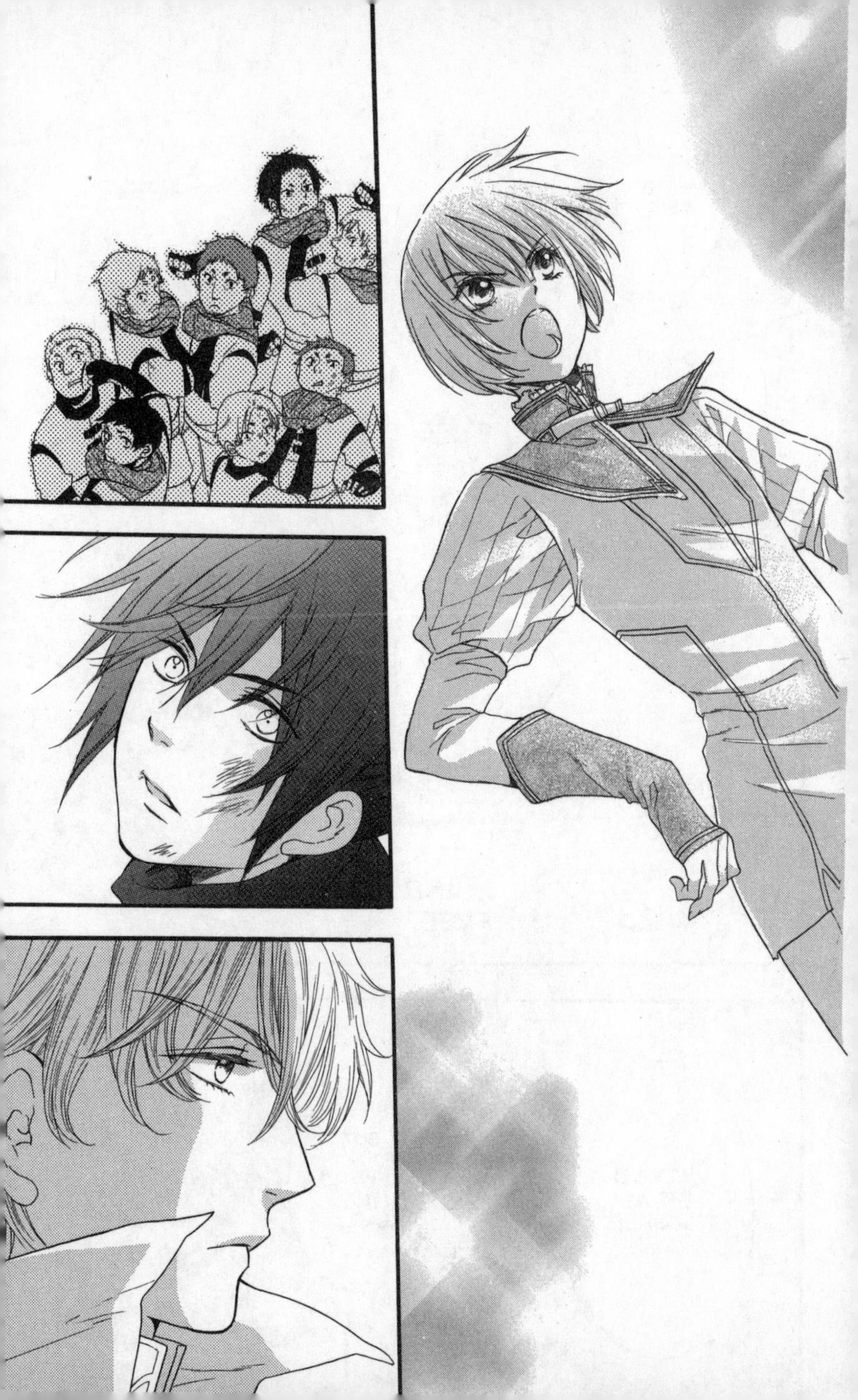

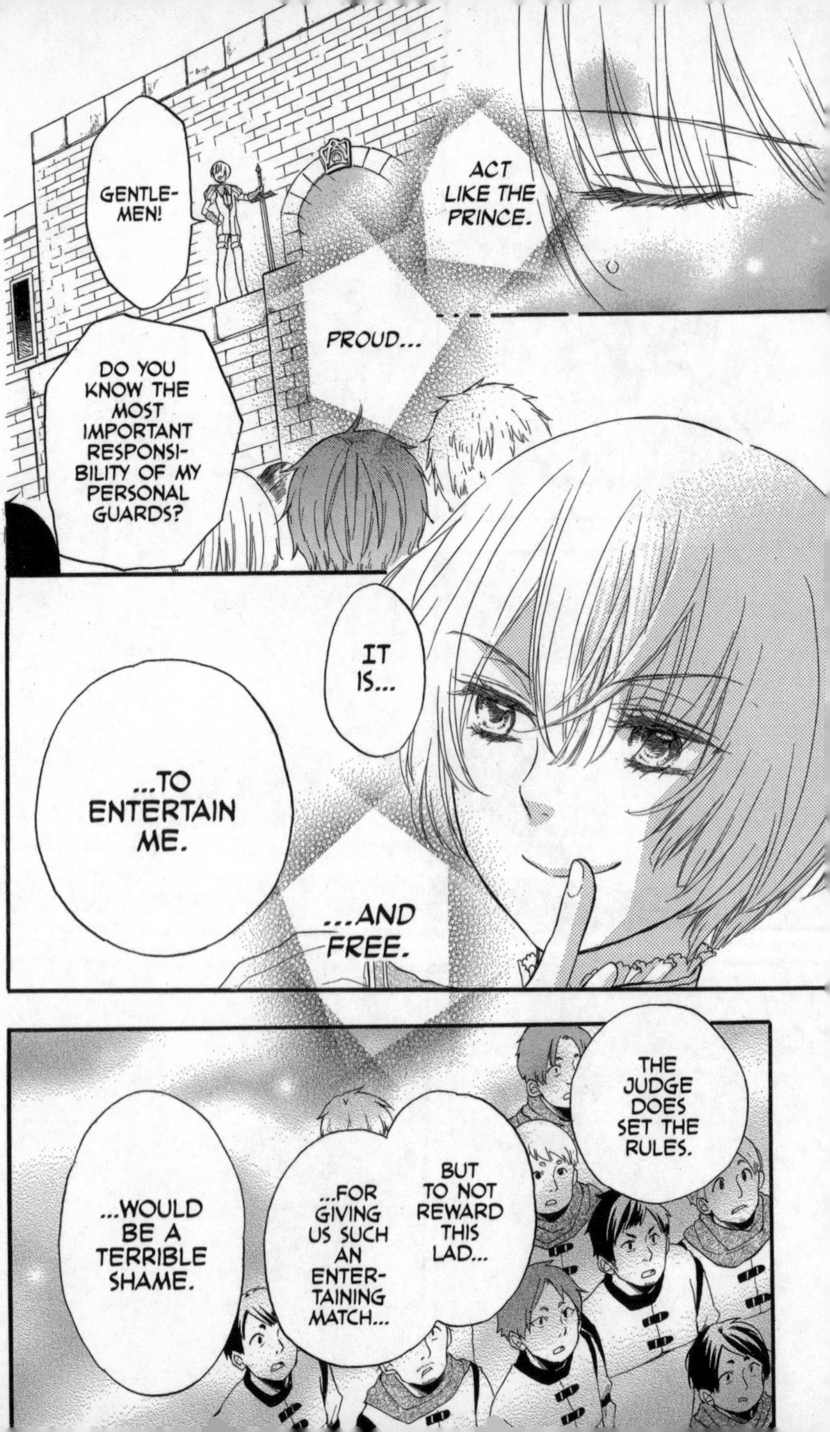
ACT LIKE THE PRINCE.
PROUD...
GENTLE-MEN!
DO YOU KNOW THE MOST IMPORTANT RESPONSI-BILITY OF MY PERSONAL GUARDS?
IT IS...
...TO ENTERTAIN ME.
...AND FREE.
THE JUDGE DOES SET THE RULES.
BUT TO NOT REWARD THIS LAD...
...FOR GIVING US SUCH AN ENTER-TAINING MATCH...
...WOULD BE A TERRIBLE SHAME.

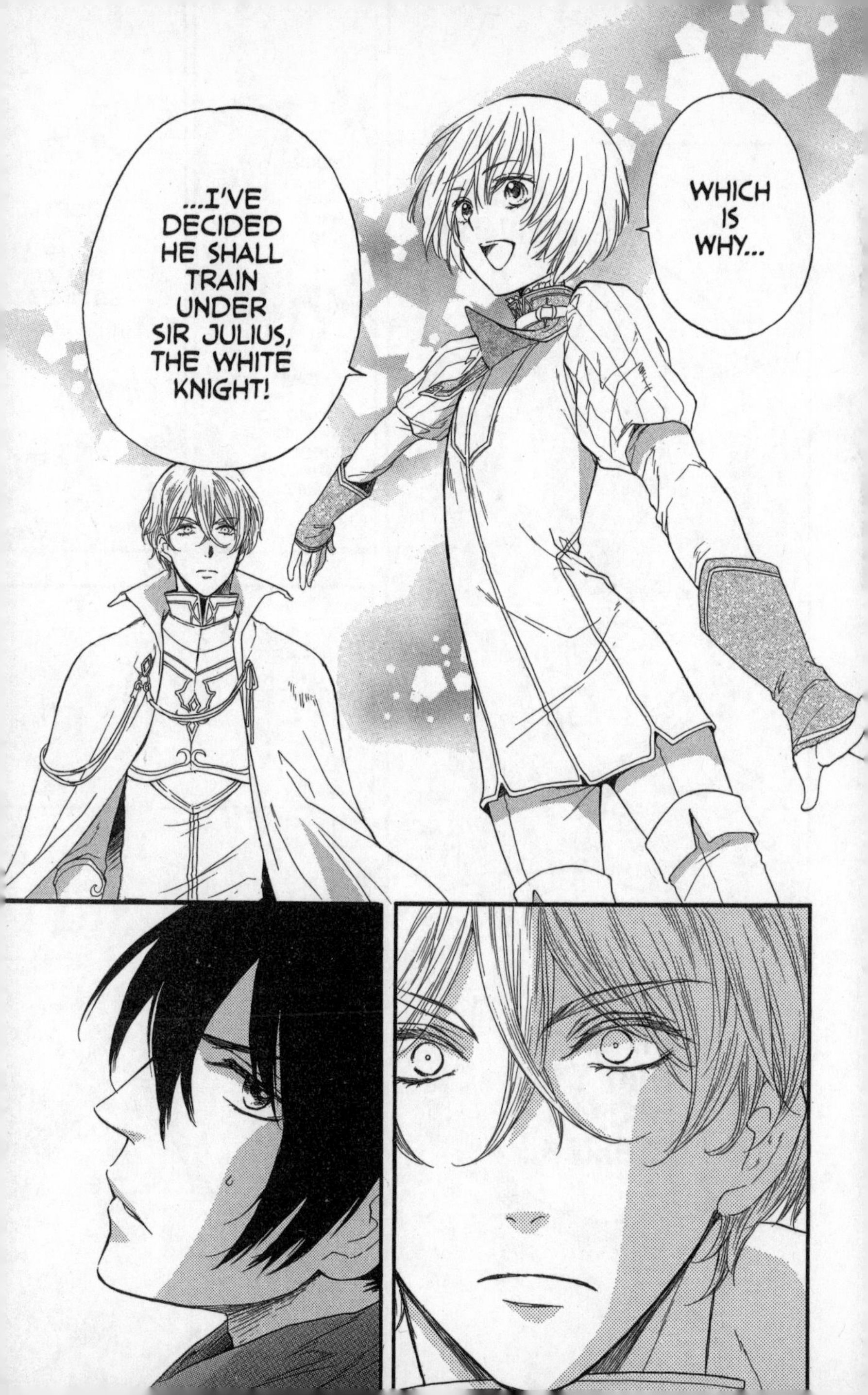
WHICH IS WHY...
...I'VE DECIDED HE SHALL TRAIN UNDER SIR JULIUS, THE WHITE KNIGHT!

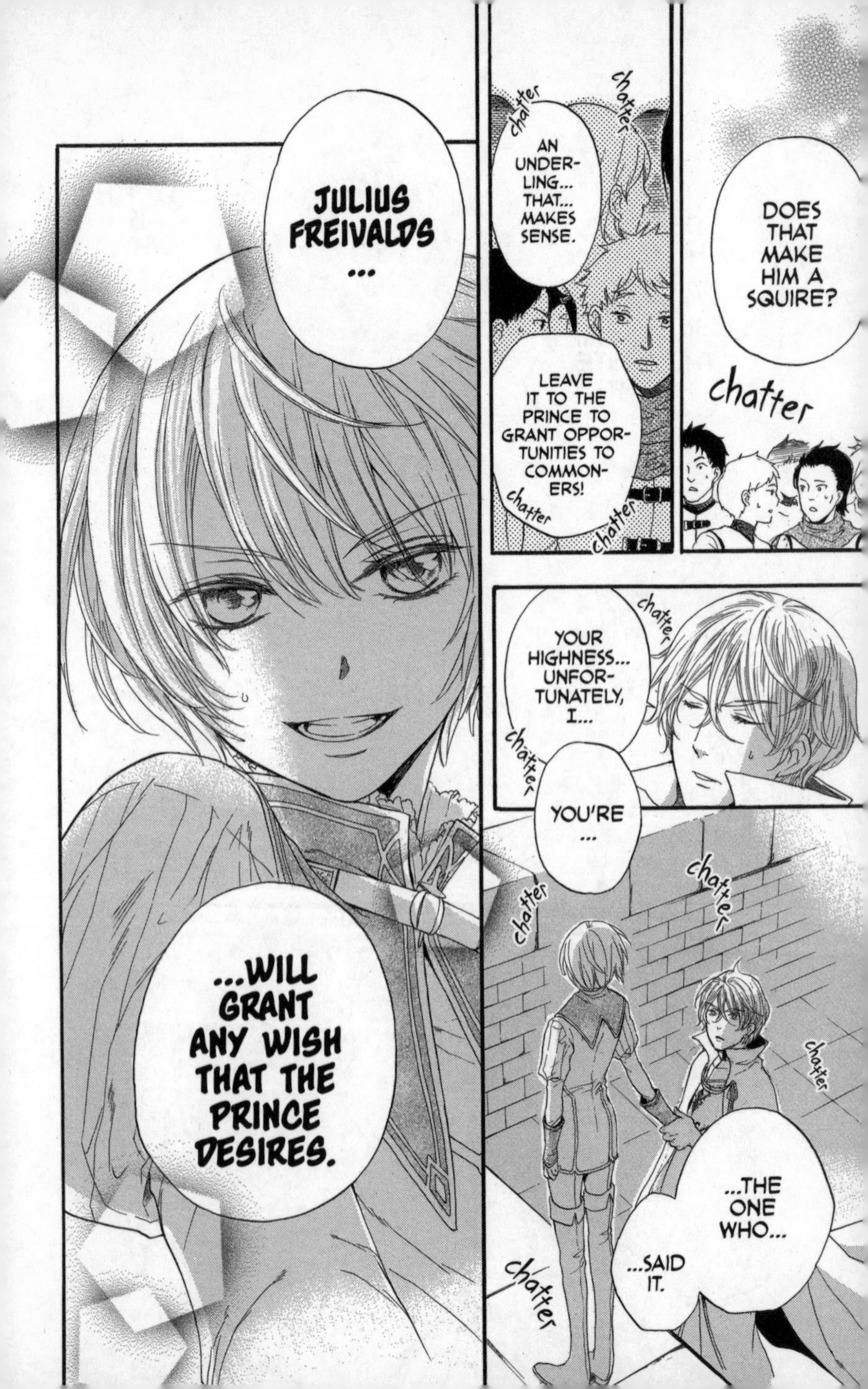
DOES THAT MAKE HIM A SQUIRE?
chatter
chatter
chatter
AN UNDERLING... THAT... MAKES SENSE.
LEAVE IT TO THE PRINCE TO GRANT OPPORTUNITIES TO COMMONERS!
chatter
chatter
chatter
YOUR HIGHNESS... UNFORTUNATELY, I...
chatter
YOU'RE ...
chatter
chatter
chatter
...THE ONE WHO...
...SAID IT.
chatter
JULIUS FREIVALDS ...
...WILL GRANT ANY WISH THAT THE PRINCE DESIRES.

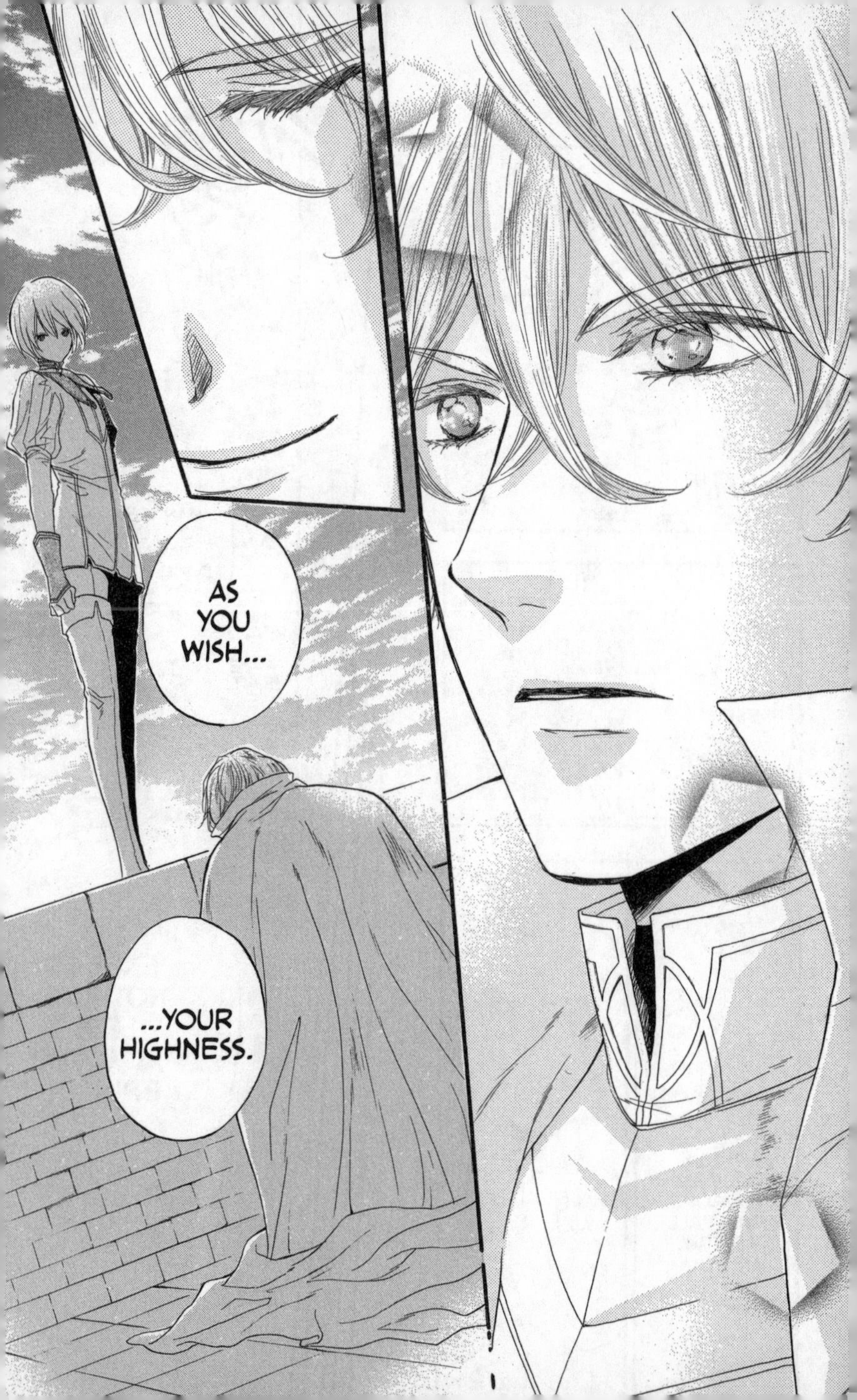
AS YOU WISH...
...YOUR HIGHNESS.

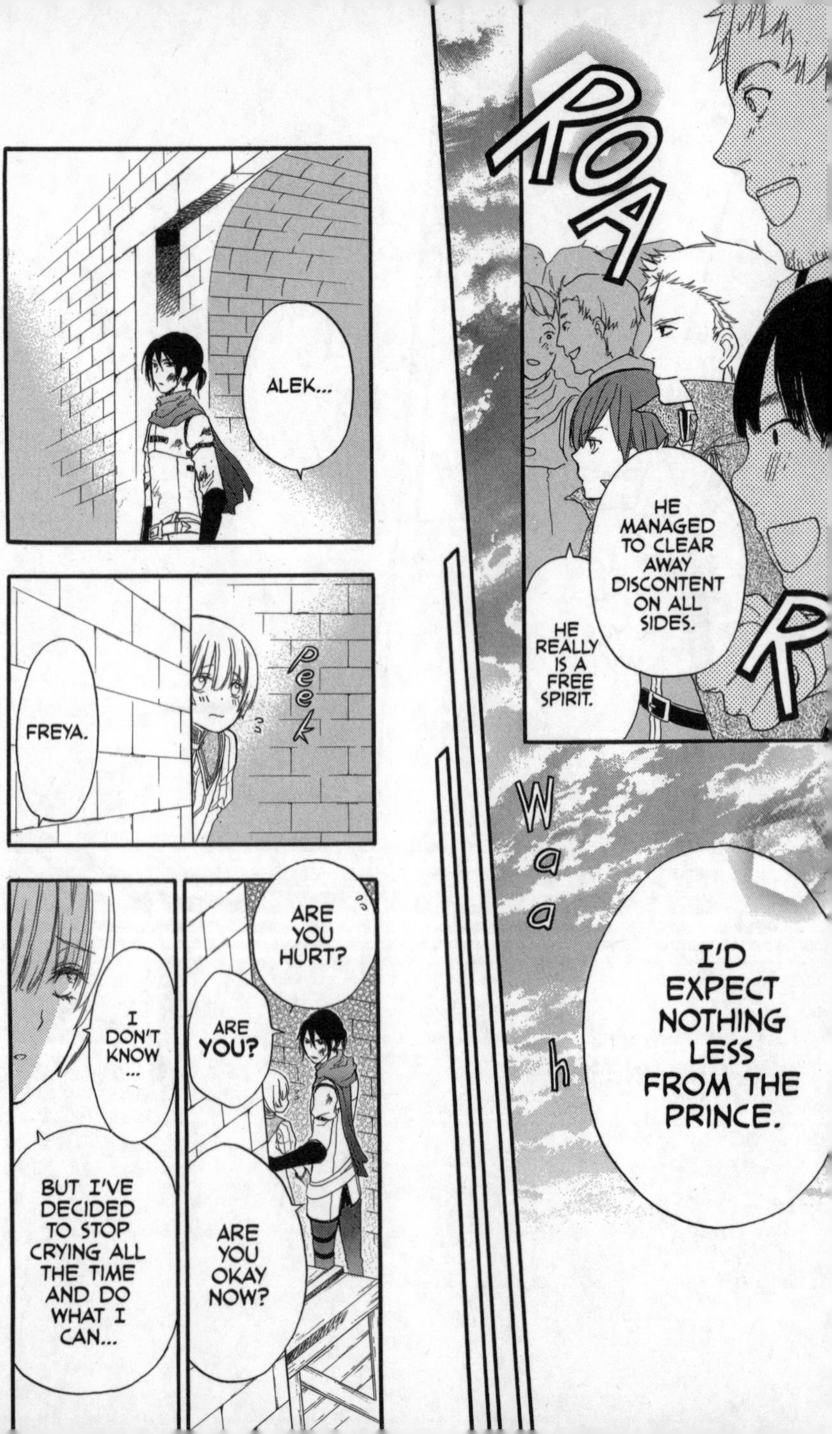
ROAR
HE MANAGED TO CLEAR AWAY DISCONTENT ON ALL SIDES.
HE REALLY IS A FREE SPIRIT.
Waah
I'D EXPECT NOTHING LESS FROM THE PRINCE.
ALEK...
peek
FREYA.
ARE YOU HURT?
ARE YOU?
ARE YOU OKAY NOW?
I DON'T KNOW...
BUT I'VE DECIDED TO STOP CRYING ALL THE TIME AND DO WHAT I CAN...

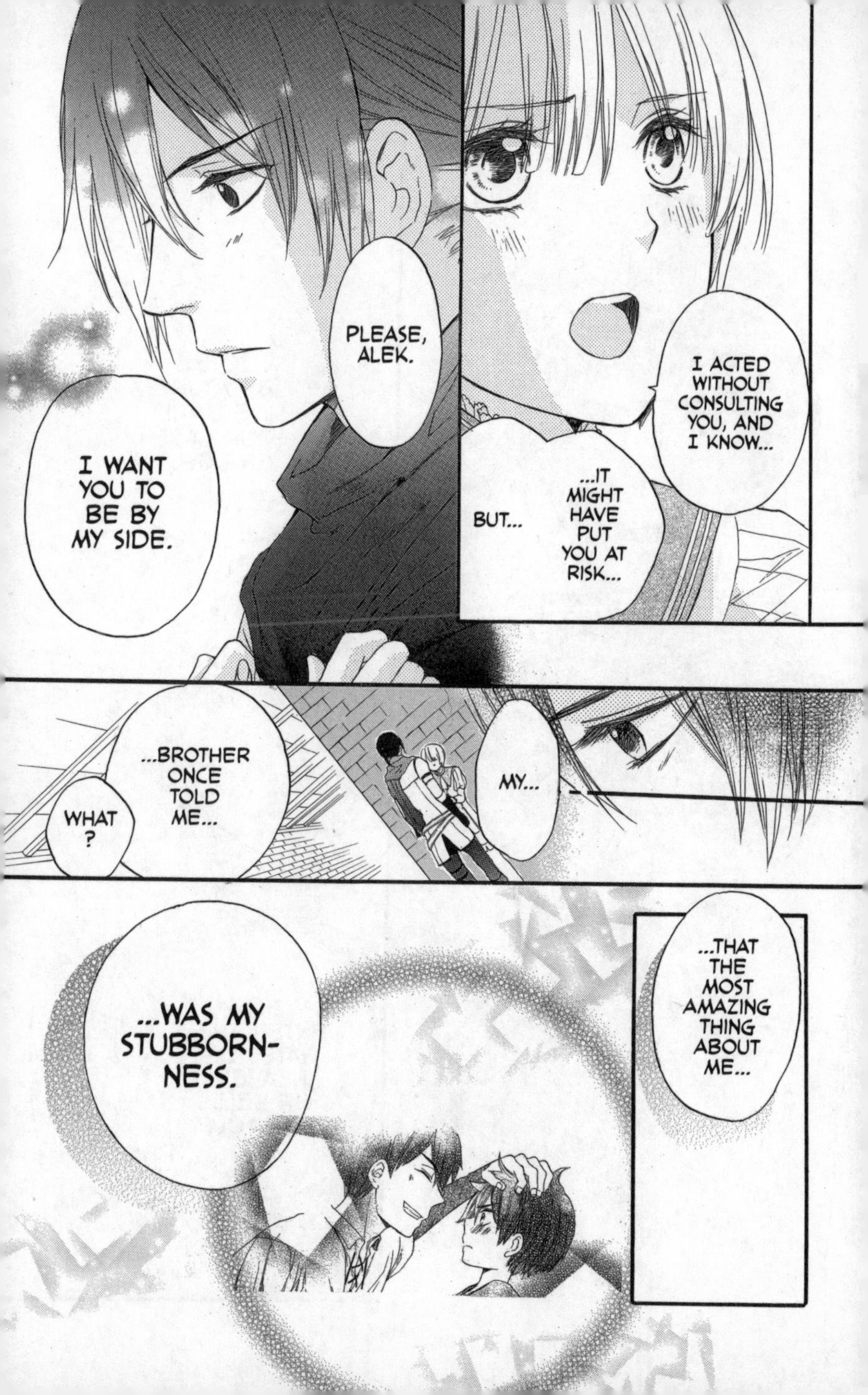
I ACTED WITHOUT CONSULTING YOU, AND I KNOW...
...IT MIGHT HAVE PUT YOU AT RISK...
BUT...
PLEASE, ALEK.
I WANT YOU TO BE BY MY SIDE.
MY...
...BROTHER ONCE TOLD ME...
WHAT?
...THAT THE MOST AMAZING THING ABOUT ME...
...WAS MY STUBBORN-NESS.

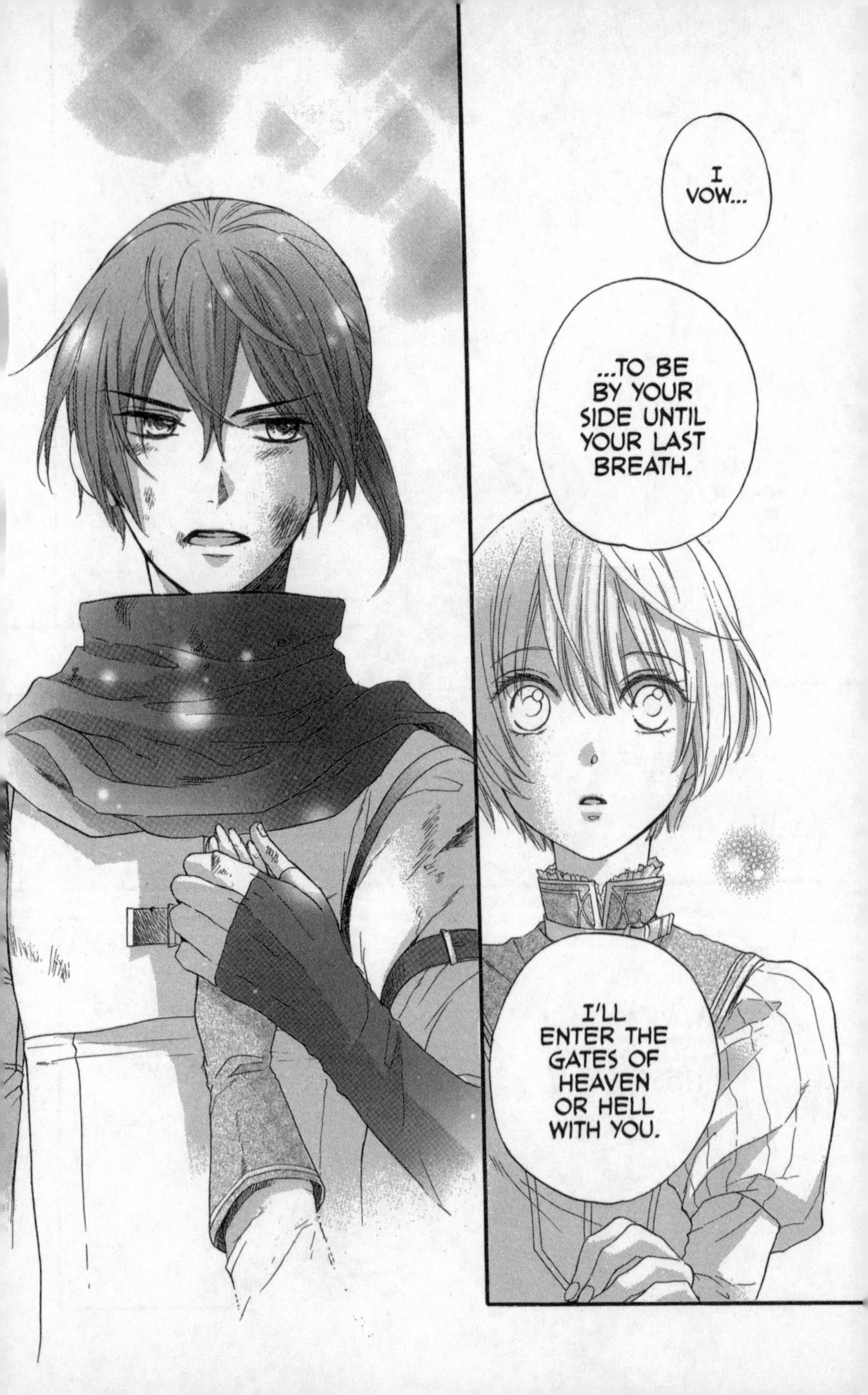
I VOW...
...TO BE BY YOUR SIDE UNTIL YOUR LAST BREATH.
I'LL ENTER THE GATES OF HEAVEN OR HELL WITH YOU.

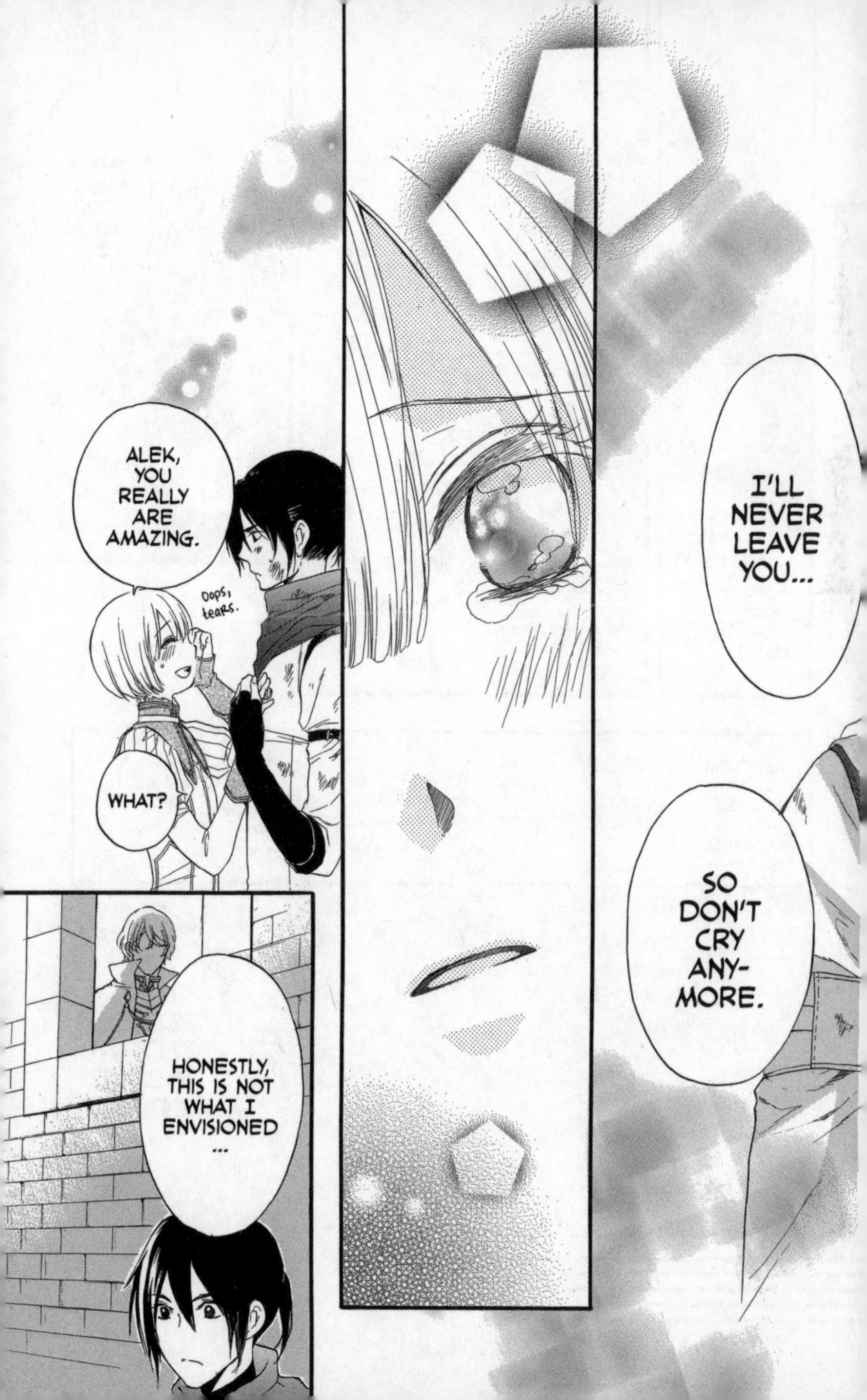
I'LL NEVER LEAVE YOU...
SO DON'T CRY ANYMORE.
ALEK, YOU REALLY ARE AMAZING.
Oops, tears.
WHAT?
HONESTLY, THIS IS NOT WHAT I ENVISIONED...

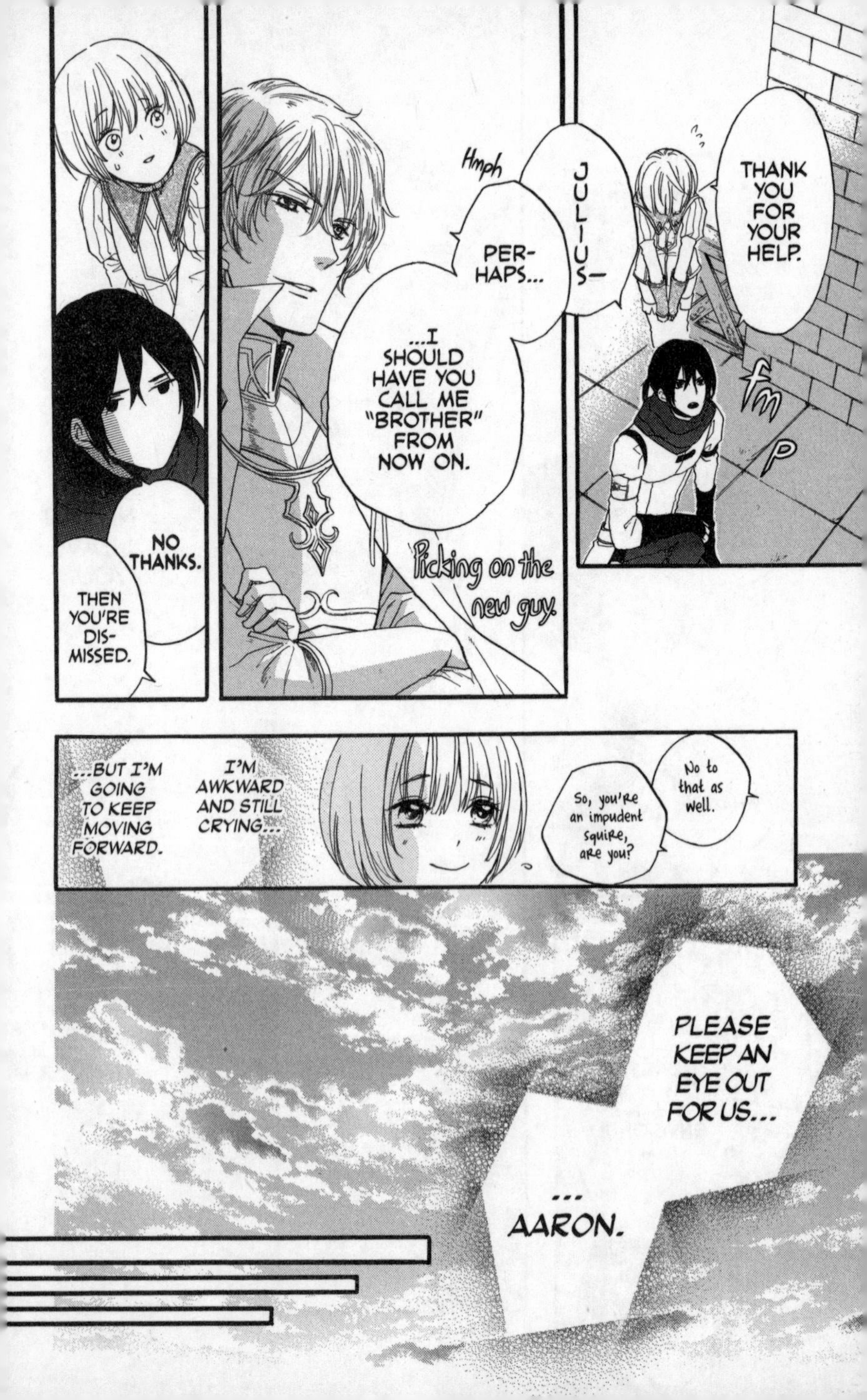
THANK YOU FOR YOUR HELP.
JULIUS—
fmp
Hmph
PER-HAPS...
...I SHOULD HAVE YOU CALL ME "BROTHER" FROM NOW ON.
Picking on the new guy.
NO THANKS.
THEN YOU'RE DIS-MISSED.
No to that as well.
So, you're an impudent squire, are you?
I'M AWKWARD AND STILL CRYING...
...BUT I'M GOING TO KEEP MOVING FORWARD.
PLEASE KEEP AN EYE OUT FOR US...
...AARON.

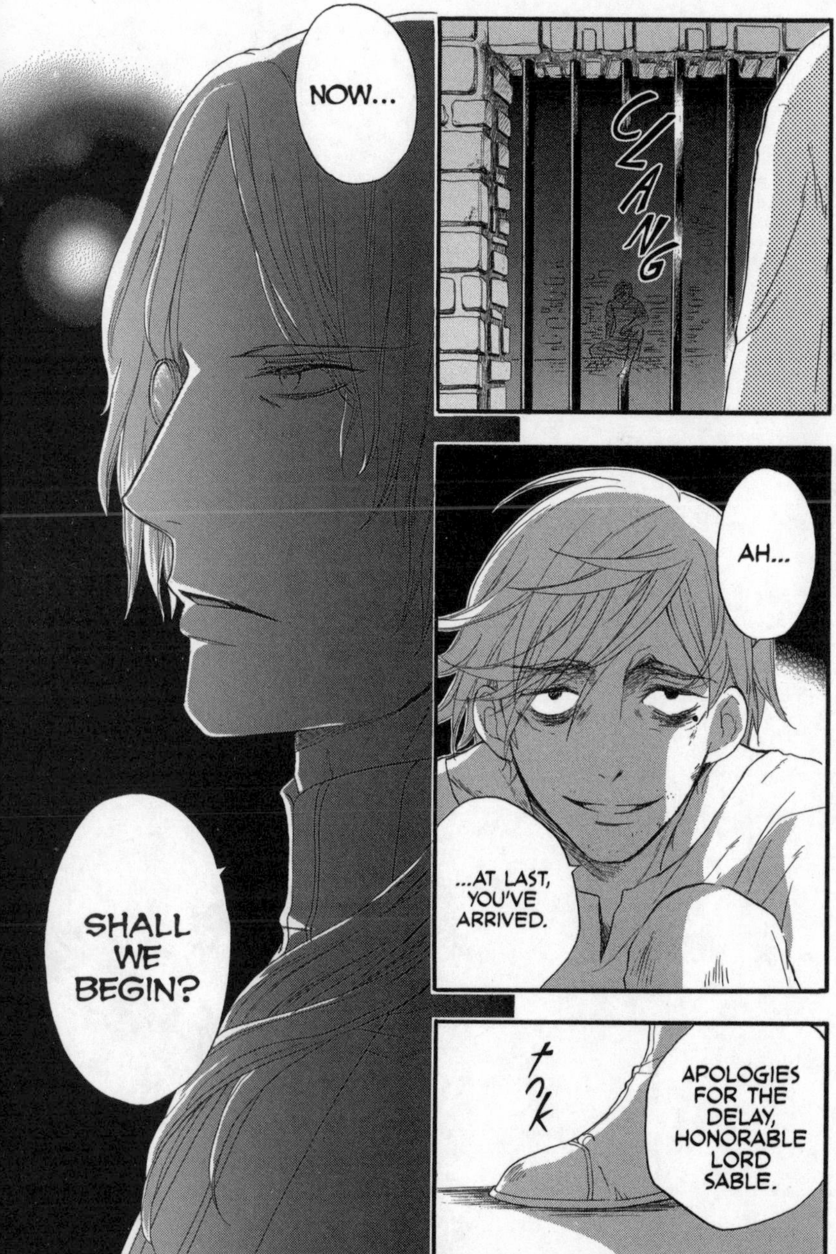
CLANG
AH...
...AT LAST, YOU'VE ARRIVED.
TNK
APOLOGIES FOR THE DELAY, HONORABLE LORD SABLE.
NOW...
SHALL WE BEGIN?

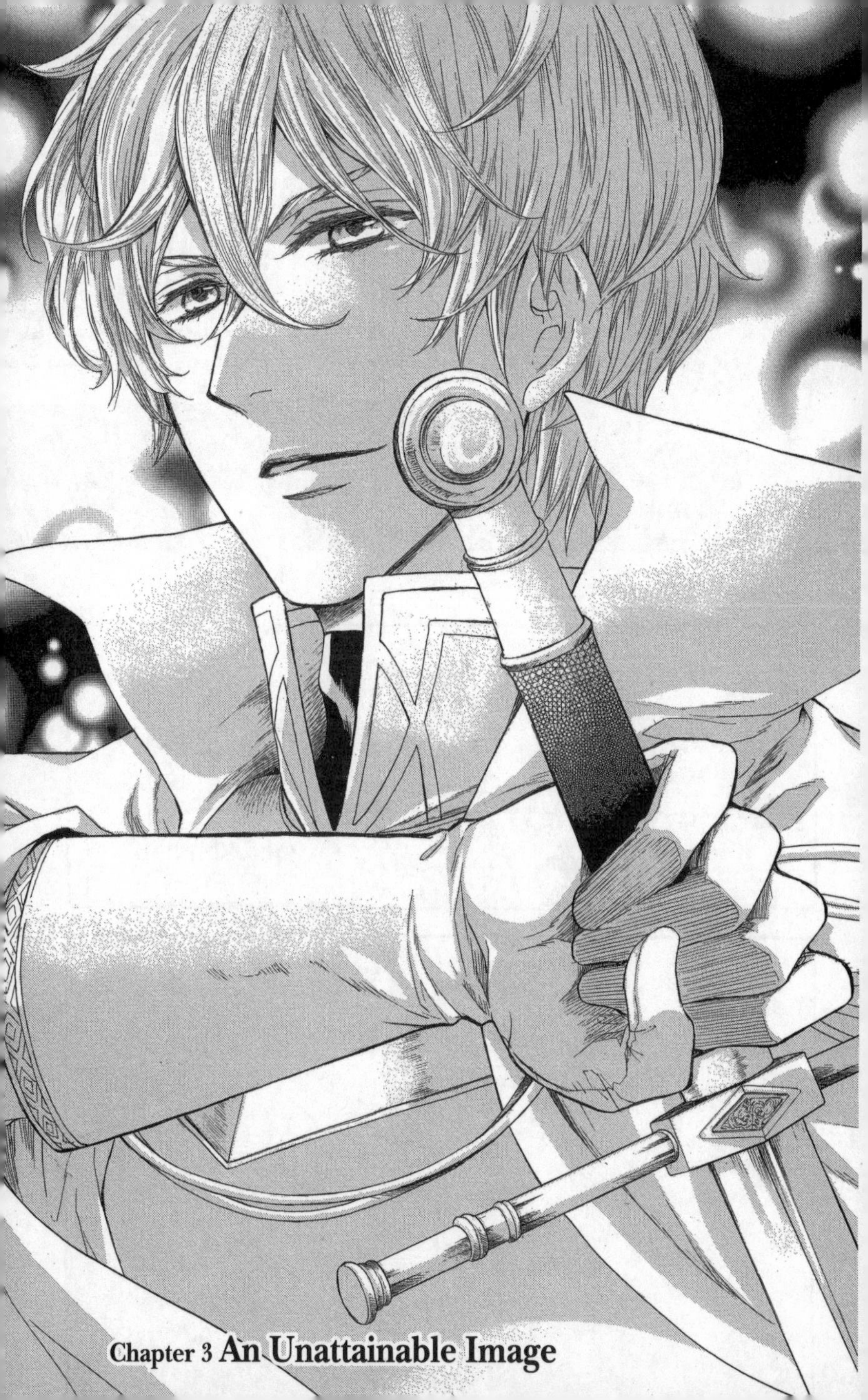

Chapter 3 An Unattainable Image

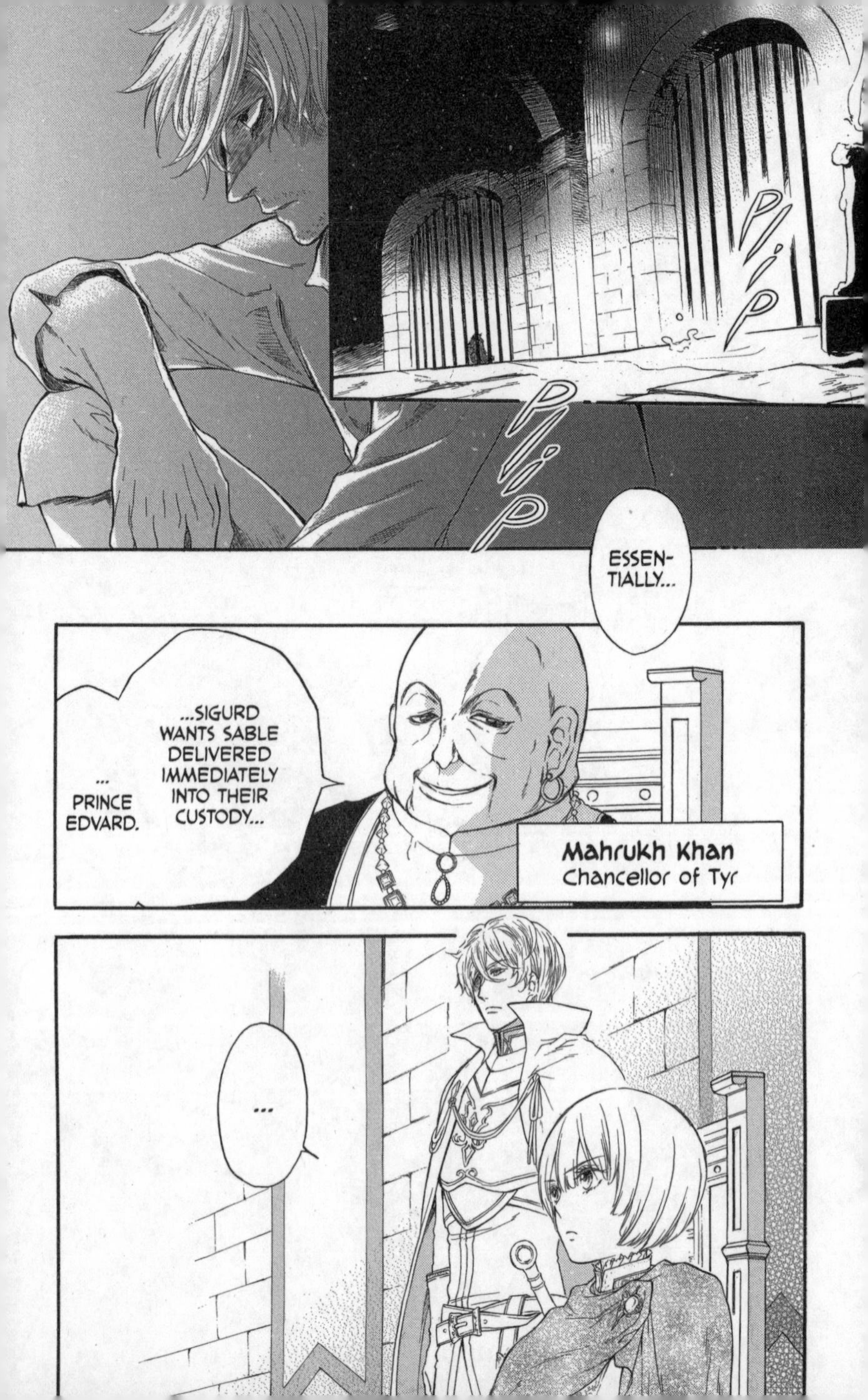
PIP
PIP
ESSEN-TIALLY...
...SIGURD WANTS SABLE DELIVERED IMMEDIATELY INTO THEIR CUSTODY...
... PRINCE EDVARD.
Mahrukh Khan
Chancellor of Tyr
...

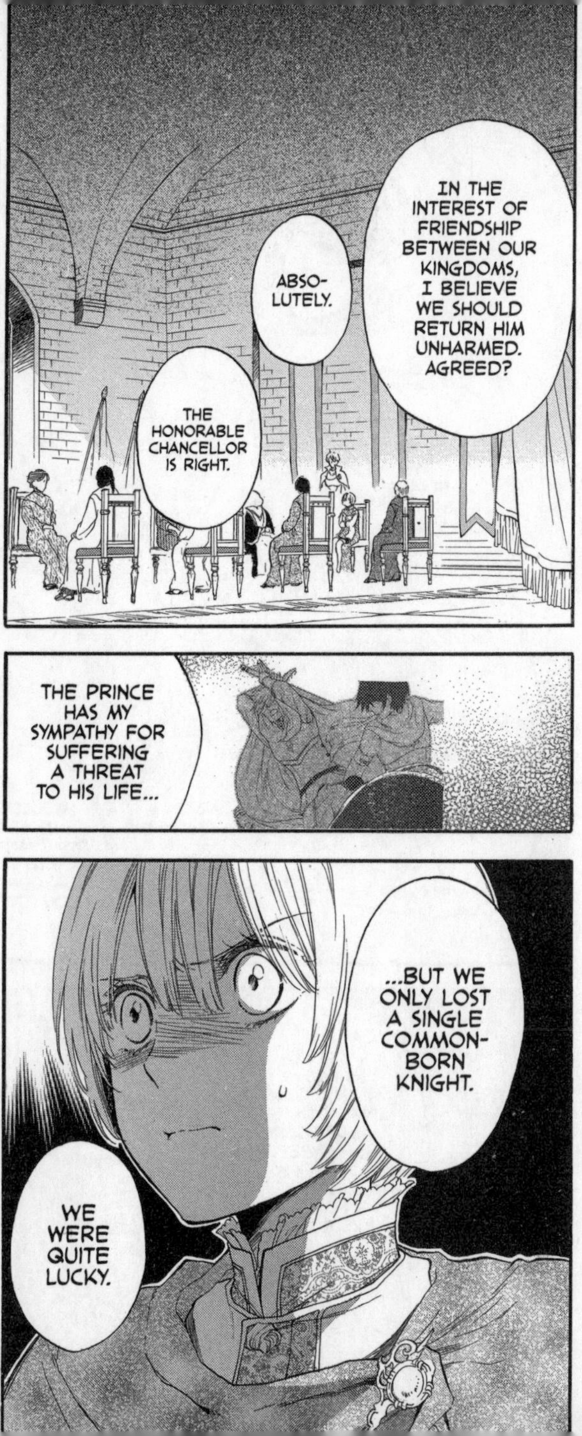
IN THE INTEREST OF FRIENDSHIP BETWEEN OUR KINGDOMS, I BELIEVE WE SHOULD RETURN HIM UNHARMED. AGREED?
ABSO-LUTELY.
THE HONORABLE CHANCELLOR IS RIGHT.
THE PRINCE HAS MY SYMPATHY FOR SUFFERING A THREAT TO HIS LIFE...
...BUT WE ONLY LOST A SINGLE COMMON-BORN KNIGHT.
WE WERE QUITE LUCKY.

J

Julius.

He's got gorgeous on lockdown.

I hear that "Julius" ranks high on the list of hot foreign names in Japan.

I didn't name him. I think that if I had, his hotness would have made me self-conscious and I would have ended up picking a really weird name, so it's a good thing that I didn't name him.

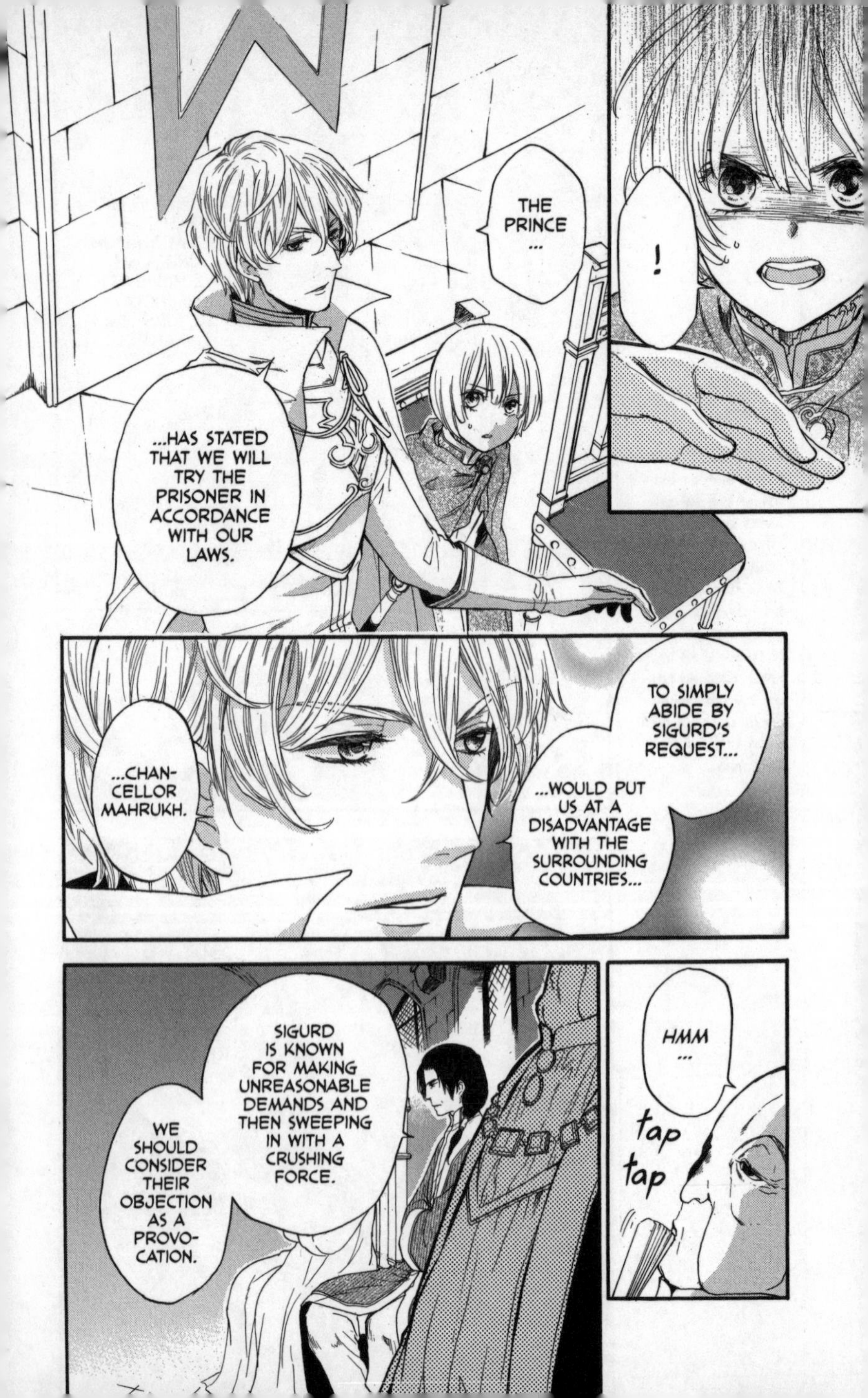
!
THE PRINCE...
...HAS STATED THAT WE WILL TRY THE PRISONER IN ACCORDANCE WITH OUR LAWS.
TO SIMPLY ABIDE BY SIGURD'S REQUEST...
...WOULD PUT US AT A DISADVANTAGE WITH THE SURROUNDING COUNTRIES...
...CHANCELLOR MAHRUKH.
HMM...
tap tap
SIGURD IS KNOWN FOR MAKING UNREASONABLE DEMANDS AND THEN SWEEPING IN WITH A CRUSHING FORCE.
WE SHOULD CONSIDER THEIR OBJECTION AS A PROVOCATION.

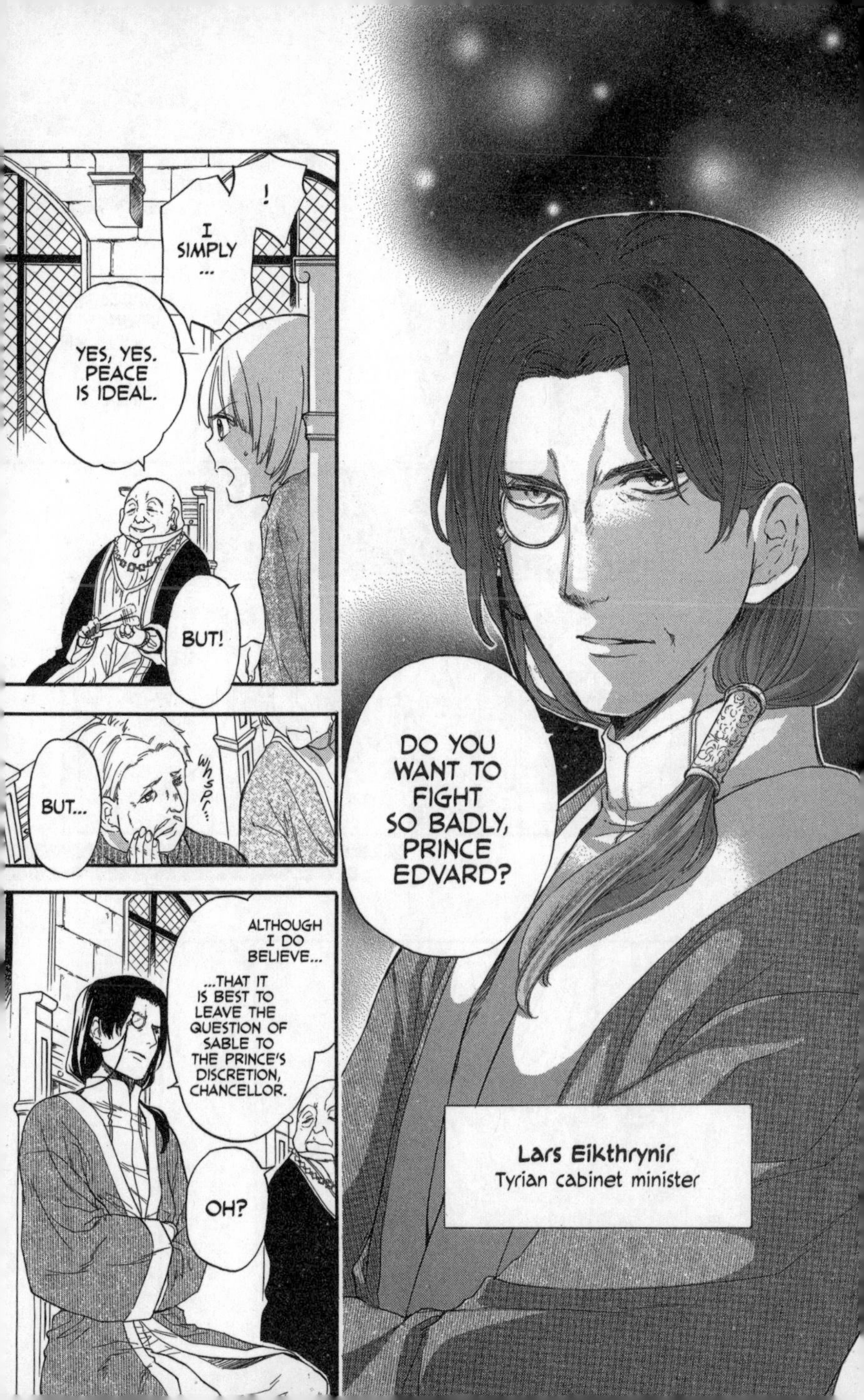
DO YOU WANT TO FIGHT SO BADLY, PRINCE EDVARD?
Lars Eikthrynir
Tyrian cabinet minister
!
I SIMPLY ...
YES, YES. PEACE IS IDEAL.
BUT!
WHSPR...
BUT...
ALTHOUGH I DO BELIEVE...
...THAT IT IS BEST TO LEAVE THE QUESTION OF SABLE TO THE PRINCE'S DISCRETION, CHANCELLOR.
OH?

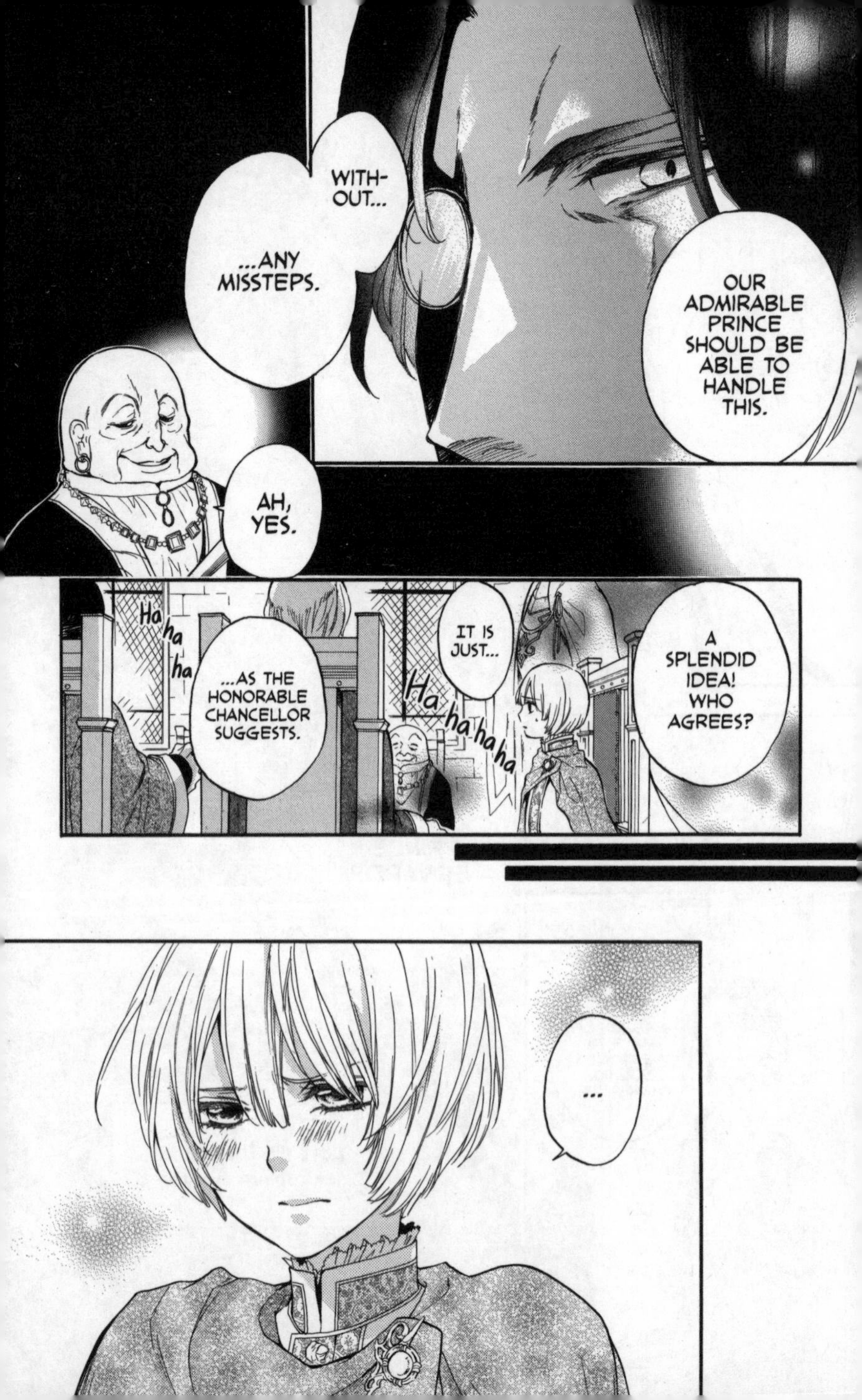
OUR ADMIRABLE PRINCE SHOULD BE ABLE TO HANDLE THIS.
WITH-OUT...
...ANY MISSTEPS.
AH, YES.
A SPLENDID IDEA! WHO AGREES?
IT IS JUST...
Ha ha ha ha ha
...AS THE HONORABLE CHANCELLOR SUGGESTS.
Ha ha ha
...

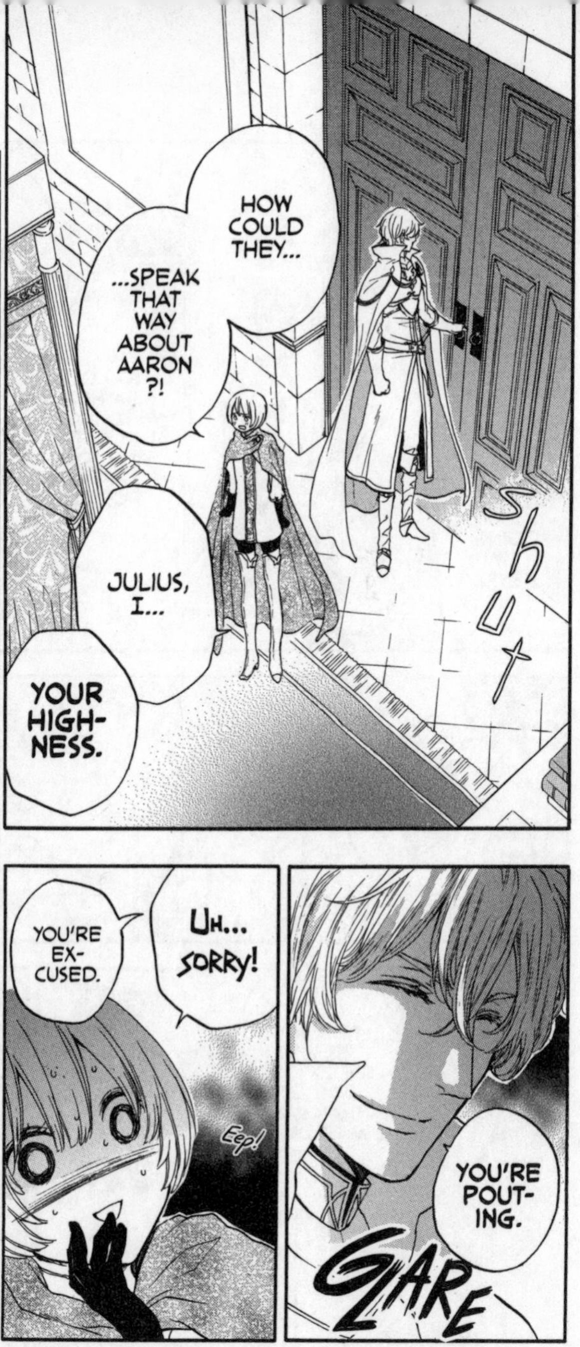
HOW COULD THEY...
...SPEAK THAT WAY ABOUT AARON?!
shut
JULIUS, I...
YOUR HIGHNESS.
YOU'RE POUTING.
GLARE
UH... SORRY!
YOU'RE EX-CUSED.
Eep!

Y M

The prince's personal guards Mikal and Yngvi.

They're often together and have probably been friends since they met.

I'd like to make them even more admirable in every way.

I'll try my best.

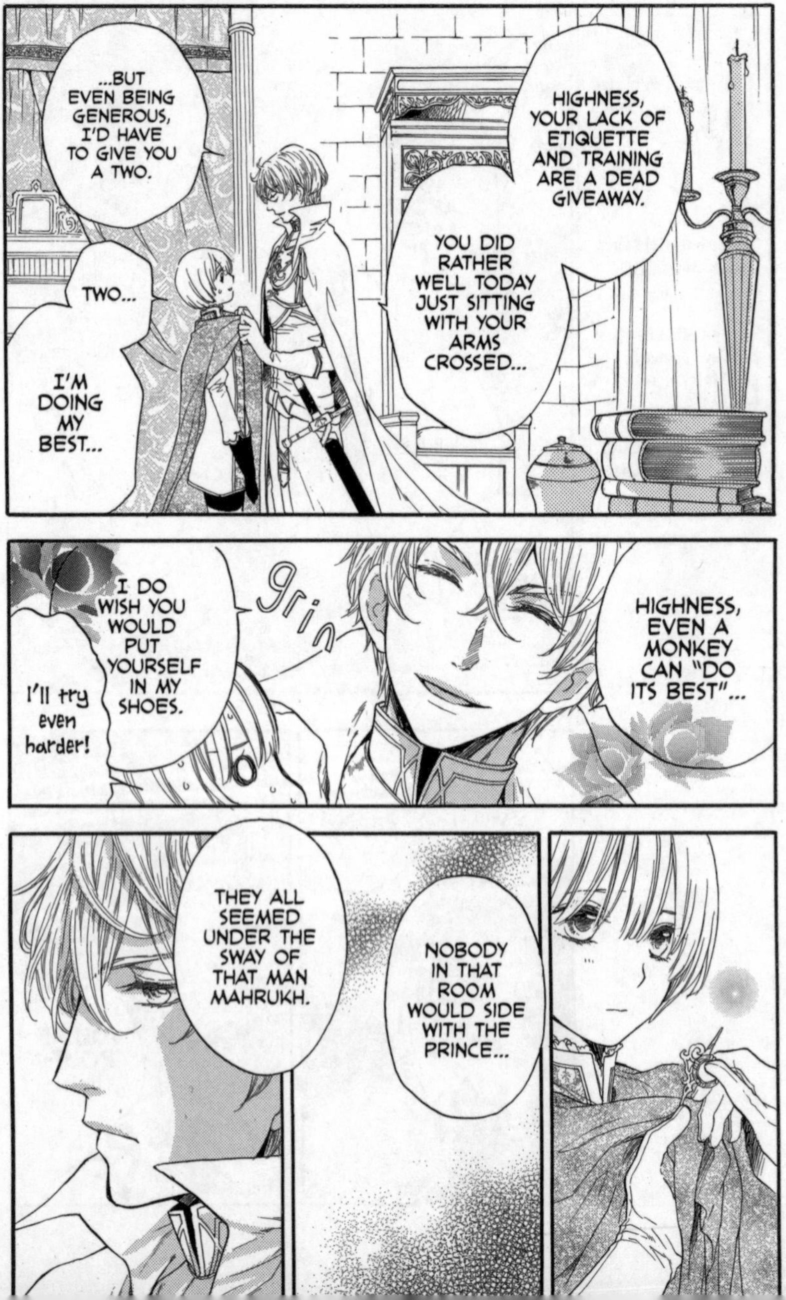
HIGHNESS, YOUR LACK OF ETIQUETTE AND TRAINING ARE A DEAD GIVEAWAY.
YOU DID RATHER WELL TODAY JUST SITTING WITH YOUR ARMS CROSSED...
...BUT EVEN BEING GENEROUS, I'D HAVE TO GIVE YOU A TWO.
TWO...
I'M DOING MY BEST...
HIGHNESS, EVEN A MONKEY CAN "DO ITS BEST"...
grin
I DO WISH YOU WOULD PUT YOURSELF IN MY SHOES.
I'll try even harder!
...
NOBODY IN THAT ROOM WOULD SIDE WITH THE PRINCE...
THEY ALL SEEMED UNDER THE SWAY OF THAT MAN MAHRUKH.

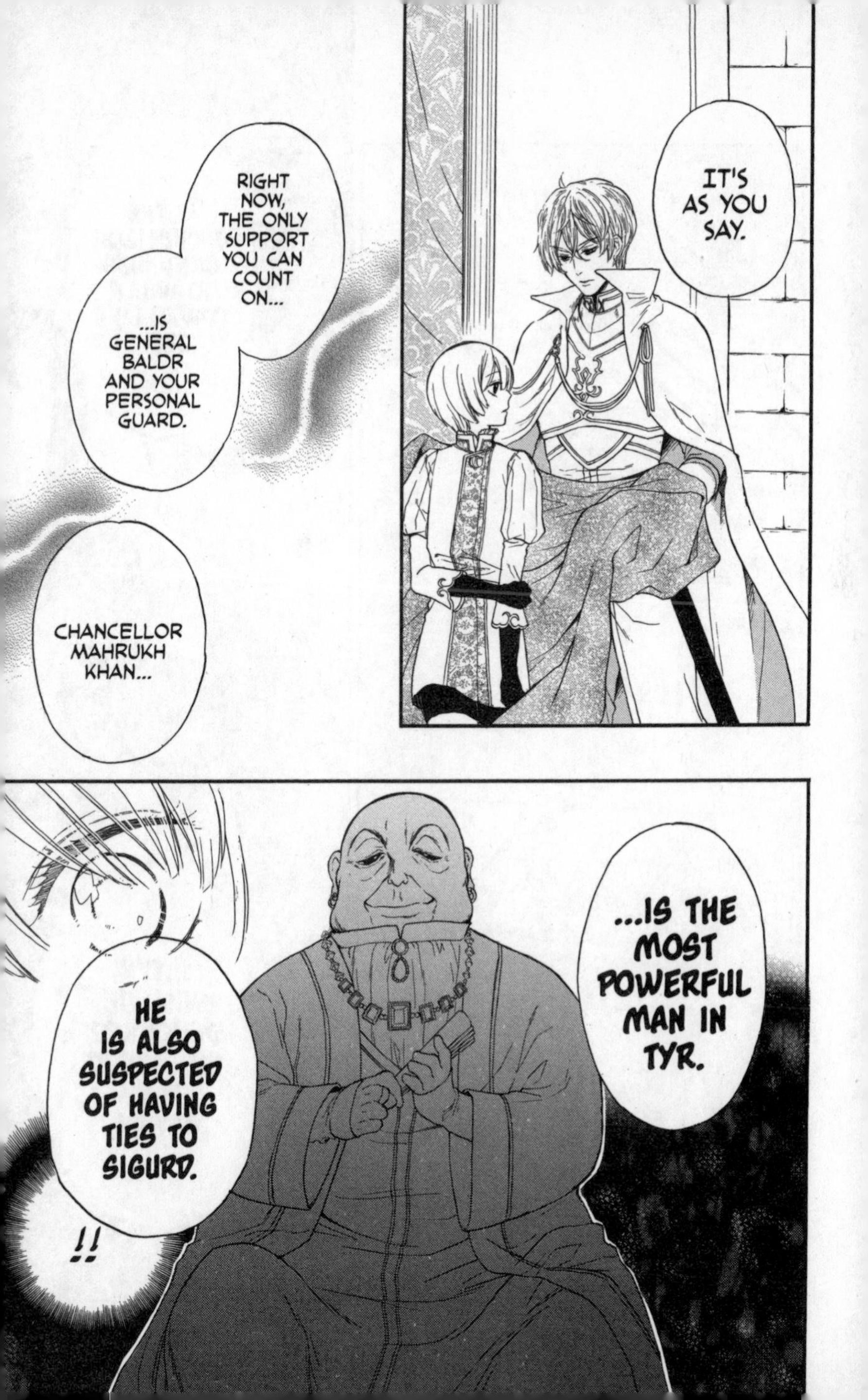
IT'S AS YOU SAY.
RIGHT NOW, THE ONLY SUPPORT YOU CAN COUNT ON...
...IS GENERAL BALDR AND YOUR PERSONAL GUARD.
CHANCELLOR MAHRUKH KHAN...
...IS THE MOST POWERFUL MAN IN TYR.
HE IS ALSO SUSPECTED OF HAVING TIES TO SIGURD.
!!

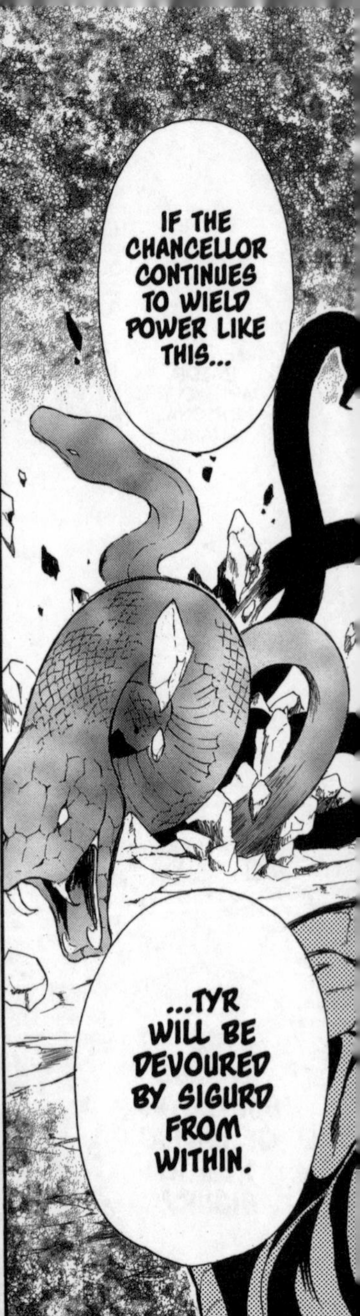
IF THE CHANCELLOR CONTINUES TO WIELD POWER LIKE THIS...
...TYR WILL BE DEVOURED BY SIGURD FROM WITHIN.

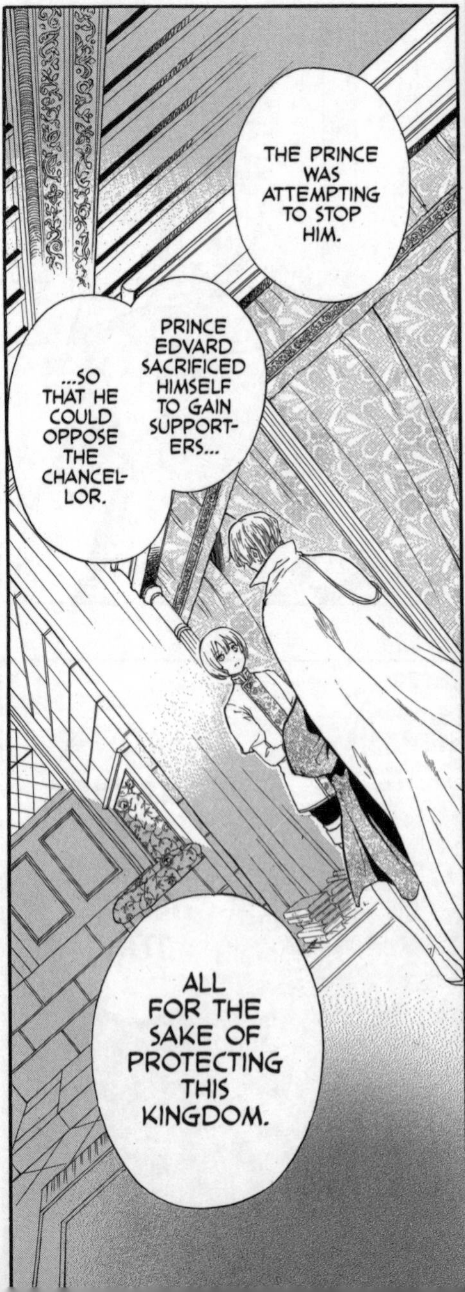
THE PRINCE WAS ATTEMPTING TO STOP HIM.
PRINCE EDVARD SACRIFICED HIMSELF TO GAIN SUPPORTERS...
...SO THAT HE COULD OPPOSE THE CHANCELLOR.
ALL FOR THE SAKE OF PROTECTING THIS KINGDOM.

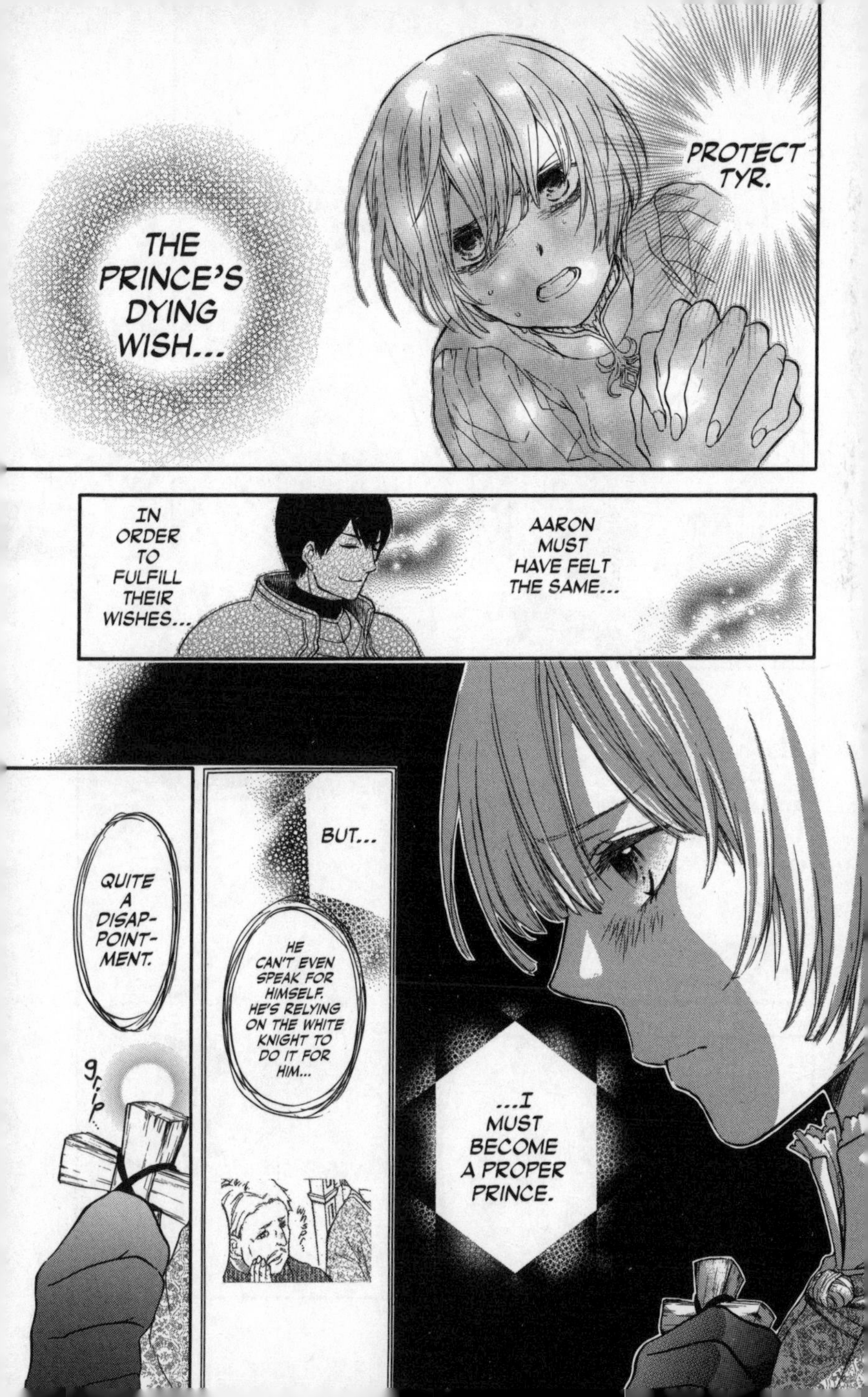
PROTECT TYR.
THE PRINCE'S DYING WISH...
AARON MUST HAVE FELT THE SAME...
IN ORDER TO FULFILL THEIR WISHES...
BUT...
HE CAN'T EVEN SPEAK FOR HIMSELF. HE'S RELYING ON THE WHITE KNIGHT TO DO IT FOR HIM...
QUITE A DISAPPOINTMENT.
grip...
...I MUST BECOME A PROPER PRINCE.

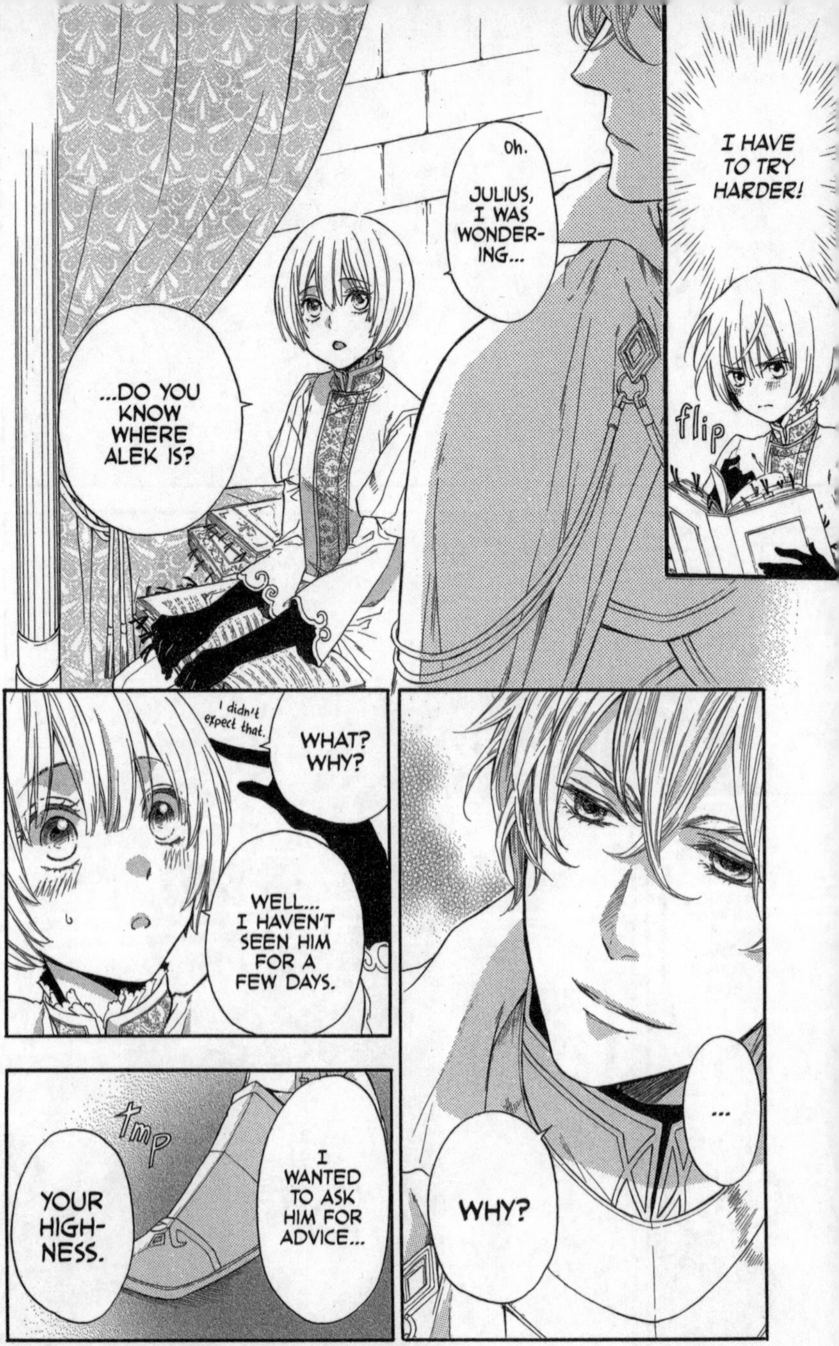
I HAVE TO TRY HARDER!
flip
Oh.
JULIUS, I WAS WONDERING...
...DO YOU KNOW WHERE ALEK IS?
...
WHY?
WHAT? WHY?
I didn't expect that.
WELL... I HAVEN'T SEEN HIM FOR A FEW DAYS.
I WANTED TO ASK HIM FOR ADVICE...
tmp
YOUR HIGH-NESS.

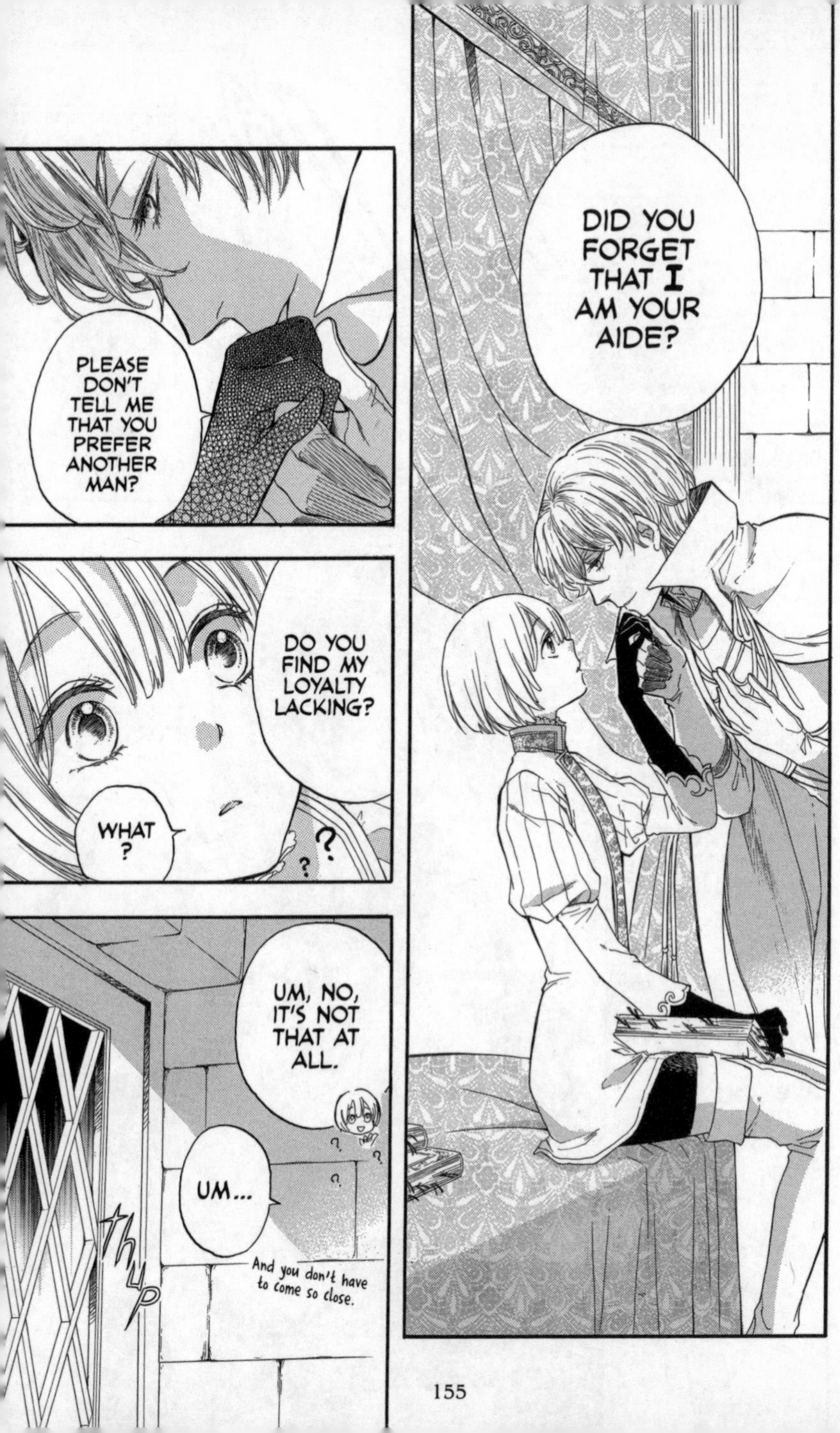
DID YOU FORGET THAT I AM YOUR AIDE?
PLEASE DON'T TELL ME THAT YOU PREFER ANOTHER MAN?
DO YOU FIND MY LOYALTY LACKING?
WHAT?
UM, NO, IT'S NOT THAT AT ALL.
UM...
thup
And you don't have to come so close.

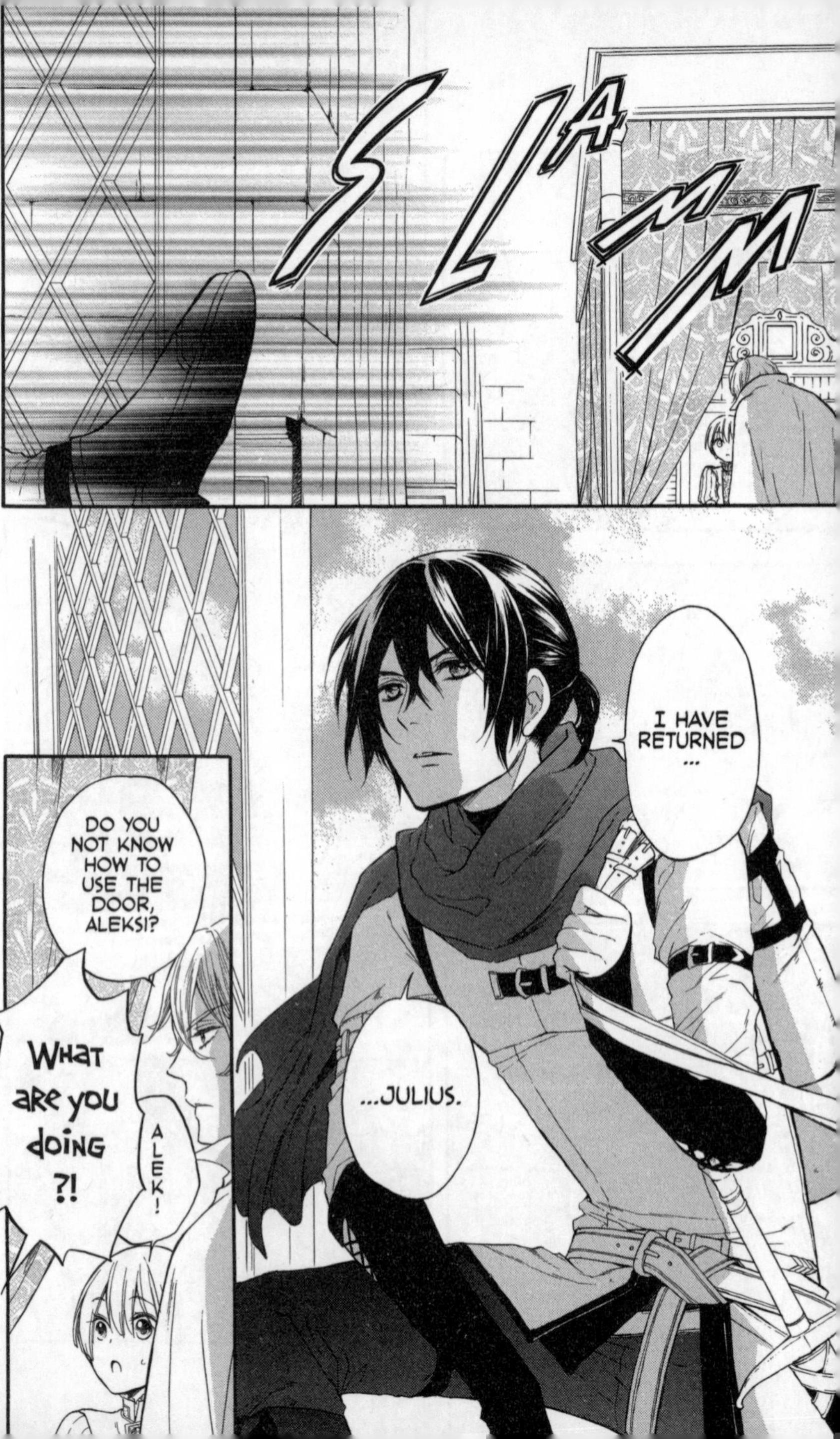
SLAMM
I HAVE RETURNED ...
...JULIUS.
DO YOU NOT KNOW HOW TO USE THE DOOR, ALEKSI?
ALEK!
WHAT are you doing ?!

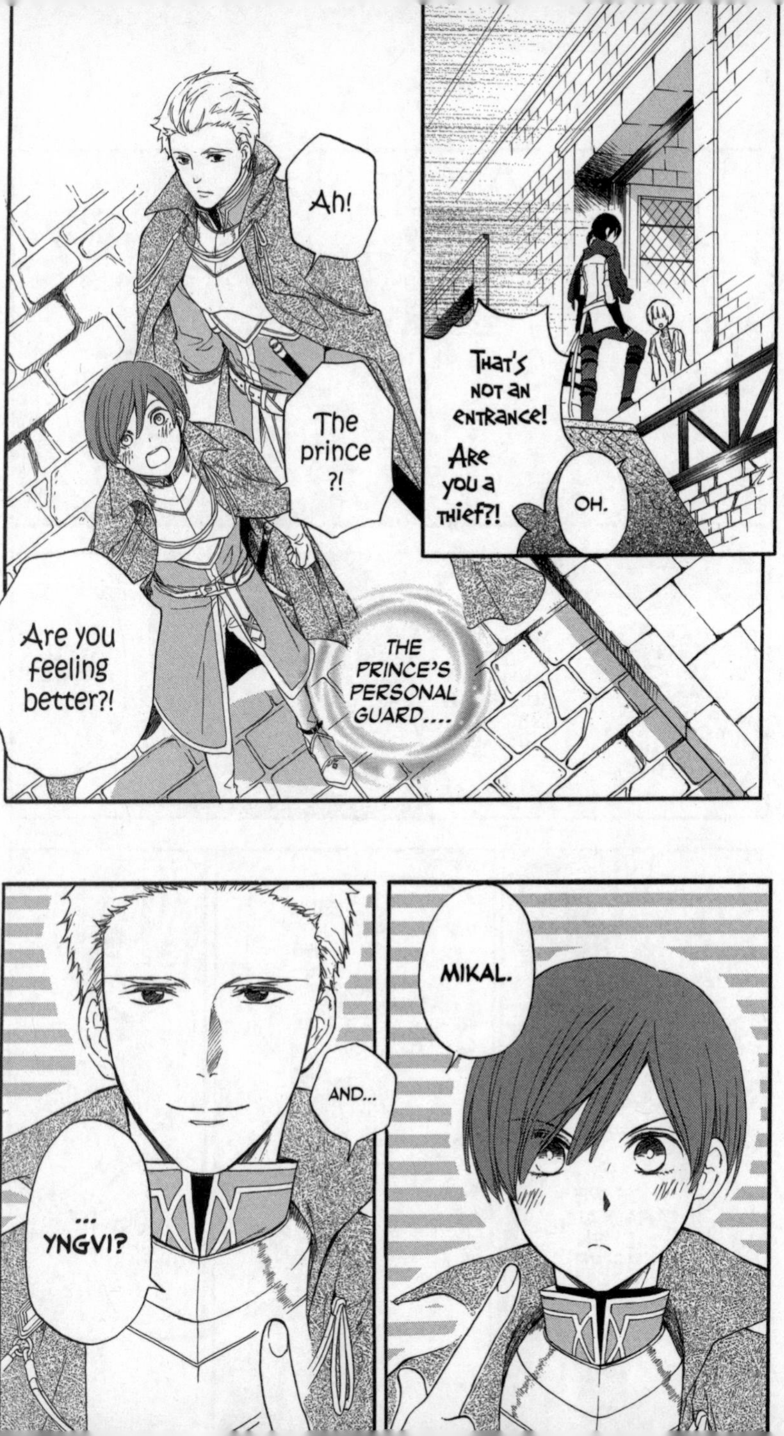
That's not an entrance! Are you a thief?!
Oh.
Ah!
The prince?!
Are you feeling better?!
THE PRINCE'S PERSONAL GUARD....
MIKAL.
AND...
... YNGVI?

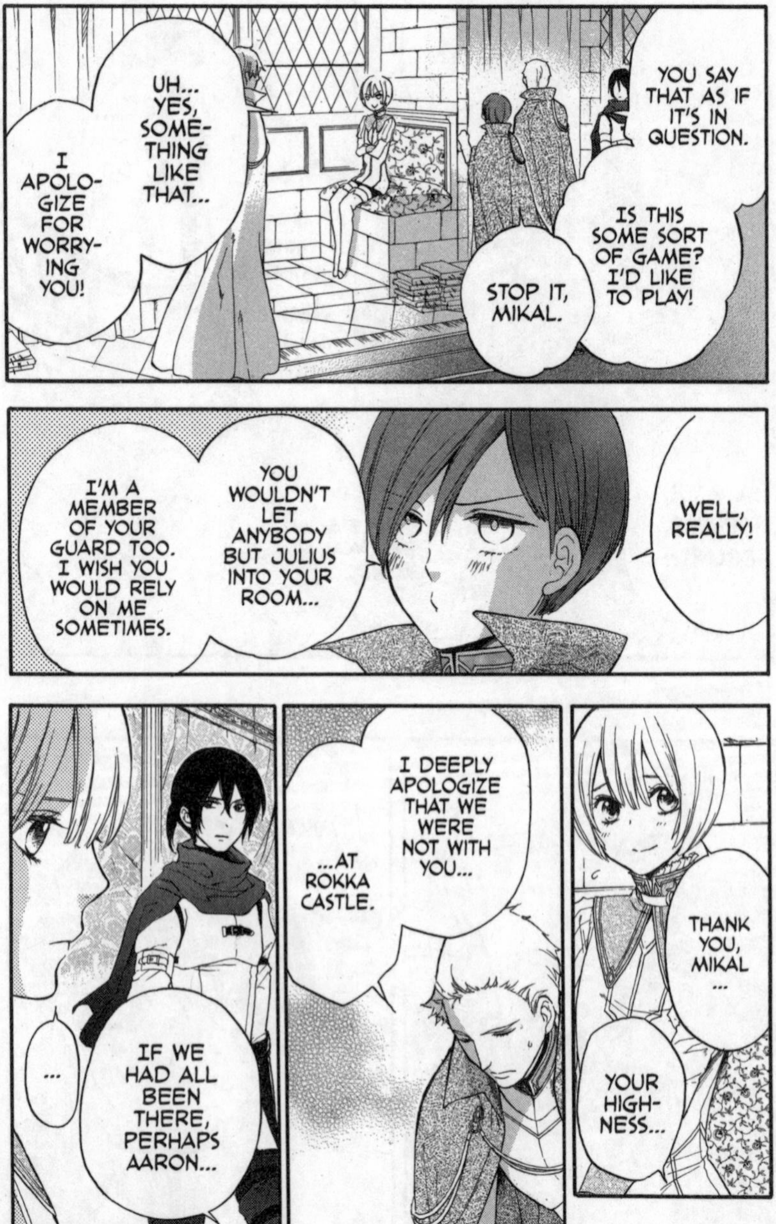
YOU SAY THAT AS IF IT'S IN QUESTION.
IS THIS SOME SORT OF GAME? I'D LIKE TO PLAY!
STOP IT, MIKAL.
UH... YES, SOMETHING LIKE THAT...
I APOLOGIZE FOR WORRYING YOU!
WELL, REALLY!
YOU WOULDN'T LET ANYBODY BUT JULIUS INTO YOUR ROOM...
I'M A MEMBER OF YOUR GUARD TOO. I WISH YOU WOULD RELY ON ME SOMETIMES.
THANK YOU, MIKAL ...
YOUR HIGHNESS...
I DEEPLY APOLOGIZE THAT WE WERE NOT WITH YOU...
...AT ROKKA CASTLE.
IF WE HAD ALL BEEN THERE, PERHAPS AARON...
...

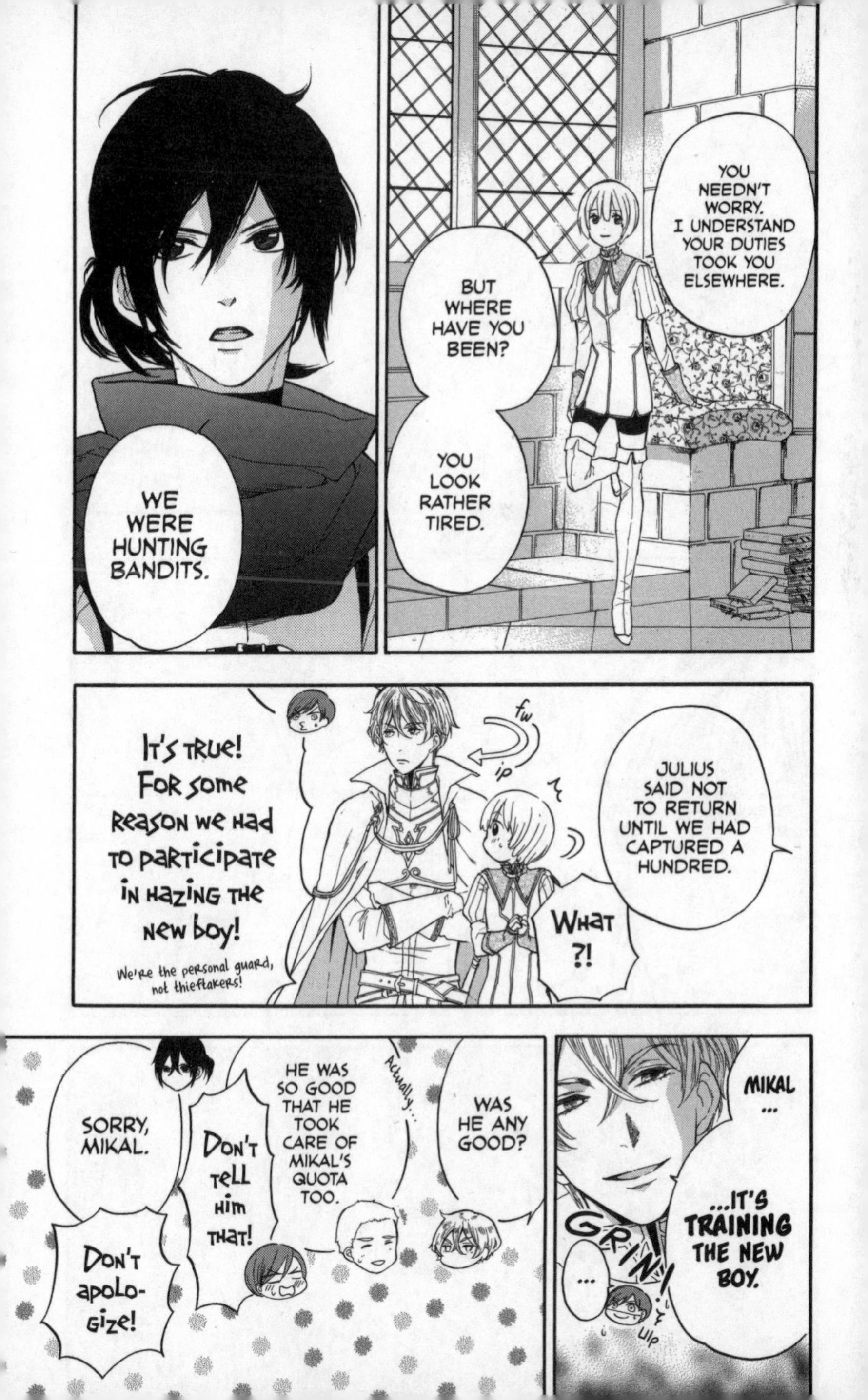
YOU NEEDN'T WORRY. I UNDERSTAND YOUR DUTIES TOOK YOU ELSEWHERE.
BUT WHERE HAVE YOU BEEN?
YOU LOOK RATHER TIRED.
WE WERE HUNTING BANDITS.
JULIUS SAID NOT TO RETURN UNTIL WE HAD CAPTURED A HUNDRED.
fw
ip
WHAT ?!
It's true! For some reason we had to participate in hazing the new boy!
We're the personal guard, not thieftakers!
MIKAL ...
...IT'S TRAINING THE NEW BOY.
GRIN!
...
Ulp
WAS HE ANY GOOD?
Actually...
HE WAS SO GOOD THAT HE TOOK CARE OF MIKAL'S QUOTA TOO.
Don't tell him that!
SORRY, MIKAL.
Don't apolo-gize!

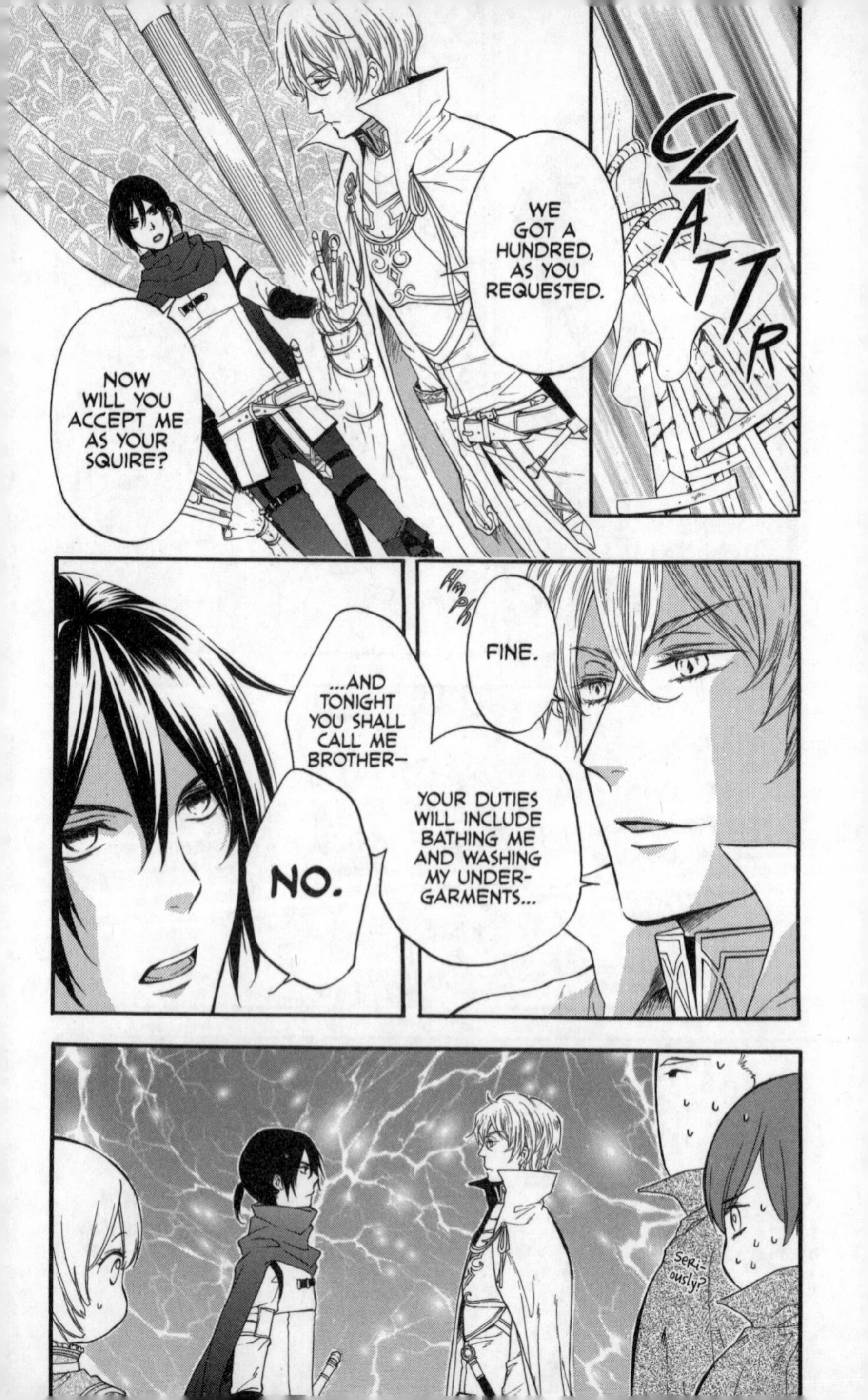
CLATTR
WE GOT A HUNDRED, AS YOU REQUESTED.
NOW WILL YOU ACCEPT ME AS YOUR SQUIRE?
Hmph
FINE.
YOUR DUTIES WILL INCLUDE BATHING ME AND WASHING MY UNDER-GARMENTS...
...AND TONIGHT YOU SHALL CALL ME BROTHER—
NO.
Seri-ously?

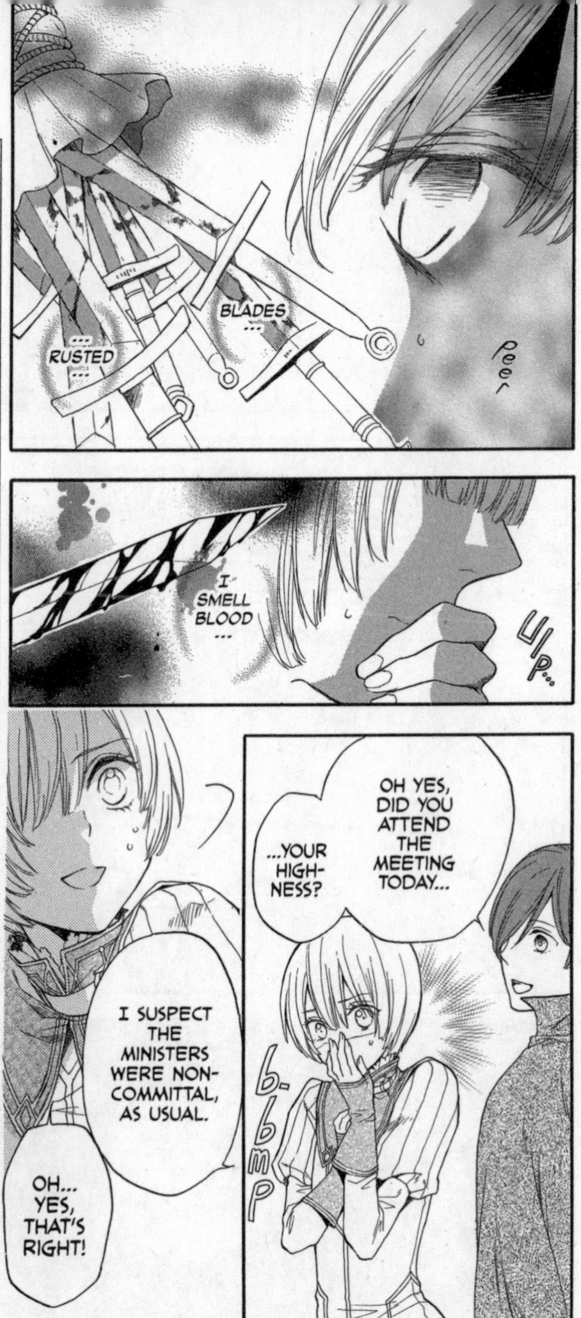
Peer
BLADES...
...RUSTED...
ULP...
I SMELL BLOOD...
OH YES, DID YOU ATTEND THE MEETING TODAY...
...YOUR HIGHNESS?
b-bmp
I SUSPECT THE MINISTERS WERE NON-COMMITTAL, AS USUAL.
OH... YES, THAT'S RIGHT!

Thank you for reading.

I'll make sure that volume 2 is even more interesting! I hope you'll read it too.

To my assistants...

Ryo Sakimiya
Miyuki Tsutsui
Yotaro Noma
Bochiko
Misaya Morifuji

My editors...

Everybody that helped with the making of this comic...

My family...

And my readers...

Thank you very much.

石原ケイコ
Keiko Ishihara

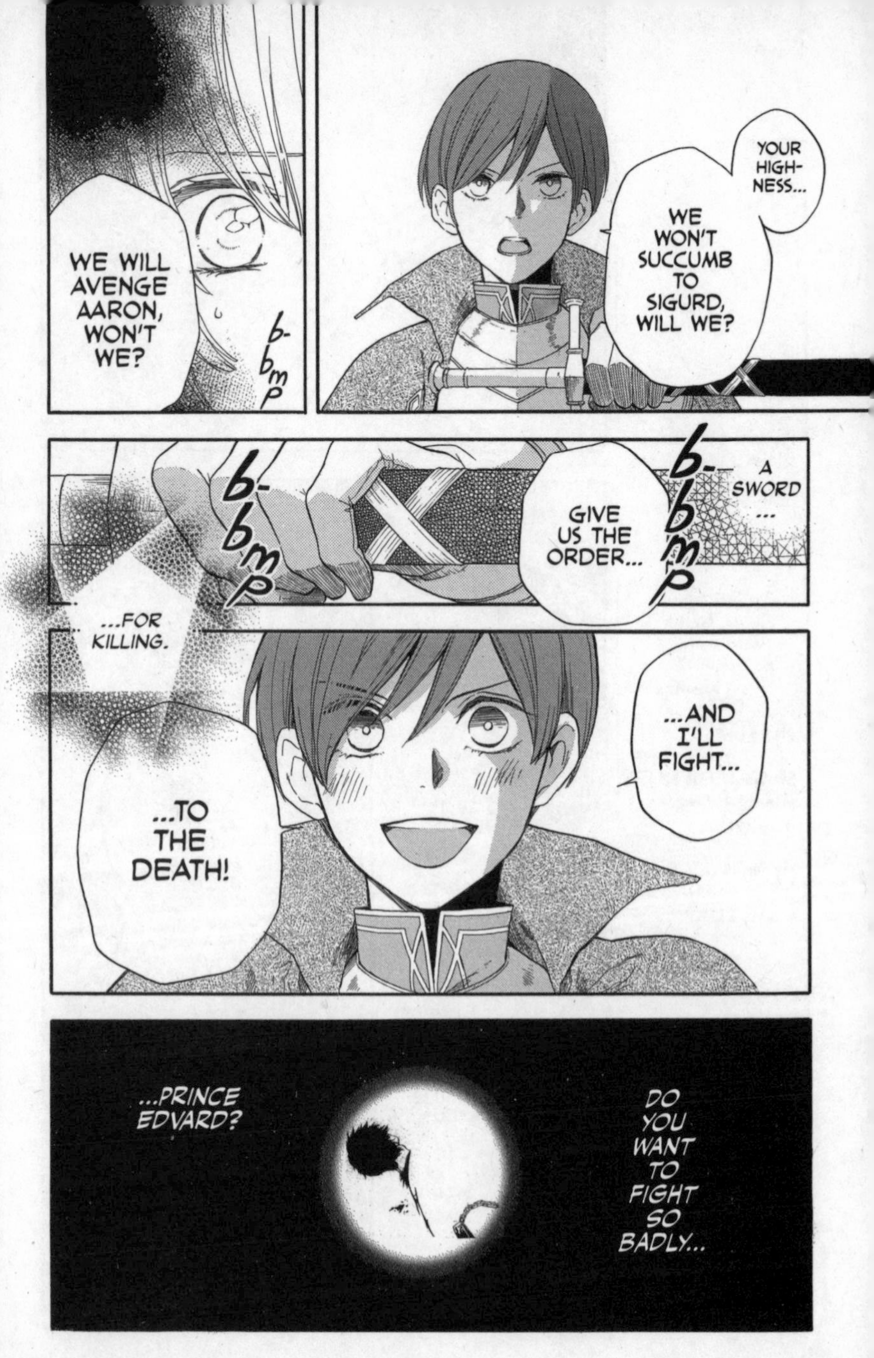
YOUR HIGHNESS...
WE WON'T SUCCUMB TO SIGURD, WILL WE?
WE WILL AVENGE AARON, WON'T WE?
b-bmp
A SWORD...
b-bmp
GIVE US THE ORDER...
b-bmp
...FOR KILLING.
...AND I'LL FIGHT...
...TO THE DEATH!
DO YOU WANT TO FIGHT SO BADLY...
...PRINCE EDVARD?

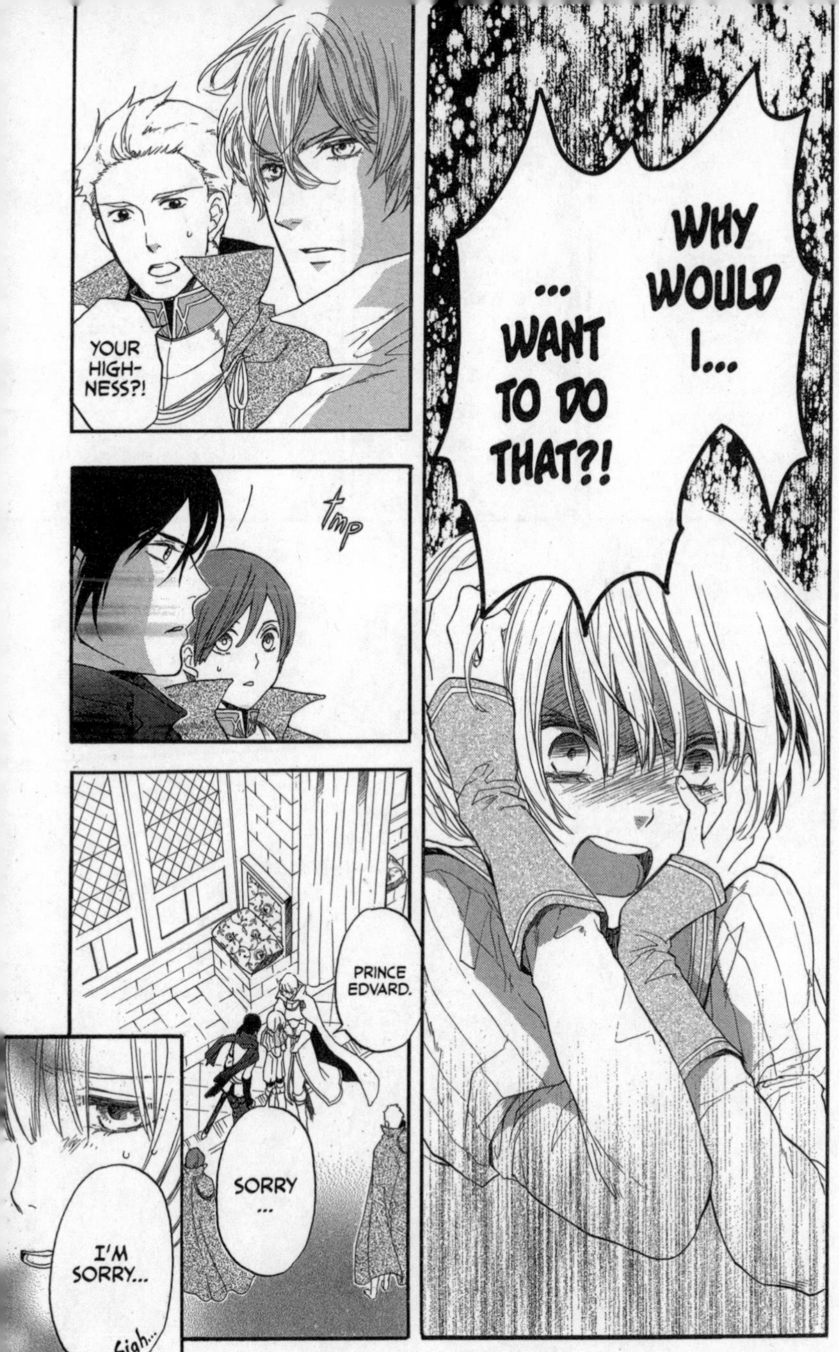
WHY WOULD I...
... WANT TO DO THAT?!
YOUR HIGH-NESS?!
tmp
PRINCE EDVARD.
SORRY ...
I'M SORRY...
Sigh...

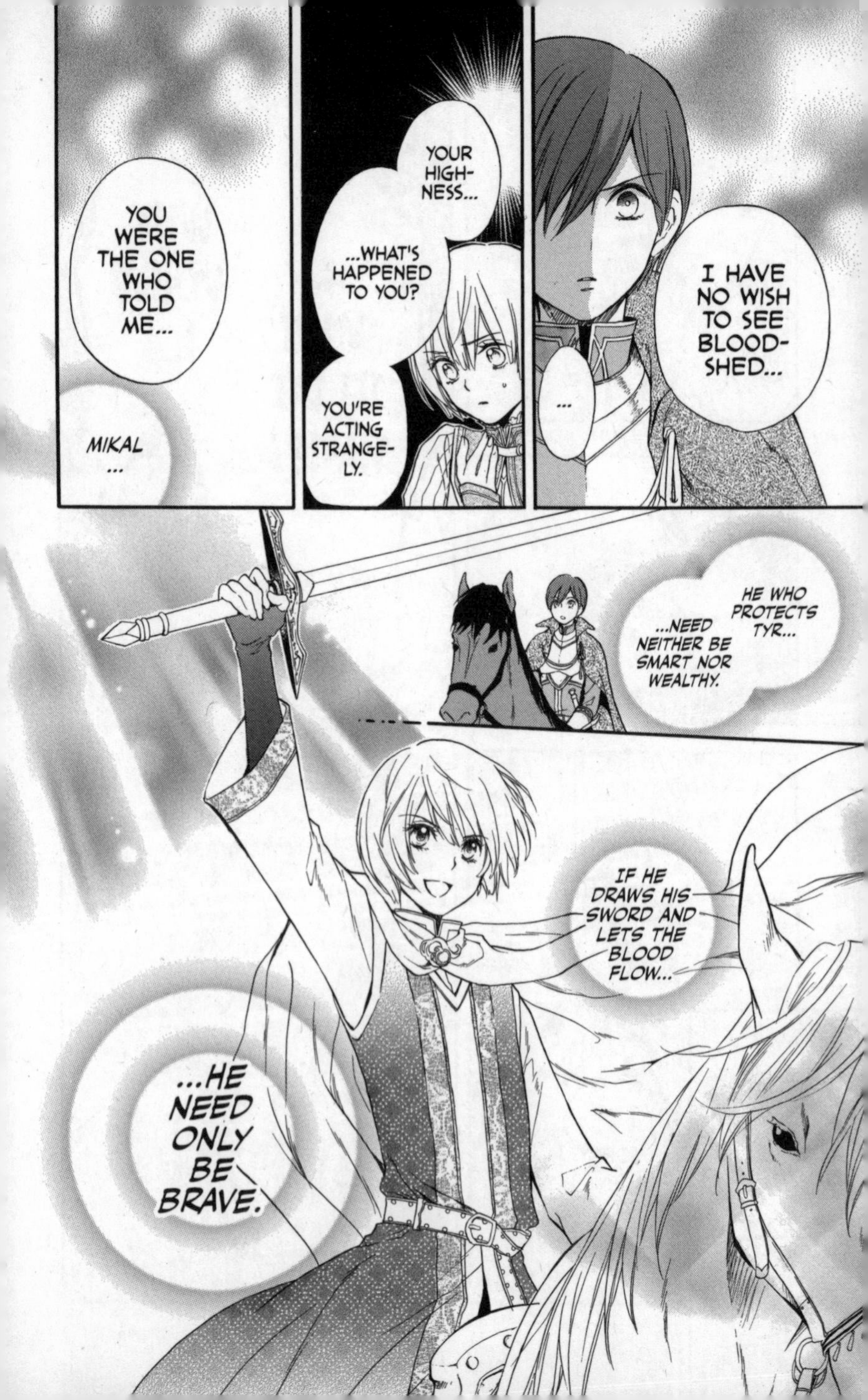
I HAVE NO WISH TO SEE BLOOD-SHED...
...
YOUR HIGH-NESS...
...WHAT'S HAPPENED TO YOU?
YOU'RE ACTING STRANGE-LY.
YOU WERE THE ONE WHO TOLD ME...
MIKAL ...
HE WHO PROTECTS TYR...
...NEED NEITHER BE SMART NOR WEALTHY.
IF HE DRAWS HIS SWORD AND LETS THE BLOOD FLOW...
...HE NEED ONLY BE BRAVE.

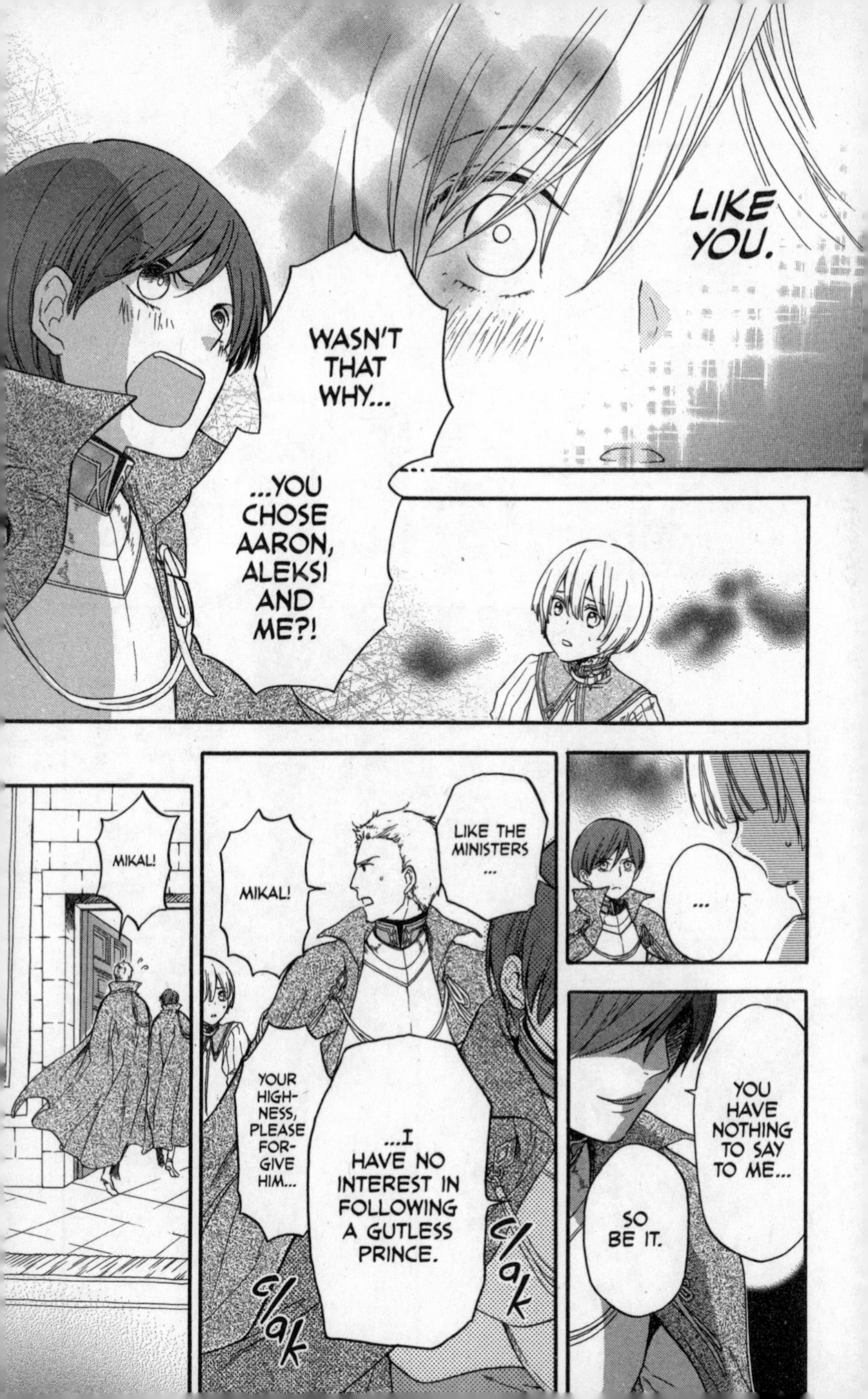
LIKE YOU.
WASN'T THAT WHY...
...YOU CHOSE AARON, ALEKSI AND ME?!
...
YOU HAVE NOTHING TO SAY TO ME...
SO BE IT.
LIKE THE MINISTERS ...
...I HAVE NO INTEREST IN FOLLOWING A GUTLESS PRINCE.
MIKAL!
YOUR HIGHNESS, PLEASE FOR-GIVE HIM...
clak
clak
MIKAL!

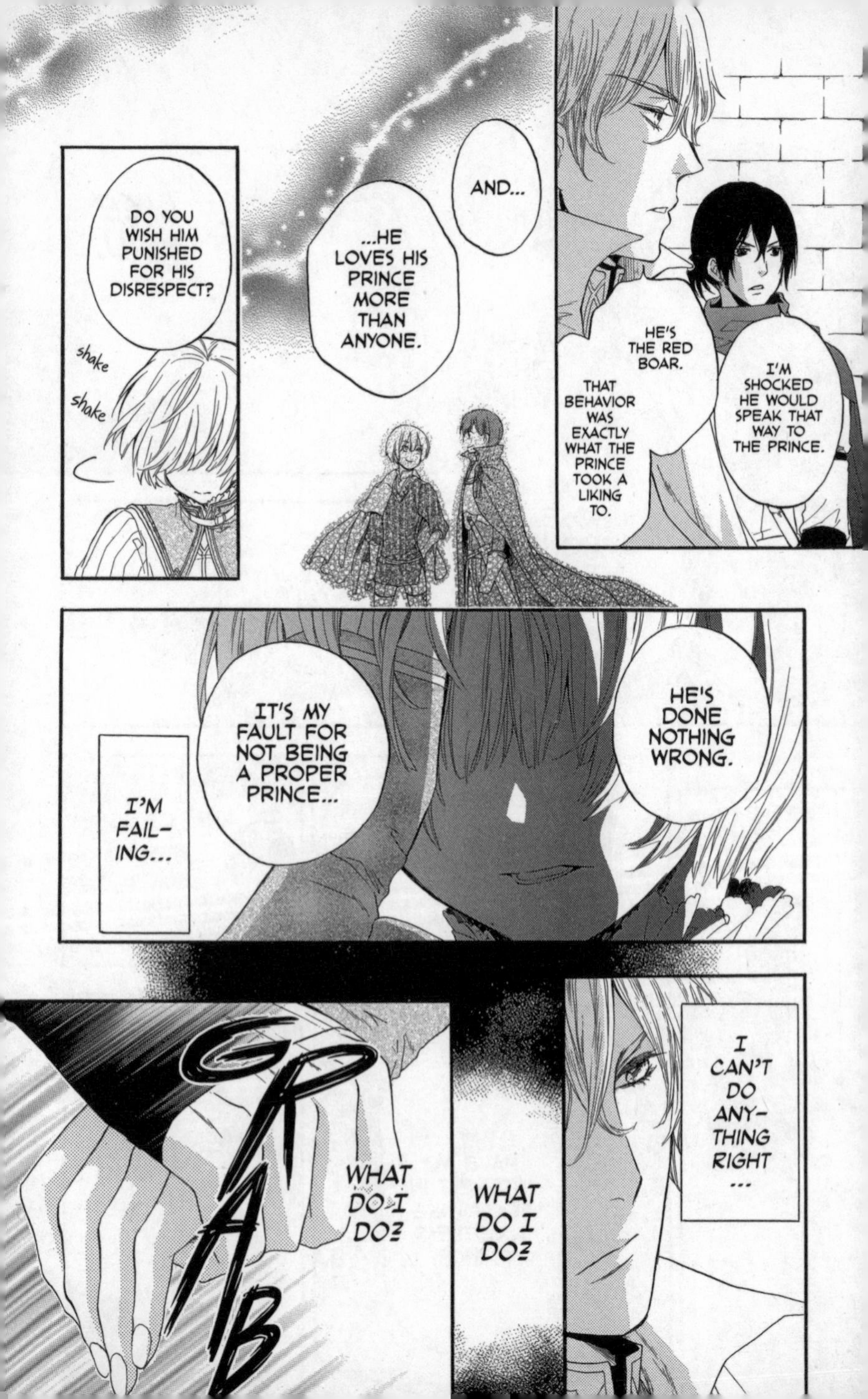
I'M SHOCKED HE WOULD SPEAK THAT WAY TO THE PRINCE.
HE'S THE RED BOAR.
THAT BEHAVIOR WAS EXACTLY WHAT THE PRINCE TOOK A LIKING TO.
AND...
...HE LOVES HIS PRINCE MORE THAN ANYONE.
DO YOU WISH HIM PUNISHED FOR HIS DISRESPECT?
shake
shake
HE'S DONE NOTHING WRONG.
IT'S MY FAULT FOR NOT BEING A PROPER PRINCE...
I'M FAIL-ING...
I CAN'T DO ANY-THING RIGHT...
WHAT DO I DO?
WHAT DO I DO?
GRAB

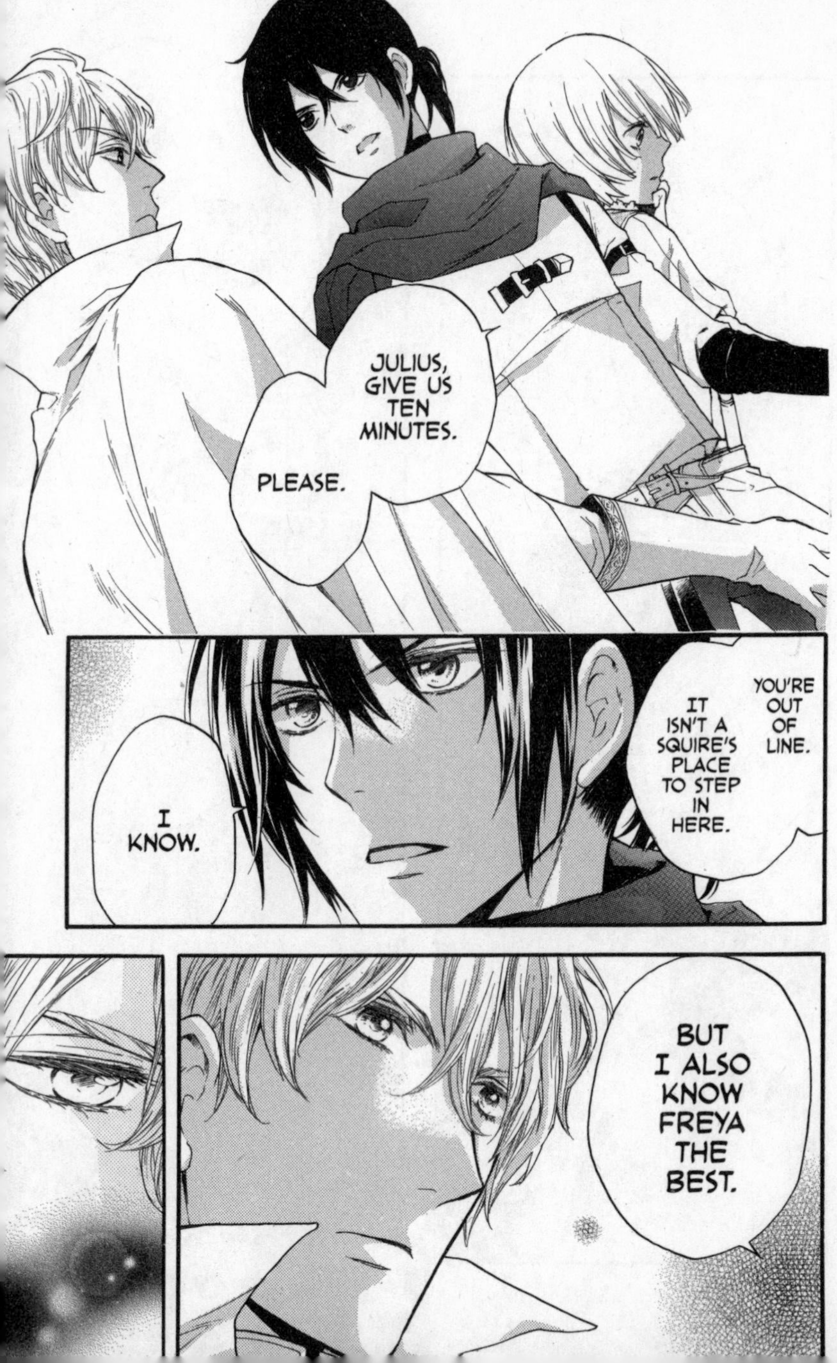
JULIUS, GIVE US TEN MINUTES.
PLEASE.
YOU'RE OUT OF LINE.
IT ISN'T A SQUIRE'S PLACE TO STEP IN HERE.
I KNOW.
BUT I ALSO KNOW FREYA THE BEST.

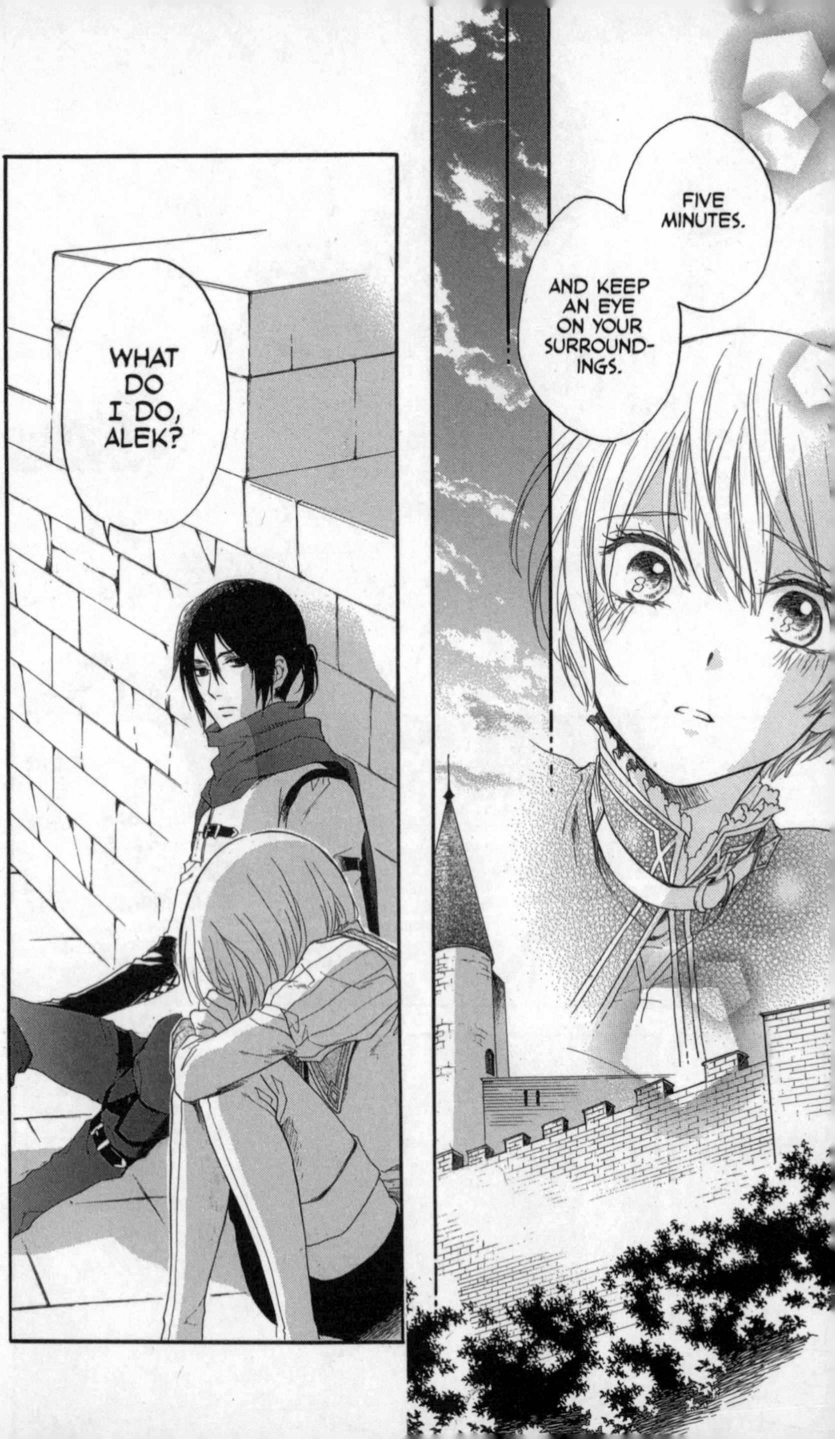
FIVE MINUTES.
AND KEEP AN EYE ON YOUR SURROUND-INGS.
WHAT DO I DO, ALEK?

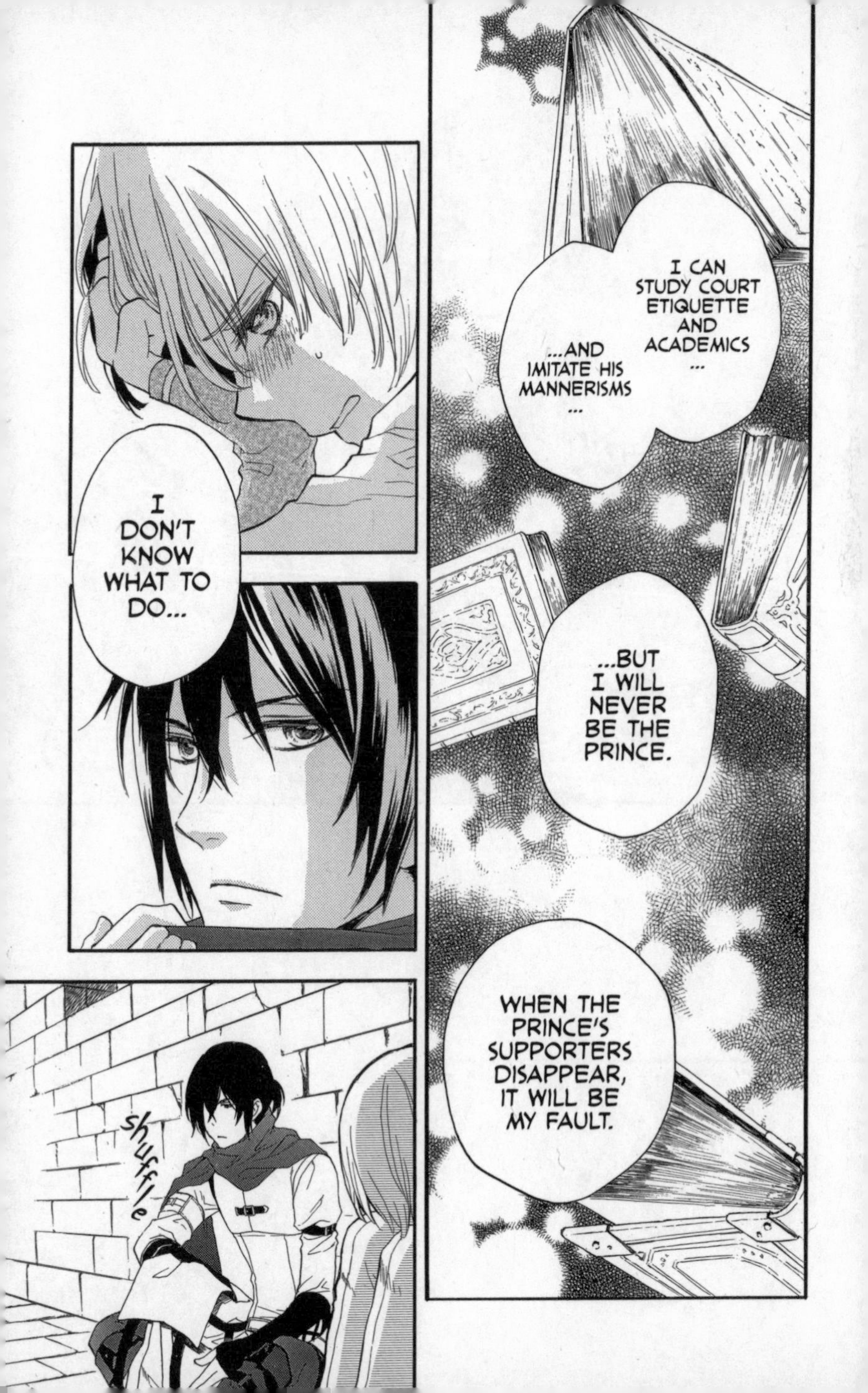
I CAN STUDY COURT ETIQUETTE AND ACADEMICS...
...AND IMITATE HIS MANNERISMS...
...BUT I WILL NEVER BE THE PRINCE.
WHEN THE PRINCE'S SUPPORTERS DISAPPEAR, IT WILL BE MY FAULT.
I DON'T KNOW WHAT TO DO...
shuffle

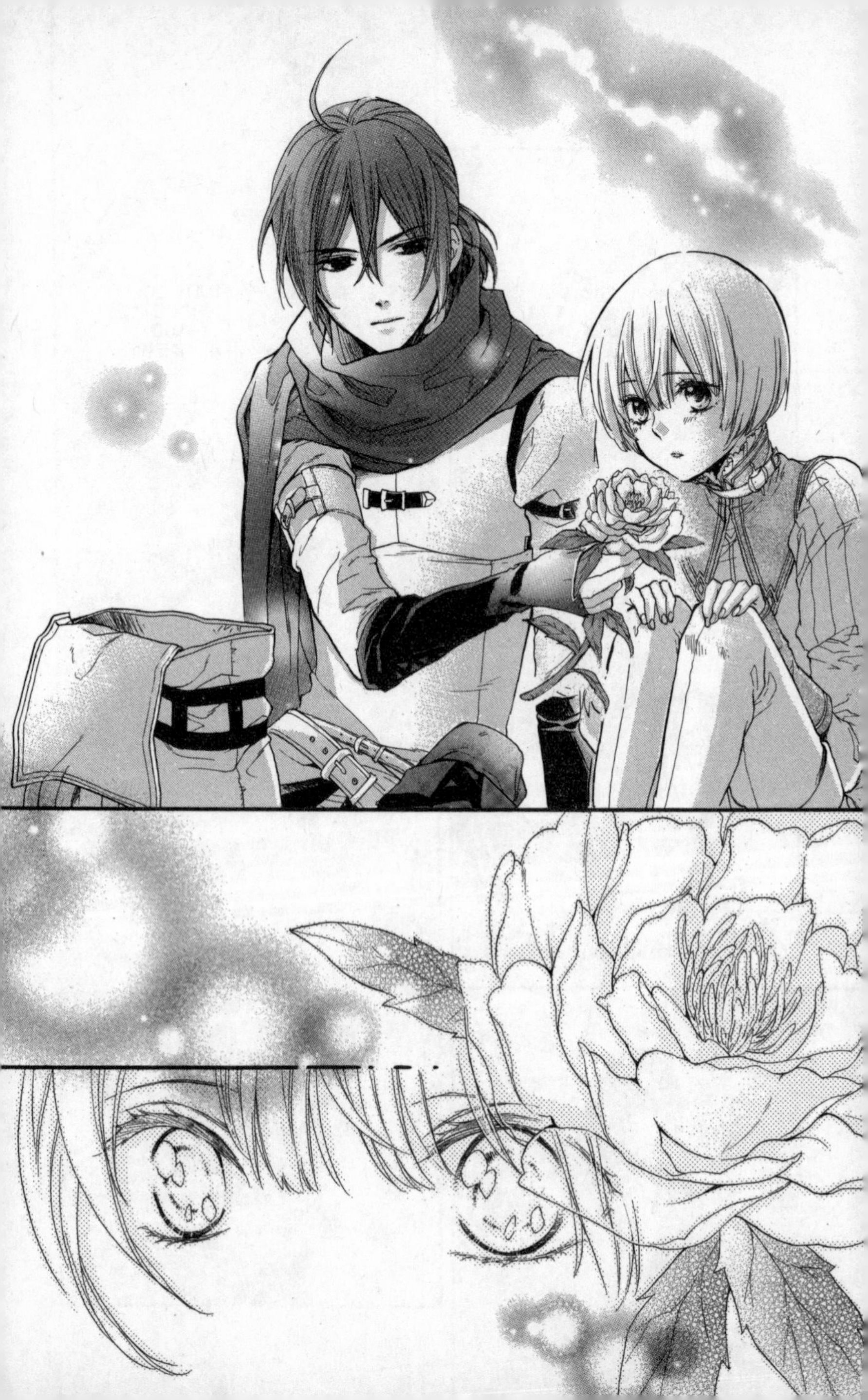

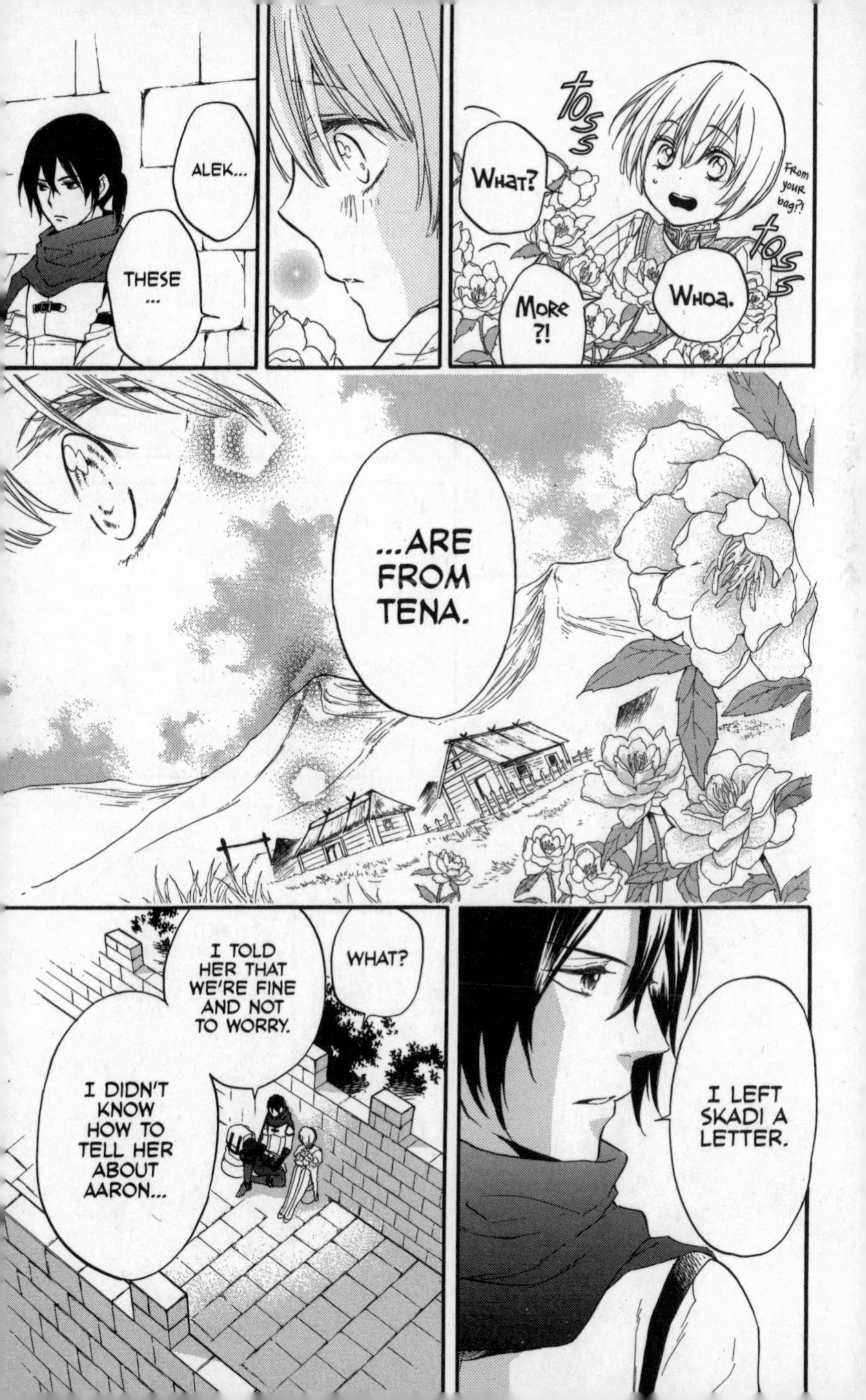

toss
What?
From your bag?!
toss
Whoa.
More ?!
ALEK...
THESE ...
...ARE FROM TENA.
I LEFT SKADI A LETTER.
WHAT?
I TOLD HER THAT WE'RE FINE AND NOT TO WORRY.
I DIDN'T KNOW HOW TO TELL HER ABOUT AARON...

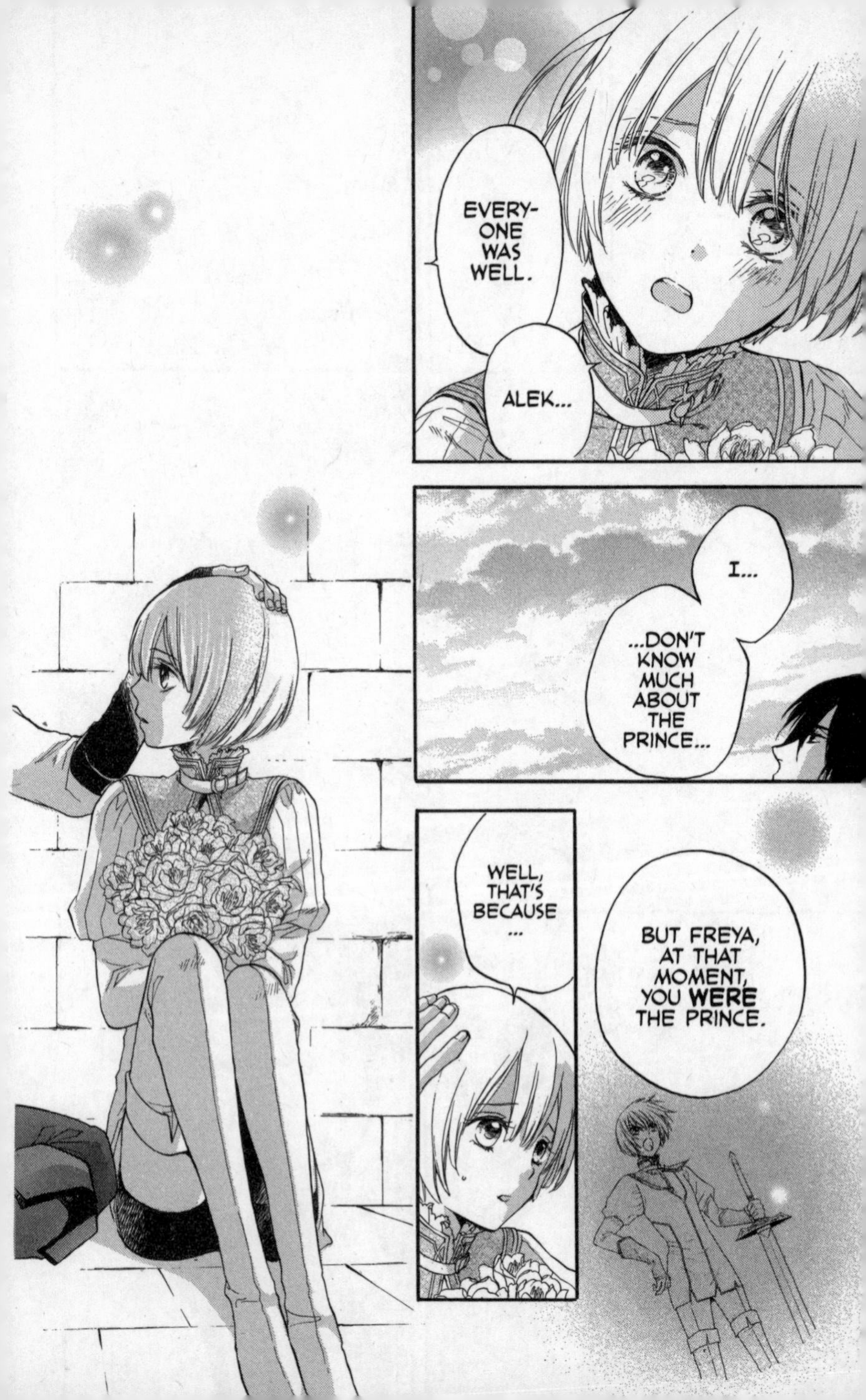
EVERY-ONE WAS WELL.
ALEK...
I...
...DON'T KNOW MUCH ABOUT THE PRINCE...
BUT FREYA, AT THAT MOMENT, YOU **WERE** THE PRINCE.
WELL, THAT'S BECAUSE...

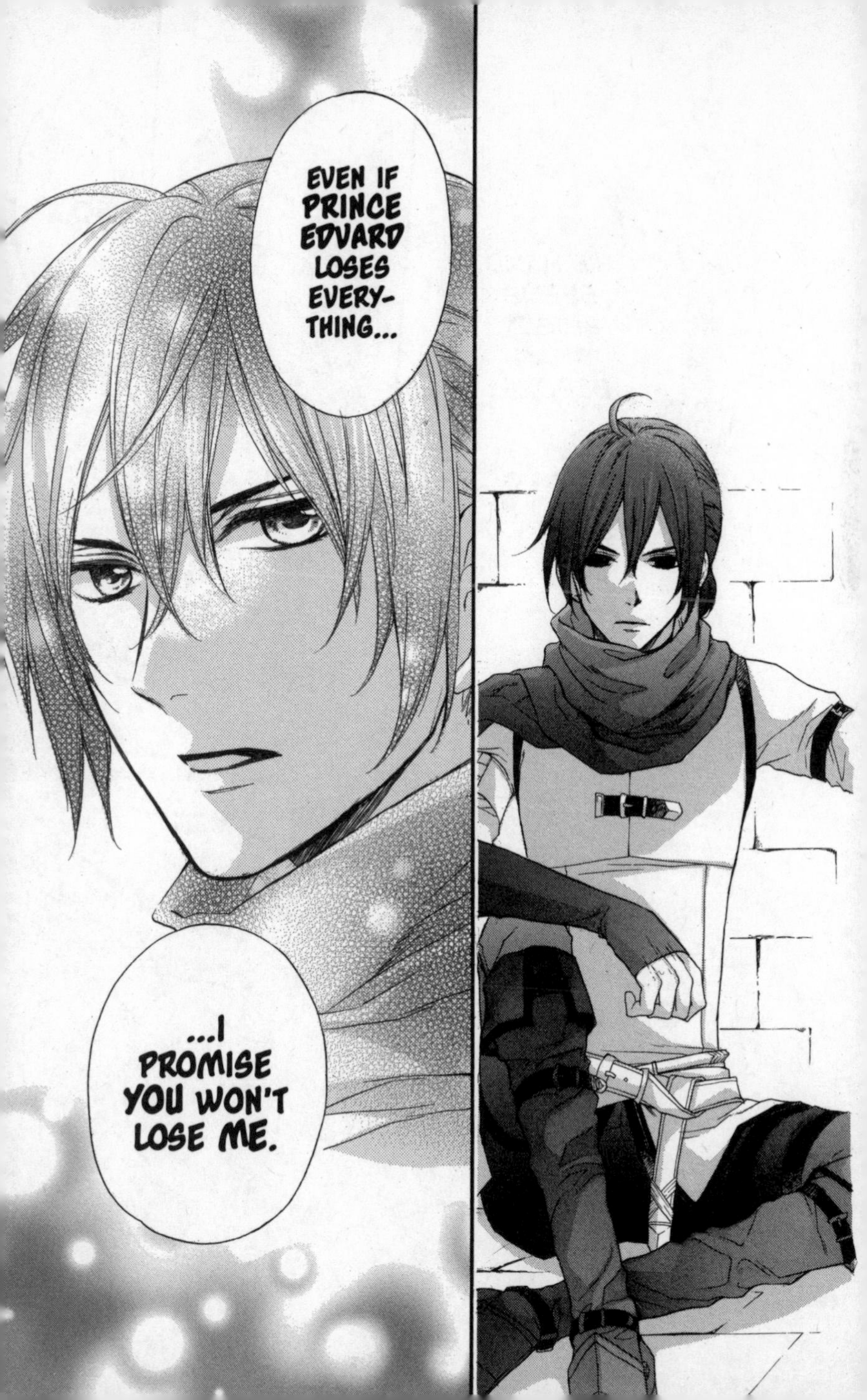
EVEN IF PRINCE EDVARD LOSES EVERY-THING...
...I PROMISE YOU WON'T LOSE ME.

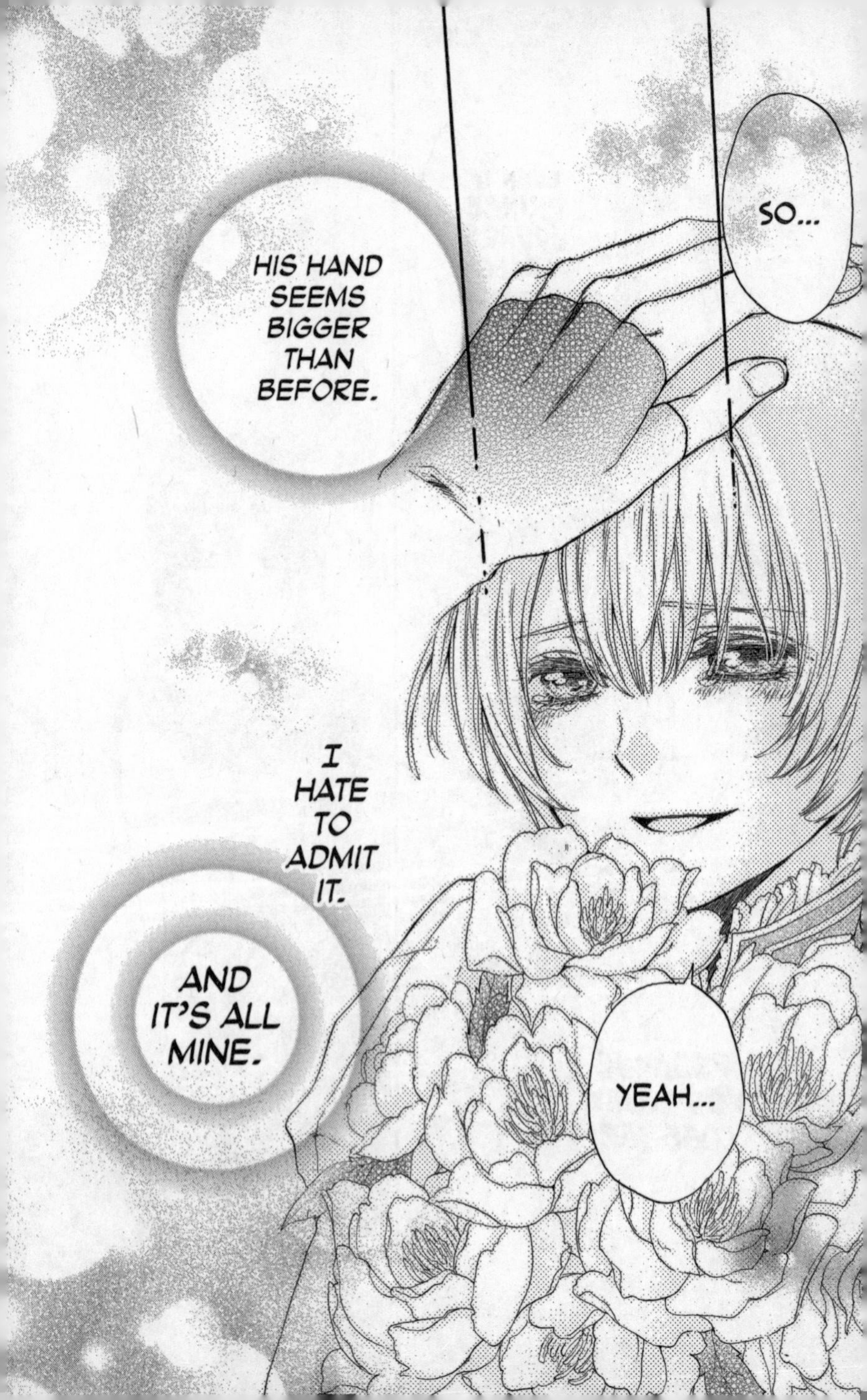
SO...
HIS HAND SEEMS BIGGER THAN BEFORE.
I HATE TO ADMIT IT.
AND IT'S ALL MINE.
YEAH...

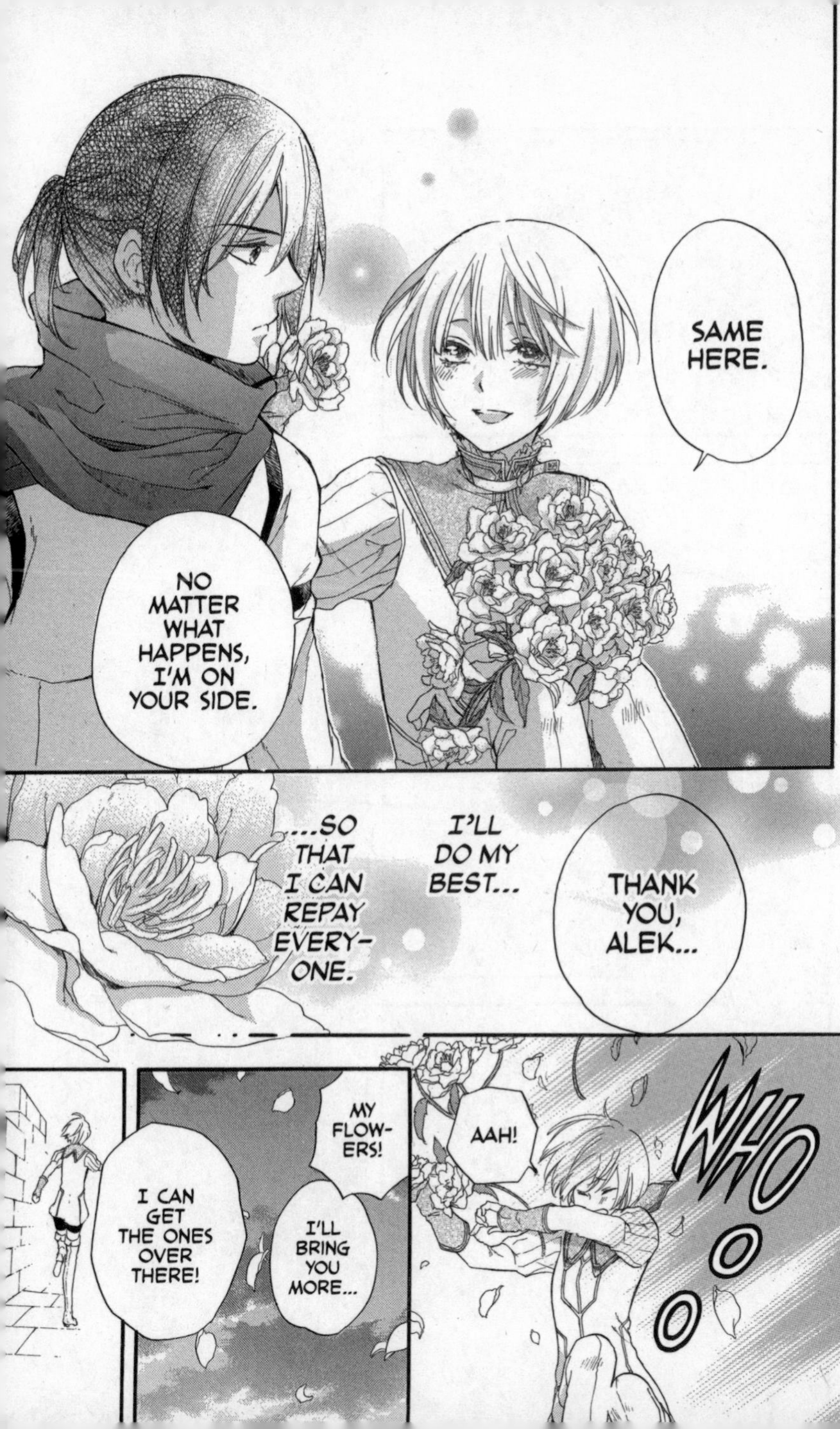
SAME HERE.
NO MATTER WHAT HAPPENS, I'M ON YOUR SIDE.
THANK YOU, ALEK...
I'LL DO MY BEST...
...SO THAT I CAN REPAY EVERY-ONE.
WHOOOO
AAH!
MY FLOWERS!
I'LL BRING YOU MORE...
I CAN GET THE ONES OVER THERE!

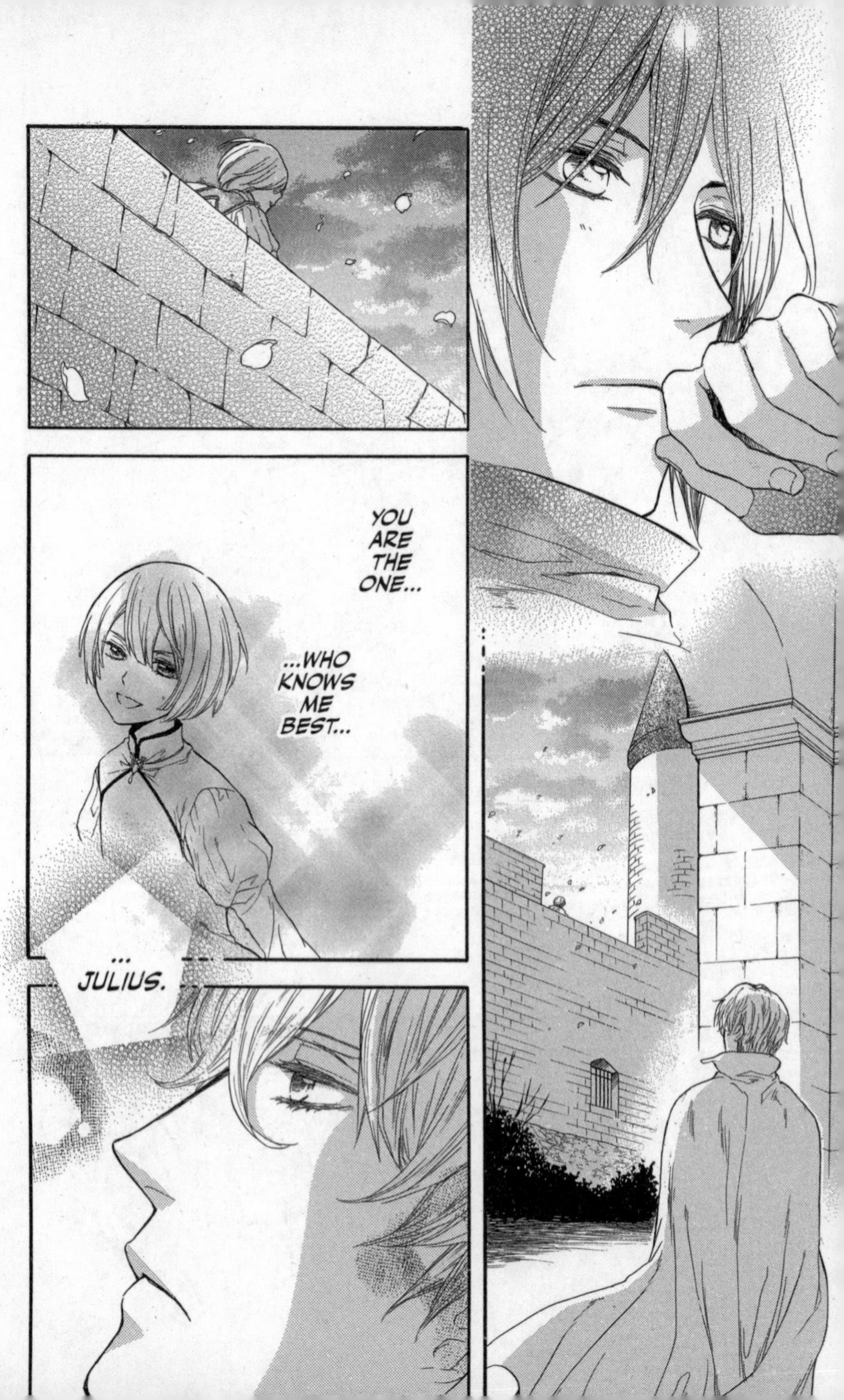
YOU ARE THE ONE...
...WHO KNOWS ME BEST...
... JULIUS.

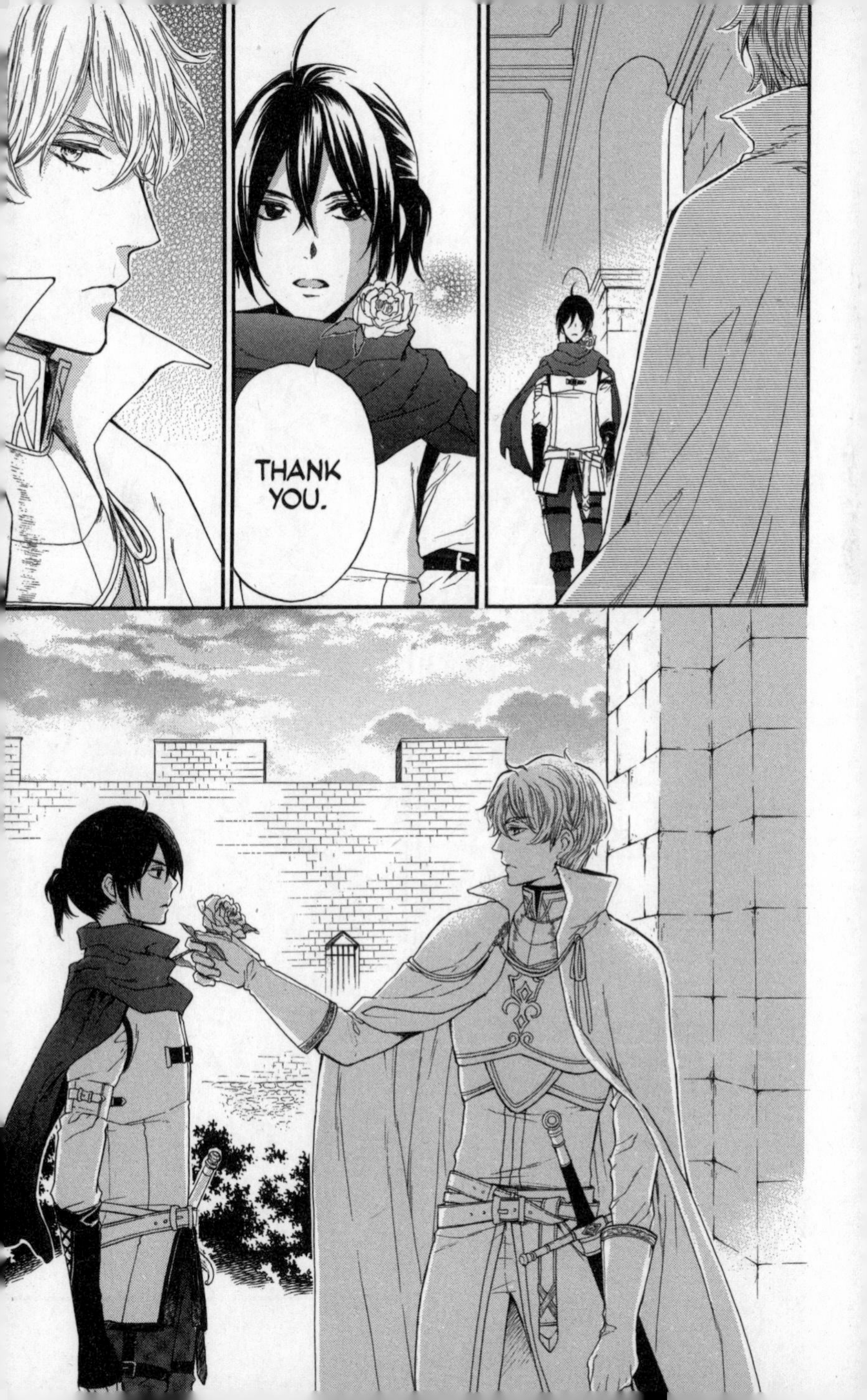
THANK YOU.

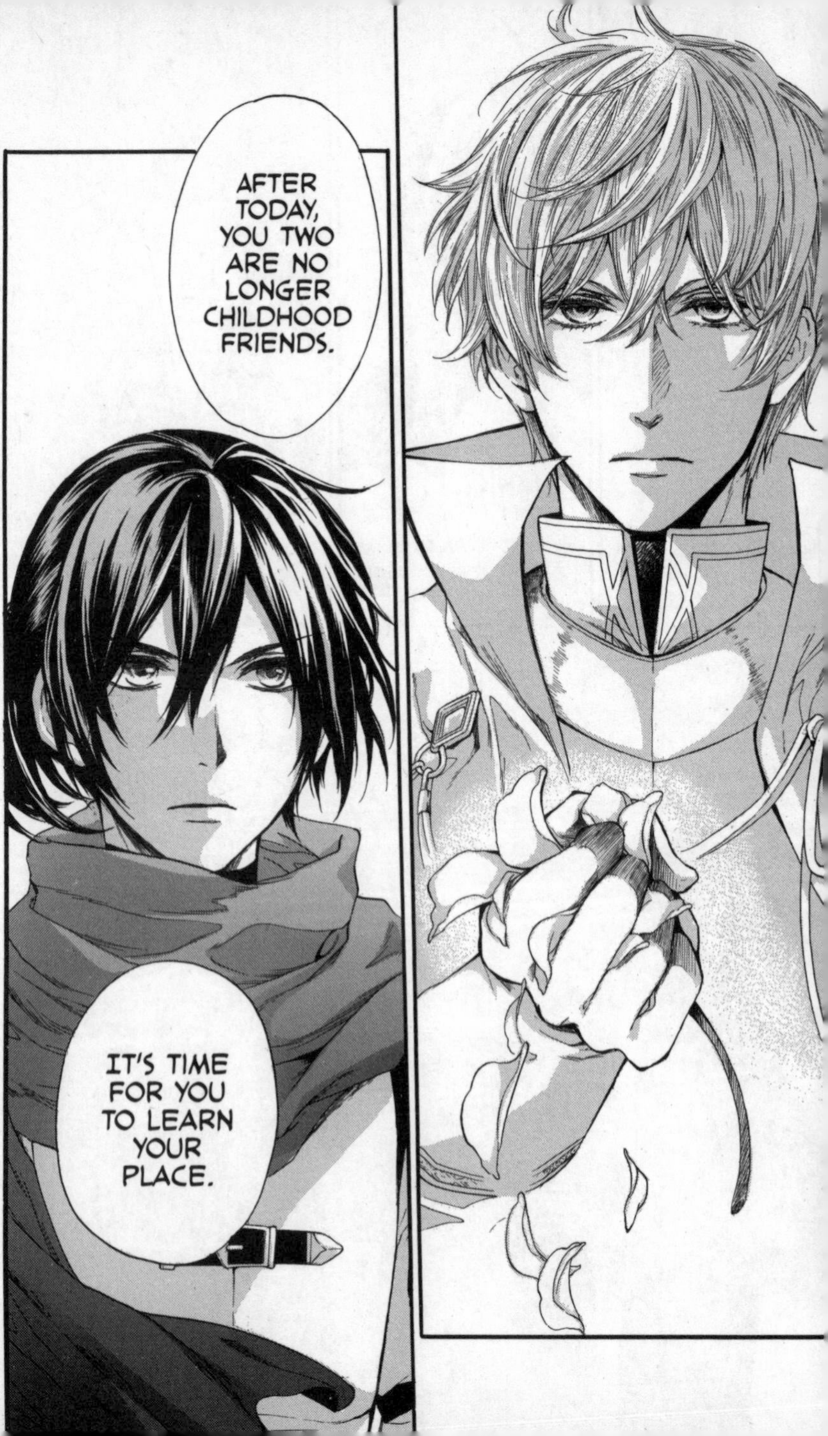
AFTER TODAY, YOU TWO ARE NO LONGER CHILDHOOD FRIENDS.
IT'S TIME FOR YOU TO LEARN YOUR PLACE.

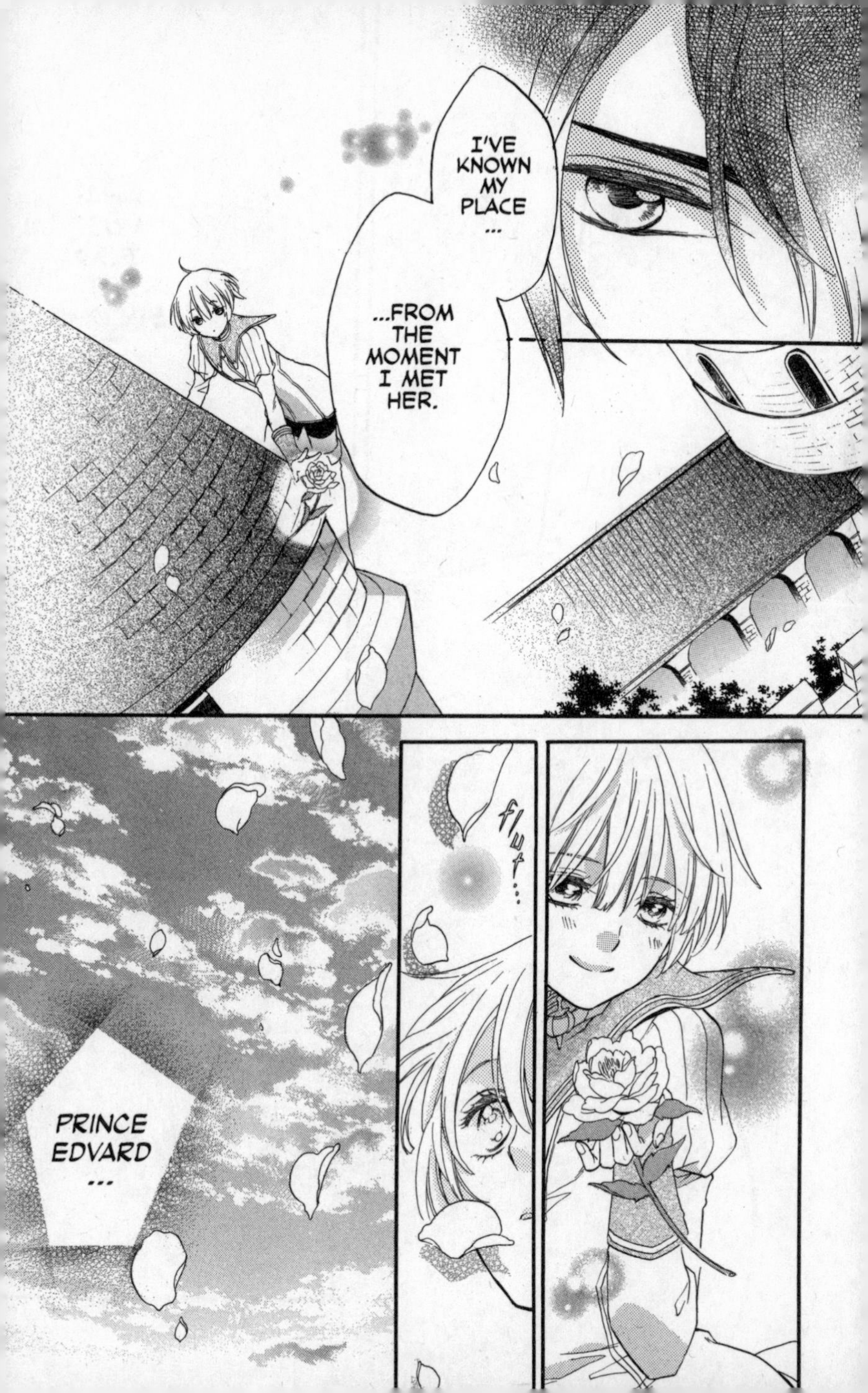
I'VE KNOWN MY PLACE ...
...FROM THE MOMENT I MET HER.
flut...
PRINCE EDVARD ...

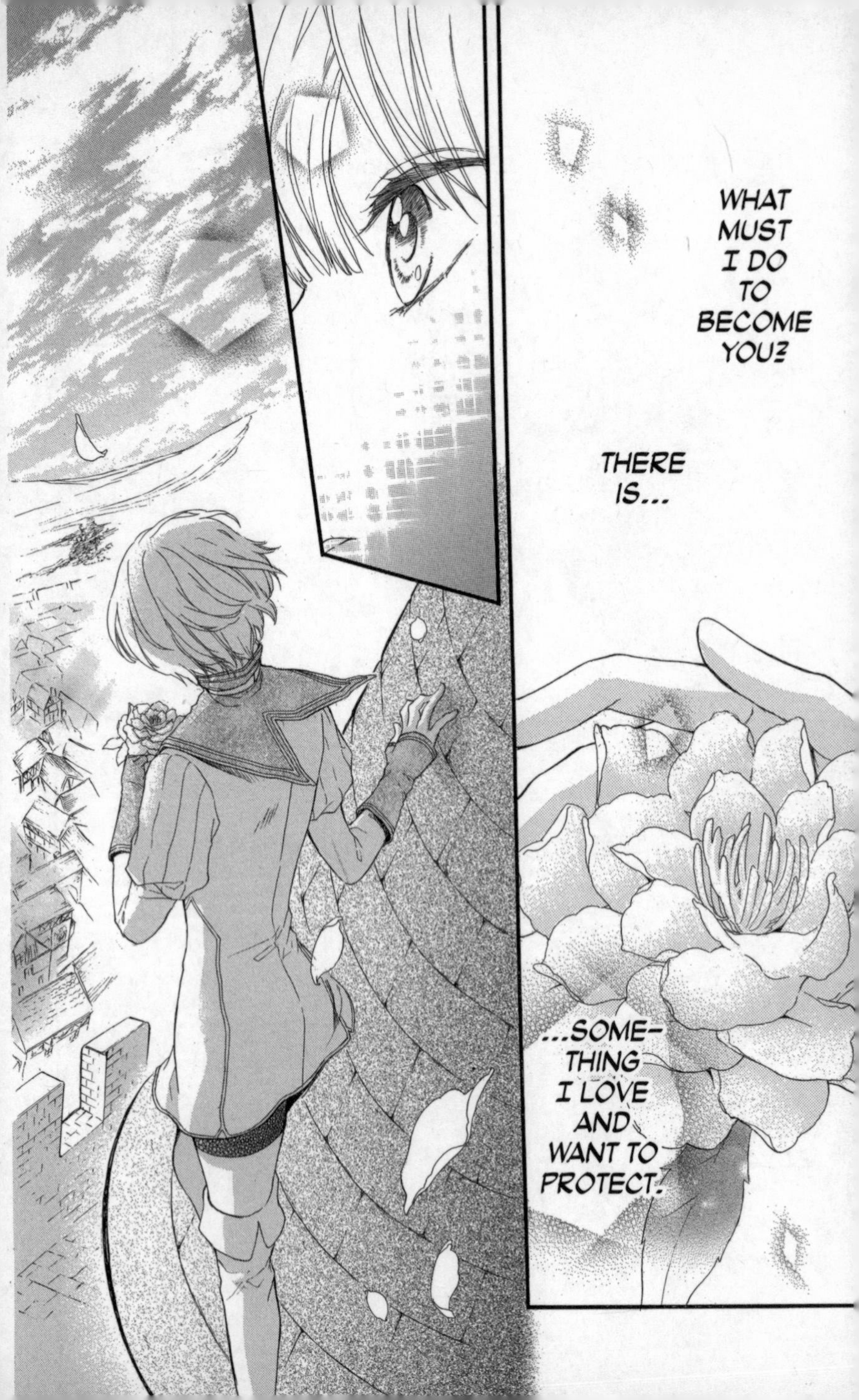
WHAT MUST I DO TO BECOME YOU?
THERE IS...
...SOME-THING I LOVE AND WANT TO PROTECT.

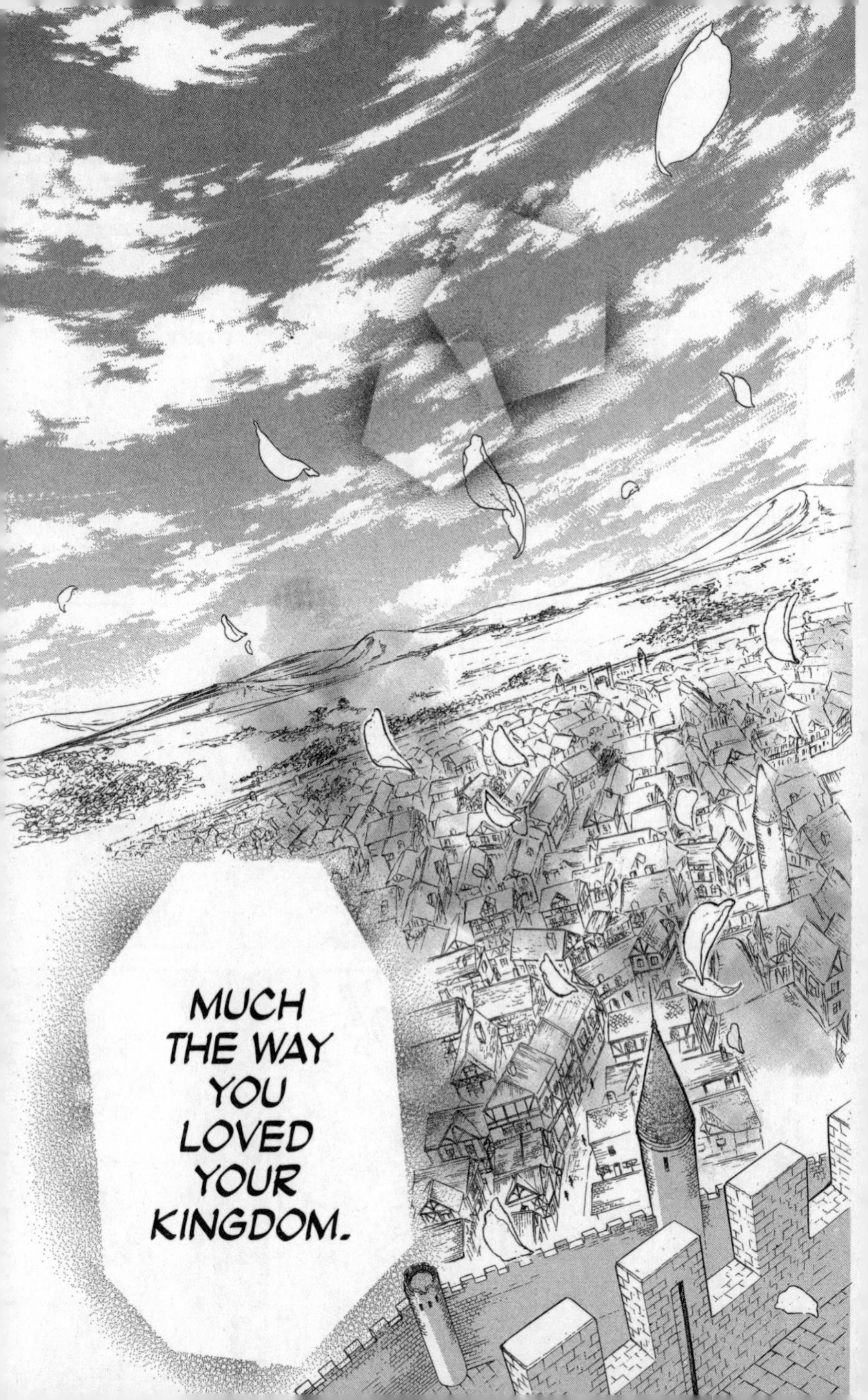
MUCH THE WAY YOU LOVED YOUR KINGDOM.

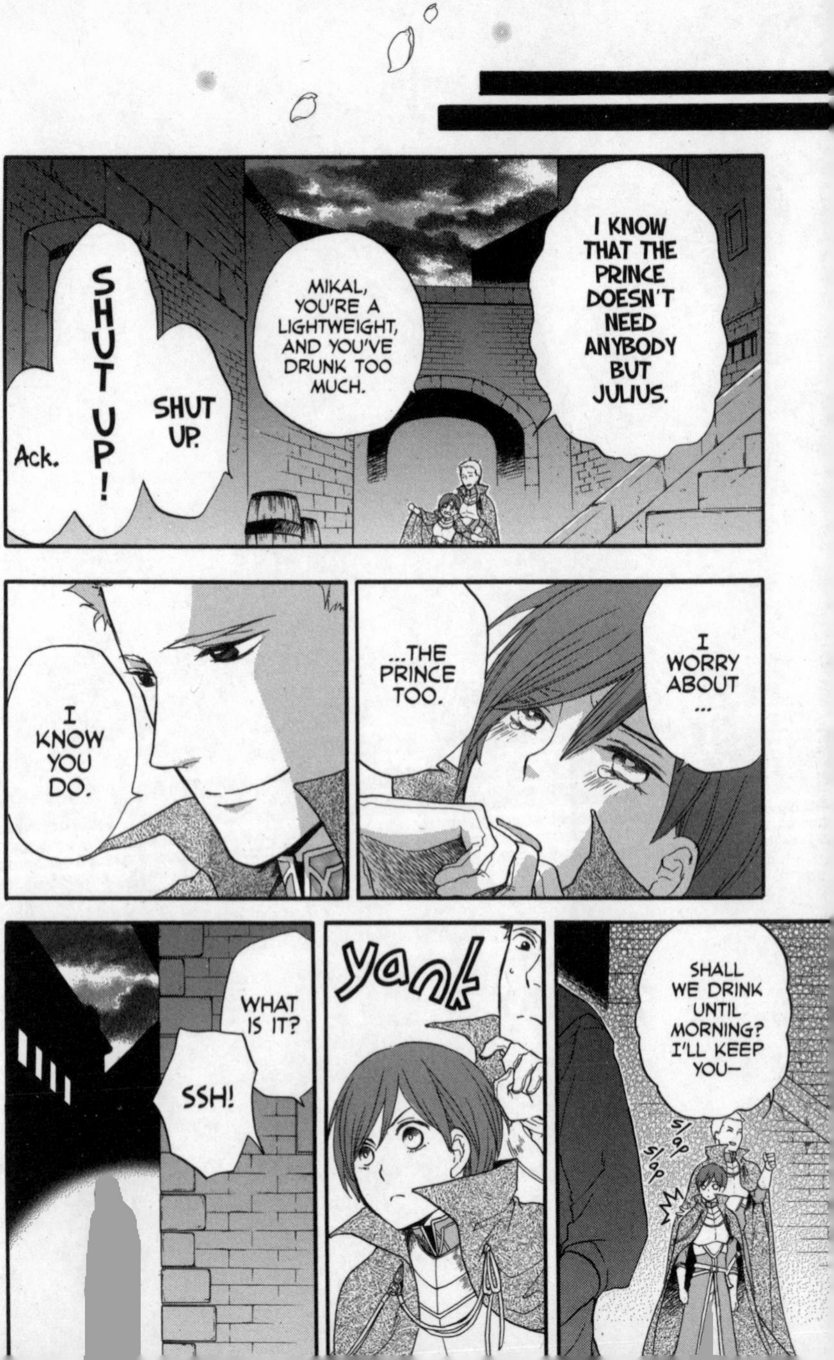
I KNOW THAT THE PRINCE DOESN'T NEED ANYBODY BUT JULIUS.
MIKAL, YOU'RE A LIGHTWEIGHT, AND YOU'VE DRUNK TOO MUCH.
SHUT UP.
SHUT UP!
Ack.
I WORRY ABOUT ...
...THE PRINCE TOO.
I KNOW YOU DO.
SHALL WE DRINK UNTIL MORNING? I'LL KEEP YOU—
slap slap
yank
WHAT IS IT?
SSH!

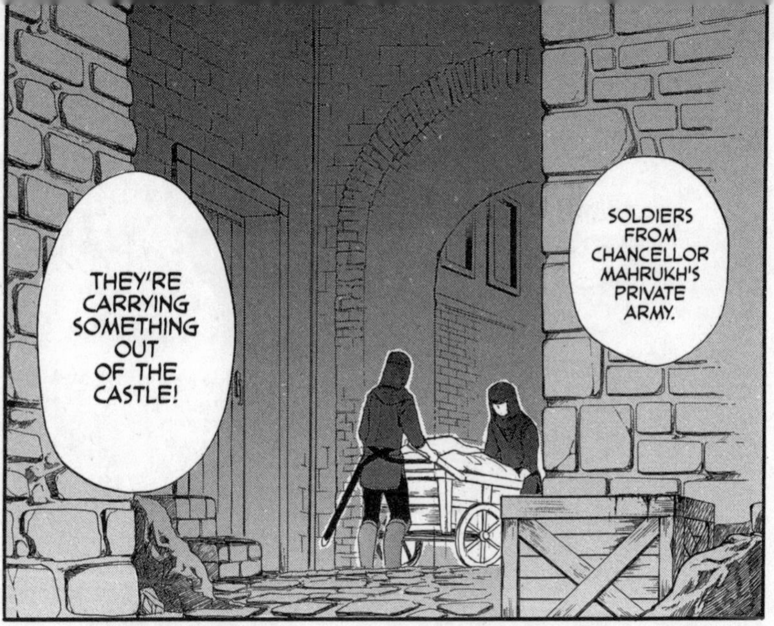
SOLDIERS FROM CHANCELLOR MAHRUKH'S PRIVATE ARMY.
THEY'RE CARRYING SOMETHING OUT OF THE CASTLE!

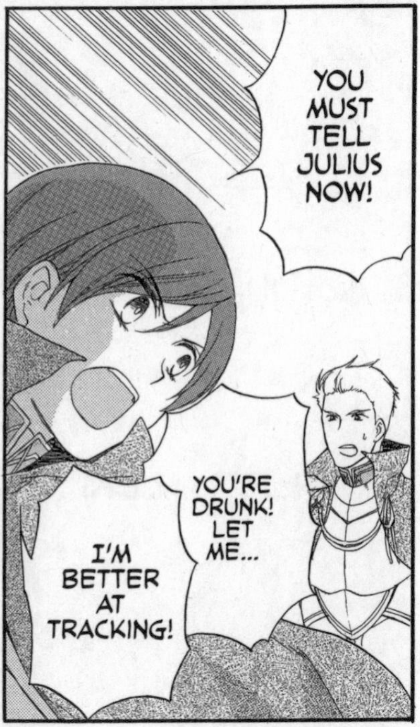
YOU MUST TELL JULIUS NOW!
YOU'RE DRUNK! LET ME...
I'M BETTER AT TRACKING!

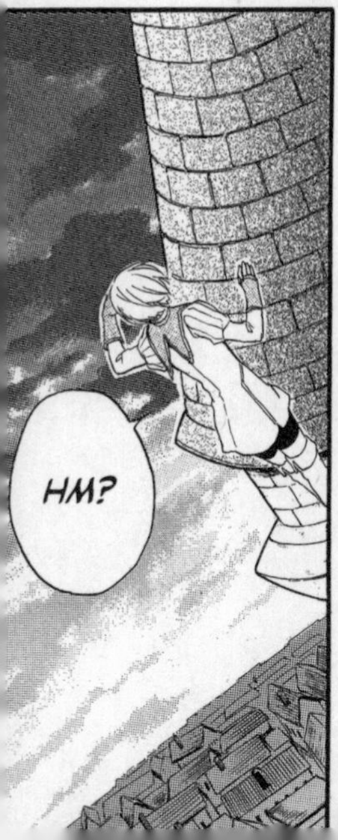
HM?

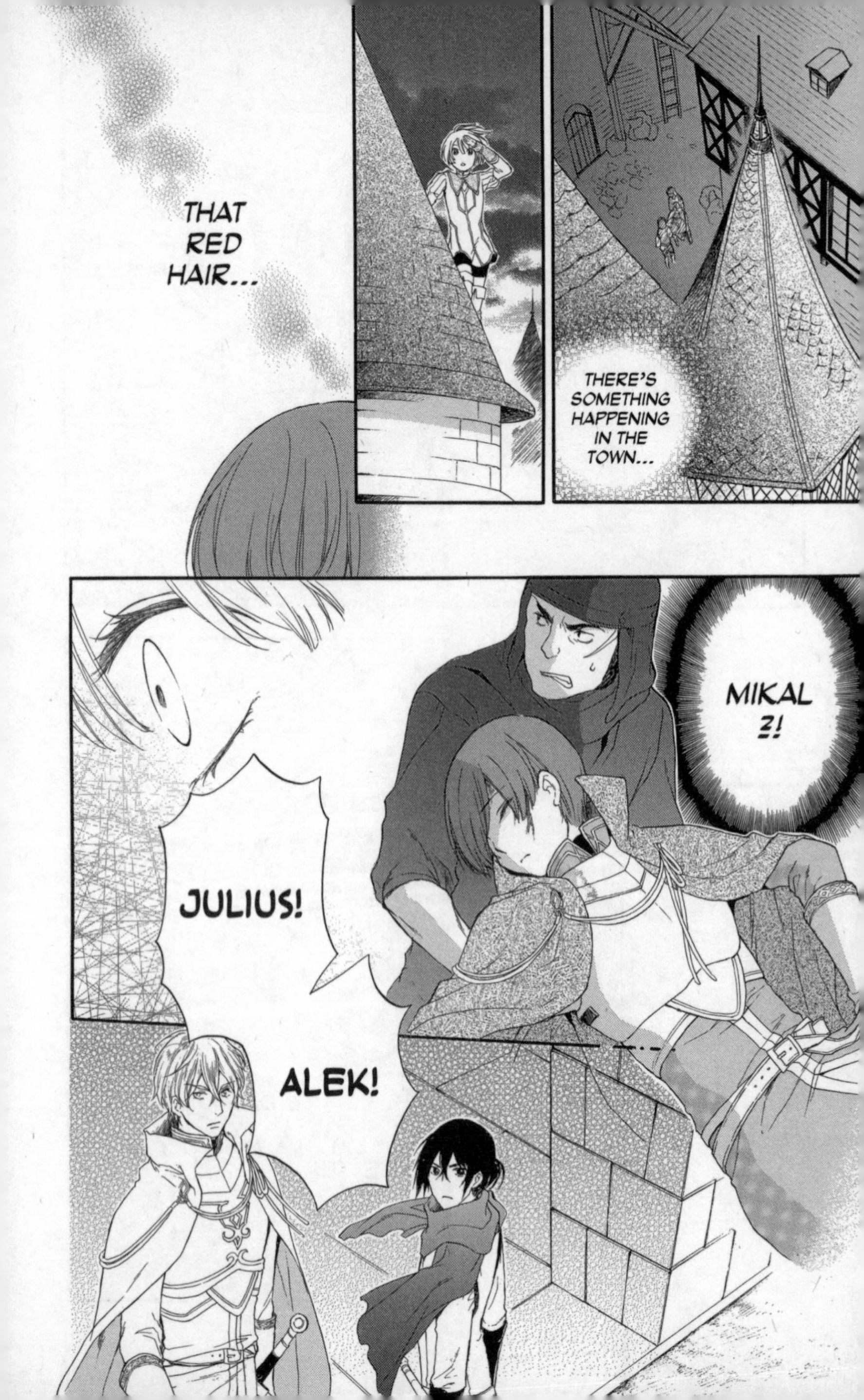
THERE'S SOMETHING HAPPENING IN THE TOWN...
THAT RED HAIR...
MIKAL ?!
JULIUS!
ALEK!

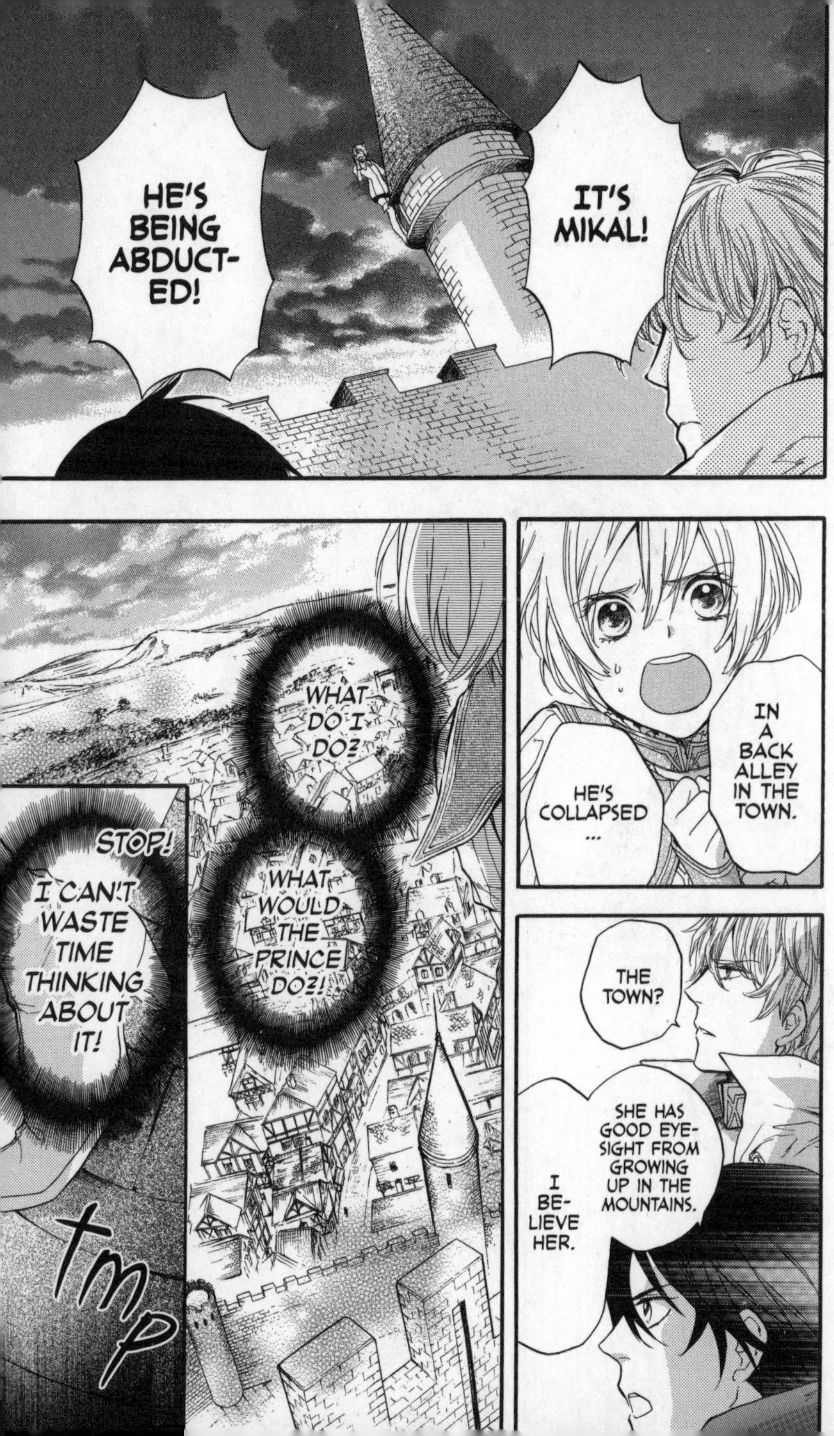
IT'S MIKAL!
HE'S BEING ABDUCT-ED!
IN A BACK ALLEY IN THE TOWN.
HE'S COLLAPSED ...
THE TOWN?
SHE HAS GOOD EYE-SIGHT FROM GROWING UP IN THE MOUNTAINS.
I BE-LIEVE HER.
WHAT DO I DO?
WHAT WOULD THE PRINCE DO?!
STOP!
I CAN'T WASTE TIME THINKING ABOUT IT!
tmp

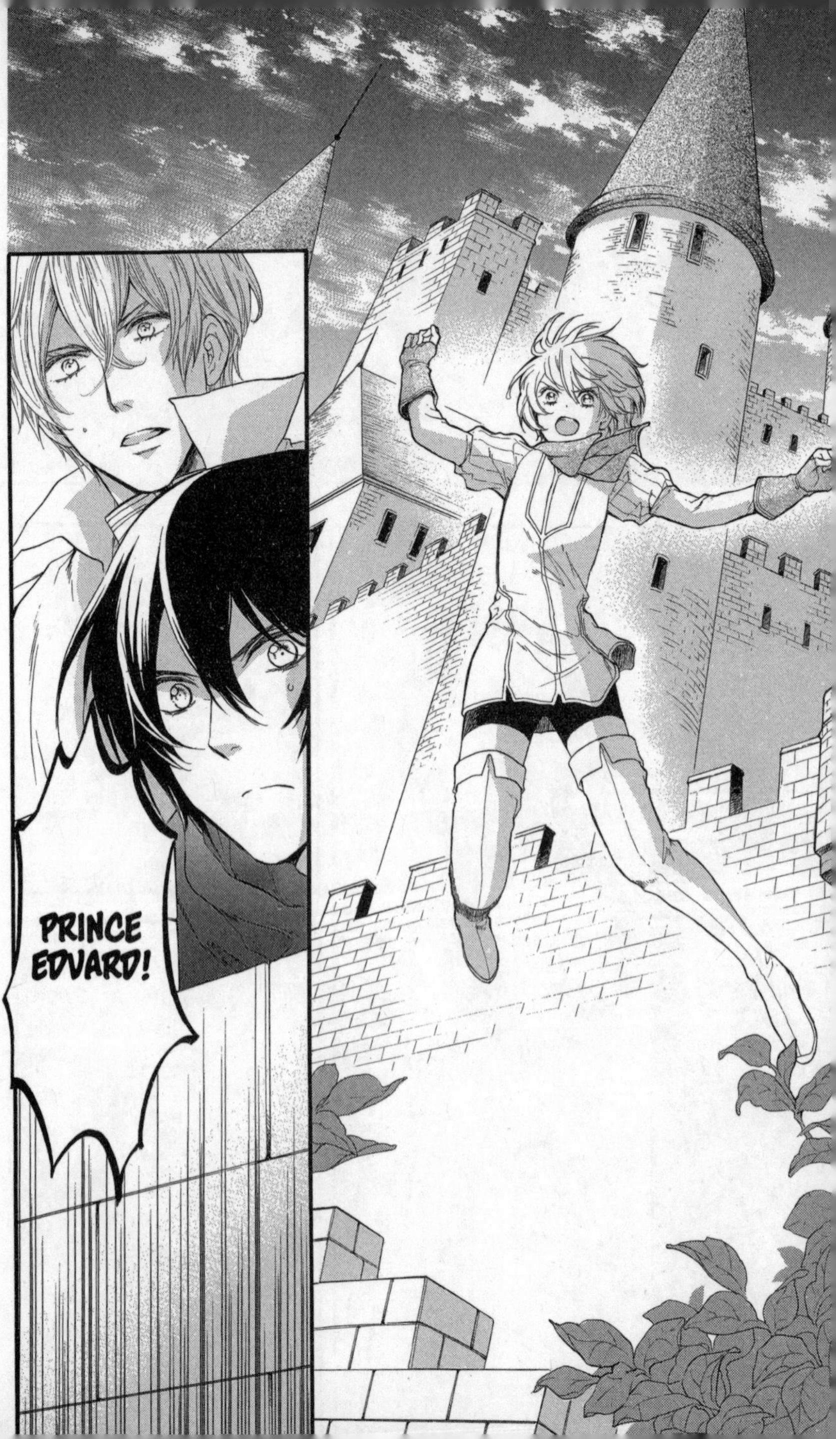
PRINCE EDVARD!

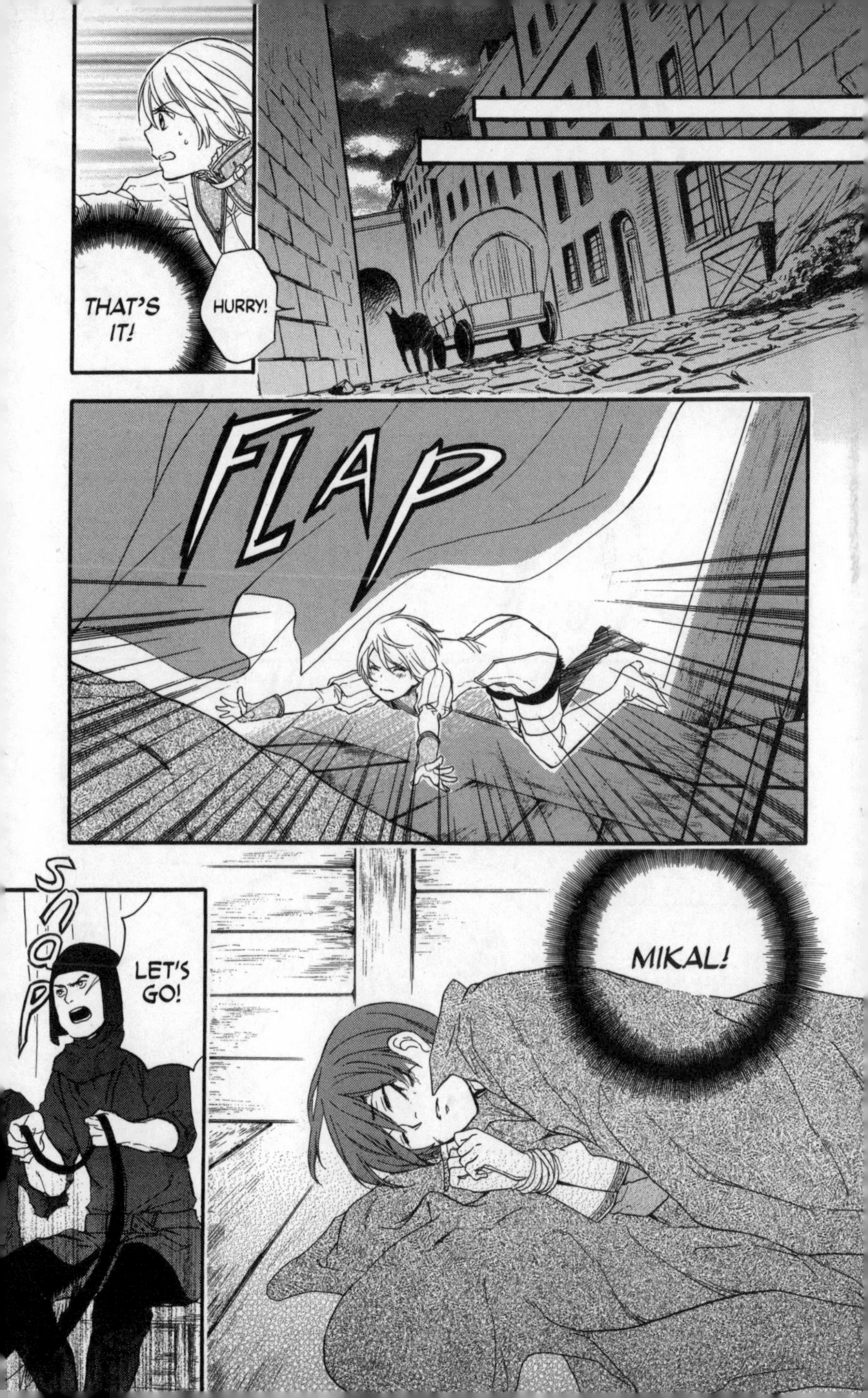
HURRY!
THAT'S IT!
FLAP
MIKAL!
LET'S GO!
SNAP

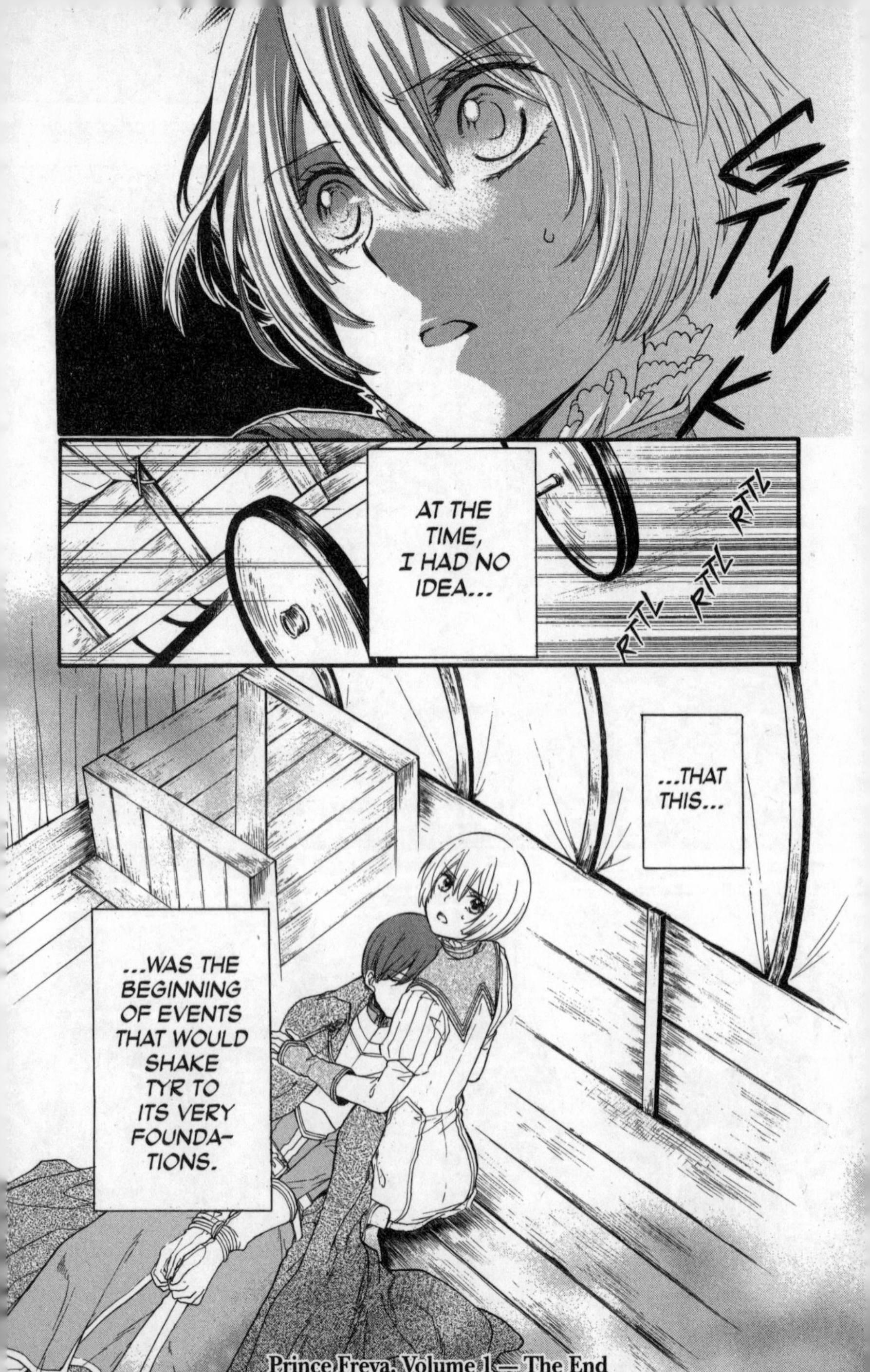
GTNK
AT THE TIME, I HAD NO IDEA...
RTTL RTTL RTTL
...THAT THIS...
...WAS THE BEGINNING OF EVENTS THAT WOULD SHAKE TYR TO ITS VERY FOUNDA-TIONS.

Prince Freya, Volume 1 — The End

Afterword

The Making of Freya

石原ケイコ
Keiko Ishihara

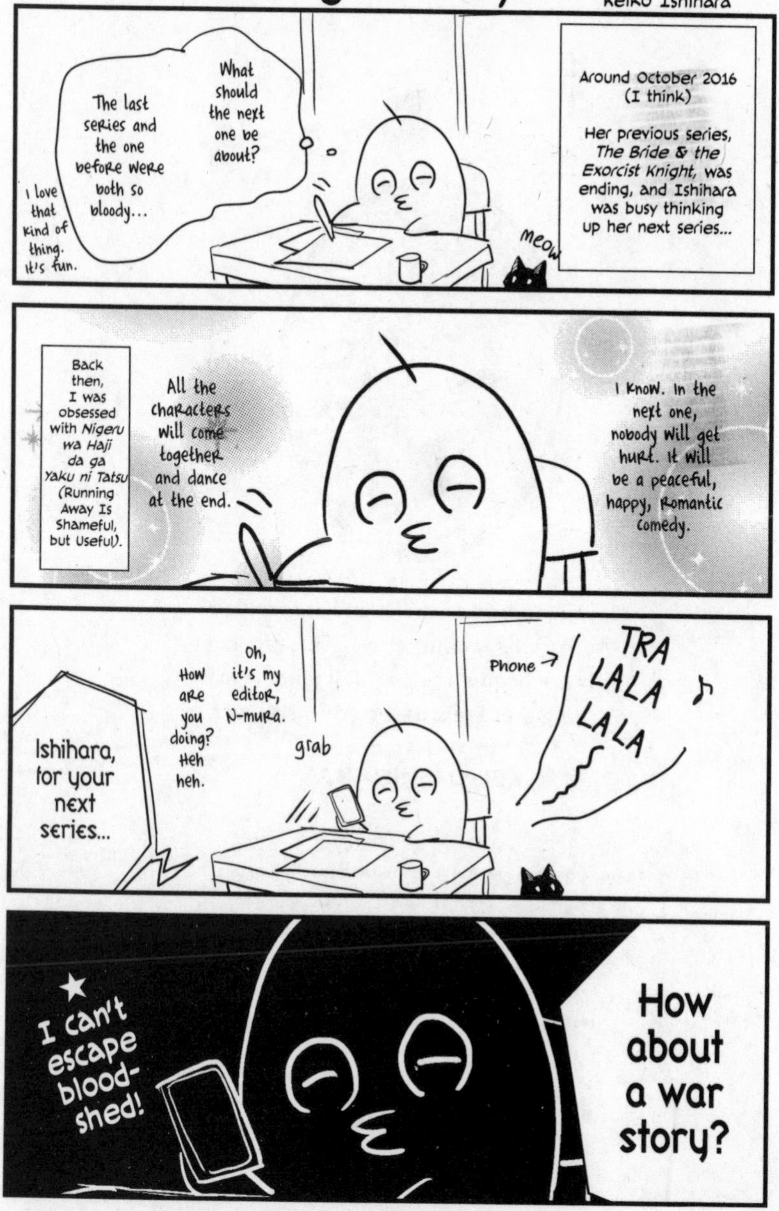
Around October 2016 (I think)
Her previous series, *The Bride & the Exorcist Knight,* was ending, and Ishihara was busy thinking up her next series...
MEOW
What should the next one be about?
The last series and the one before were both so bloody...
I love that kind of thing. It's fun.
I know. In the next one, nobody will get hurt. It will be a peaceful, happy, romantic comedy.
All the characters will come together and dance at the end.
Back then, I was obsessed with *Nigeru wa Haji da ga Yaku ni Tatsu* (Running Away Is Shameful, but Useful).
TRA LALA LALA ♪
Phone →
Oh, it's my editor, N-mura.
How are you doing? Heh heh.
grab
Ishihara, for your next series...
How about a war story?
★ I can't escape bloodshed!

I love European fantasies and am thrilled
to be working on this series! This story has
only just begun. I hope you'll join me in
watching over Freya as she grows stronger.

KEIKO ISHIHARA

Born on April 14, Keiko Ishihara began her manga
career with *Keisan Desu Kara* (It's All Calculated).
Her other works include *Strange Dragon*, which was
serialized in *LaLa* magazine, and *The Heiress and
the Chauffeur*, published by VIZ Media. Ishihara
is from Hyogo Prefecture, and she loves cats.

PRINCE
Freya

VOLUME 1 · SHOJO BEAT EDITION

STORY AND ART BY
KEIKO ISHIHARA

ENGLISH TRANSLATION & ADAPTATION Emi Louie-Nishikawa
TOUCH-UP ART & LETTERING Sabrina Heep
DESIGN Yukiko Whitley & Shawn Carrico
EDITOR Pancha Diaz

Itsuwari no Freya by Keiko Ishihara
© Keiko Ishihara 2018
All rights reserved.
First published in Japan in 2018 by HAKUSENSHA, Inc., Tokyo.
English language translation rights
arranged with HAKUSENSHA, Inc., Tokyo.

Printed in the U.S.A.

Published by VIZ Media, LLC
P.O. Box 77010
San Francisco, CA 94107

10 9 8 7 6 5 4 3 2 1
First printing, April 2020

 MEDIA

viz.com   shojobeat.com

This is the last page.

In keeping with the original Japanese comic format, this book reads from right to left—so action, sound effects, and word balloons are completely reversed. This preserves the orientation of the original artwork—plus, it's fun! Check out the diagram shown here to get the hang of things, and then turn to the other side of the book to get started!

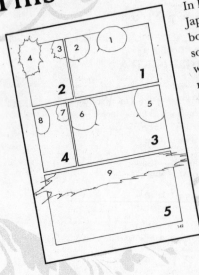